RENAISSANCE ITALY
1464-1534

RENAISSANCE ITALY

1464–1534

PETER LAVEN

G. P. Putnam's Sons, New York

Preface

While writing this book on Renaissance Italy I have held constantly in mind the need (that most teachers of European history of this period must have experienced) for a manageable volume to recommend to students whose prime historical interest might not necessarily be in this period of Italian history and whose linguistic accomplishments might not be sufficient to make up some of the deficiencies in the English literature on the subject. The book should also prove useful to students who choose to specialise in some aspect of Renaissance history. Such students are usually presented with a limited but detailed course on Florentine history. They might deal at some length with perhaps Venice or the Papacy as well. But it is my experience that such students seldom have a reasonable grasp of what is going on in other parts of Italy, and names like Ferrante of Naples, Andrea Doria or Francesco Gonzaga haunt a uniformly nebulous background. It is hoped that this book together with its bibliographical guide should serve to minimise the problems some of these students encounter. My intention, however, has been more than to provide useful background information to students or general readers. No one can explore so fertile an area of history, which has given rise to countless controversies of interpretation, without suggesting some conclusions of his own. Mine emerge at appropriate places throughout the book, and an attempt has been made to make a few salient points about Italy as a whole in the final chapter.

My approach has been guided by a further principle: that history is only fully revealing when it is looked at from a wide variety of viewpoints. The economic historian, the art historian, the historian of politics or technology, in order to get the most out of his researches must have a broad familiarity with the works of specialists in other fields of the period and place he is studying. Literary movements affect political thinking, industries affect scientific investigation or political organisation, religious beliefs affect business methods or artistic styles. The permutations of such interactions are endless. That I have not included, for instance, chapters on the music, poetry or popular attitudes of this period of Italian history

5

is partly due to a desire to prevent the book from becoming too long for the main purposes for which it was designed. It is also due to a lack of confidence in my competence to do so. But I believe that I have shown enough of the economic and political life of Renaissance Italy, of its culture and beliefs, to present some idea of the complex interactions of various aspects of the life and society.

Certain working decisions had to be taken before writing began. I found it necessary, for example, to use the names Florence, Milan, Venice, Naples, Genoa in most contexts instead of writing the Republic of Venice, the Kingdom of Naples, etc. Because of this there might be some ambiguity at times concerning whether I refer to the city or the state. The index, however, makes the distinction. I have used population figures and occasionally other statistics without indicating their controversial nature. If the figures are sometimes rough approximations, their comparative relationships are, I believe, sound. One is sure, for instance, that Naples grew into a great European city in the sixteenth century, that Cremona did not partake of the general urban decline in Lombardy during the first decades of that century, and so on. Finally, after much thought it was decided to do without footnotes. It was felt that a book of this nature depends a great deal on the use of secondary material, and that one's debt to other historians could be adequately indicated in a bibliography. Since this book is thought of, for some, as an introduction to Renaissance Italy, it is hoped that it will lead readers on to delve into the vast literature on the subject, and that those authors I am indebted to myself will be read later by some of my readers.

Burckhardt wrote his *Civilisation of the Renaissance in Italy* over a century ago. It is a great work of original research and full of revealing insights. Since it was written many new aspects of Renaissance Italy have been investigated, but no one has attempted to bring them together between the covers of a single short book. There have been first-class histories of individual states of Italy, excellent art or economic histories of the whole of Italy, but nothing of a comprehensive nature such as has been attempted here. Burckhardt could never be replaced: his work is not only one of the great historical classics; it is also the starting-point of innumerable subsequent investigations, which only become fully comprehensible in the light of what the Swiss historian had to say. But it is a difficult book for an undergraduate to read without any previous background in the subject and it certainly does not treat of some aspects central to the period such as the economy. It is therefore hoped that the present book will serve students as an adequate introduction.

Perhaps one reason why no work of this nature has appeared before is the vast literature on all aspects of the period. One never reaches that point at which one is reasonably confident that the basic material has been mastered. Perhaps one has to come to a place like Western Australia, where there are manageable limits set upon what one can read, in order to embark upon so risky a project. I have had the generous co-operation of the university librarian, Mr Leonard Jolley, whose library must hold more recent books and periodicals dealing with Renaissance Italy than most college and university libraries in Britain. But it certainly has not the resources to make up its shortcomings in depth such as can be found, for instance, in some American libraries. Here, there comes a point when it is possible to stop reading and begin to write.

I should like to thank my friends in the History department of this university, Dr Isabel Durack and Mr Iain Brash, for their constant and valuable criticism and for their encouragement. I would also thank Mr John Barnes of the English department and the librarian for helpful criticism of parts of this book.

October, 1965
Peter Laven
University of Western Australia,
Nedlands, W.A.

7

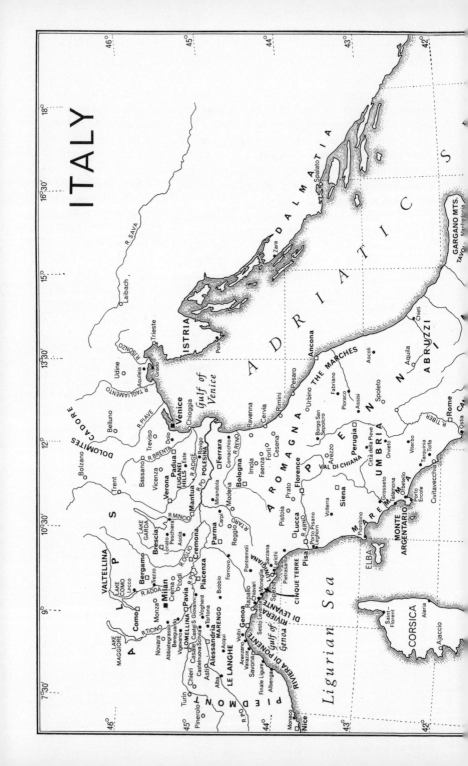

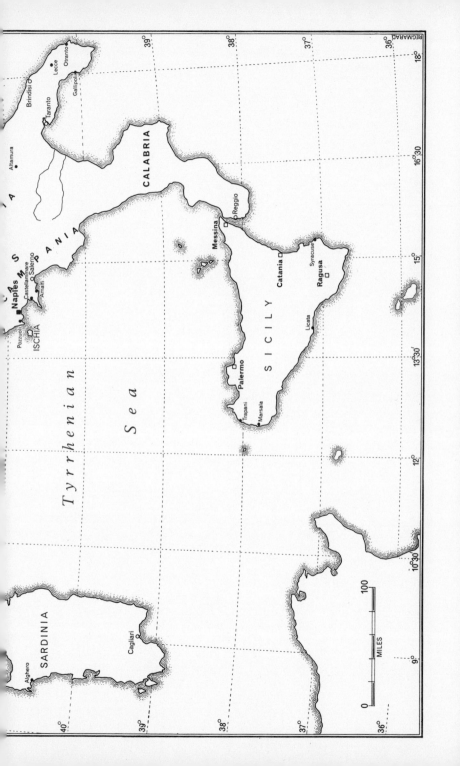

Contents

Preface   page 5

Map of Italy   8–9

Map of the Mediterranean   72–3

Chapter

  1   The Country   15
  2   The Manufacturing Industries   35
  3   Trade   59
  4   Finance   91
  5   External Relations   108
  6   Internal Affairs   130
  7   History, Political Thought and Language   149
  8   Science, Medicine and Technology   172
  9   Religion   197
 10   Art and Architecture   220
 11   Conclusion   246

Bibliography   257

Index   277

RENAISSANCE ITALY
1464–1534

I
The Country

If agriculture is limited by the inherent possibilities of land and climate, there is also much that man can do to influence its ultimate form. This was so even in an age ignorant of soil chemistry, in which fertilisation was largely accidental, and when technology was not always able to hold its own with nature. There were in Italy in the fifteenth and sixteenth centuries varied instruments of man-made change: the hill-sculpture which in all its variety of terracing was chiefly a soil-break against the erosion of heavy rains; and the canalisation of the water of the winter rain and the spring thaws which reduced marsh, avoided the havoc of flooding and irrigated the parched wastes. The demand from the city or from abroad for vegetable dyestuffs or for raw materials for textiles, successful foreign competition, or changes in taste, also dictated to the farmer what he should grow. Transhumant sheep ate into the plains with disastrous results and over-zealous wood-cutters denuded the hills of trees that held the soil, while war and depopulation by disease repeatedly removed the constant care that was necessary for this artificial landscape to survive. The aim of this chapter is to show the state of change the countryside had reached by about 1464, and to sketch the main developments that occurred over the next 70 years, hinting at later trends in the agrarian economy in Italy.

From the tenth century until towards the end of the thirteenth century, the Italian economy steadily revived from the low level it had been left in by the decline of Rome and the barbarian invasions. A symptom of this revival was the great amount of land brought under cultivation during this period. Then, as in the rest of Europe, there ensued a period of regression accentuated by a corn crisis in the second decade of the fourteenth century and a financial crisis closely followed by the Black Death. The north of Italy in the first period developed most and in the second period, owing to a remarkable resourcefulness and adaptability, suffered least, and in parts not at all. It was in the south, in the kingdom of Naples from the Abruzzi and Campania to the southern tip of Italy and in the islands of Sardinia and Corsica, that the least progress was followed by the greatest setbacks. Sicily, for reasons to be seen later, avoided to a great extent this general backwardness.

Naples had small pockets of intensive mixed agriculture, carried on often by the owners of small holdings. This was the case with much of the land around the city of Naples itself and in the south of Calabria. But a great part of the kingdom was in the hands of the barons, who owned huge tracts of land in the tradition of the Roman *latifundia*. These estates were added to by usurpation, especially in the fourteenth century, when the peasant was leaving his land to the invasion of the marshes and seeking security in the hilltop but jobless villages, which the barons themselves were bringing under their protection and control. One such landlord, the prince of Taranto and Altamura, was master of half Apulia and independent enough to align himself with Venice against the succession of King Ferrante in 1458. The land of these often uncontrollable feudal lords was not cultivated systematically. Sometimes wheat and fallow alternated biennially; sometimes the land was freed to grazing. Through shortage of labour, soil exhaustion or turning over to sheep farming, much of the land was lost to the plough. But Apulia exported grain in abundance, especially to Venice, never sufficiently supplied with bread during this period by her mainland territories, the Terraferma. Likewise, the small ports of the west coast of Naples, Gaeta, Castellammare, Salerno and others, discharged their grain to small Genoese coasters. Campania, wetter than the other grain-growing areas of the kingdom, produced some of the cheaper, coarser and sturdier grains, buckwheat and dhurra grass, but most Neapolitan grain was high-quality wheat. Even in the Abruzzi around Aquila to an altitude of about 5,000 feet wheat and barley were produced in quantity. Neapolitan agriculture, of course, was not limited to grain. Aquila was famous for the excellence of its saffron, which provided a dye in great demand in the textile industries of Europe and which was also used in paints and hair colouring, as a laxative and a preventative against plague, and for cooking, especially in sweetmeats. Saffron, which largely accounted for the thirteenth-century origin of Aquila and for its later growth, by 1500 was no longer able to hold its sales, and Aquila's prosperity declined. Apulia produced large quantities of olive oil, much of which was used in the local export industry of soap-making, centred at Gallipoli and Brindisi, and in the sixteenth century particularly at Bari. Often the oil itself was exported to Levantine and Aegean soap manufacturers from the great olive-growing centre of Andria, by way of the port of Barletta. Oak from the bear-haunted forests of the Gargano mountains furnished Adriatic shipbuilders on both sides of the sea with much of their timber, and some cotton was grown in Apulia and exported north to the industries of the Po Valley. In the west, Calabria was the centre of an increasingly prosperous production of silk, and reaped large profits as the Genoese silk industry expanded in the sixteenth century. There was a comparatively small production of silk also in Campania. But here wine production was becoming increasingly more important and famous; for it was in Naples that the vagaries of connoisseurship were now being understood and wine was being produced in variety to suit the tastes of a farflung *clientèle*. Pope Sixtus IV collected a long list of prized wines, but the Neapolitans also considered the cruder tastes of their customers in England or the Netherlands.

Naples, with Sicily, did much towards feeding the north of Italy and other countries of the Mediterranean. Without the help of grain from southern Italy, the Spain of Ferdinand and Isabella, and then later of Charles V, could not have survived the pastoral economy of the Mesta and the expulsion of the Moors. But if sheep were largely responsible for Spain's agricultural decline, the same process was to occur in Naples. With the fourteenth-century drop in population and the corresponding loss of labour and of cultivable land, stock farming grew increasingly tempting. Stock had always been kept to a minimum: oxen for the plough, mules as pack-animals, pigs for meat or sausages and sheep for milk. As sheep-farming grew, the cultivated land retreated, and King Alfonso I tried to check the devastation in the middle of the fifteenth century by controlling the seasonal migrations of transhumant flocks. The main pattern of transhumance was for the sheep to summer in the Abruzzi and come down into the Tavoliere of Apulia, where the big wool market of Foggia grew up, and winter there after the wheat harvest. A toll was levied on their passage. In 1463, 600,000 sheep made the journey; in 1536, over a million. The peak of $5\frac{1}{2}$ million was reached in 1604. But the quality of Italian sheep's wool was not good, for the pastures were not suitable. In the fourteenth century sheep from North Africa had been introduced into Naples with little effect. Then Alfonso brought in merino sheep from Spain, but the quality of the merino wool did not equal its Spanish counterpart, which in turn failed to reach the standard of the best English wool until well into the seventeenth century. Accordingly Neapolitan wool never carried the price to justify commercially the near extinction of a well-developed agriculture. In fact there was some resistance to the process. About 1500, in Apulia, those whose living depended largely upon agriculture strongly opposed the yearly invasion of the pastoralists from the hills; but, as the figures show, their protests had little effect, and under Philip II of Spain grain production in Campania and Apulia declined dramatically in an economy that increasingly reflected Spanish habits and ways of thought.

The islands of Corsica and Sardinia were the seats of feudal anarchy and neglect. Both were homes of piracy rather than industry; yet both made their contributions to the agrarian commerce of the western Mediterranean. Especially in the south and west of Sardinia livestock predominated over agriculture and sustained a trade in salted meats and cheeses, products greatly relished around the north-west coast of the Mediterranean. At the same time a moderate wool production brought all the consequences of transhumance. In Corsica irresponsible brigandage of great Ligurian families, of the aristocratic Fieschi or the so-called 'popular' ducal family of the Fregosi, made agriculture a losing battle and converted the island into a wilderness. For bread the Corsicans used the chestnuts from the hills; and there was timber enough to make a considerable export trade to the ship-building industries of Genoa and, with its rise in the sixteenth century, Leghorn. Wine was exported from the little port of Saint-Florent, especially to Genoa and Rome. Work, however, was scarce and Corsica's biggest export perhaps was its men. Seasonally, Corsicans left the island for the wheat harvest in the Tuscan Maremma; but more often they emigrated for good. Genoese officials tried to plug this drain of manpower on two separate occasions, in 1475 and 1489, by having Corsicans forbidden from living in Rome.

Sicily more than Naples was the great wheat-growing region of the central Mediterranean. In the fifteenth century its exports were high. Merchants, mostly Genoese, had their businesses centred in Palermo, where the absentee landlords from the south lived. They sent small ships to pick up grain along the south coast of Sicily from Marsala to Licata, to distribute it to wherever grain was short or to take it home. The grain was grown on huge estates in the south of Sicily, stretching back high into the mountains. The land was well drained and the summers good for ripening and harvesting, with the result that Sicilian wheat was of high quality and the crop was less open to destruction than most. Some buckwheat and other coarser grains were grown and so was rice, until towards the end of the fifteenth century it was successfully introduced into Lombardy. In the sixteenth century the export of wheat from Sicily dropped markedly. This is possibly not so much an indication of a decline in wheat-growing as of the rise in the island's own consumption with the development of its large cities.

The Sicilians did not have to face difficulties similar to those that wool production had brought to Naples, and they had alternative products for export. Chief amongst these were silk and cane-sugar, both of which found a big market amongst the Genoese. The sugar was distributed throughout Europe; and, although from the second half of the fifteenth century strong competition came from the Atlantic islands of Portugal so that by 1496 Atlantic sugar could be bought even at Venice, Sicilians had no difficulty in selling their sugar right up to the end of the sixteenth century. Cotton, salted cheeses based on the big salt industry at Trapani, aloes for purgatives, indigo for dyeing, hemp and citrus fruits were all produced in large quantities, principally on the small northern coastal plains of the island and in the plains behind Catania where often smaller holdings, intensively worked, contrasted strikingly with the vast wheat estates of the south, where the fields were left fallow in alternate years. Thus, partly by avoiding the problems caused by the perennial hostility between stock-raising and agriculture, but also because of its ideal position on the trade routes of the Mediterranean, Sicily was able to maintain its arable land through a period when big reductions were being experienced in the other islands and in the south of the Italian mainland.

The Papal States divide roughly into two: those of Romagna and the Marches going from the eastern slopes of the Apennines to the Adriatic on the one hand, and Umbria and the western coastal plain corresponding roughly to Latium on the other. These territories were neglected in the period of chronic indiscipline during the Avignon papacy and the ensuing schism, and especially so in the west. That these circumstances coincided with the period of population decline in which marginal lands were left to waste only accentuated an already disastrous process. The Pontine Marshes to the south of Rome expanded to absorb previously cultivated land and became the refuge of the wild boar and buffalo. North along the coastal plain, continuous with the Sienese Maremma, swamp had encroached on much of the land. Even inland in the Val di Chiana between Florentine Arezzo and the papal Città della Pieve it had predominated. Some recovery was made in the fifteenth century and corn was sown in the Roman countryside. But this land was held by local barons in large estates. Particularly when there was a labour shortage was it tempting to turn to pastoralism, for which shepherd labour from the Abruzzi was readily available. From Sixtus IV the popes vigorously fought this tendency, since bread was basic to the tranquillity of Rome. But the very policy of placing restrictions on grain commerce in order to satisfy the city's food supply had already made the growing of cereals a less attractive commercial proposition by limiting the free exploitation of the best market prices. Accordingly, as late as 1523 Clement VII was making efforts to ensure a local grain supply, and figures for the following year showed that there was only half as much grain produced then in the district around Rome as had been common in the previous century. In Umbria certainly, where the agriculture was to a large extent determined by communal needs as in the region of Perugia, grain production, in particular wheat, was more widespread. However, there were not sufficient reserves to draw on when the crop was poor, and the hardships that followed were severe. Such was the case in 1529 when the crops failed for 50 miles around Perugia, and again in Umbria in the summer of 1538 when hail-storms destroyed the crop and winter snow and spring floods accentuated the misery.

Baronial feuds and the instability of papal government were reasons for the inability of the popes to enforce a successful corn policy in the west. In the Marches and in Romagna the hold of the professional captains, the *condottieri*, and other local rulers over the communes, together with the strong propensity of the communes themselves to support policies markedly independent of the papacy, gave the popes no greater scope to influence the development of agriculture. Moreover, the barrier of the Apennines coupled with the insecurity of the country made transport of grain from east to west on a large scale hardly a feasible proposition. Grain was far more cheaply furnished from Sicily, Naples and the Maremma by sea. In the east the problem was not one of choice between wheat and sheep. It was a matter of providing the peace and security for maintaining the level of agriculture already reached and creating the confidence to embark upon improvements. Up to the first decade of the sixteenth century, when Julius restored papal authority over most of the Papal States, only Bologna (Ferrara will be dealt with separately later) was able to create such confidence. In other major regions agriculture declined with the insecurity of the times. The large area over which the Malatesta exercised their influence from Rimini was prosperous in the first part of the fourteenth century. In the second half of the century it was continually subject to disputes. Territory was lost and in that which was retained production decreased. Worse, the population of the town and its surrounding country from the end of the fourteenth century to 1524 dropped to a quarter of its original total, so that Rimini became a mere village and its land was largely deserted.

Bologna, as a prosperous university city with a sound industrial development, provided a steady demand for food and raw materials from its countryside, which enjoyed the advantages of comparatively peaceful Bentivoglio rule. North and east towards Ferrara and the Valli di Comacchio corn, flax and hemp were grown in considerable quantity, although there was still a great deal of waste and marshland as yet unclaimed. Here also cattle were kept, the wet and naturally manured pasturelands being used for fodder in alternate years. Generally Bologna could supply her own bread. In bad years, years of too little or too much water, or when earthquakes, plague or civil strife interrupted the normal conduct of affairs, she sought imported grain at Venice, the normal market for her own surplus. In 1477 she hired Venetian shipping to bring grain directly from Calabria, a costly method since the Venetians exacted a huge profit on the cargo. Behind Bologna the lower slopes of the Apennines were covered with olive-groves and vineyards, and with the growth of the silk industry mulberry trees became an increasingly prominent feature of the landscape. Already in the fifteenth century the Bentivoglio had extended the Canale del Reno to the walls of Bologna and so had completed a continuous waterway from the Po to the city. The canal, if it priced itself out of business as far as the transport of produce was concerned, nevertheless contributed to the drainage of the surrounding country. Also the people of Bologna, led by the Bentivoglio, invested the profits of profession, industry or commerce in the building of country villas and the reclamation of land to increase the pleasantness and productivity of their estates. After the papal subjugation of Romagna the popes looked more carefully at the agricultural potentialities of the region, but little of distinction was attempted until Clement VII tried to recover saturated land north of Ravenna, a project the first stage of which had been tentatively begun by Julius II in 1504; but this did not achieve very satisfactory results until the end of the sixteenth century. Likewise in the west Leo X had seen a chance of profit for his family as contractors for reclamation from the marshlands, but his impulse had no tangible result. The popes had won back the papal lands, but it was long before they were really to enjoy the fruits of their success.

In the republic of Siena the cultivators of wheat held off the extension of marshland in the Maremma as well as they could. But the fevers from the swamps were hostile to human existence. That is why the migratory, seasonal workers from Corsica were so welcome there. If the lords had their castles there too, they only used them for refuge or as haunts of conspiracy, preferring the safety and salubrity of a house in Siena. In the long run Sienese agriculture prospered. It supplied Florence with its deficiencies in corn and meat and regularly supplied Rome, Genoa and the Ligurian Rivieras with grain. Lucca on the other side of Florence was even more successful. By the fifteenth century the old mediaeval silk industry had so developed that surrounding hills were richly cloaked with mulberry trees for the intensive rearing of silkworms.

The countryside or *contado* of Florence had perhaps developed more than anywhere in the fifteenth century the distinctive feature of the cultivated, Mediterranean hillside, the terrace. In limited areas in the north of Sicily, on the steep slopes around Amalfi, on the southern side of the Ligurian Apennines, in the Euganei Hills and in many other parts of Italy terraces in varied forms could be found, but nowhere did they dominate the hills as they did in the territories of Florence. Terracing had been going on throughout the later Middle Ages and, as terraces required the unremitting vigilance of the farm-workers to keep them in repair, they drew the cultivator from within the walls of a hilltop village down into hillside farms. As a result, the countryside became more populated and the landscape was widely scattered with farm-buildings, whilst the large villages were partially deserted. By the fifteenth century the land was generally divided into small units and owned by the peasant himself or by a merchant from the town. Even the old estates of the nobles had tended to subdivision, if only for the purpose of leasing out. However, the tendency by the fifteenth century was to buy up contiguous land to form larger blocks, especially at the expense of the peasant owner. The main form of tenure was that of *mezzadria* or share-cropping, in which ideally the landlord and the tenant shared the produce of the farm equally. In fact, it was not unusual for the agreement to give the landlord a greater share. The contracts, which were usually for a short term of years, had innumerable individual variations. Sometimes the landlord would take the greater share of wine but would expect money instead of grain; it might be the tenant's task to deliver produce to Florence, but the landlord's burden to pay the toll on the wine, grain or oil entering the city; there would be special agreements about who provided the seed, the farm implements and farm animals, how the bacon, fowl or eggs were to be distributed and so forth. Most of this small-scale farming yielded a wide variety of produce. There would be perhaps grain or high-class Tuscan saffron produced for the market, but the share-cropper would be self-sufficient and he would be expected to supply the needs and the additional delicacies demanded by his landlord.

The land itself was a highly negotiable commodity, passing frequently from owner to owner. While the noble from the country invested in the city, the successful artisan, the professional man, the big merchant, invested in the land. Why money from the city was spent on the land is not certain; it was probably the product of several varied and interwoven motives. By city standards land was not an especially paying investment; a good Florentine business always yielded more, more quickly. Nor was it only because land was a safe investment; if this was true, investment in land often took place when city business did not involve great risk. If there was an ideal fostered by writers like Leon Battista Alberti about the gentlemanly delights of the country life, there were always those who deprecated the flow of money away from trade and industry which were the foundation, they said, of Florentine greatness. But those who could afford it were probably attracted by the prospect of a country retreat in a countryside which was becoming increasingly friendly as a place that was lived in. However, the mill was one extremely profitable country investment, and from the fourteenth century mills fell under the dominance of city capitalists.

The Florentine coastal plain resisted less the encroachment of the marsh than did Siena's to the south. The tiny ports of Porto Pisano, by the end of the fifteenth century almost abandoned, and of Leghorn, by the same time scarcely having emerged, were both—a few hundred yards apart—surrounded by marshlands, which spread south to meet those of Siena, and remained for long untouched by the plough. In 1469 some attempt was made to reclaim Florentine territory for cultivation by making artificial lakes, but in the sixteenth century attempts at reclamation were still meeting with little success. This was chiefly because the people were settled before the land was reclaimed, with the result that most of the settlements were devastated by malaria before any effective reclamation had taken place. As in Romagna, the occupation or passage of enemy troops in Florentine Tuscany and particularly the dreary fifteen years of the Pisan war, which exercised the republican, anti-Medicean régime at the turn of the century, did nothing to improve matters; and it was left to the emasculated Florence of the dukes to accomplish some of the frustrated agrarian ideals of the fifteenth century. Yet in this period, nowhere in Italy except in the Po Valley did agriculture flourish as in the Florentine *contado*, where, moreover, the man who provided the labour worked under better conditions than perhaps obtained anywhere else in his time.

The main state in the valley of the Po was Milan, the great coastless duchy dominating several of the Alpine passes to the north, and cut off from the sea to the south by the Ligurian Apennines. The further north the territory of Milan pierced the sun-starved, Alpine valleys and rose into the mountains, the less the land was farmed. Here there was wide-spread heath; and peasant small-holders strove for self-sufficiency, while enduring a hungry independence. In the friendlier hills a little to the south much more specialisation occurred, about a third of the land being sown with grain; and after the legislation of Galeazzo Maria Sforza in 1470 each 15 acres of suitable land in this region was to carry at least five mul-berry trees. The higher part of the adjoining plain was not irrigated; yet it was planted with grain, vines and some forage, and as much as three-quarters of the area was farmed. The irrigated plain was cultivated to an even greater extent and most intensively in the Cremona district on the Po and in the land around Lodi to the west of the Adda. In these areas there was scarcely an acre of waste, and there was an abundance of water from the rivers, carefully controlled in a complex system of canals and irrigation ditches, as well as from a belt of warm springs. Thus there were lush meadows for the development of cattle farming in the fourteenth century, and swamps that were used for the cultivation of rice from the end of the fifteenth century. Although cattle became widespread in the duchy, they were especially dominant in the district of Milan, important for its meat as well as its dairy produce, and south of the Po from Parma to Piacenza whose cheeses were already famous. The development of rice culture took place principally in the areas around Vigevano and Pavia and in the intervening Lomellina. The Pavese had previously been an import-ant flax-growing region, but rice—once the initial outlays had been met—was a much more rewarding crop. It had a good yield and required only a very small permanent labour force. Although the demand for flax was falling as a result of successful competition in the fifteenth century from the south German fustian industries, it was still grown locally for the manufacture of fustian at Cremona, the second city of the duchy, and at Alessandria. East of Alessandria, in the Marengo, woad had replaced the old madder production, partly on account of a shift in taste from reds to more practical blues. The woad crop was sometimes sandwiched between a wheat harvest and approaching winter; at other times the land was given over to woad altogether and four or five crops were gathered successively in the same summer. From the point of view of the farmers, therefore, this leaf crop was in all ways more satisfactory than the old biennial root crop of madder. Fifteen thousand of the 60 or 70 thousand mule loads that crossed the Apennines from Lombardy to Genoa each year were given over to woad on the first leg of its distribution to England, the Low Coun-tries or Spain. It was also sent in large quantities from Lombardy into Tuscany and to Venice. But by about 1480 the woad production of

Toulouse had grown so vastly that the Lombards were pushed out of the international trade.

Rice growing expanded so fast that by the second half of the sixteenth century the grain was produced for export, while at the same time multiple fodder crops made the export of dairy produce also possible. Despite this and a wide diffusion of industrial crops, like mulberries for the silkworm and woad and saffron for dyes, of the half of the land that was cultivated in about 1550 nearly three-quarters was given over to grain and leguminous crops. Even cereals were produced for export, for in the sixteenth century and later the Swiss looked to Lombardy for their bread. But still, as in the time of Francesco Sforza, there was a shortage of white bread and the important grains were rye and millet. At the same time the total amount of land cultivated had already contracted owing to the wars of Italy, which had continually brought troop movements, occupation by foreign soldiery or actual warfare during the first half of the sixteenth century.

In a period when the rest of Europe was suffering from an economic depression and a decline in population, northern Italy and especially Milan was adapting itself not only to survive, but indeed to expand. The opportunity may have been fortuitous, but the method, if self-interested, was calculated and original. The Church was rich in land accumulated haphazardly from the bequests of the devout, largely in the interests of their departed souls. What it lacked in the later Middle Ages was money, which in a developing money economy it needed more and more urgently, particularly since it was so difficult to enforce the services due to it from its scattered peasants and was having to go over to the employment of wage-earners. To get money the churches were forced to lease their lands. Investors—feudal lords, successful city merchants, soldiers or lawyers, shopkeepers or artisans—saw their chance. A form of contract including improvement clauses was used. It required at the expiry of the lease that the lessor make good money used by the tenant for improving the property. Failing this the tenant was able to repeat the lease under the same conditions as before. Seldom could the Church, owing to its cash shortage, meet the first alternative. Accordingly speculators got hold of land made increasingly valuable by improvement—at very low rents, which were even relatively reduced during periods of rising prices. These speculators aimed at gathering together blocks of land, and thus they altered fundamentally the pattern of landownership, the scattered possessions that had characterised the past. Even the old feudal nobility tended to consolidate much of its property. Consolidation had several attractions.

Improvements such as the provision of irrigation ditches or farm buildings were far more economical if they were to serve a compact stretch of land. The tenants, virtually the new owners of the land, were capitalistic speculators aiming to produce for the biggest and most profitable markets. They were behind the big dairy farms, the large-scale woad production, the experiment in rice. To farm for a commercial market, everything had to be streamlined. Labour charges and equipment costs were lower, marketing facilities were more efficient, if production was centralised. Ultimately, despite early fifteenth-century ducal legislation forbidding it, the Church in return for a slight rise in the rent granted perpetual leases. The new owners usually did not live on the land. They sublet it on contracts of *mezzadria* extremely favourable to themselves or used hired labour to work it for them. Sometimes they acquired the land from the Church by exchanging for it other land, not of equal extent but of a real value equal to the absurdly low nominal value of the land in question. Land acquired one way or another was often resold at enormous profit. The dukes—in the first place the Visconti, later the Sforzas—were generally in favour of what was going on. They built roads which encouraged the commercial exploitation of the land, but which at the same time helped them to control the feudal lords. With the increase of rural works on canals, farm-buildings and so forth, and with the revival of the land, the countryside and the villages were repopulated and rural industries returned and made possible the dispersal of the unemployed or discontented to perhaps a more satisfied existence in the country. A new class of supporters of the dukes was being fostered, men whose vision could only be realised if the whole weight of the community were harnessed to it. The dukes won them by developing the canal system which provided cheap transport and by extending the drainage and irrigation networks of Lombardy to their advantage. Farms became more efficient; the duchy more prosperous. Finally, by taxing the Church, the dukes speeded up the process of capitalists acquiring Church lands, for the Church's need for money was accordingly aggravated.

The process of capitalistic exploitation was ultimately self-defeating. Sometimes the turnover of land at a profit became more important than the use of the land itself. At others the money-making urgency did not survive many generations and the speculator or his descendant became the country gentleman, enjoying rather than exploiting his possessions. By the end of the fifteenth century the Church had little more land to filch, and the properties of small owners had fast disappeared into the consolidated properties of the big landowners. As the sixteenth century progressed the landowners had to look outside Milanese territories to the mountains behind Bergamo to find workers willing or available to accept unfavourable *mezzadria* contracts. Then with the Counter-Reformation the Church began to acquire land anew. No longer was it on the defensive. No longer had it to surrender its land to city speculators. Now the economy was dominated by the demands of Hapsburg Spain; and a régime in which Church, landlord and foreigner held sway was doomed to lose the dynamism formerly bestowed upon it by the expedients of capitalistic enterprise.

To the west of the duchy of Milan were the small states of Asti and Montferrat and the Piedmontese territories of Savoy. Much the same pattern of development took place here as in Milan. Irrigation allowed the change to cattle farming, and rice culture was developed somewhat later in the sixteenth century than in Lombardy. Local flax supported the fustian industry of Chieri, which like other north Italian examples of the industry suffered from the competition of south Germany. The Piedmontese silk production, which flourished in the fifteenth century, was severely hit by the wars in the first part of the sixteenth century, and it was only under the active encouragement of Emmanuel Philibert of Savoy that a silk industry restored the successful growth of the mulberry. At the same time, hemp cultivation continued to expand, despite the presence of French troops, and by 1529 huge exports were recorded, while behind the juncture of Alp and Apennine the vineyards of the Langhe bore a prosperous and well-famed wine industry.

The duchy of Mantua, pushed back by Venice from the shores of Lake Garda and watered by the Mincio and the Po, was famous for its horses, and to feed them it grew large amounts of spelt and oats, although by the second half of the sixteenth century wheat took up over half of the cultivated lands of the duchy. Sheep farming was encouraged by the privileged position of the woollen industry at Mantua, and the north Italian process of replacing sheep with cattle was checked, even though transhumant cattle from Venice encroached upon Mantuan territory. That wolves were still a menace to the livestock of Mantua perhaps indicates the limits of man's control over his environment at this stage of the history of northern Italy. Ferrara, consisting of the technically papal state of Ferrara and the no less technically imperial fief of Modena, was also mainly concerned with the production of wheat. This was actively encouraged by Borso d'Este, duke in the third quarter of the fifteenth century, and by Ercole II, who inherited the duchy in 1534. But in the meantime, even in bad years, Ferrara was always sufficiently supplied with corn, while in good years as much as two-thirds of the crop was used for export, with Venice the chief

27

customer. Finally, the sodden meadows of Ferrara like the rest of the Po Valley saw a growing cattle industry, and Ferrara cheese was well known beyond the confines of the duchy.

Changes that took place in Milanese Lombardy and Piedmont, also occurred to some extent in the Venetian Terraferma, although with Venetian frontiers continually expanding during the fifteenth century the initiative for these changes often predated Venetian control. Moreover, the long series of wars with Milan and the Turk in the fifteenth century and with most of Italy and Europe on various occasions during the first three decades of the sixteenth century allowed little opportunity for official or private development to be planned from the capital. Crema—and Cremona while Venice held it—were both typical centres of Lombard agriculture. Cereals rather than cattle tended to be produced there, so that, as in Lombardy, despite the advances in new crops and produce, grain still predominated. In the districts of Brescia and Bergamo, iron deposits, not agrarian interests, brought people to the valleys. A little grain was grown in them too but most came from the plains of the Bresciano, cut by the Mella and artificially irrigated by canals from the Oglio. Sheep and cattle were kept in the summer along the slopes of the valleys and brought down to the plain to winter. The landowners of Brescia complained bitterly at this invasion of their stubble fields and their vineyards, but the Venetian government's bans on transhumance had little effect and the practice continued. Nor did the costs of controlling the Oglio, over which the landowners were often in conflict with Cremona, ease their problems and in 1534 they protested about this too to the government. The plains of Crema, Bergamo and Brescia were also the main centres of Venetian silk production, and their countryside acquired the mark of the mulberry.

Rice came later to the Terraferma than to the duchy of Milan. Its introduction was under urban influence and ricefields consequently were developed near the towns. This produced ill-feeling between official and landowner: the one in the interests of public health trying to enforce laws keeping the rice swamps at a distance from the town populations, the other in the interests of profit continuing to grow rice on the city outskirts. In the 1520s such a conflict was aroused on account of ricefields around Verona. Furthermore the innovation of rice was to the detriment of local wheat and beef production. To check the decline the government of Venice in 1529 fixed a quota of 1,000 beef cattle to be provided by Verona annually. This did not alter things and a quarter of a century later Verona was pleading that it was impossible to provide so many head of cattle. In spite of the official attitude the growing of rice continued to expand in Venetian territories until it reached a peak in the last decades of the seventeenth century.

It was the policy of sixteenth-century Venice to compensate for its loss of buying power, resulting from reverses suffered in its position in world trade, by being able to provide more of its own food from the mainland. Much of what was done officially to achieve this end did not take place until after the end of the period covered by this book. This was owing to a lack of opportunity rather than to any lack of desire. The office of the *Cinque Savi della Mercanzia* was established at the beginning of the century, primarily to consider ways of maintaining the Levantine trade, but it also set the tenor of future thinking connected with economic and therefore agrarian policy: a state policy was to be enforced by government officials rather than, as had been the case in Milan, development being left to private initiative, to acquire later the stamp of official approval. The reason is not difficult to see: in the past the provision, that is to say the import, of food had always been a matter of government responsibility. Now the manner of providing the food had changed but the government did not relinquish the responsibility. This was unfortunate because the Signoria could seldom see beyond the limits of corn. Especially in the second half of the sixteenth century a great deal of land was reclaimed: by 1545 a third of the Venetian mainland was still uncultivated waste; but the reclamations were turned over to corn production with the effect that the recovered land was often quickly exhausted by the unbroken culture of cereals. Even pasture was taken over by grain, and rotational techniques that were effectively emerging in the Po Valley from Piedmont to Bologna seemed not to find their way to the more newly cultivated parts of Venetian territory. In the west, Lombard, in the south, Ferrarese traditions were followed; and where there were well-established agricultures as around Padua, important for its wheat and cheese, mistakes like this were not made. But, because the government over-emphasised wheat in its requirements from the cultivators whose land it had helped to retrieve, its effect on agriculture tended to bring disaster.

Venetian farming was much more varied than has hitherto been indicated. Sheep-farming was not limited to the far north-west of the state, but followed the valleys and foothills right around the south-eastern regions of the Alps. Likewise vineyards were to be found terraced on the shores of Garda or at Chioggia, on the hills about Padua or on the islands of the lagoon. Pig-farming was important in the wheat country of Friuli, where the hams were reputedly of good quality, whilst in the south the

Polesina di Rovigo sent its poultry to Venice. Later in the sixteenth century maize was introduced, but it was not before the eighteenth century that it began to dominate the landscape. Hemp too was an important crop of the Terraferma, partly answering the needs of the shipbuilding industry at Venice. Timber for the ships was floated down from the Dolomites, for instance on the Adige, to be towed from south of Chioggia into the lagoon, and firewood was brought to Venice from Istria. But the use of timber was reckless, and Venice was confronted with a crippling wood famine by the end of the sixteenth century.

For long rich patricians and citizens of Venice had bought properties on the mainland in territories which had not yet been brought under Venetian control. As the frontiers of Venice advanced they continued to buy land, cashing in on the sequestrated properties of uncooperative land-lords or on their loss of prosperity resulting from changed political con-ditions. As civil governors or military captains in subject territories, the Venetian patricians had every occasion to buy up land on very favourable terms, and they did not fail to do so. The property gathered together in this way was fairly scattered, because the opportunities to buy did not necessarily give the purchaser the chance to accumulate large consolidated blocks. But with the vigorous reclamation of the sixteenth century, estates emerged as considerable units, although one owner might have such blocks in three or four different districts. There was also great competition for the control of mills, and very often a mill would be divided into three or four shares. Despite the considerable possession of landed property by the rich Venetians, little seems to have been done to work or improve it until Venice had extricated herself from the terrible conse-quences of the wars following the League of Cambrai. This was also the case with consolidated blocks of land acquired by monasteries. Perhaps in the 1520s, when the first real opportunity arose to compensate for trade losses to the Portuguese by developing the Terraferma, attention was turned to the land. Soon the patrician would learn the delights of the countryside and adorn his estates with a villa, perhaps built by Palladio. Certainly the second half of the century and the first half of the next saw a great expansion of such settlement and the merchant nobility cast itself in the mould of a country squirearchy.

The only major part of Italy still to be described is Liguria: the two Rivieras of Genoa, scarcely coastal strips hemmed in between sea and mountain, and the barren mountains themselves. Here the land was owned by feudal lords or peasant proprietors. There was no bourgeois investment from the city, although country lords might very well have considerable business interests in Genoa. This was not inevitable either; for the powerful Malaspinas, to take the most prominent example, kept themselves out of Genoa and developed interests only in their own considerable territories and in Tuscany. In contrast the Spinola di Luccoli at times virtually dominated the vast and complex business world of Genoa. In the absence of bourgeois landowners the feudal relationship was still very real, although services were generally commuted for money payments during the fifteenth century. The *mezzadria* contract was accordingly never employed by the big landowners, although it did occur when a prosperous peasant with more land than he himself could farm would lease out his surplus property to another peasant. To the west, on the Riviera di Ponente, terraces rising almost from the sea bore mulberry, olive and fig trees, vines, melons and gourds, even hay. This was not an inconsiderable production, and, for example, dried fruits from Finale Ligure were sold as far afield as Salonika. In the small plains around Albenga and Savona a more ambitious agriculture took place. Albenga grew grain quite extensively, and had good crops of fruit and beans. Savona prospered on the production of hemp, which was made into packing-cloth for the transport of fragile ware, and coarser material from which sacks for wool and grain were made. Farther east on the Riviera di Levante the terraces bore similar crops—for instance, grapes and figs, citrus fruits, olives, on the most southerly slopes in Cinqueterre. At Moneglia slaves were disembarked especially to work in the silk production there. Around Sestri Levante and Rapallo some cattle were kept. Nearer the capital, especially in its eastern suburbs stretching across the mouth of the Bisagno, intensive market gardening took place, whilst in their suburban villas around Genoa the rich families grew grapes for wine. Mulberries for silkworms were grown here too. In the hills to the west, a few animals were kept and the chestnuts were harvested for flour. In the eastern hills, particularly in the Lunigiana between Pontremoli and Sarzana, panic grass was the poor grain from which the local bread was made. In Genoa, everyone ate white bread; but it was made of imported wheat from Sicily and Naples or on occasion from the Sienese Maremma.

The farming produce of Italy was even more varied than it might seem from this brief survey. Beans were grown almost everywhere for local consumption and chick peas were common. Wine was drunk in greater quantities in the Italian Middle Ages than today and alms of bread and wine, not bread and water, were given to the poor. Thus the vine was almost ubiquitous and the peasant of the Alpine valleys of Lombardy took his independence so far as to make his own vinegary wine. Every farm kept a minimum of livestock: sheep, as less destructive than goats, often for milk and cheese; hens for eggs; working animals, generally oxen for the plough; and mules as pack animals for transport. Carts and wagons were not yet common in Italy, as they were in the north of Europe. In Naples there was no route across the Apennines that the wheel could safely negotiate. In the *contado* of Florence wheeled casks were used for transporting wine. Wagons were sometimes used for the middle stretch of the journey between Geneva and Genoa from the Alps to the Apennines. But most transport in Lombardy used the big riverways and canals; salt—to take one major example—was imported through Genoa to Milan on mule and barge. The mule was consequently in great demand and Tuscan muleteers and those from the Ligurian Apennines gained considerable repute. Despite the specialised breeding of horses in Mantua and less famously in the Milanese, there was a very serious shortage of cavalry horses in Italy as in the other countries of the Mediterranean in the sixteenth century; on the other hand, a lady's carriage in Milan might well be drawn by as many as four finely-groomed horses, such were the values of the time.

In Italy as elsewhere the wildlife of the country was plundered, and there was a great deal to be found in the swamp and waste that covered a considerable part of the land. A wide range from the buffaloes and boars already mentioned, hares, rabbits, ducks and geese spread to such delicacies as quails, thrushes and finches. But in a Christian country fish were also important. The Mediterranean is not over-lavishly provided with fish, and it was not exceptional to import North Sea herring, salted cod from Andalusia, caviar—especially to break the monotony of Lent—from the Don and the Dnieper or salted fish from the Nile delta. At Genoa rock fish from the Provençal coast was also imported. There was, however, a big tunny-fishing industry based on Sicily, where the fish was preserved in local oil. This was supplemented by tunny bought in the south of Spain and imported to other parts of Italy. Fishing was carried on around the whole Italian coast, but there was nothing to compare with the great herring fishery of the North Sea. Inland, naturally, fish was less often eaten and it was always salted or preserved in oil, except for the comparatively infrequent occasions when freshwater fish were to be had. But for the most part, meatless days were not confined to Fridays and Lent, and fish was not an invariable substitute. Not even cheese was necessary. The usual diet for many was bread, beans, *pasta* made of the flour of beans as well as of grain, fruit and wine. Perhaps this was no great deprivation. An English traveller, William Thomas, although a great meat-eater who had barely been able to 'brook' fruit in England, wrote in 1548 that in Italy he 'desired no meate more', being happy to live on such fruits as pomegranates and pumpkins, melons and figs, oranges, peaches, pears and apples.

Several points emerge from a broad glance at the Italian countryside during this period. The first is that stock-raising expanded vastly. In the south the sheep population rose steadily and its growth accelerated rapidly in the remainder of the sixteenth century. On the other hand, in the north cattle began to change the aspect of the Po Valley, although sheep at least were able to hold their own on the Venetian Terraferma. Whereas to a very large extent the southern sheep destroyed the land, the northern cattle helped utilise land that before had been only waste. Moreover, they fertilised it, and fodder was often grown the year after the cattle had grazed on it. The north was also more open to the introduction of new crops than was the south. It is true the mulberry gained ground in Sicily and Calabria, but there it was a tree of comparatively remote origins. Lucca apart, the mulberry was not exceptionally widespread in the north, until its striking development in almost every state in the fifteenth century. By the end of the sixteenth century it had completely changed the landscape of Tuscany and modified profoundly that of the Po Valley and elsewhere. But the north was further changed by the vast expansion and dramatic decline of woad production, the conversion of marshland to ricefield, the spread of drainage and irrigation. Lombardy, although it regressed in the early decades of Valois and Hapsburg occupation in the sixteenth century, had already won by 1500 considerable tracts of previously unused land. Venice at the end of this period was about to embark on big schemes to clear her eastern lands for farming and to control her waterways and drain her swamps, and Tuscany had already conquered her hills for cultivation. This victory over the land contrasted vividly with the spread of wasteland in the south and around Rome.

In the developing areas people began to move into the country. It has already been remarked that to maintain the terracing of the Italian hills it was best to have the worker on the spot. This was true of the maintenance of irrigation ditches, canals, even rivers and the multitude of other improvements made above all in Tuscany and the north. The result was that the countryside in such regions became populated, and with the presence of people it became more secure. There were opposing factors contributing to a loss of security: the maintenance of *condottieri* and their men, periodic warfare between the Italian states and, later, foreign invasions; but generally these northern areas enjoyed a greater security encouraged by their rulers. The Sforzas in Milan tamed the old feudal lords. The Bentivoglio, professional warriors, kept Bologna generally at peace; so did the Gonzaga, Mantua. The Medici forged good relations with the *contado*. The popes, from Julius II, exercised a growing control over their states and alleviated the troubles between *condottieri* and papal nephews. Venice emerged from a long succession of wars to find her main chance of salvation in the peaceful development of her mainland territories. In general, then, a period which is known for its violence, its treachery and its instability in fact offered a great deal of opportunity for the peaceful development of its agriculture and the secure occupation of the land. If Milanese speculators did not settle, their successors did. So did the Venetian patricians; and Florentine and Bolognese merchants built country villas and farmed their estates. The landlords followed the farm-workers into the countryside.

2
The Manufacturing Industries

Italian wool was generally of poor quality. Wool in the kingdom of Naples even after serious attempts to introduce new strains of sheep and selective breeding did not improve significantly owing to the deficiencies of the pasture, and it was from such inferior local wool that the Florentine cloth-making industry began. But the skills of Florentine textile manufacturers developed rather in the finishing of cloth from Flanders and northern France, an industry controlled by the traders and refiners, whose guild was known as the *Calimala*. This cloth was bought at the Champagne fairs and brought overland to Florence. By the time these fairs had declined at the end of the thirteenth century a new woollen cloth-making industry had outstripped this finishing industry. The new industry was based on the import of English wool that had developed into the finest product of the west. This was supplemented by the cheaper, lower quality wools of Spain, wools which nevertheless were far superior to anything Italy herself could produce. In the fifteenth century the cloths from English wools, *panni di San Martino*, sold at three times the price of the *panni garbi* made of Spanish wool. A large range of cloths was produced and a new and even more powerful guild, the *Arte di Lana*, organised the trade and industry. Especially when those limitations imposed on importation by the difficulties and costs of bringing wool and cloth overland from the Low Countries and the north of France had been overcome by the opening of the sea route through the Straits of Gibraltar in the early fourteenth century, the size and number of firms employed in these industries based on foreign wool and materials increased considerably. The financial crisis which destroyed the great Bardi and Peruzzi banks in the 1340s seriously shook the whole of the Florentine economy, including of course the basic woollen industry; but the resilience of Florentine business founded on its advanced financial and manufacturing techniques led to a remarkable recovery. Nevertheless, in the fifteenth century the Florentine wool industry began to decline seriously.

The main reason for the decline was that cloth-makers in Flanders and England were beginning to learn, often from imported Florentine artisans, the technical skills upon which the pre-eminence of Florence had been based. The demand for fine luxury cloths in the north was being increasingly satisfied by local manufacturers, and Florentine sales were falling. But the republic's markets were far-flung: it sold its cloth in central and eastern Europe, as far north as the Baltic and throughout Italy, and there was a growing demand in the Levant for Florentine quality cloths made out of English wool. If the growing difficulty of selling on the western markets was a blow to Florentine prosperity, it was certainly not fatal by the middle of the fifteenth century. During the supremacy of Cosimo de' Medici in Florence wool-workers still outnumbered the workers employed by any other industry, although the reduced profits from woollen cloth were being overhauled by those of the rising silk industry. Moreover the industry was still important in the sixteenth century for the towns of the Florentine territories such as Prato, Arezzo and Pistoia.

The woollen industry had been as developed in the towns of Lombardy as in Tuscany, and the local wool was often of a higher quality than further south. Good cloth was manufactured at Como; and Milan itself, Cremona, Monza and other centres in the duchy had all had a flourishing cloth production. In Venetian Lombardy, Brescia and Bergamo, which until 1426 and 1428 respectively lay within the Visconti territories, were also important producers of woollen cloth; but as in Florence these industries all experienced grave setbacks during the fifteenth century. In the Venetian Terraferma, the Lombard towns apart, the woollen industry had never been so highly developed, although there were manufacturers at Verona who produced fairly high-quality cloths. The output there was small and did not suffer the vicissitudes that the woollen industry experienced elsewhere in Italy. Mantua also manufactured woollens under the protection of privileges bestowed upon it by its dukes, and Genoa had an industry which in part used poor-quality North African wool.

Where woollen manufactures declined, the manufacture of silks often rose to compensate for the losses. This has been seen to have happened in Florence. It was certainly true of Milan in the fifteenth century, while Venice until the middle of this period for long had had a more advanced silk industry based in the first place on its imports of raw and spun silk from the Near East. The remarkable growth of Italian silk production, which has been widely illustrated already with the spread of the mulberry tree, is an indication of how silk came to be universally regarded as a remedy for declining business in wool. But, if silk was a substitute, it was also a reason for the decline. As the techniques of silk production were successively mastered, so the profits became increasingly attractive. Demands for Italian silks rose and tempted private investment in and government support for the expanding industry. It became universally more popular to use silk for adornment and trimmings; and, especially when supplies of furs were limited by the Turkish control of the Black Sea after the fall of Constantinople, the use of silk further reduced the prosperity of this trade.

The wool industry in Lombardy was also adversely affected by difficulties brought about by war and changes in farming practice. About a quarter of the huge import and export trade of Venice in normal times was carried on with the portless duchy of Milan; for even when Milan held Genoa, as intermittently she did, the difficulties of transport across the mountain passes were always a barrier to the full use of that port. Export via the Po, which was navigable as far inland as Pavia, was generally preferred; but Venice controlled the north bank of its outlet to the Adriatic and, by the end of the fifteenth century, territorial gains had given her a far greater dominance of the Po traffic. Even the land route to Venice was easier to negotiate than that to Genoa. Furthermore, Venice as a port and, as it were, a crossroads had marketing and distributing facilities which made it profitable to trade there. But with the incessant warfare between Venice and Milan in the first half of the fifteenth century much of this traditional trading was interrupted, the trade became insecure and accordingly the industries upon which the trade was based suffered. Prominent among these was the woollen industry; but its decline did not initiate the change in Lombardy from sheep-farming to cattle-farming, for like the development of silk production, dairy farming grew in response to a new set of economic attractions. The growth was a consequence of the process whereby speculative farmers acquired land from the Church by way of cashing in on improvement clauses, and one such improvement, the recovery of land, produced a terrain suitable for cattle. That this class of speculator was able to enlist the powers of the dukes to accelerate the process by large-scale works on canals and irrigation made the new type of farming so attractive that sheep-farming and wool production were badly hit by the changes.

From the invasion of Louis XII in 1499 to the Peace of Cambrai 30 years later there was hardly a town in northern Italy whose economy was not severely shaken for much of this time. Yet by 1534 there was distinct indication in places of a revival of manufacturing activities. In some instances this revival occurred within the wool industry. The general economic decline in Lombardy during the first three decades of the sixteenth century was partly due to population movements. During these troubled years workers left the city of Milan. Many of them worked in Rome under Leo X where they were often employed on building houses to cope with a rapidly expanding population. Later they took part in the building connected with the growth of Naples and they also went to the smaller towns of the duchy. Repeatedly, legislation from 1527 to 1535 was aimed at preventing this loss of man-power, but it clearly had little success. More dramatic, the population of Brescia in 1505 was something like 65,000; by 1517 it was no more than 24,000. This was due to successive occupations of the French, Spanish and Imperial troops, which led to a large exodus from the town. Again, Pavia's population declined from about 16,000 in 1500 to only 5,000 in 1529. The same story could be told of other towns in the north too. No industry could continue to function properly under such conditions. Yet before the sixteenth century had passed, those towns that had not gone entirely over to silk production had once again developed impressive woollen industries. Bergamo increased its output threefold from 1540 to 1595; Como by 1580 was as flourishing as ever. Milan and Florence both achieved levels of production, which if they did not match those of their heydays, indicate a notable recovery. But Venice which had hitherto lagged so far behind, outstripped all rivals in its amazing expansion as a manufacturer of woollen cloths.

At the beginning of the sixteenth century the economy of Venice was challenged from all sides. In a war with the Turks from 1499 to 1503 the Venetian hold on her Levantine trade was threatened by further Ottoman successes at the expense of Venetian colonial possessions. Then in 1516 and 1517 the great spice ports of Beirut and Alexandria fell into Turkish hands. In the first decade of the century news of the growing successes of the new Portuguese spice trade produced uncertainty and fear in the lagoon, when a new threat from the forces of Europe in the League of Cambrai started a period of invasion, destruction and financial stress that brought the republic to the verge of annihilation. It was under such conditions that hard thinking about Venice's economic future produced several imaginative possibilities. One of these was that a woollen industry, eschewing the finer stuffs of international trade in luxuries, should be developed to serve the needs of Venice herself and her mainland territories. This was in no way to prejudice her traditional activity of distributing the luxury materials of others. It was to tap a market which reached beyond the very real limits of a commerce for the rich, to serve the wider and less pretentious needs of a greater section of the people. The result was startling. Between 1516 and 1521 Venetian woollen-cloth production increased threefold. It held this position until 1530, except for a sharp fall in production during the plague year of 1525. Then up to 1535 there was a steady rise, followed by a further check from 1536 to 1538, but in the next ten years production more than doubled, while in the 20 years from 1549 to 1569 it climbed a further 250 per cent. From then only slight increases took place until the peak year of 1602, and during these last decades of the century there were some setbacks due to the war of Cyprus and plague. Altogether, from 1516 to 1602 Venetian woollen-cloth production multiplied 22 times. Although the overall value of this industry was not comparable to that of the production of similar quantities of luxury stuffs, by 1600 Venice was in some years making nearly as much cloth as Florence and Milan combined.

In the fifteenth century Cremona was the only Italian town with a large output of fustian. Chieri, Alessandria, Acqui and Monza were still producing a certain quantity of the material, as were country manufacturers of the Ligurian Apennines, and there was a small fustian industry on the Venetian Terraferma. However, the competition that had arisen from south German towns such as Nuremberg grew to such dimensions that these industries were reduced by 1500 to only local importance. This decline of the Italian industry can be measured to some extent by the drop in the cultivation of flax. Piedmont by the end of the fifteenth century had gone over largely to silk and hemp production, whereas rice had superseded flax in the Pavese. Then, as in most industries in Piedmont and Lombardy, the manufacture of fustian was unable to escape the effects of war in the early decades of the sixteenth century. In so far as this applied too to Cremona, it was not the reason for the death of the industry and the town. In 1502 Cremona was a town of 40,000 people. In 1570 she was holding her population, but by 1660 could count no more than 14,000 inhabitants. This is not to say that the causes for her decline lay after 1570. It was the industrial traditions of Cremona which enabled her to fight a losing battle for the three and a half decades before that year; but at the same time it was this vitality that had invited the artificial reasons for her decline. Because Cremona had survived foreign occupation and the disruption of trade and industry better than most of her Lombard neighbours, when it came to making assessments for the *mensuale*, a tax imposed by the government of the Emperor Charles V on his Lombard acquisitions, Cremona was penalised heavily for her comparative success. Her quota was higher than that of Pavia, Novara, Como, Tortona, Alessandria and Vigevano combined. It was set at 60 per cent of that of Milan, a city whose population was three times as great as hers, and which had all the advantages of being a capital city and administrative centre, with a highly diversified industry and trade. Whereas less taxed cities like Como and Pavia revived to become important wool and silk towns, Cremona eventually succumbed to the unequal competition. Except where land was turned over to a church exempt from taxation, a thriving countryside was transformed to a great extent into a deserted waste, and a resilient industry was sucked dry as its artisans left for kindlier circumstances. The south Germans were left without an opponent in Italy.

Silk was brought from the Muslim world of the Levant in the Middle Ages by Moor and Arab, crusader and adventuring merchant. It is not surprising therefore that its earliest appearance in Italy was in Sicily. But it was at Lucca where the industry developed significantly. Here the whole range of techniques from farming to cloth-making and finishing was mastered, and it was the Lucchesi who initiated the rest of Italy into these skills. With the Pisan sack of Lucca in 1314 and the subsequent years of war and unrest, silk-workers of every kind sought refuge from their troubles and were welcomed everywhere. In the first instance, Florence above all attracted the exiles, but as the advantage of borrowing their skills became more generally perceived the Lucchesi were sought after when they no longer had to seek refuge on their own behalf, and they gave to Venetians, Genoese and Lombards the mastery of their trade. After a while Florence, like Lucca, became a teacher; and early in the fifteenth century she learnt the arts of interweaving brocades with threads of silver and gold, so that she captured not only the rich markets of the West but also sold her materials on the brilliant stalls of the Levant. The silk for these north Italian industries was at first imported to the centres of manufacture. It came from Messina or across the straits from Reggio, from Persia, Turkestan and even China. The silk from the East was often bought by Italian merchants at inland markets such as Samarkand and Tauris or, nearer at hand, Aleppo. It was transported especially by the Genoese from Trebizond and other Black Sea ports, and by the Venetians from Tana and from Beirut and the Syrian ports. A huge demand led to the planting of mulberries and the development of silk farms throughout Italy. This process was speeded up by the closure of the routes across Asia by the fourteenth-century territorial advances of the Turks and, with the fall of Constantinople, by the Turkish control of the Black Sea trade with the Mediterranean. Persian and Levantine silks, however, were still available at the great Turkish market of Bursa and in the Syrian markets of Aleppo and Damascus. The Florentines bought large quantities at Bursa between 1488 and 1512, after which their purchases began to decline, partly on account of home-produced silk. Genoa from 1453 imported increasing quantities of Calabrian silk, which was also bought in significant quantities by the Florentines at the fairs of Salerno. Genoa then turned more to the excellent silk of Granada until her supply was badly hit by the Castilian conquest of the Moorish kingdom. After the fall of Granada in 1492, the Genoese relied more and more on their supplies through Chios of silk bought at Bursa. Most Lombard silk imports came through Venice, but Messina, a great redistribution centre of Levantine goods, sold silk both from the East and from Sicily to all parts of Italy.

In 1442, Filippo Maria Visconti offered privileges to Florentines to bring their skills to the duchy of Milan in order to develop the manufacture of high-class silks. By the last years of the ducal reign of Francesco Sforza there were 15,000 silk-workers in Milan alone, although the population of that city had not then reached 100,000. But it was not until the sixteenth century that the Milanese mastered the art, practised 100 years earlier in Florence, of using gold and silver thread. Other towns in the duchy, such as Pavia after 1550, turned to the silk industry as their woollen industries declined. Likewise, after 1516 the Venetian government encouraged the growth of a silk industry in Brescia by holding out privileges to foreigners who would be willing to settle there and practise their skills. The success of the policy can be gauged by the fact that by 1540 Brescia was producing eight times as much silk as woollen cloth. When it is recalled that the population of Brescia recovered from its low level of 24,000 in 1517 to 44,000 by 1546, it is clear that this revival was due in no small part to the encouragement given to this new industry. Bologna, too, developed silk manufactures, and was notable for ingenious mechanical innovations in the industry. Its produce was so fine that Matthias Corvinus singled it out for the purchase of certain special materials and Bolognese silk stuffs were even exported overland to Genoa. Florence produced an original technique for weaving cloths of a mixture of fine wool and silk, which were in great demand in the Levant. Verona and Vicenza were both important silk producers on the Terraferma, and their products sometimes found their way *via* the fairs of Lyons even to Genoa, itself a far greater producer of silk stuffs. Lucca in the time of Leo X was still the largest and best producer and biggest exporter of silks in Italy; whilst Naples, which under the Emperor Charles V set European fashions very much in the way that the France of Louis XIV was to do later, manufactured her own much-demanded silks and silken goods. But by the end of the century Venice, which had developed so magnificently her woollen industry, had also maintained a thriving silk industry, and from the end of the fourteenth century Venetian imports of Levantine silk steadily rose at the expense of Genoa's. Genoa therefore relied increasingly on Calabrian, Sicilian, Spanish and home-produced silk.

In 1531 Genoa had 2,000 silk-weavers compared with only 400 wool-weavers. The proportion was greater than it had been in the previous century. By the end of the sixteenth century she owned 3,000 active silk looms, compared with 2,000 at Venice and 1,600 at Lucca. Despite her trade losses in the Levant she was still clearly able to build up a great industry. Some of the products of these widespread and prosperous industries have been mentioned, but the variety was impressive. The cloths ranged from gold or silver threaded brocades and silken damasks with their patterns to velvets, taffetas, satins and dozens of lesser-known cloths of the time. Ribbons were an important speciality of Venice and decorative trimmings were characteristic of Naples, whilst some industries were known for their fine colours. Of all these Genoese black silk was the most notable. This of course had a rich and assured *clientèle*. Dignitaries of all sorts, from the higher reaches of the Church to holders of government offices, and professionals in law, medicine or the universities, would wear the black silks of Genoa. Mourning, of course, was always in demand, and widows, if sufficiently wealthy, would don Genoese silks for the rest of their lives and, if not, they might well have a garment put away to be worn only on special occasions. The rich bourgeois, less flamboyant than the aristocrat, would usually prefer a tasteful unobtrusiveness in black to the more obvious appeals of colour. Genoese black was worn widely throughout the Christian world and was certainly not confined to any local demand. Of the silk industry of Genoa as a whole, the Doge Antoniotto Adorno declared in 1523 to the Maona of Chios, the organisation which controlled the great commercial monopolies of the island, that the art of silk was more than the right eye, it was the soul, of his time. This soul above all was black.

No textile industry was complete without its dyes, and dyes determined the quality of the cloth almost as much as the fabric itself. Accordingly the dyeing industry was vital to the success of much of Italy's industrial wealth, and for this reason dyes were sought all over the known world and dye crops were cultivated widely in Italy. Brazil, a wood dye giving a range from scarlets to pinks, was imported from the East Indies, Ceylon and Calicut. Indigo came from the Malabar coast and the mainland opposite Ormuz, although it was grown in Sicily. Gall-nut, an oak-growth started by an insect injection, was used for blacks and was brought especially from the lands bordering on the Black Sea. Lac for crimson was bought with indigo on the markets of Damascus and came from as far afield as Cambay and Calicut. Ultramarine from *lapis lazuli* was imported indirectly from Persia, whereas a substitute pigment from aloes came mainly from the island of Sokotra. Cramoisy was the crimson dye of the scarlet grain insect and was imported from Asia Minor, Greece and Spain to be used for the colouring of superior cloths. Madder for cheaper reds was grown in Lombardy, as has been seen, in decreasing quantities. Woad was the great source of blue. Saffron was cultivated in many hilly parts of Italy, but with the best effect in east Tuscany and around Aquila. It produced a range of orange dyes almost from yellow to red. Greens and yellows came from dyer's weed, also widely grown in Italy. But the basic material required for many dyeing processes was alum.

Alum had a variety of uses in the tanning, glass-making and sugar industries. It took the absorbency out of paper. It was good for desalting salted codfish, and in medicine it was piously hoped that alum would prevent haemorrhages. In the textile industry it was used for taking the fats and impurities out of fibres and cloths and also, most importantly, as a mordant for reds, yellows and blacks. Mixed with the dyes it not only helped fix them, but it endowed the colours with a brightness and delicacy, which substitute mordants failed to achieve. There were substitutes: potassium, tartar, *aqua fortis*, gall-nut and the ashes of pinewood and lime. None of them were as efficient as alum, although a mixture of alum and tartar was thought best for brazil-wood red. Clearly, whoever could get a hold on the sources of alum would be in a very strong position. In the middle of the fifteenth century such a position was almost held by Genoa who controlled the trade in the best alum then mined at Fokia and other parts of Asia Minor. The fall of Constantinople was followed by the fall of Fokia three years later in 1456 and, although Genoa managed to hold on to much of the Asia Minor alum trade for a while from her base in Chios where the alum had always been assembled and stored for transshipment, she was eating into her reserves, and prices rose between 1453 and 1458 by nearly 500 per cent. Moreover, her rivals—especially Venice who had always managed to supply herself independently—were bargaining with the sultan for the trade. In fact, Asia Minor alum was eventually farmed out to the Venetian Bartolomeo Zorzi until the outbreak of the Venetian-Turkish War of 1463–79. The threat to the alum supplies made Christendom re-examine its resources. Old deposits of inferior alum were reopened by the Genoese, for example in 1459 on the island of Ischia and at Pozzuoli in the kingdom of Naples, and new sources were found in 1462 at Mazarron in Castilian Murcia and at Tolfa in the Papal States. It was this last discovery of an abundant, high-quality supply which transformed the situation entirely. The discovery was regarded by the Pope, Pius II, as a providential blast at the Infidel; but it turned out to be a powerful instrument of papal policies and the object of political and economic manœuvres which had profound effects on the fortunes of the western world. The textile industries of England, the Low Countries, Italy and elsewhere had been delivered from a partial reliance upon the predictably self-interested sultans only to become semi-dependent upon the unforeseeable shiftings of papal policy as successive popes were enthroned.

Italy's industry was largely dependent upon specialised farming for the production of raw materials, which made the importation of large quantities of food necessary. It also required the import of raw materials themselves, so that without a great shipping industry it could not have existed. Even as it was there were many Ragusan, Portuguese, Basque, Catalan and Cretan ships engaged in the Italian carrying trade. But in the fifteenth century it was Venetian, Genoese and to a lesser extent Florentine shipping that dominated the Mediterranean. Up to the mid-fifteenth century much of the bulk-carrying in the Mediterranean and from the Mediterranean to the Channel and the North Sea was in the hands of the Genoese. Genoa held a monopoly of the export of Lombard woad which flourished until 1480 and she carried the alum of Asia Minor to England and Flanders. The Venetians, however, had a growing interest in big cargoes in the second half of the century, which is manifest in the fact that the papal alum of Tolfa was shipped in great quantities by the Venetians and the Portuguese in the first decade of the trade. The Genoese in the 1460s only carried 20 per cent of the Tolfa alum. Accordingly the losses of two important, partial monopolies in bulk-carrying by the Genoese in the second half of the century gave added impetus to others, especially the Venetians, to develop big ships.

The importance of Genoese shipping at this time lay in her big sailing-ships and, although Venice used big ships too, she and Florence relied more on the galleass, a large galley dependent on sails except in calms and when entering and leaving port. The galleass had little more than half the carrying capacity of the Genoese sailing-ship. This big vessel, usually in the middle of the fifteenth century of something like 700 tons but sometimes reaching even 1,000, was normally clinker-built with one mast, square-rigged and at times 150 feet tall. At the beginning of the century the process of having the huge single sail broken down was begun with the appearance of a small topsail. During the century more than one mast became more common and lateen-rigging was mixed with the predominantly square-rigging. The castles were becoming permanent: a forecastle for fighting, with artillery under the platform; a sterncastle with cabins. The storage room was ample and generally better than that of the galleasses. It was also a safer craft, sturdier for bad weather and more easily defensible against the raids of pirates. The galleasses, sometimes used by the Venetians and always by the Florentines, had some advantages over the big ships. They were more manoeuvrable and therefore, if they could not face the same weather as the big sailing-boat, they could be beached when conditions were bad. They were not becalmed because they could always revert to oars. They were smaller, generally less than 500 tons; but they were used for more precious cargoes, and more harbours and river ports were accessible to them. A Venetian galley under pressure was known to make the voyage from Southampton to Otranto in 31 days, a feat which the big sailing-ships could not match. These heavy galleys, broader in the beam than the sleek fighting galleys used by all three states for naval purposes, usually had three oars to a bench each side of a gangway with maybe 25 pairs of benches. They could be as long as 140 feet with a beam of 25 feet, standing eight or nine feet out of the water. The fighting galleys which relied less on sails often carried reserve oarsmen. They were generally not quite so long, much narrower in the beam and sat low in the water. By the middle of the sixteenth century the big round ship usually had five men to a bench, but sometimes even eight, all tugging at the same oar. By the end of the fifteenth century some enormous sailing-ships had appeared, although these were mainly used for naval and military purposes. Venice had already built a ship of over 2,000 tons. But during the sixteenth century, although sailing-ships were becoming more popular, they were still regarded as big when between 700 and 900 tons, whilst galleys still played a significant role as for example at Lepanto. The galleys were pulled by slaves and criminals, and it was in part the difficulty of finding the manpower that attracted the Italians from oar to sail.

These three states of course did not monopolise the shipping of Italy. Anconans were a great sea-faring people who, with the Ragusans, were only prevented from wresting the supremacy of the Adriatic from the Venetians in the sixteenth century by their dependence on Venetian marine insurance. Naples was a big enough sea-faring state to be able to send a merchant fleet to Antwerp before the end of this period. There was also a great coastal traffic that all states took part in, even if it was dominated by the Genoese in the Ligurian and Tyrrhenian seas and by the Venetians in the Adriatic. Boats of 120 or 150 tons carried much of the commerce in grain and little craft of 25 tons looped from harbour to harbour around the coast engaged in an active and variable trade. Finally, there were local fishing vessels, the skiffs often carried by the great cargo ships, the river and canal craft of the Po Valley and at Venice the ferries of the lagoon and the barks and gondolas of the canals.

This wide range of shipping was necessarily backed by an active building and repair industry which involved a multitude of subsidiary industries as well. The Arsenal at Venice and the beach at Sampierdarena, the western coastal suburb of Genoa, were perhaps the busiest centres of this activity. The Venetian Arsenal was indeed reconstructed between 1472 and 1487 for a flourishing industry. However, at the Battle of Lepanto in 1571 Venice was already using foreign-built ships, and by the turn of the century most of her new ships came from the Netherlands or from her old possession in the Aegean, since 1537 held by the Turks, the little island of Patmos. This was due in large part to the improvident use of wood by the Venetians. No urgent understanding of the possibilities of reafforestation had yet occurred, and the Trentino from where the Adige and the Brenta fed Venice with timber and the Cadore from where it was floated down on the Piave had both been largely denuded of their woods. However, the republic had by then very much turned its gaze inland from the sea. The wood for the Genoese industry was brought from further afield. Apart from the sweet chestnuts, the hills of Liguria were largely bare of trees. Some timber was obtained from behind the coast between Varazze and Arenzano, although most came from more distant sources: from Corsica or the Alpes Maritimes behind Nice, but mostly from the Dauphiné. From here it was floated down the Rhône to Arles where it was bound into rafts and towed out into the Mediterranean and along the Provençal coast to Genoa. Because of the difficulty of getting wood, the Genoese often built their ships near where they found it. They built as far afield as Famagusta until they lost influence over Cyprus at the beginning of this period; and since ships often needed repairs done far from Genoa, a big industry used by ships of all nations, Venice included, was developed on the island of Chios, where the local terebinth tree provided pitch for caulking. Pitch was also imported to Genoa from Provence and Catalonia. Big docks used mainly for repair, but also for building, were located at Genoa, and all along the coasts of Liguria, especially at Savona, craft of all kinds were built. At Genoa and along the Rivieras and on the Terraferma of Venice sail-cloth, rope, big iron nails and so forth were manufactured for ships. Hemp brought from Savona, Catania and Alessandria was the basis of a rope industry at Genoa which exceeded local needs and allowed a considerable export to Catalonia; even oars manufactured at the little Ligurian port of Chiavari found a ready market at Marseilles. The development of the Tolfa alum deposits brought a renascence to the little port of Civitavecchia, but its fortress rather than its port facilities were developed. Leo X did, however, order that the docks of the inner harbour should be deepened to take ships with a draught of six feet. A similar comment on the times lies, perhaps, in the fact that Leghorn was for long rather a fortification than a port despite the silting up of Porto Pisano and the obvious need to develop Leghorn if Florentine aspirations to become a real challenge to her Venetian and Genoese rivals were to be realised. In the sixteenth century port facilities were developed. Coupled with a liberal customs policy this made possible the striking growth of Leghorn into the surrounding marshlands. However, during the 70 years that are the main focus of this book it was only Venice and Genoa of the Italian ports which offered the facilities of really imp ressive maritime powers.

Public works were not ignored by governments. Sometimes their scope was dictated by political rather than economic considerations. Even so, large-scale building and engineering activities are an important part of the industrial life of a country. When the great mass of private and ecclesiastical building achievements are added, there can be no room for doubt that, even if the economies of Italy were overtaxed, they were on the whole magnificent economies that were strained by magnificent aspirations. The last part of the fifteenth century witnessed a great step forward in the city of Venice. Before, there had been wooden houses and palaces, likely to flare up at any moment to destroy the riches that many of them held. This was why the glass industry had long ago been moved to Murano. Now the republic was to undertake a series of public works and to encourage its people to follow suit. New houses were built of stone, and old wooden buildings often made way for new stone ones. The government itself replaced the wooden bridges with stone as it occupied itself with a programme to excavate the canals, pave the footways or *calli* and make public buildings at once grander and safer. After a fire in 1483 work was undertaken on the east façade of the doge's palace, but building went on there through the centuries so that the palace acquired a variety of styles in the manner of a great Gothic cathedral. Particularly in the sixteenth century was its interior decorated with the works of Venice's great painters, not to create a legend but to round off what was still a powerful reality. In the vice-royalty of Pedro de Toledo, which began in 1532 towards the end of this period, Hapsburg Naples foreshadowed the reign of Louis XIV. It has been seen how it was fashionable to buy Neapolitan as later it was to be fashionable to buy French goods, not from any intrinsic value in the wares offered. It was also the policy of the government to attract unruly barons into the comforts of a rich, cultivated and, it was hoped emasculating environment. The parallel will not be pushed too far. However, the great capital was adorned with new administrative offices, palaces for barons and officials, new churches to accommodate its exploding population. Toledo only accelerated a process. The population of Naples had doubled to more than 100,000 in the fifteenth century. By 1547 it had grown to 245,000, the second city in Europe after Paris, if Constantinople is left to the East. During this expansion the walls of the city had been extended twice—under the direction of Alfonso of Calabria for King Ferrante by 1484 and by King Federico between 1499 and 1501. The building of houses had been a continuous concern and their protection a matter of public policy. The expansion of Venice statistically was not so dramatic; but there was a limit to what could be reclaimed from the lagoon. The increase in population from about 90,000 in 1493 to a peak of about 170,000 in 1563 presented therefore no less of a problem. The solution has already partly been seen: the stone house containing several apartments was able to hold more families than the wooden house that had preceded it. It was the solution of Genoa clinging to a narrow ledge of land: to build upwards.

In the middle of the fifteenth century Rome's population was probably no more than 30,000 and it was not until the beginning of the next century, even as late as the reign of Leo X, that it began noticeably to increase. It reached 100,000 around 1600. Such a growth was perhaps not too difficult to accommodate. The problem was to prevent the attending misfortunes of seasonal fluctuations as pilgrims poured into the Holy City. These might be multiplied hugely in jubilee years. It was in fact an epidemic blighting the jubilee of 1450 which set Nicholas V to work in the first place on the modernisation of Rome. For this he probably consulted Leon Battista Alberti, who about this time was writing his work on architecture and whose views in it on town planning reflect those of the Roman architect, Vitruvius. But the Pope had neither time nor money to rebuild Rome, certainly not with the fundamentality of Vitruvius, and if Alberti's hand lay behind Nicholas's achievements, the architect was, as so often, responsible for a face-lift rather than a completely original undertaking of his own. The Acqua Vergine was restored, although most of Rome still relied on the Tiber for water; bridges and walls were repaired; the Vatican library was built. A decade or so later Paul II invited more trouble by succumbing to the temptation of a profitable tourist trade and scheduled a new jubilee for 1475. He did not live to see his scheme a failure, nor could Sixtus foretell that it would be so. Sixtus accordingly embarked upon a continuation of Nicholas's work. He built a new bridge across the Tiber to facilitate circulation and a papal barracks to ensure order. He started the Sistine chapel and improved the library. If both these popes were aware of Rome's problem of invading pilgrims, neither of them pursued the solutions with great energy, single-mindedness or consistency. Nicholas was shocked so much by the news that Constantinople had fallen that his programme was brought to a standstill; Sixtus was too involved in his family's aggrandisement to complete a policy that would produce no more than the good of Rome. The three sixteenth-century popes of this period who had a great influence on the future of Rome—Julius II, Leo X and Clement VII—have all been seen to have turned to the task of retrieving the land for use; but they had little success, and their efforts in this respect can hardly be said to have amounted to a significant contribution to industry. But the city itself, particularly during Leo's reign, was transformed. Alexander VI and Julius II had done much by any ordinary standards, embarking on plans to widen vistas and build palaces and churches, and their work was crowned by the efforts of Bramante. But the development of new suburbs; the employment of wide spaces to reveal old architecture; and the fantastic crop of new palaces for cardinals; mansions for rich merchants, princes and barons; churches; building at the Vatican itself—a fervid activity of architecture and planning, founded on the designs of the leading architects of a leading period in Italy's long history of building creativity, was the result of the encouragement of Leo X. If Rome was made more spacious and therefore more able to cope with the movement of visiting throngs, was given more buildings and was therefore better able to house her visitors during their stays, she was also made more attractive and, except where they shared Luther's reactions of horror, drew people to herself for reasons other than devotion. Merchants came to exploit the expanding market; workers necessarily came to enable the development itself to take place; visitors came as much to enjoy the gaiety and admire the beauty of the city as to fulfil their spiritual aspirations. Like many solutions this one served largely to intensify the problems. Moreover, it is not surprising that unpaid mobs of soldiers belonging to the Imperial Army should descend on the city to redress their grievances with loot, so that much of this vast work was destroyed by the brutal sack of Rome in 1527.

One could tour Italy and never exhaust the examples of an industry which was the greatest of arts: the palaces at Florence of the Medici, the Pitti and the Pazzi, of the Rucellai and the Strozzi; the Palazzo del Te of the Gonzagas at Mantua; the Palazzo Piccolomini at Siena; the Palazzo Raimondi or the Palazzo Fodri at Cremona; villas along the Brenta or behind the industrious sands of Sampierdarena; churches everywhere from Turin to Venice, from Naples to Como. All over Italy the excitement of anticipation was felt as buildings were in various stages of completion; for, although money was not always forthcoming, or building was often interrupted for some other reason, generally there was a well-grounded expectation that an undertaking would eventually be fulfilled. Even so, it is a little sad to notice how many half-finished buildings in fact there were; but it was a great self-confidence that embarked upon so many glorious projects and the greater part of them were brought to their intended ends.

The dukes of Milan provided no exception to the eager patronage of architecture which has been described. The Visconti had had many grand ambitions for the embellishment of Milan and Pavia, the political and cultural capitals of the duchy. Francesco Sforza took over some unfinished projects and embarked upon new ones of his own. Work was thus done on the cathedral at Milan and the university and the *Certosa* or Carthusian monastery at Pavia. Building was begun at Milan on the Ospedale Maggiore under Francesco too. Later in the century Bramante and Leonardo da Vinci were amongst the architects, artists and engineers who were gathered by Ludovico Sforza to Milan for the embellishment, the gaiety and the utility of his state. However, Lombardy had been traditionally a leader in canal engineering and it is her achievement in this that should be emphasised.

A few miles south-east of Milan the Cistercian monks at the monastery of Chiaravalle had built irrigation canals in the first half of the twelfth century. A 100 years later similar work was done publicly in the district of Lodi. Before 1300 much of the Lomellina and to its north the Novarese was irrigated and in the fourteenth century a canal built from Milan to Binasco irrigated the land south-west of the capital. Meanwhile between 1179 and 1257 the Naviglio Grande linking Milan to Abbiategrosso, a few miles from the Ticino, was built and improvements were made from 1269 enlarging the canal and adding sluices. It fell 110 feet in a matter of 31 miles. The canal was extended several miles north to join the Ticino.

There was also a small canal or moat encircling Milan which was used for transport. Thus before the fifteenth century Milan had a system of irrigation and boat canals that was perhaps bettered nowhere outside the Low Countries. In his last years Filippo Maria Visconti took an active interest in the development of the Milanese canal system, which was taken up immediately by the Sforzas. Earlier in the century the Naviglio Grande had been extended to join up with the moat or Naviglio Interno, so that marble from near Lake Maggiore could be brought by water to the Ticino, then by the Naviglio Grande and the moat to very close to the cathedral site. The arrangement was not very effective since there was only one sluice-gate and the moat was considerably higher than the big canal. However, a second gate was added in 1438 to make Italy's first pound-lock. Subsequent improvements were made to the moat right up to the end of the century. Meanwhile, a beginning had been made to an impressive development of navigational transport facilities, which produced between 1439 and 1475 more than 55 miles of canal south of Milan including 25 locks and which fed lesser waterways and irrigation ditches. Amongst these developments was the canal joining the Abbiategrosso end of the Naviglio Grande to Bereguardo, which included in 12 miles a fall of 80 feet negotiated by 18 locks. From Bereguardo the land portage to the Ticino was shorter and to a lower and more navigable part of the Ticino than had been the case previously from Abbiategrosso. Parma, comparatively remote from the centre of Milanese activities, also had five locks built during the reign of Francesco Sforza to facilitate its communication with the Po. An even greater development was the connection of Milan to the Adda by the 50-mile long canal, the Martesana. This project was conceived in 1456, but the bulk of the work was carried out between 1462 and 1470. This great canal, which was enlarged in 1573 for more effective use as a navigational canal, led from Trezzo to Milan, crossing the Molgora on an aqueduct, while the Lambro was carried under it in a culvert. Leon Battista Alberti showed interest in sluice techniques in his work on architecture, but Leonardo da Vinci seems to have been actively involved in improving them. Certainly he was interested in mitred lock-gates while he was in Milan at the court of Ludovico and it was at this time that they were used in irrigation canals at Vigevano. At the same time they were installed in the Naviglio Interno. Another great design, the building of a canal to produce an outlet from the Lecco branch of Lake Como to the Po, was frustrated by the loss of Milan by the French to Charles V in 1522 after work had been in progress for some three years. Except for this unfinished enterprise of the French the canal building of the period between 1464 and 1534 was under the direction of the dukes. It was a sign of how the capitalistic landlords and merchants had influence in the ducal government and how the dukes were aware of the advantages of their activities. Irrigation and transport were the sinews of the state, certainly a fact that was to escape the Emperor Charles. Yet, perhaps already the energy which had produced such ardent activity in the development of fifteenth-century Milan was already running out; for, as has been noted, the process upon which Milan's development had largely rested was in its very nature self-exhausting. New inspirations were necessary for its greatness to survive. The Hapsburgs were the last people to look to for such a lead.

Milan in the fifteenth century was already beginning to feel the challenge from Nuremberg and other south German towns to her supremacy in the iron industry. The loss of Brescia and Bergamo, in whose neighbouring valleys iron was mined, did not materially affect the Milanese industry, for the old links remained. It was easier to distribute the raw material along ready-made routes to industries ready to utilise them, than to forge new routes and new industries to replace the old. Thus the political and military humiliation did not bring a corresponding economic setback. Milan's industry was very largely centred on armaments, although there was a wide variety of manufactures from iron wire and nails to decorative wrought-irons. As the German industry grew, Milan turned more to artistic metal-work for which she was to become famous in the sixteenth century. Genoa, too, had a small iron industry. Forges were scattered through the hills and the great feudatories collected dues on the industry. The iron was imported from Elba and the Basque Provinces and stored at Voltri in readiness for distribution. The wood from behind Varazze and Arenzano, just west of Voltri, was more than sufficient for the *carbonari* and charcoal was exported with re-exported iron to Palermo. This industry manufactured armaments, most notably cuirasses, for export, but its chief function was to supply the shipping industry with essential commodities such as nails, wire and needles for sewing sail-cloth. The glass industry at Murano followed a similar pattern to that of Milan's iron industry, moving from the manufacture of utilitarian to artistic ware. This was partly due to a refinement of the techniques of the glass-makers enabling them to produce better and more varied glass, but it was also due to the growth of competition from elsewhere which continually exercised the Venetian government. Much of this transition had already been achieved by the middle of the fifteenth century, by which time many of the colouring techniques had been evolved.

Italy was the home of several other industries. In Venice alone there was a leather industry, soap-manufacturing, sugar-refining, bead-making; the glass industry there made spectacles as well as cruets or chandeliers; tallow candles were manufactured and precious stones were cut; there were rope-makers and there were goldsmiths. But the two remaining industries of major importance in Italy were paper-making and printing. Paper became a widely demanded commodity long before the invention of printing. Two little towns, Pioraco and Fabriano, on streams flowing down the eastern slopes of the Roman Apennines, built from such needs a famous industry. With the invention and spread of printing they could not satisfy the hungry demand for paper. Yet, although Venice had by the end of the fifteenth century developed a considerable industry of its own at Padua, the famous Aldine press imported its paper from Fabriano. Like the silk-weavers of Lucca, the paper-workers of Fabriano spread their skills around Italy. Voltri, with the aid of immigrants from Fabriano, and using the fast-flowing waters of the Leira, began to produce a wide range of paper from scrap to quality, the watermark of the latter being widely recognised outside Italy as far as Africa and the Orient. The Voltri paper-workers like the Genoese silk-workers, having mastered their borrowed craft, spread it abroad. As silk-making was taught to Frenchmen at Tours under the auspices of Louis XI, so paper-making with all the refinements of the Italian industry was taught at Marseilles and in Spain.

The invention of printing was a north European achievement, but nowhere in Europe was its commercial exploitation more profitable and on a grander scale than in Venice, which, although not the first Italian state in the field, managed to print over half the books printed in Italy during the fifteenth century. It was only in the middle of the sixteenth century that Lyons appeared as a serious rival to the Venetian book trade. The secret of Venice's superiority was her ready realisation of what would best sell. If she had idealistic publishers such as Aldo Manuzio who saw publishing as an instrument for the spreading of culture, her vast sales were in popular trifles—almanacs or works of devotion. Also, works in the mediaeval traditions of the university took priority over the publication of the classics with their appeal to the leisured dilettante, and manuals useful to tradesmen were numerous. Yet much that was important for the development of European civilisation came off the presses of Venice. The great Greek undertakings of the Aldine Press were the principal contribution, and Latin versions of Ptolemy and Euclid were among earlier publications. But, as always, it was the popular press that made the profits.

The structure of industries varied considerably from one business to another, from one industry to another and from one state to the next. However, there are perhaps some broad lines worth noticing. In Florence and Milan big business concerns usually spread their interests through a range of industrial, commercial and financial activities, providing as it were an insurance policy against a serious failure in one particular line of business. The firms were also in conception permanent, although in Florence they often did not survive for more than about 30 years. In Genoa on the other hand business arrangements were mostly on a short-term basis, and groups of businessmen would bring their capital together to exploit some given and limited venture of a more specialised nature. This type of arrangement held good for most undertakings which did not involve specialised equipment. In most big industrial enterprises the place of capital was dominant, whether in Venice or Genoa, in Florence or Milan. The big Florentine woollen and silk industries were linked indissolubly to the merchants and merchant-bankers, who provided the capital, organised the industry from the point of buying the raw material in London or at Bursa to marketing the cloth at Adrianople, Bruges or Lyons. Many processes were carried out in the establishments of these firms, although weaving was often put out to domestic workers and dyeing was usually carried on in independent dyeing establishments run by prosperous artisan-owners. The Florentine worker was most often a wage-earner. Such capitalist organisation was general in industrial Italy, although the relationship between the capitalist and the worker varied greatly. Wage-earners, for instance, were not uncommon in Genoa, but there was a great variety of alternatives. Weavers other than those in the silk industry, most metal workers and workers in the paper industry worked for wages. The silk-weavers were often forced to work for a share of their produce which in turn was over-priced, and they formed themselves into a movement in order to oppose the pressure put on them to accept these unfavourable terms by the capitalistic merchant. Putting-out was a widespread practice, especially amongst silk-weavers. However, in the silk industry there was a manufacturer, playing a middle rôle between worker and capitalist, organising the industry himself and often owning much of the equipment, although he was ultimately in the hands of the man who provided the financial backing. The weaver apart, the employees of the manufacturer often worked in his workshop for wages. In contrast Genoese dyers were growing in independence throughout the fifteenth century. Precious cloths to be dyed in the highest quality cramoisy were sent to specialist dyers who by this trade became very prosperous. Indigo dyeing was another highly specialised task which led by the end of the century to the formation of a separate indigo-dyers guild. Generally, dyers would have their own workshop with stove, cauldron, ironing and drying equipment and so forth. In fifteenth-century Venice wage-earning was virtually unknown outside the government-run *Arsenale*. Industry was often a cooperative effort between skill and capital, with the capitalist taking at least half the profits. This was especially true of the dyeing and leather industries, lace-making, embroidery and the big silk and woollen industries. The Murano glass industry, however, was developing techniques which were allowing it to change over to the employment of large numbers of wage-earners by the end of this period. As in Venice the Florentine state galleys were built by the state itself; and the building was controlled by the *Consoli del Mare*, the officials of Pisa and Florence appointed to organise the state convoys. The situation of an industry in Italy was often determined more by the local availability of capital than of raw materials. Thus feats of transport were accomplished to assemble materials in great bulk so that industry could be carried on smoothly; but clearly in this respect a port such as Venice or Genoa had an advantage over inland towns like Florence and Milan, a fact which determined the political expansionism of the last two centres towards the sea. Occasionally, however, a process might decide the situation of a subsidiary industry. Fulling, for instance, required water that Venice could not provide, so that Venetian fulling was done at Treviso. Likewise Genoese fulling used the streams from the Ligurian mountains and as a result was controlled by the big territorial lords.

Guilds were still an important element in the organisation of Italian industries, but generally speaking in the large industrial towns they had lost their directive powers over industry to capitalistic pressures. The major guilds in Florence under the early Medici still had a constitutional position of some prominence in the government; but it was the powerful members of the guilds rather than the guilds themselves who exercised political power, and even this was limited by the degree to which the Medici were able to make themselves the real rulers of Florence. In the organisation of industry the rich merchant-banker-industrialists were scarcely constrained by industrial and guild regulations. Guilds, in fact, proliferated in Genoa during the fifteenth century; but, although they might enforce certain regulations, it was ultimately the capitalist aristocrats and *popolani* who called the tune. In Rome several guilds grew up in the fifteenth century without influencing the economic policies of the popes, who were of course dependent upon very special sources of wealth. And in Venice the guilds, closely controlled by the legislation of the government,

were rather an instrument of state policy than the holders of power themselves. The guilds of Bologna numbered amongst their members all the
powerful families of the city, including the Bentivoglio, members of the
guild of notaries and the guild of butchers; but here the important guilds
were not industrial. Moreover, as in Florence, a guild was only powerful
in so far as it had members who were powerful irrespective of the membership of the guild. If a guild lent a faction political support, this support
was not the basis of power so much as a confirmation of it. Rather did the
guild hope to gain advantages from a propitious alliance.

The position of the workers in Italy, as anywhere at this time, would perhaps best be described as depressed. Entertainment was turned on for
them by rulers who saw advantage in keeping the people reasonably con-
tented. The carnivals of Lorenzo de' Medici and the endless pageants and
jollities under Ludovico Sforza are cases in point, while the gayer of the
festivities of the Church, although not peculiar to Italy, were enlivened
there by a plentiful flow of wine. When workers were short and their skills
were in demand the normal economic forces that raised their value came
into action. The classic example was perhaps a century before this period
when the Black Death put a premium on the weaver. But this happy
position was soon modified as demands became less urgent. The privileges
extended to attract workers away from their home towns to launch new
industries always gave those workers a temporary advantage in their new
surroundings. That there was sufficient freedom of movement to make
such policies effective was in itself an indication that the worker was
something more than the chattel he has been described as in many accounts, and legislation against such movement was on the whole ineffec-
tive. In an elective monarchy such as Rome the populace was able to use
its power over each inexperienced ruler to maintain its privileges, and it
was a new pope's custom always to confirm the people in their liberties.
But when towns offered attractive conditions to workers, they tended to
flow in to make a superabundance of labour and therefore to depreciate its
value. This was so, for instance, of Venice whose good food supply under
government control always attracted people from the Terraferma in hard
times with the result that Venice had to expel, usually on racial or religious
pretexts, its superfluous population. Yet Venice to a large extent owed her
survival to foreign workers whose skills helped her to adapt to the demands of changing industrial circumstances. Notable amongst these were
the Candiotes whose crowning contribution was a knowledge of Greek
that was used in the ambitious programmes of editing the Greek classics.

The general tendency in Italian industry during the fifteenth and sixteenth centuries was to move towards the manufacture of luxury articles with a rich but limited market. In cloth-making the great movement was from woollens and fustians to silks. Florence especially, Milan, Verona and other centres produced some very fine and expensive woollen materials, but the profits did not compare with those from the silk industry. The south developed some rather specialised silk interests that made Neapolitan articles under the Empire become much sought after, although it went ahead with an overwhelmingly rural economy based on poor-quality wool production. Venice was outside the main stream. The republic, although it developed luxury crafts in glass, wood and leather, laces, embroidery and stone-cutting, built up its tremendous manufacture of cheap woollen cloths for a popular home market. Nevertheless, the trend from wool to silk was, in direction, one from commodities of a wider appeal to others for a richer market. But if the market was richer, it must be remembered that with the emergence of bourgeois elements throughout western Europe the rich were more numerous. The major reflection of this whole tendency outside the textile industries was the way the metal industry in Milan went over to the manufacture of artistic ware. Venice in general acted as though she were not subjected to the normal processes of the time. If she preferred wool to silk, and in this central development of her industrial economy the mass-produced to the exclusive, she was also out of step in so far as her industries depended less on private capital and initiative than most in Italy. There was, it is true, a capitalistic exploitation of the skilled artisan; but in the main the state kept all economic activities under a close surveillance and was over-ready to intervene where it deemed it necessary. Such readiness to control the economy was increased in answer to the challenges Venice had to face in the early sixteenth century. However, at Rome and at Naples the authorities in the sixteenth century were beginning to play an increasingly important part in directing the resources of the economy. In Milan on the other hand the fruitful alliance between the dukes and capitalistic enterprise, after 1500, began to decline, a process which was furthered by the government of Charles V.

Italy's economy was clearly tied to a successful shipping industry; yet, in the next chapter, Italian shipping will be seen to be giving way to competition from elsewhere. This was in part due to Italy finding herself suddenly removed from the main shipping routes of a wider world opened up by Columbus and da Gama. It was also due to the exhaustion of wood supplies that were never overabundant in the Mediterranean. Causes and effects were inextricably mingled, but whatever the reasons for it the decline in Italian shipping was closely tied to the fact that Italy turned her attention inwards and depended more upon the land and her resources at home than upon a precarious maintenance of far-flung connections. However, except for the interruption in her development during the difficult years between the invasion of Louis XII and the Peace of Cambrai, in absolute terms Italy increased her industrial production up to about 1600. It was rather in relation to the great windfalls of the Spanish and Portuguese empires and later the development of England and the Dutch Republic as commercial states that Italy appeared to decline economically; as, Venice apart, politically she succumbed to France, the Empire and to Spain.

3
Trade

Only a wedge of Italy consisting of north Piedmont and north Lombardy had territory more than 6o miles from the sea. Moreover, north Lombardy had waterways connecting it to the Adriatic except for small unnavigable sections of the Adda and the Ticino—mainly compensated for by boat canals. This wedge together with the northern territories of Venice also lay astride the routes to the Alpine passes. Accordingly the greater part of Italy turned naturally towards the sea, whereas those areas which were not well placed had negotiable contacts with the north, for the Alps never presented the same problems to the traveller as did, for example, the Pyrenees. Italy was in a particularly strong position for the development of commerce, in an age when the sea connected rather than separated and when it was generally a faster medium of transport than the land, besides being more appropriate for the transportation of larger cargoes. Only personal travel or the delivery of news or mail were faster by land than sea, and Italy was well placed for this form of communication with its passes fanning out to the north. But a cargo of silk was not only delivered more quickly from Genoa to Flanders by sea; it was also four times as cheap. Furthermore, Italy lay across the Mediterranean in a position to dominate its traffic in all directions; and until new perspectives were given to the world by the ocean voyages in the middle of this period, the Mediterranean was the connecting link between Europe and the great eastern sources of many luxury and some essential goods. When Italy is extended to incorporate her colonial possessions, and when the colonial quarters of various Italian states in distant ports and market towns, the branches of her important firms and her consulates are considered, it is clear that her influence reached far beyond the Adriatic and the Tyrrhenian, and that developments in distant places might have considerable reverberations in Italy.

Venetian territorial expansion was initially directed more towards the eastern sea routes than towards the Terraferma. In the fourteenth century

Venice acquired much of the Dalmatian coast and stretches and pockets of coastline in Albania, Epirus, Morea, together with some important islands from the Ionians to the Aegean. Before the fall of Constantinople in 1453 there had been a large colony of Venetians there, and there was another at Tana in the Sea of Azov, where both Venetians and Genoese possessed fortified quarters. The Tana colonies survived the Turkish control of the Black Sea for some time, but they were reduced largely to local trade and became increasingly less a part of the Italian economy. Inland at Aleppo members of important Venetian trading families had establishments and, in the big Levantine ports, Venice and her competitors generally kept a consul or representative to look after the interests of their merchants and to supervise the behaviour of their visiting subjects and to exercise a degree of jurisdiction defined by individual agreements. Western trading nations might also be entrusted with a *fondaco* or warehouse, with marketing facilities, offices and hostel incorporated. As a result of her greater volume of trade, Venice had two *fondachi* at Alexandria as against one each for her rivals. Yet the influence of the Venetians overseas was always in flux; and even as she was still amassing possessions Venice was losing a hold elsewhere. If in 1453 Venetian interests in the Black Sea had become precarious, the Aegean islands of Skiros, Skopelos and Skiathos were occupied by Venice in that very year, and in 1462 Monemvasia, which had close links with Crete, another important Venetian possession, was taken to forestall Turkish occupation. Cyprus under Jacques II developed close relations with Venice from 1466 and eventually fell to her as an Egyptian tributary after the king's death. Meanwhile the Turks expanded into Morea and across the Balkans towards the Adriatic coast, took Negropont or Euboea in 1470, eventually threatened Venice herself from the north, and set well under way that process whereby the Venetian empire was whittled down to Crete and a diminished hold on the Adriatic.

The other big colonial empire was that of Genoa. Like Venice, Genoa had consuls and *fondachi* scattered through the Levant. Genoese merchants settled in Damascus and Aleppo; in Pera, the northern suburb of Constantinople; in every important Black Sea port including Sinope, Trebizond, Simisso, Tana and above all Caffa. Until the rise of the Venetians in Cyprus, Genoa had long held a privileged position there; Chios was the centre of all her Levantine operations; and she had merchants settled the length of the Barbary coast. In the middle of the fifteenth century the Gattilusii, a Genoese family, still held sway over the island of Lesbos or Mitilíni and several smaller islands. However, the expansion of the Ottoman empire was to pare away the influence of the Genoese in the Black Sea and the Aegean, so that at the beginning of this period it had already become much less significant. The fall of Constantinople and Pera was followed quickly in 1456 by the occupation of Fokia on the mainland of Asia Minor opposite Chios, which the Genoese had developed on account of the local alum deposits. Lesbos fell in 1462, and the last hold that the Genoese had on the Black Sea coast was lost when Caffa fell in 1475. The Turks left Chios to Genoa, as it was to their advantage to maintain the trade which the Genoese had built up and which could only be carried on with the experience and connections of those who had organised it in the past. It was only after radical changes had taken place to Mediterranean and world trade at the beginning of the sixteenth century, when moreover Turkish influence had spread vastly in all directions, that the Turks no longer felt it necessary to use the Genoese who had by then turned to Spain, the enemy of the Turks. Accordingly, Sultan Suleiman the Great demanded in 1533 that the Genoese *podestà* should be expelled. The demand was resisted until 1552, but when the Genoese gave way it was the beginning of the end. In 1566 the Turks occupied Chios.

The object of Venice's string of colonies was primarily to protect her trade and to control the traffic of the Adriatic. It was the notion that the Adriatic was a Venetian lake that prompted the republic to occupy on several occasions various ports of Apulia, although such violation of the territory of Naples was generally given some less aggressive justification. Nevertheless, ports and stretches of coast including Gallipoli in Apulia, Brindisi, Bari and Otranto were occupied from time to time between 1483 and 1528. Her hold on any part of the Apulian coast, however, was always uncertain and Venice therefore particularly prized her possession of Corfu, from where she dominated the Straits of Otranto. The routes from Venice to Constantinople, Beirut or Alexandria were littered with stopping places—Zara, Spalato, Durazzo, Corfu, Zante, Modon, Coron, Nauplia— all of which served as refuges, victualling places, markets for selling and buying and bases for protection. The two islands, Crete and as it became more under the republic's control Cyprus, were also used for these purposes but they became important for their own produce and industry as well. Crete, which was held by Venice until 1669, was famous for its malmsey and its muscatel, which even Genoese ships picked up on their way from the Aegean to the west. The wine apart, Venetian shipping loaded at Candia raisins, cheese, cypress-wood for building very large ships, oil and, on their way east, especially soap. But Candia also exported raw cotton, sugar and some silk, and she imported cloth for tailoring and re-exported the finished articles to the Levant. While the demand was great and many Greek texts were still little known during the last half of the fifteenth and the first decades of the sixteenth centuries, copying and the sale of manuscripts was carried on on a significant scale. Perhaps her greatest export to Venice was men. The employment of Cretans by Aldus and others for work of all kinds in the publishing and printing trade has already been noted; but Candiotes worked as sailors, as merchants' assistants, soldiers and in many other trades or occupations in Venice. As a refuge for Greeks from Constantinople and Morea the island was highly over-populated and the people spilled over into the republic. In 1478 it was estimated that there were as many as 5,000 Greeks at Venice.

Cyprus was made by the Genoese a distribution centre for the spice trade. Their monopoly had forced Venice to seek spices further afield in the ports of the Levant, so that by the time Venetian influence developed on the island the spice trade was well established at Beirut, Tripoli in Syria and Alexandria, and by-passed Famagusta. Barley and wheat had become Cyprus's main home-produced exports under Genoese dominance, and port restrictions imposed by the Genoese meant that only Famagusta and the inland capital of the ruling family, Nicosia, were of importance. Venetian dominance brought new enterprises. The salt at Larnaka was exploited; sugar was grown for refineries at Limassol and Paphos; wines were produced; and cotton was planted, particularly by members of the Venetian family of Corner di San Luca, who irrigated the land systematically for this purpose. At Nicosia and Famagusta textile industries were developed and at the former town dyeing became an important industry. Boccasins and camlets were among the richest cloths produced on the island. Ladanum was extracted from the rock rose for medicines, embalming mixtures and plasters. A reflection of the Venetian occupation was the growth in population of the small Cypriote towns, Nicosia and Famagusta; and Larnaka grew as a port. On the other hand Limassol was reduced to no more than a village despite its sugar industry, whose growth was limited by the more important production of Sicily and the Atlantic islands. An important feature of Venetian exploitation of its overseas possessions was the introduction of Latin bishoprics, which collected dues previously going to the Greek Church, and the republic often managed to get its patricians appointed to them. Venetian appointments occurred also where the Latin Church already had a hold. Thus Church revenues found their way into the pocket of frequently absentee Venetian bishops, even if as in Crete the population remained overwhelmingly Orthodox.

Chios in the eleventh and twelfth centuries, in so far as it played a part in Italian trade, had been a centre of Venetian commercial influence. From the fourteenth century it fell within the orbit of Genoa, which held it consistently from 1346 to 1566 except for a brief occupation by the Venetians in 1431–32. In the fifteenth century, with the Genoese development of Fokia alum, reinforced by rights from the sultan to exploit the deposits of Karahissar and elsewhere in his territories, Chios' most important function was to re-export this mineral, so vital to the dyeing process, to the textile industries of Europe. The Venetians alone in the first half of the fifteenth century kept themselves free from dependence upon the Genoese-borne supplies, which served Italy, France, Flanders, Brabant and England in particular. It was due to the alum trade that the Genoese tendency to use large ships was reinforced, and Genoa became the great bulk-carrying state of the Mediterranean. Because of this she was forced to develop large entrepôt centres with deep-water ports. Thus at Chios and elsewhere such as at Malaga or Majorca fleets of small boats assembled cargoes to be loaded on big sailing-ships. In this way alum was brought from Fokia, Lesbos and so on, wheat and barley from Gallipoli or Salonika, slaves from the Balkans or the Black Sea, cheese from Thrace and many other commodities from surrounding ports and islands, to be loaded at Chios for the longer voyages south or west. As the Turks expanded, they found this system of exporting through the Genoese at Chios a useful way of maintaining sales to the west. They were also able to exact from Chios a considerable and increasing tribute. However, Chios lost its important alum trade to the Venetian, Bartolomeo Zorzi; and from then, especially after the discovery of the Tolfa alum, Chios was forced to develop the alternative trade of re-exporting purchases from the flourishing market of Bursa. Silk was the main commodity in this alternative trade. But the Turks were developing the overland caravan routes from the Persian Gulf and the Red Sea to Bursa, undermining as far as possible the markets of Damascus and Aleppo. Thus spices, pearls and other oriental produce were brought with the silk by pack-animal overland to Fokia and shipped to Chios for re-export to the west. Rice grown around Scutari was also carried in this manner. The silk export involved a change of traditional Genoese shipping routes. Instead of sending alum direct to the Atlantic and North Sea, shipping from Chios now carried silk to be used in the silk industry at Genoa. Before the fall of Constantinople the Genoese transported slaves from Caffa to the Mediterranean: young men were usually sold to the Egyptian sultans for soldiers; young women to the West—some were taken home to Genoa itself—for domestic work, sometimes combined with concubinage. The trade was modified after 1453. The export of Muslim slaves was forbidden by the

Turks, and the source of slaves tended more often to be the Balkans. They were shipped to the great slave-market at Chios from where they were distributed in much the same way as before. Like Crete and Cyprus, Chios had important products of her own. Of these terebinth or turpentine pitch for the ship-repairing industry has already been noticed. Wine was produced to be exported together with other wine brought to Chios from the Aegean islands. This was mostly of the sweet malmsey variety so relished by the west European, but also imported for their own consumption by the Muslim countries to the south, such as Egypt. The local silk production became important as Genoese demands grew, and citrus fruits were grown in quantity. But the great local monopoly was mastic, which was grown nowhere else. Most of this was exported to the Muslim world, especially to Egypt, Syria and the Barbary coast as an ingredient in chewing pastes, although some was used in the west in perfumes.

Chios was dominated by the *Maona*, an organisation formed in 1347 by the most notable Genoese trading families on the island to exploit its commercial possibilities. In 1364 most members of the *Maona* adopted the Venetian name of the palace they occupied for their business, Giustiniani, according to the Genoese custom of forming *alberghi* and employing a common surname to denote their close association. The *Maona* monopolised the important trades in alum, salt, pitch and mastic. It had representatives in Genoa and all the main centres with which Chios did business. Accordingly, the name Giustiniani was as widely known throughout the business world as the names of Medici, Strozzi, Centurioni, Lomellini, Affaitadi, Borromei or Bonvisi, and its standing was a measure of the importance of Chios to the economy of Europe.

The great importance of the colonial territories of Venice and Genoa is evident, but the great centres of the eastern trade were Constantinople and Pera; Aleppo, Damascus and Beirut; and Alexandria. The fall of Constantinople hit most those states that had a well-established trade with the south-eastern corner of Europe, Asia Minor and the Black Sea. From then on it was the sultan who called the tune. The Ottoman empire, however, was no more willing to forsake the commercial benefits that her new conquests bestowed upon her than were the Italians to give up their ancient supremacy in that trade. But the Turks drove as hard a bargain as they could. Tributes were exacted from Venice for the continuance of her trade and a high price was set on the alum farm which was then acquired; whilst Chios, as has been seen, was also forced to pay a considerable tribute to the sultan. Florence entered the field when Cosimo de' Medici sent ambassadors to the sultan in an attempt to take advantage of the losses of the

Genoese and Venetians. But Venice in the first instance came out best. She immediately negotiated a trade treaty with Mehemmed II, whereby she was allowed to have a resident representative, a *bailo*, at Constantinople to watch over her commercial interests. Her merchants and shipping were given free rights of entrance and departure, only a two per cent sales tax was placed on her goods, and goods in passage were left untaxed. Christian, but not Muslim, slaves were allowed transit through the Bosphorus and Dardanelles, although all shipping was to report at one of the forts set up on either side of the entrance to the latter before proceeding. In all, these were not unfavourable terms. However, the officially sponsored trading voyages, the *mude*, arranged by the government for the most important trade routes and auctioned out to contractors, had been fairly regular for the 120 years preceding 1453. From then until 1478 there were none; and such voyages were only undertaken in less than a third of the next 37 years ending with the last Constantinople *muda* in 1514. Despite this, trade with Constantinople and the surrounding region did not halt so abruptly as it would seem. Official trading voyages of this nature never surpassed the bulk of private trading in any section of Venetian commerce. During this period this private trade was to a noticeable degree reorientated towards Salonika, the Maritsa and elsewhere along the Thracian and Macedonian coast rather than beyond the Dardanelles. At the same time direct contacts between Venice and the Black Sea lasted longer than those of the Genoese, despite the predominance that the latter had previously held in this area. When sailing conditions were difficult, especially in the periods of Turkish-Venetian war, more or less successful attempts were made by the Venetians to maintain this eastern trade overland from Spalato or Durazzo across the Balkans to Adrianople, by this time a great Turkish market, and to Constantinople. These overland routes were policed sufficiently by the sultan to keep this trade comparatively free from banditry. The object of this great commercial activity was variable. In times of food shortage, as for instance during the war of Ferrara, 1482–84, it became extremely profitable as well as necessary to import wheat. Silks were brought from Bursa, although the Venetians had no immediate dealing with that market and relied upon the Genoese to carry the goods to Constantinople for them. Cloths from Flanders, or Lombardy, or even Verona and Vicenza, metal goods especially from Germany and soap from Venice and Apulia were amongst the main items the Venetians took to Constantinople, whilst they brought home a variety of produce gathered together from the Balkans, the Danube delta, the lands north of the Black Sea, Asia Minor and beyond. These included furs and hides, caviar, musk for perfumes, rhubarb for medicinal purposes and a wide variety of other produce. It is an indication of the changes that had taken place in Venetian trade that, whereas at the beginning of this period Venetians bought very largely from the Turks with ducats, towards its end they were exchanging goods for their own gold coins.

Florence tried to capitalise on the misfortunes of Venetian and Genoese merchants. Already in the early 1460s she was spying on Venice for the sultan by intercepting letters that would have an adverse effect on Venetian-Turkish relations, and passing them on. When Pius II tried to unite Christian forces into a huge effort to regain Constantinople, Cosimo de' Medici held aloof. But Florentine trade with the Turk really had to wait for the fall of the early Medici before it assumed significant proportions. Florentine convoys accompanied by armed galleys went yearly to Constantinople, Chios and Fokia by the end of Cosimo de' Medici's life. About 1460 they even appeared at Caffa and Trebizond, but lacked the marketing facilities and experience of their Venetian and Genoese rivals. When Mehemmed II died in 1481, Lorenzo unlike his grandfather was dilatory in sending ambassadors and lost any advantage that Florence might have had; but during the Turkish-Venetian War of 1499–1503 Florentine merchants were not slow to profit from the difficulties Venice was undergoing. They delighted at her inconvenience and did their best to prolong it. By 1507 Florence had developed an important trade at Pera, Bursa, Adrianople, Sofia, Moncastro and Gallipoli, a trade that amounted to half a million ducats a year. An important element in the Florentine trade with the Levant was the sale of English cloths finished in Florence or of Florentine cloth made out of English wool. Under Henry VIII, however, English shipping and cloth manufacture by-passed Florence, and between 1511 and 1534 the English exported directly to the Levant. It is true this trade fell off until by 1552 it was negligible, but it revived again in the 1570s under Elizabeth I. Its magnitude can be seen from the fact that the cloth was carried in Venetian, Portuguese, Candiote, Spanish and Ragusan bottoms as well as by the English themselves. While the Florentine trade was prosperous, it used Sienese and Anconan shipping as well as its own. However, much of the trade was sent overland to Ancona, shipped to Ragusa and then sent on to Adrianople and Pera by pack-animal. Only a luxury trade of the highest order could survive the transport costs that were involved.

The trade in pepper and spices of many kinds, in dyestuffs, herbs and drugs from the Orient which generally goes under the inclusive name of the spice trade, was centred mainly on the ports of Beirut and Alexandria.

Before the Portuguese came on the scene the produce of the East was usually assembled at the ports on the Malabar coast or further north at Cambay. It was brought by Chinese junk or the ships of Arab, Gujerati or East Indian seamen. Although these towns were predominantly Hindu, Muslim merchants organised most of the trade, which was facilitated by their connections with other Muslim merchants in the Malay peninsula or in the East Indies. Occasionally Gujerati seamen by-passed the Indian ports and delivered their goods directly to Ormuz at the entrance to the Persian Gulf. Through this Far Eastern trade, cloves were brought from the Moluccas; gum benzoin for perfumes and medicines from Java, Sumatra and Indo-China; ginger and rhubarb (although the latter deteriorated on the sea) from China; camphor for drugs from Sumatra; nutmeg and mace from Celebes and the Moluccas; cassia, a purgative, from Java; precious stones, cinnamon, brazil-wood and pepper from Ceylon. A mass of other commodities, especially valued in the West, were gathered at Cochin, Cannanore, Calicut, Goa and Cambay. To these were added local produce and other Indian goods from further afield. Cannanore was known for its poorer quality but cheap ginger. Cambay, apart from the usual goods, exported such unusual produce as costus, a member of the thistle family which was used for perfumes and incense and was brought down to the Indus from the north of India. It also exported locally produced lac. Pepper, the basis of the whole spice trade, was important along the Malabar coast, especially towards the south. Indigo, brazil-wood and medicinal plants like zedoary, a stomach-warming medicine, were also products of this region. The produce of eastern Africa became identified with this trade, especially the trade in ivory and in amber with its multifarious uses in medicine, perfumery, the making of buttons and crucifixes, and as an ingredient in embalming oils.

There were two main routes by which these goods were distributed to the Occident: they went by way of Ormuz and the Persian Gulf up the Tigris to Baghdad and by caravan to Aleppo or perhaps Bursa; or they went *via* the Red Sea to Jeddah where they were disembarked and followed the caravan route to Damascus, or were transshipped to Tor and thence taken by caravan to Cairo and down the Nile especially to Alexandria or direct from Tor to Damascus. Along these routes other goods were picked up: aloes from Sokotra; amber in south Arabia, generally sent overland in order to preserve it better; indigo from the mainland opposite the island of Ormuz; pearls from the southern part of the Persian Gulf. In the markets of Aleppo and Damascus or at the ports of Alexandria and Damietta the oriental produce was sold together with goods of local origin or imported from elsewhere; but it was particularly the rich eastern trade that attracted the western, predominantly Italian, merchants.

Venice was always the most important trading power with these great, eastern markets, sending her ships regularly to Beirut and Alexandria. From 1346 to well beyond this period *mude* regularly set out for Egypt. Only six years were missed between 1464 and 1534. These were all years when Turkish expansion or Egyptian enmity made it dangerous for the Venetians to undertake the voyage, or when there was a demand on Venetian shipping to supply naval needs. There were no years omitted between 1467 and 1498, nor from 1517 to the end of the period central to this book. Thus, during a dozen years of the Venetian-Turkish war from 1467 and for a long time after the Portuguese had established the regularity of their voyages around the Cape, Venice still found it worthwhile to pursue her trade with Alexandria; so much so that, even if shipping was needed for military purposes, it was often thought advantageous to use some for the Oriental trade.

The Genoese and Florentine trade during the period was less systematic. Florentine shipping, as will be seen, never succeeded in challenging the greater sea-faring states, whereas Genoese shipping was completely in private hands and therefore its direction was controlled by the immediate prospect of profits. Venetian policy, on the other hand, was to maintain continuity in her commercial contacts, so that even low bidding in the auctions for the *muda* contracts did not deter the republic from pressing forward with these voyages. A virtually subsidised voyage was better than letting a rival steal a march on her spice trade. But in the fifteenth century Venice more than any Mediterranean sea-faring power was in a better position to prosecute this trade. If the East poured its produce into the West, it wanted something in return. The assembly trade, as it were, the gathering together of goods on the west coast of India, caused little problem. Much of this was done on the basis of an exchange of local produce. But those who ran the trade—the merchants from Egypt, east Africa and Arabia and local Indians of the ports—needed goods that were in demand in India itself. First and foremost were precious metals. This is where Venice's advantage lay. European supplies were not great, but the biggest sources were in the hands of the merchants of Augsburg and other south German towns. They controlled the silver of the Tyrol, Hungary and Saxony and the small deposits of gold in central Europe. The most convenient outlet, through Venice, was on the route to the most profitable markets in the East. Thus Venice throve on a geographical accident. The important centre for managing the German trade and storing its goods, the *Fondaco dei Tedeschi*, was thus a crucial link in the Venetian spice trade. Germany had large supplies of another metal in great demand in the East. This was copper, and it too was exported through Venice either as raw material or in the form of manufactured utensils. Genoa and Florence simply had no comparable advantages. Another prominent element in the Far Eastern trade was the export of Arab and Persian horses to India, and although these did not concern the Italian states directly they were instrumental in obtaining spices to be sold on the Italian markets. The Italians also sent other European metals like tin and lead, European wines or high quality woollen cloths to the markets of India. But the one other important export to the East was coral, a trade exploited by Florentine, Genoese and Venetian alike. The coral fisheries off Mers-el-Kharez, near Bône, were under Genoese control, and from the beginning of the sixteenth century the Lomellini of Genoa controlled the Tabarca fisheries. The fishery centred on Alghero on the west coast of Sardinia was also in Genoese hands. But remarkably the most powerful coral merchants of all, the Venetian Contarini, had a branch at Genoa, and in 1469 René of Anjou, Count of Provence, gave the Contarini together with two Florentine merchants rights over the coral fisheries from the Rhône to the Var. Most of this coral found a market in Damascus or was sent on to India by the Damascus caravan and sea routes, while the Florentines in particular sent it also *via* Egypt.

The Italians sought local produce from Egypt such as cotton, balm and fine linens; sugar and dates; emeralds, beryls and rubies; and senna and cassia for use in purgatives. In return they sent goods for local consumption. The mastic, wine, and slaves from the Genoese Aegean have already been mentioned. But the Genoese on their occasional round voyages which touched in at Alexandria also took salt from the Balearic island of Ibiza; oil from the isle of Djerba; nuts from Provence, a much sought commodity; raisins from the Aegean; and wood, always in short supply for cooking-fires, from Asia Minor. Much the same list of commodities would apply to the Venetians, but crystal from Murano, silverware, and falcons, much demanded by the sultans for hunting, should be added.

The market of Alexandria was controlled by the sultan from Cairo. When each ship arrived it was boarded by port officials, who took minute details concerning, amongst other things, where it had come from, the number of persons aboard and the nature of the cargoes. This information was sent to Cairo by pigeon and instructions were sent back. Normally, steering gear and sails were removed until the time for departure and were returned only if everything was in order in the eyes of the Egyptian officials.

Foreign consuls were often maintained at Cairo as well as at Alexandria, not only to represent the trading nation, but also as hostages to the sultan who paid them a considerable salary himself and provided them with accommodation. The great city of Cairo relied very much upon this trade between East and West, profiting greatly from customs dues levied upon it. The sultan, moreover, forced an overpriced quota of spices on each western vessel. These spices were frequently of low quality, even full of impurities. But if this quota were not accepted the ships would not be allowed to sail. Transport costs and taxes levied at Jeddah, Tor, Cairo, Alexandria and perhaps elsewhere kept spice prices very high; this accounted for the hopes underlying the drive for cheaper spices undertaken by the Portuguese. A sea route would eliminate such intermediary expenses and allow a greater profit margin even at reduced prices.

For precious cargoes such as spices, fine silks, dyestuffs, and less precious light cargoes such as cotton, loading periods also known as *mude* were specified by the Venetian government. Ships were not necessarily bound to sail in convoy, but they had to load and depart from the port, not only at Alexandria but at Beirut also, not later than a specified time. There are several possible reasons for this restriction. That it tended to avoid the worst weather conditions in dangerous seas accounted for its timing rather than its institution, for bulk cargoes were carried the year round. The restricted loading period may well have been designed to facilitate the organisation of convoys or their resumption when it was thought necessary to sail under protection. It certainly would have put a term to the haggling over prices which was a constant feature of the negotiations that took place in these Levantine ports. By doing this, a quicker turnover was assured. Consequently there was a saving in shipping costs and a greater amount of trade undertaken. The *mude* also established a rhythm in trade, so that merchants could expect with confidence favourable trading conditions at given times. Moreover, the success of a controlled enterprise of this nature was easily assessed and merchants could plan their future investments on solid information. It was only with great reluctance that the republic made exceptions to the strict enforcement of these loading periods and then, as in 1503 and 1527, the goods were impounded until the normal marketing times, presumably so that no unfair profits were made on the Venetian market and so that a system, which was to the advantage of smooth marketing and which benefited all, was strictly maintained.

The trade with Syria was equally dominated by the Venetians. It had its origins in the Genoese spice control on the island of Cyprus, which forced the Venetians to push further afield to Beirut, Tripoli, Tyre, Acre and Alexandretta. Beirut, the port of Damascus, developed into the largest and most important of these ports and regular *mude* were organised by the Venetian republic from 1374. In the period from 1464 to 1534, only in 1499, 1501, 1505 and 1511 were official voyages to Beirut not undertaken. The finer spices like mace and nutmeg (both considerably more expensive than pepper, even discounting the greater transport costs), amber, pearls from the Persian Gulf, tragacanth or Persian gum for drugs, rhubarb, silks from Persia and further afield, the products of local industries such as carpets and tapestries, preserved fruits, damasks and other linen and silken cloths, damascened dishes, raw cotton, copper utensils, arms—a varied array of goods such as these produced the exciting and busy atmosphere of the Damascus market. Aleppo reproduced the scene with slight variations. Sugar-cane was grown near Beirut, Tyre and Tripoli; cotton near Acre and Beirut; camlets were manufactured at Tripoli. Often these were bought at a smaller market such as cotton at Hama or sometimes at the ports themselves. Venetians, Genoese and other Europeans regularly frequented the ports and the markets. The Venetian names of Barbarigo, Morosini, Quirini, Soranzo would not be unfamiliar at Aleppo or Damascus. Apart from Syria being an important adjunct to the spice trade, its cotton was important for the fustian industry at Cremona and great quantities were imported for that purpose for re-sale by the Venetians. It was also the dominance of Venice in this sector together with her favourable contacts with central Europe that gave the republic a long lead in the business of carrying pilgrims to Jaffa *en route* for Jerusalem.

The Portuguese efforts to undermine the traditional spice routes by rounding the continent of Africa had been encouraged by the Genoese. Alexander VI by his bull *Inter caetera* of 1493, fixing the boundaries between Spanish and Portuguese spheres of influence, had given the Portuguese a free hand. As soon as da Gama's success had been affirmed, the Florentines and the Genoese jumped in to grab a share of the spoils. They helped fit out and finance spice fleets and even took part in the voyages. The Venetians, who at the time were at war with the Turks, were slow, perhaps reluctant, to admit the danger of this competition. It was not usual for a patrician to be allowed to refuse a government order to undertake an important mission: the republic's will was law. Yet when it was eventually decided to send an ambassador to Manuel I of Portugal the first two asked declined and were permitted not to go, and the third choice was a young and inexperienced patrician, Pietro Pasqualigo. By the summer of 1501, in reaction to the voyage of Cabral, Venetian thinking had become more serious, even if completely divided. There were those

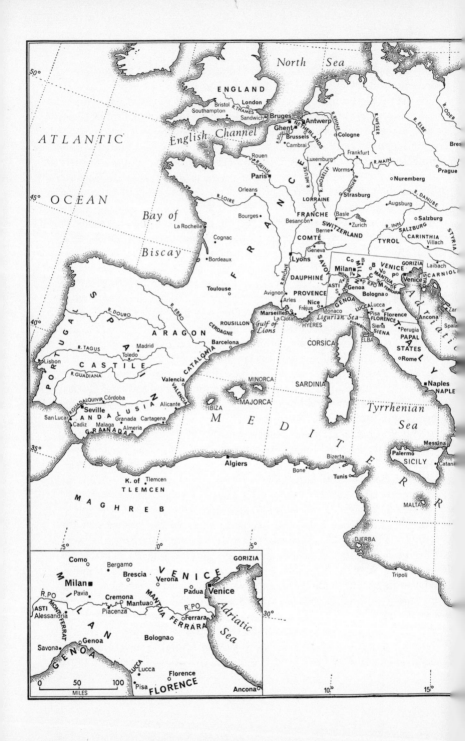

THE MEDITERRANEAN

50°

R. DON

R. VOLGA

UKRAINE

Kievo

R. DNIEPER

R. DNIESTER

Astrakhan

45°

Caspian Sea

R. TISA

R. DNIEPER

Tana

Sea of Azov

Y

ANSYLVANIA

MURES   Sibiu   Brasov

Moncastro

Caffa

R. DON

R. DANUBE

Black   Sea

Sofia

R. MARITSA

Sinope

40°

Adrianople

Samastro

Simisso   Trebizond

CEDONIA

Salonika

Constantinople   Pera   Scutari

THRACE

Gallipoli

Sea of Marmara

Bursa

Taurus

LESBOS

Dardanelles

ASIA   MINOR

R. TIGRIS

SKIROS

Mitilini

Karahissar

epanto

Athens

Chios

Fokia

Smyrna

CHIOS

PATMOS

Alexandretta

35°

Nauplia

Aleppo

R. EUPHRATES

MOREA

Hama

Baghdad

Monemvasia

Nicosia

Famagusta

don

CYPRUS

Larnaka

Candia

Paphos

Limassol

Tripoli

S

Beyrut

Damascus

CRETE

Y

Tyre

R

Acre

I

A

N

S

E

A

Jaffa

Jerusalem

30°

Damietta

Alexandria

Tor

Cairo

EGYPT

100   200   300   400

Red

MILES

Sea

25°

R. NILE

25°   30°   35°   40°   REGMARAD

who believed that as the Portuguese traffic became more regular, the cheaper alternative route would grow and menace the established contacts and traditional channels of the trade. There were many, however, who were inclined to question the ability of Portugal to consolidate her position. She would have difficulty in recruiting enough men to keep the trade going. Portugal had a population of only a million and a half people, perhaps no more than that of Venice and her Italian territories at the time. Her resources were limited too, and she could not sustain for long the inevitable expenses and losses that so difficult a route would bring. In the event, this may well have been so, had not, as it were, a conspiracy of capital intervened. The Florentine firms of Bruges, the Gualterotti and Frescobaldi, the Marchioni and others from Florence, Welser, Fugger, Hochstetter of Augsburg, Hirschvogel and Imhof of Nuremburg, the Lomellini of Genoese origin and so on, all poured their capital into the enterprise of Venice's rivals. So that Venice might compete with the Portuguese on a more equal footing, in 1503 and 1505 Venetian ambassadors were sent to the Egyptian Sultan, Kānsūh al-Ghaurī, to try to persuade him to grant better trading terms. Both missions failed. The Venetians becoming increasingly anxious even considered building a Suez canal. Then a new committee, the *Cinque Savi della Mercanzia*, was set up in 1506 to consider and advise upon Venice's future commercial development in the light of these changes. There was little Venice could do immediately because she was embroiled in disastrous European war. She emerged from her immediate dangers in Europe only to be faced by a new situation, the Turkish conquest of Syria in 1516 and of Egypt in the following year. She re-negotiated her rights for trading with Beirut and Alexandria and transferred her tribute for Cyprus to the Ottoman sultan. Otherwise her position was unchanged.

If from this time there was a powerful stimulus for Venice to re-direct her economy towards the mainland, her oriental trade showed remarkable resilience. Portugal's conquest in the East was aimed not only at securing a foothold there from which to carry on trade, but also to monopolise the shipping in the Indian Ocean and the East Indies, so that none of the old Muslim-dominated trade could survive. She therefore tried to cork up any leakages to the Red Sea and Persian Gulf. The completeness of her victory was astounding. After establishing herself in Malabar and inflicting heavy losses on Arab and Gujerati shipping, she took Goa in 1510, Malacca in 1511—thus dominating the main outlet to the East Indian trade, Calicut in 1512 and Ormuz in 1515. Thence she proceeded to expand further, acquire mastery over strategic routes, and, if she never succeeded in dominating the Red Sea (the Turks advanced so far as to take Aden in 1538), she was at least in a position to prevent Indian and African shipping entering or leaving it without great risk. Had she been able to discipline her officials, she might well have killed the Mediterranean spice trade. She could not, however. Her officials proved venal; and Portugal, as was forecast by those Venetians who had from the beginning been optimistic, had not the resources in the end to maintain her stranglehold on her Muslim competitors, who were to a great extent reinforced by the growth of Baber's Moghul empire. Venice, moreover, had her own advantages. Her spices, especially those that suffered badly from long sea voyages, were generally of higher quality than Portugal's. The experience of the merchants who had governed the old routes was also important: they had their old contacts and trained judgment to aid them. Venice's marketing experience in Europe, the excellence of which underlies the fact that spices imported from Alexandria through Marseilles to Lyons were more expensive than Venetian spices taken directly overland from Venice to Lyons, again acted in favour of the republic. Her proximity to central Europe countered in part the cheaper Portuguese transport costs to Antwerp. Finally, her experience in supplying the needs of the eastern merchants, which held good until New World precious metals spread sufficiently to alter the pattern of trade, was important for the maintenance of the Venetian trade.

In 1508 Portuguese spices imported through Antwerp, the centre of Portuguese spice distribution, were being sold at Lyons; by 1516 they had reached Marseilles; and in the 1530s they could be bought, even at Venice. Venice certainly experienced bad years. In 1499 and 1500, in 1504, 1506 and 1512 there was no pepper to be had at Alexandria or at Beirut. 1517, 1519, 1523 and 1529 were also meagre years for the Venetian spice trade. Yet in 1515 Venetian pepper and ginger were still on the market at Antwerp, the very home of the Portuguese trade. Whereas in 1525–26 Levantine spices from all sources only just predominated over Antwerp spices at Lyons, in 1533–34 85 per cent of the spices at Lyons were Venetian. The Venetian hold over the French trade was partly due to the protective policies of Francis I, which were aimed at promoting a trade between Marseilles and Alexandria; but Venetian marketing techniques and experience were able to confound them. Therefore Francis' encouragement of the Mediterranean route served Venice. In an attempt to combat the Mediterranean predominance in France, Portugal transferred her trade from Antwerp to Lisbon. Even so, by the 1560s Venice had a spice trade greater than it had ever had in the past. This did not last long.

After the defeat of the Turkish fleet at Lepanto, in which the Venetians played an important part, the eastern Mediterranean came increasingly under Turkish control; and, although things were going badly for the Portuguese in the East, the Venetian spice trade declined. With the deterioration of Venice's shipping it had no well-founded hope of revival.

The commerce in the western Mediterranean as far as the Italians were concerned was partly a comparatively local matter and partly integrated with the through traffic to the Atlantic, the Channel and the North Sea. In the early decades of the fifteenth century the local trade was largely organised by Pisans, who established themselves at Palermo after the fall of Pisa to Florence. By the middle of the century the Genoese predominated in this trade, although by no means did they limit themselves to their own shipping. During the fifteenth century even Venetian *mude* entered the coastal trade of western Italy and the Gulf of Lyons, while much of the indigenous, coastal trade of the Maghreb was in the hands of the Genoese. It was even the Genoese who carried Muslim merchants and pilgrims on their journeys along the North African coast. Some of this trade of the western Mediterranean has already been mentioned incidentally: Spanish wool to Florence, the timber of Dauphiné and the silk of Granada to Genoa, the importation of salt by Lombardy through Genoa, Sardinian cheeses sent out in all directions. One or two salient aspects of the trade will be dealt with in brief.

Majorca, Malaga and Valencia were used by the Genoese as entrepôts. Small shipping gathered together the produce of North Africa, Andalusia, and the kingdoms of Granada and Valencia at these centres, and the big ships of Genoa then redistributed them to more distant parts. The pattern was similar to that of Chios, and was forced upon Genoa by the size of her long-distance, bulk-carrying shipping. Messina was also a distribution centre, but by no means a monopoly of the Genoese. Big shipments of spices and other oriental produce were unloaded there by ships of all origins for delivery to a variety of centres in Italy and the western Mediterranean. This method grew up in part to save bigger ships from making too many diversions. Accordingly Messina developed experienced marketing channels, contacts and techniques; it became advantageous, if not necessary, to distribute silks and spices to certain areas through this centre.

Trade patterns at this time therefore were not simple, bilateral exchanges of mutual necessities, but far more complex. The Genoese were particularly fond of three-cornered arrangements. For instance, they would carry salt from Ibiza to Civitavecchia or Corneto (Tarquinia) in the Papal States and exchange it against wheat for use at Genoa itself; although later it was exchanged against Tolfa alum, which would be for further, wider distribution and traded for perhaps English woollens. The Genoese precious metal shortage produced another triangular solution. Gold brought across the Sahara was obtained at Tripoli, on the Guinea coast or in the north African kingdom of Tlemcen and was used to balance the favourable trade situation that Genoa had with her African customers; for against woollen cloths, Levantine cotton, Lombard fustians, Genoese paper and silks, the Africans could only trade poor quality wools and skins, and small quantities of generally low-valued commodities. The gold in turn was used to make up an unfavourable trade balance with Castile. This pattern lasted through the second half of the fifteenth century, but the first small beginnings of a gold flow from America was too great a rival to Sudanese gold. Even here, although the basic pattern was tri-angular it relied on Genoese imports from a variety of places and was therefore involved in a far greater complex of negotiations.

Both the bulk and the value of the trade carried on by a variety of small coastal craft weaving in and out of a string of tiny harbours, spaced roughly a day's sailing from each other, were certainly greater than the magnificent commerce that passed through the Straits of Gibraltar. The Straits traffic, however, is more characteristic of the highly organised, capitalistic enterprise of the times. Like the Levantine trade, too, it illustrates well the dependence of Italian economies on remote circumstances beyond the reach of direct control from Italy. This accounts greatly for the growing sophistication in diplomatic methods that occurred during this period, especially amongst the Venetians and the Florentines.

Venice generally employed the big galley with sails for her long distance trade. Accordingly rivers, fairly shallow waters and poorly equipped harbours could be used. When necessary the galleys could be beached. Unlike the big Genoese sailing ships, these galleys could consequently be used for a considerable amount of intermediary trade. Thus on outward voyages Spanish goods in particular were picked up for sale in the Low Countries and in England. Cartagena, Almeria, Malaga, Cadiz, Seville even, and Lisbon, together with a number of other places were ports of call at which the Venetian galleys bought and sold *en route* for the Channel and the North Sea. There was no limit to the trade done during these voyages, which often merged with the local Mediterranean business of the smaller vessels. Thus Spanish wines, dried fruits, silks from Granada, oil, soap, cochineal and other commodities became important elements in the Venetian trade with the north. As on the other great trade routes, the republic sponsored voyages in its own ships which were auctioned to contractors, while at the same time there was a great traffic in privately owned ships. *Mude* developed in frequency during the fourteenth century, until they became regular at the same time as those to Beirut in 1374. From 1464 to 1495 there were no gaps in the voyages which called in the Low Countries and then England, where they delivered, apart from Mediterranean goods, others from across the North Sea. After 1495 there were only two Flanders *mude*, in 1507 and 1520. This sudden falling off in the Venetian trade with Flanders and Brabant reflects a complex of circumstances. In origin it was probably due to the Emperor Maximilian's expansionist designs in northern Italy, where he had ideas of reasserting the imperial title and by doing so forced the Venetians to pin their faith on a dubious relationship with France. Following the Franco-Venetian agreement at Angers in 1499, Venice was caught up in war with the Turks, in which she got little more than token support from other Italian and European powers. Then in 1508 she was invaded by imperial forces, and in the following year by a European coalition. Meanwhile, the Portuguese spice trade flourished in Antwerp, robbing Venice of much of the *raison d'être* of her trading relations with the Low Countries. Venetian spice galleys were in fact at Antwerp in 1504, 1505, 1508 and 1510; but there was no large-scale trade, which can be accounted for by the fact that Venetian prices were up to 25 per cent above those of the Portuguese. The Flanders *muda* of 1520 thus appears as a forlorn attempt to maintain a trade against overwhelming odds. The English voyages, which now of course—except for 1507 and 1520—were no longer connected with the Low Countries, continued irregularly. There were 15 *mude* from 1498 to 1533. But, as has been said, the English themselves were now making direct contact with the Levant and by-passing Italy, even if sometimes they employed Italian shipping. Thus the Venetian western *mude* were by no means so tenaciously clung to as were those to the spice ports of Beirut and Alexandria. This marked a change in the Venetian methods of distributing her spices from the north Mediterranean: in response to the Portuguese challenge land routes became increasingly popular.

In 1406 Pisa and its territories were conquered and passed under Florentine control. Thus Florence had an outlet to the sea around the mouth of the Arno. By 1421 she had acquired Porto Pisano and Leghorn, and thereby had better prospects of developing a sea traffic of her own. Although in the second half of the fourteenth century Pisa had granted free transit to over a hundred Florentine firms, the rivalry between the two cities had made such an arrangement extremely precarious for Florentine trade. Accordingly, Venice with its flourishing commerce—that of

Pisa had long fallen from its mediaeval greatness—became very much the port of Florence. It was to counter her dependence in this respect that Florence made her drive to the sea. *Consoli del Mare*, three at Pisa and three at Florence, were appointed to organise a Florentine commerce to supersede the services of foreign shipping. By 1425, after some trial runs to Corsica and the Gulf of Lyons, two or three galleys a year set out for northern waters. These voyages were run on similar lines to the Venetian *mude*, although there was a greater insistence by Florence on sailing in convoy. Voyages followed a given route, as was insisted on wherever possible by Venice. The ships were government built and government owned. Each scheduled voyage was undertaken by contractors who secured their rights by auction. However, contractors after an initial enthusiasm found themselves not sufficiently rewarded to finance the voyages. Soon the trade became highly subsidised by the State, which by 1441 had taken over the entire responsibility of sponsoring the trade. There was a gap in these voyages between 1449 and 1455, firstly while Francesco Sforza was laying claim to the duchy of Milan with Florentine financial backing and secondly during the war waged by Milan and Florence against Venice and Naples. After Alfonso of Naples had decided in 1455 to adhere to the League based on the Peace of Lodi of the previous year, the Florentine voyages were resumed, but with no great success. Discriminatory measures against foreign ships were abolished in 1465 in order to encourage them to bring wool and other much needed raw materials for the maintenance of Florence's industries. In the following year a ban on the importation of foreign cloths was lifted, and English cloths for finishing were readmitted. The attempt to compete with the great Mediterranean shipping powers had failed. The woollen industry clearly needed to be protected from the consequences of a fruitless policy. True, Florentine galleys sailed west in the four years from 1465 to 1468; and from 1467 to 1472 galleys, built by Florence for Charles the Bold of Burgundy for the abortive crusade of Pius II and now owned by the Medici, made the voyage annually. But after this there was only one official voyage in 1478. In 1480 the convoys were officially withdrawn for a period of four years in order to encourage foreign shipping in an attempt to maintain a steady flow of wool, which Florence independently had failed to do. This policy was also aimed at keeping prices down. Although even some English ships had brought wool and cloth to Florence, the republic had not really solved her problem of supplies. In 1490 she negotiated a treaty with Henry VII, whereby all English wool entered Italy through the Pisan ports, except for a comparatively small quota for Venice insisted on by the English. Previously Richard III had forbidden Venetian ships to load wool unless they were bound for Pisa, an irksome if unenforceable regulation; but Henry VII saw no advantage in alienating Venice further. The agreement also included a safe conduct for six years for English merchants in Florence and Pisa, but before the period was over Florence had experienced a further setback to her imports, in the revolt of Pisa. Pisa was not recovered until 1509, and two years later Henry VIII opened up direct contacts with the Ottoman empire. Thus Florence's efforts to control the commerce in fabrics made out of English wool were frustrated.

With the decline of the sale of her luxury cloths in England and Flanders because of the improvement and increase in the manufacture of their own local cloths, Florence found it difficult to balance her trade with these areas. Even the respite given to Florence, by the Medici acquiring an important share in the exploitation of papal alum at Tolfa, lasted only about ten years; and during that period profits declined. This accounts for the importance of the intermediary trade that Florentine shipping engaged in. A Florentine convoy would call at a dozen ports on its way to Flanders and England. It would carry silk from Catalonia and raisins from the south of France; while wine, mercury and wax were loaded at Cadiz. Dyestuffs and spices brought from the Levant would be included in the original cargoes, and madder would also be taken from Flanders to London. A vast array of goods assembled with difficulty was transported, so that Florence could be provided with English wool and unfinished cloth. Florence also imported from England calfskins, squirrel furs, household goods, lead and tin. But these were not essential cargo. The great justification of so much effort was the English wool. In striking contrast to Florence, Venice sought a market for her rich oriental cargoes, not a source of raw materials necessary to keep an industry in progress. The fortunes of that trade have been seen. In fact, Portuguese spices first arrived in the Thames in 1504. Consequently around the turn of the century Venice, a few years after Florence, lost a significant reason for her connection with the West. It was Genoa, and not her politically more powerful rivals, who managed in the long run to sustain an important trade by sea with the north, because it was she who managed to gain control of one commodity, alum, essential to the textile industries of England and the Low Countries.

The hold of the Genoese on the alum of Fokia, Karahissar and its other sources in the Aegean and Asia Minor up to the middle of the fifteenth century has already been described. With the fall of Constantinople and Fokia the Venetians managed to take over the trade, but new sources of alum were soon found as a result of the effort to release western industry from dependence upon the Turks. That the main new source fell within the territories of the Papacy, the one European power whose law in a measure knew no frontiers, was all important. At once it was perceived by the popes that spiritual sanctions could be put to economic advantage. It became a matter now only of who might grab their share of the papal profits. Under Pius II, who died about two years after the discovery of the Tolfa deposits, there were already big sales of alum to the Spinola, Centurioni, Doria and Giustiniani of Genoa and to the Medici of Florence; but the initial exploitation of the alum was given to its discoverer, Giovanni di Castro, together with a papal official from Genoa and a Pisan merchant at Rome. Most of the profits were to go to a crusading fund. It was not until 1466 that the Medici officially entered the society to exploit Tolfa. Thus, although the great business families of Italy were eager to gain advantage from this new turn in events, the Papacy and a handful of relatively obscure businessmen were the first to profit. The Genoese at best could be said to have recouped some of their losses in the Levant.

In 1463 Pius II forbade merchants to buy any but papal alum; but the great attempt to enforce the Tolfa monopoly was made by his successor, Paul II. That he was a Venetian had a great effect on the solution he arrived at. His favouring of the Medici rather reflected his need for ready cash than any deep love for that family or Florence. To buy off the claims of the Frangipani, lords of Tolfa, he used a large advance from the Medici bank. Paul II reasserted the claim of Pius II to a monopoly of alum sales in Christian countries with the backing of the spiritual powers of the Church and, although at the time it was always felt by Christian countries to be desirable to obey the Church and avoid its strictures, there were limits beyond which a pope could not push a ruler. Consequently these papal claims in regard to alum were a signal for negotiation. The two most important markets for alum were the Flanders and English textile in-dustries, and these received high priority in Paul's attempts to monopolise their alum supplies. In 1468 a 12-year agreement was made with Charles the Bold of Burgundy, whose dominions included most of the Low Countries, that only crusade alum, as it was called, should be used in states under his control. This was to be sold only at Bruges by Tommaso Portinari, the Medici branch manager there, or by papal commissioners. Substitutes for alum in dyeing and the treatment of hides were to be banned, and the Duke himself would get a considerable commission on the sales. On the other hand the price was not to exceed that of neighbouring territories and the agreement was not to come into force for two years until existing stocks had been used up. The Pope had clearly not had it all his own way. The following years were to show the limits of papal powers in enforcing an agreement such as this. In 1471 Portinari was forced into giving Charles a loan in return for the implementation of the agreement. Then in 1473 the Estates-General in the Burgundian Netherlands stipulated that alum should be admitted in equal competition from all Christian countries in return for a loan to the hard-pressed Duke. In the event the Medici's rivals at Florence, the Pazzi, imported to Antwerp and Bruges between 1473 and 1475 alum from Naples and Spain, and even from Asia Minor and the Barbary coast. When at Rome the Pazzi replaced the Medici in the papal favour they turned to exporting to Flanders only alum from Tolfa. Paul II had also sent papal commissioners to negotiate with Henry VI of England. The immediate result was that England took only crusade alum from 1466 to 1475, but after that, as in Flanders, the papal restrictions were not always heeded. Likewise in France, Tolfa alum was taken in large quantities by Louis XI who nevertheless sought to bring alum from North Africa. The same could be said for most Christian states in and out of Italy. Castile with the help of Genoese capital and management began to exploit the newly discovered Mazarron deposits. In times of enmity with the Papacy Florence used alum from Volterra, although the supplies there were quickly exhausted. Local alum was used wherever it was found and, if there was enough of it, it was marketed further afield.

Because papal alum had two great advantages, its abundance and its high quality, the Papacy, its succession of papal salesmen and the specially privileged Venetian government profited greatly from their control of alum sales, despite the inability of the popes to enforce their monopoly completely. The position of Venice was interesting. In the first place Paul II bought off a potential rival, Bartolomeo Zorzi, who had farmed Fokia alum before the Venetian-Turkish war interrupted his activities, by giving him in 1469 a monopoly of the sale of crusade alum in Venetian territories, Romagna, Austria and southern Germany. In the following year, with the threat to Negropont, the Papacy, as a contribution to its defence, gave Venice the Tolfa alum stocks that were there in the city in return for the transport costs and some other comparatively small amounts of money. Nevertheless, Venice only engaged to respect the Tolfa monopoly until her stocks were used up. She certainly resumed the import of Turkish alum later in the century. Meanwhile, Paul II had come to an agreement in 1470 with Ferrante of Naples, whose territories held several not insignificant deposits of alum. The Neapolitan and Tolfa alum was to be controlled by one sales organisation. Both sides of the business were to be open to inspection by the other. Expenses were to be shared equally by king and pope, as were the profits. Naples and Rome would undertake to export half each of an agreed quota annually, but over and above this the pope would export full quotas to Bruges and Venice, only a sixth of the profits of which would go to Naples. Cash sales were stipulated and only a year's credit was to be allowed. Losses would be met by the partner responsible, and if one side failed to produce its half of the quota the other was to profit proportionately as it made up the deficit. On the face of it, this was a liberal agreement and it was intended to be an important element in a rapprochement between the Papacy and the kingdom. In effect, Neapolitan alum could never meet the commitments laid down in the agreement and the alternative clauses came into play, giving Tolfa a far greater share of the trade. Naples was soon to import crusade alum for her own use. But the Venetians came off well, controlling the distribution of papal alum in their own territories, in Lombardy and north to Austria and southern Germany. Moreover, it was Venetian together with Portuguese shipping which carried most of the alum from Civitavecchia during Paul's reign.

The farming of papal alum was always in the hands of the Italians. The important element of this farm was distribution. This was granted to the Medici for the ten years from 1466, during which period the profits dropped off markedly, largely owing to the policy of Charles the Bold. During the next two years, when Sixtus IV was abetting the Pazzi opposition to the Medici in Florence in the hope of gaining advantages for his nephews, the Pazzi themselves acquired the Tolfa farm. For nearly a quarter of a century the farm changed hands rapidly, coming under the control at various times of Genoese families like the Centurioni and the Gentili and of Florentines—Lorenzo de' Medici again and later Paolo Rucellai. In 1501 the chief share was taken over by the Sienese banker, Agostino Chigi, until his death in 1520, when the controlling interest was seized by the Spannocchi of Siena rather than by Chigi's sons. In 1530 a Florentine firm gained control for a while, but the following year saw the start of a long series of Genoese farmers. The Genoese hold was only broken in 1578, again by the Florentines. From the 1470s until the Genoese success in winning back the Tolfa trade at the end of this period the Papacy met many challenges to its monopoly. Julius II in 1506, for instance, was forced to renew the bull of Paul II of 1465 forbidding the import of Muslim alum. The papal alum profits of Clement VII were only half those of Sixtus IV. The exploitation of central European alum was ever increasing, and in 1534 important deposits in Silesia were opened up for exploitation. In 1504 Philip of Burgundy gave permission for Turkish alum to be delivered to Antwerp, which from 1491 had become the alum staple of the Low Countries in place of Bruges. In the 1520s under Charles V considerable quantities of Spanish alum were taken in Basque ships to Antwerp and Zeeland. The exploitation of Spanish alum fell largely into the hands of the Genoese; and when Ansaldo Grimaldi and Girolamo Venturi of Genoa took over the papal farm in 1531 they promised to wipe out competition. Owing to the favourable relations established between Genoa and Spain by Andrea Doria in 1528 it was believed by Clement VII that Genoa was best able to assert the Tolfa monopoly, but by then competition was too widespread and lost ground was never made up.

As a bulky material in relation to its value alum naturally was generally carried in big sailing ships. The shipping used, as has been seen for the first years of the Tolfa trade, was by no means limited to that of the state of the farmer. After the first decade or so Genoese shipping began to reassert its place in the alum trade and a great deal of the alum which was sent to the North Sea ports went by way of Genoa. This was just as well, since it compensated for the decline of Lombard woad exports that occurred at the same time. The Genoese maintained this predominance throughout the period, although Venetian shipping usually ran it a close second. Some interruption occurred in the Venetian sea trade, when for a period in the 1530s export overland to Pesaro on the Adriatic coast was preferred to the risks of the sea route from Civitavecchia to Venice, threatened by Turkish and Barbary shipping. It is significant of the importance of alum that even this laborious and costly process was considered worthwhile. Another important interruption of the pattern of the alum trade occurred in the great years of Chigi between 1501 and 1513. He shipped the alum out of papal territory to the new Sienese alum ports of Orbetello, Porto Ercole and Talamona, close to where Siena's own alum deposits were located at Monte Argentario. By storing alum in these ports, Chigi created an artificial shortage in order to maintain high prices. He also acquired control over the Agnano and other supplies of alum in Naples so that he could control the market even more closely.

A great deal has been mentioned already concerning trade within Italy: the reliance of the duchy of Milan on supplies of cotton, silk, alum and salt through Venice or Genoa; grain shortages in Italy being made up from better crops elsewhere and the Genoese and Venetian dependence on grain supplies from the south; the small coastal trade that went on all round the peninsula; regular Sienese food supplies to Florence; Elban iron to Genoa, Brescian iron to Milan. These exchanges were enormously important for the economies of the Italian states, and they add to the complex interrelationships upon which depended the survival of Italy as an important factor in the economy of Europe, the Mediterranean, indeed of the known world. To complete the picture, the Alpine routes to the north will be dealt with.

The four powers most engaged in overland trade to Europe were Genoa, Milan, Venice and Florence. Lucca also played an important part in it on account of her valuable silk industry. Florence—a continual rival to the Genoese in the Ligurian and Tyrrhenian Seas from the capture of Pisa and in bitter competition with Venice from when Cosimo threw in his lot with Francesco Sforza—depended very much on passage through Milan for her distribution of goods by land. Genoa on the other hand had feasible alternatives through Milan or Piedmont and was not so tied to the good offices of a single state. Milan and Venice were completely free, in so far as they had a variety of routes to choose from through the northern passes, leading into different states. Before the fall of Constantinople the Genoese had regularly distributed Italian goods throughout eastern Europe through the Black Sea. Some Italian trade to Moncastro and elsewhere continued to pass through the Bosporus afterwards; but alternative routes were made more popular. The Venetians, for example, sent cloths from Verona, Vicenza and Bergamo by way of Vienna to the Transylvanian markets of Sibiu and Brasov, or they used a more southerly route through Hungary. High quality Florentine cloths were taken to Cracow, Breslau, even Danzig, by land. This east European trade, however, was modest in comparison with the great volume carried on with south Germany, Geneva, Lyons and other parts of France.

The Genevan fairs were an important centre of distribution for Italian goods during the middle of the fifteenth century. From Geneva they were taken on by the French or northern merchants to Lyons and thence throughout a large area of France, or across Switzerland to Strasburg, Basle, Cologne and a multitude of other places. Conversely goods from the north were brought home by the Italian merchants in exchange. Normally the merchandise distributed in this way was light and transport costs were kept at a low level in relation to the value of the goods. Accordingly Venetian spices and silks from Lucca, Genoa and Florence formed the basis of Italian relations with Geneva. Milan, Asti and Montferrat profited more from tolls and customs and from providing transport facilities than from a more direct part in the trade. On the other hand, Piedmont tended to view Geneva with its political ties with Savoy as a commercial capital and marketed there such produce as Pignerol cloths. An ominous challenge was presented to Geneva by the institution of the Lyons fairs in 1446, although their competition was not acute until after their reorganisation by Louis XI in 1464. In the first instance it was the Germans rather than the Italians who were deflected from Geneva, but a reduction in French and German patronage reduced the value of the Genevan fairs to Italian merchants. The Medici moved their Geneva branch to Lyons in 1466 and the Centurioni were present at Lyons from 1470. Nevertheless the Genevan fairs continued to attract the Italians and received a new lease of life when the Lyons fairs were closed from 1483 to 1487. Within a decade of their re-opening Lyons had captured the Italian trade from Geneva. The eventual dominance for a time of Venetian spices at Lyons has already been considered. Lucca, Florence and Genoa vied for the silk market. The pro-French policies of Florence under Lorenzo and in the republican period of Savonarola and Soderini are largely explicable in economic terms; Florence's success in the Lyons silk market was an important element in this economic relationship. To avoid the effects of the preferential, protective policies of Francis I, Italian businessmen at Lyons sometimes adopted French nationality, so profitable were their affairs. During the sixteenth century, despite attempts to establish a French silk industry, Lucca and Florence dominated the Lyons silk trade. Not so the Genoese. From 1494 Genoese silks and jewels were widely sold at Lyons. The trade depended, however, on the capricious relations between France and Genoa. It was good from 1499 to 1512 and from 1515 to 1522, periods when the French intervention in north-western Italy was successful; but, despite the determined attempts to keep the trade alive, French hostility as Genoa threw in her lot with Charles V made the continuance of the Lyons commerce impracticable, especially since the conditions imposed upon Genoese transit through Piedmont by Charles III of Savoy were often unacceptable. By 1534 Genoa recognised the hostility of Francis I to be implacable, and when he occupied Piedmont in the following year Genoese trade northwards was deflected back to the routes through Milan. Alternative fairs were established at Besançon in the Franche-Comté in 1535, not as an act of Charles V to deprive France of Genoese trade, but as a result of the short-sighted and rapacious policies of the king of France and the duke of Savoy. The marriage of Genoese interests with the policies of Spain was complete.

In the thirteenth century the Venetians built the *Fondaco dei Tedeschi*, where German merchants put up, stored and marketed their goods and had their offices. Although some Venetians themselves took part in the overland portage of their merchandise, they tended to rely much more on

Germans coming to Venice to transact their sales and purchases. Whereas the Genoese went half way to meet the French, Flemish or German merchants they did business with, the Venetians considered their job done, apart from sales, when they had assembled their goods by water at the warehouses of the Rialto. The *Fondaco dei Tedeschi* was burnt down in 1505. Yet, despite the current fears about the future of the spice trade, the republic was sufficiently hopeful to replace the *Fondaco* by 1508 with a far bigger and better building. They were right: the big German firms like Fugger and Hochstetter continued to disperse a considerable part of their trade through Venice. In the bad years between 1509 and 1515, when the Emperor Maximilian I was at the throat of the republic, this trade was not good; but by 1531, to take one example, the Fuggers exported great consignments of Hungarian copper through Venice. Indeed, the duty paid by German merchants to the republic in 1561 was as much as 41,000 ducats, whereas in a year when Venetian trade was at its height, 1490, the duty had been only 18,000. Various reasons apart from a discrepancy in the volume of trade would help to explain the disparity between these figures. They nevertheless represent the continuance and growth of a flourishing overland commerce.

The Milanese, using the waterways of the Lombard plain, exported their goods in large quantities to Venice. Even much of their export of manufactures north into Europe took this course. Nevertheless, the *Camera dei Mercanti* set up in the thirteenth century organised trade in all directions, including a great deal through the Simplon pass and later, when it was opened up as a route in the fourteenth century, the St Gothard pass. The Valtellina was also used for traffic directed towards Austria, whilst the big lakes formed a prominent part of Milanese communications. However, the Milanese were primarily specialists in light, fast traffic. In 1436 the *Camera dei Mercanti* was given the right to carry on a postal service, despatching letters and small packages and bringing back replies between all parts of Europe from Naples in the south to Spain and Brabant in the west and north.

The great difficulty in the development of land transport for goods was that a sufficient bulk of expensive material had to be carried, so that the carriers were numerous enough, without over-inflating the costs, to defend themselves against highway banditry. If Mediterranean shipping had always to be alert for Provençal pirates raiding from La Ciotat, Fréjus or the Grimaldi principality of Monaco, for Catalan pirates lurking off Sardinia or the islands of the southern Aegean, for Barbary and Turkish pirates stealing into Christian waters, or even the official piracy of the

Venetian republic during food shortages waylaying grain ships and presenting their captains with an official chit with a dubious promise to make good their losses later; land routes, for instance across the Ligurian mountains or the Neapolitan Apennines, had to contend with armed bands whose raids were often organised by a powerful local feudatory. Thus merchants whose business was not done on a considerable scale seldom risked the uncertainties of taking their merchandise overland, and looked to the sea for the disposal of their produce. It was this situation that led to the development in the sixteenth century of specialised transport businesses, big enough to lend security to the overland trade. The transporters did not provide wagons for this new kind of enterprise; but if a merchant or a group of merchants could fit one out, these firms would see to its transportation in convoy and arrange for delivery from a series of stages along the route, where they kept agents. By the middle of the century there were six such firms which had reached a stage of highly sophisticated development. Of these two were German, one was from Lorraine, two from Milan and one from Genoa. Each of them eventually connected parts of Italy to Antwerp. However, their routes were so diverse that between them they provided important connections with a wide selection of towns and villages: Cologne, Augsburg, Nuremberg, Salzburg, Villach, Venice; Luxemburg, Lorraine, Basle, Milan; Bolzano, Trent, Bassano; alternative routes through Austria and Switzerland; Ancona, Pesaro, Bologna, Florence, Genoa, Naples. Most of the traffic south made for Italian ports, especially Ancona and Venice; and it is interesting that by and large the German carriers went to Venice whereas the Italians used Ancona, a reflection of the old Venetian dependence upon German transport overland and the nature of the business this had engendered. This highly developed carrying trade to some extent compensated for losses which occurred to Italian exports by sea to northern Europe from the beginning of the sixteenth century. It was an example of the fertility of capitalistic insights at this time: a crisis might always very well be turned into a new source of profit; but whereas this flexibility which adapted to the needs of the time had once been very much a north Italian property, by now in the age of Fugger this ability had clearly been mastered north of the Alps.

The utter dependence of the economies of the Italian states on their commercial relations and the extent to which their trade reached out from China or the Moluccas to England, from the Baltic to the Sudan or Madagascar, meant that political, military and economic occurrences the world over found a reflection in the business world of Florence, Venice, Milan or Rome, Genoa or Naples, Palermo or Bologna. This is perhaps one reason why the Italians developed that system of limited warfare based on *condottieri*, whose interests were often served rather by retreat than the risk of an open conflict which would result in the destruction of life and property. That was a business rather of the rising nations, more self-sufficient with their vast territories and less dependent upon the provisions of others. All Italians shared the belief that war must not destroy trade. The Portuguese expansion in the east in so far as it was successful shocked the great commercial traditions of Venice into a period of experimentation. The limitations imposed upon free commerce in the Levant by the Ottoman empire forced Genoa to look to the west and ultimately tie herself to the fortunes of Spain. Struggle between Valois and Hapsburg forced Italians to decide where in Europe their profit really lay. The Reformation caused Venice to resist papal pressures in order to maintain a vital trade with heretical Germans. As the English and the Dutch felt their own strength in the commercial world and began to market their own produce, all Italy was impelled to find a new solution. As the colonial powers of Venice and Genoa lost their possessions to the Turk and as Spanish and Portuguese, Dutch and English shipping began to dominate the Atlantic and the northern waters, so Italy turned inwards to the land. Although Italy's industrial and urban expansion continued generally up to the seventeenth century, her horizons became more limited. The trade routes over the Alps replaced the great shipping ways of old. Merchants became farmers, and food crops tended to replace industrial crops in the country around the industrial centres of the north. Yet the constant shifts of the investment of capital into new, less challenged spheres marked the whole period as one of positive evasion and gainful retreat. It was this resourcefulness of the Italian businessman that ultimately enabled him to accept and work towards more limited goals. It enabled him also to play off one great challenger against another.

Genoa met a succession of setbacks that ultimately landed her in the arms of Spain: the loss of Fokia, her initial failures to compensate for this by controlling Tolfa, the fall of Caffa, the conquest of Granada, the successive difficulties posed by Geneva and Lyons as markets until Besançon emerged as the answer. Ultimately she came through by selling her experience and her techniques to Spain. Venice had to face a similar string of reversals. The gradual loss of her colonies in the eastern Mediterranean, the challenge of the Portuguese trade in the orient, the war of the League of Cambrai, all strained her resources to the point where only an adaptability, almost a slipperiness, of a most remarkable kind extricated her from what appeared to many to be most certain disaster. Florence too had to meet repeated challenges: the new independence of the cloth manufacturers of England and Flanders, the irritating Pisan wars, the invading powers of France and Spain, the internal unsettlement of rival factions. Yet she too emerged, as a respectable duchy, even a grand duchy, more glamorous but less significant perhaps than the virile republic of old, but at least for the first time able to develop a flourishing port at Leghorn with the shipping of others where her own had failed. Rome became a great centre of a dwindling Catholic world. Naples grew to become the second city of Europe in the train of the Spanish monarchy, if only to be shaken by imported causes like those at work in Castile. Milan, beautifully placed for a landward-looking people, profited as a centre of distribution and communication. The prolonged vitality of the Italian peninsula had a variety of reasons: that Rome was there, that the momentum of traditions was not lightly overcome, that its greater freedoms endowed it with qualities of flexibility, that its skills inflated its resources. Of these skills perhaps the most important were those related to both private and public finance.

4
Finance

During the Middle Ages the Catholic doctrine of usury was flexible. It allowed for a reasonable compensation for risk or for the loss of the use of money on loan. But as it was defined more rigidly in a bull of Clement V in 1312 it influenced profoundly the development of financial procedures in the Catholic world. If, owing to the pressures on governments to borrow in the age of Charles V, loans at interest were widely recognised as a necessary adjunct of economic survival, usury could still worry the consciences of its practitioners; and popes—Pius V, for instance —frowned their disapproval of such loans. Governments, such as Genoa's in 1467, legislated against usury not only to avoid the censures of Rome but because of uneasy consciences. Some theologians—the Franciscans were forward in this respect—recognised the old principle of compensation for risk or for compulsion, when money was lent with the technical possibility that it might not be returned or when a government collected a forced loan. Dominicans and Augustinians tended to be more stringent: particularly did they question the many dodges that businessmen invented to get round the letter of the prohibition on interest loans. But even the businessmen themselves were disturbed. Restitution of usurious interest was carried out according to the instructions of his will for Giuliano di Giovenco de' Medici 50 years after the interest had been taken, and the will of his son, Francesco, contained similar instructions; while Alessandra Macinghi Strozzi seems to have been tortured with doubts after speculating in entitlements to interest payments on the Florentine public debt.

An important function of banking as it had developed by this time was exchange. So important was it that the Florentine bankers' guild was known as the *Arte del Cambio*, and certainly exchange transactions were the foundation upon which the greatness of the Medici bank rested. Exchange consisted of the changing of foreign into local coins, gold into silver coins, or in the dual transaction of taking money in one place and currency by selling a bill of exchange and repaying it after a stipulated period in another place with a different currency by realising the bill. It is this aspect of exchange which was most important. It was in fact tantamount to borrowing money for a given period and paying it back only in part; for the exchange rates were generally such that the banker made a profit on them. Thus a dual profit was made, since the money involved in the exchange was used in other profitable ventures. There were further refinements on this procedure, whereby the banker in effect paid interest on a loan, and it was here that the usury laws of the Church were evaded. A fictitious exchange of Florentine florins for Venetian ducats, for example, was made at rates current in Florence. After a period calculated as though a real exchange had taken place, the ducats were converted back to florins according to Venetian exchange rates. Technically there was the risk involved that the rates would prove unfavourable to the virtual lender. In practice this was rarely so. Accordingly a loan had been made and repaid with interest. This technique was also widely employed at Genoa. Another use of the bill of exchange that became in effect a loan at interest and a form of insurance at the same time was also practised at Genoa. A loan was made to a ship's owners before a voyage, and repaid in a different currency at exchange rates favourable to the lender at the end of the voyage. The loan would be used to help provide the ship with its cargo. The difference in rates would amount to interest on the loan or the premium on the insurance; for such a loan would not be repayable if the ship were lost, in which case the owners' losses would be reduced by the amount of the loan. The lenders would generally protect themselves by insuring their loan. Borrowing at interest which was concealed from all but the two parties involved and the eyes of God was another common practice. The method was to lend a given amount of money and to have written in the promissory note or promise to repay not the amount lent but the amount lent plus interest. If an extension of the loan was negotiated, the further interest was paid over at the time of the new agreement. Accordingly there would be no written record of the interest payment. This was the case with the two Medici who made provision for restitution in their wills. It was fairly common practice also at Genoa. At other times interest was simply represented as a gift.

There were two types of deposit accounts, both of which were of a fairly local nature. Small deposit accounts were often kept in order to facilitate foreseeable transfers. No interest was paid on these accounts, which gave the banker money with which to speculate and enabled depositors to settle their accounts simply and without the dangers of carrying money with them. Transfers, moreover, could be made by written instructions, either in the form of a cheque to the creditor, or as an instruction direct to the banker. Accordingly the transaction could take place with only one or even with neither party being present. This was found useful by people not wishing to be present in town. The other type of deposit was known as a discretionary deposit. This was made for a fixed period, and amounted to a loan at interest. The banker would employ such investments in commercial ventures and other business activities, and the interest payment on the loan would be represented as profits. This was common practice in Florence, Venice and Genoa by the fifteenth century. Much of the *raison d'etre* of bankers was clearly of the nature of acquiring money which could be used in further money-making activities, perhaps underwriting the ventures of others, perhaps taking part in profitable enterprises themselves. Thus beyond their capital, the bankers' financial resources consisted of deposits and money held temporarily during exchange procedures, to which should be added undistributed profits and extra investments of the partners over and above their share of the capital. This last element in the case of the Medici bank was withdrawn with interest before the share-out of profits for a particular venture was made.

The cheque has already been mentioned as a technique in use in this period. It was used in Pisa as far back as the fourteenth century, although not extensively. By the mid-fifteenth century it was common in Genoa; but it was not characteristic of European or even Italian banking until the seventeenth century. The same should be said of endorsement. Examples are known in Florence as early as the fourteenth century. In Genoa it was a common practice by about 1450. Yet it was not common in Florence until the seventeenth century, when it was used in particular to transfer the right to draw on a bill of exchange to a third person. In its origins its equivalent—transferring the right by a separate statement on another piece of paper—was sometimes, but not always, used. Often in fifteenth-century Genoa, however, endorsed entitlements changed hands several times and therefore gathered a list of signatures. Endorsement was in effect a form of paper currency. Another development of such currency was the transfer of shares in public debts. This is found in Genoa, especially in relation to the interest payments which were made in the form of new share issues. Accordingly share certificates were broken down into small fractional amounts with denominations of *libbre*, *soldi*, *denari*. This development, together with the increasing use of credit in Genoa, is a reflection of the precious metal shortage, which was so acute that, to restrict the flow of gold and silver into industrial uses, gold and silver coins were valued higher than the metals themselves. Thus it became more profitable to sell these metals to the mint than to manufacturers of gold and silver threaded cloths or jewellers. A further effect of this situation was to encourage merchants to sell abroad in areas where coins were not so highly valued in relation to their precious metal content.

Loans against pledges with commission or interest payments were also common in Italy, but unless they were made on the grand scale to princes and governments they were not in the province of the great bankers. Milan, where banking was not so sophisticated, was the exception. In Florence for instance the pawnbroker, the resort and ruin of the needy, was tolerated, made use of, but ostracised. Pawnbrokers in Florence paid the government a yearly fine collectively, which was in effect no more than a fee for a licence to carry on their business. After 1437 only Jews were allowed to take part in this form of business. The great loans to princes were regarded in a different light, and will be dealt with later.

The minimisation of risk was a great concern of the Italian businessman. This was achieved by two methods: the diversification of his interests and the development of insurance. Most Florentine bankers were merchants and industrialists as well. As merchants they sold the produce of local industry, especially silken and woollen cloths. But their shipping carried mixed cargoes, some of the goods being picked up *en route*, for instance in Spain. They also returned with mixed cargoes, especially of silks and spices, drugs and dyestuffs from the Levant. Trade was generally speculative, the vendor taking his wares to the buyer who would require to see the goods before embarking upon a transaction. Clearly there was a risk for the former which could best be overcome by variety. As industrialists these same men had often at least interests in both the silk and the woollen industries. They also farmed the land, the produce of which, for example citrus fruits or saffron, might become a significant part of their business interests. If one looks further into their banking activities the same will be found. Apart from their exchange activities, deposit banking, loans to princes, the Medici—the classic example—farmed for two periods the papal alum deposits. As papal bankers, they handed over bulls appointing to benefices on payment of the required sums; they collected annates; they delivered subsidies to princes fighting the Turks. These transfers of moneys to and from Rome were carried on by the normal exchange procedures, as were smaller transfers to priests resident at Rome whose benefices were perhaps in northern Europe. They advanced money through their branches, still using the principles underlying the bills of exchange, for buying wheat in Naples to be delivered to governments other than their own. The Venetians, too, diversified their shipping cargoes, especially when spices were being carried. A shipload of spices alone would have been of fabulous value, as spices were so light. Therefore, even had it been feasible to load a ship only with spices, the risk would have been too great. Thus space was given over to a variety of goods. The Genoese with their big ships carrying bulk cargoes of woad and alum were not forced to diversify to the same extent; but commercial partnerships were formed for single voyages and the interests of business-men were often spread over several different enterprises involving different commodities and activities. On the other hand the Milanese channelling of investments into one main activity, land speculation, although it brought with it a new and imaginative approach to land use, tended to exhaust itself and leave few activities for alternative investment. This was partly due to new political situations that arose in the sixteenth century; but the lack of diversification by individual capitalists, stemming from the safe and enormous profits entailed in landed investments, limited the adaptability of the Milanese economy very largely to experi-mentation with new kinds of farming.

Diversification, however, was not the farsighted planning of an adaptable state economy. It was the protection of the individual businessman, looking after his own interests and safeguarding himself against crippling losses. For this insurance, which like most financial devices of this period had its roots remote in the Middle Ages, was an extremely important instrument. By the last decade of the fourteenth century the Florentines led in marine insurance, underwriting for instance two-thirds of the Venetian shipping of that time. By the middle of the fifteenth century almost every kind of risk was insured against in Genoa; whilst the Venetians had taken a lead by that time in marine insurance. A century later Venetian shipping was protected to some extent by the dependence of its main Adriatic rivals, Ancona and Ragusa, on insurance taken out at Venice. The Venetians regarded the insurance of galleys as safer and requiring a lower premium than sailing ships, whereas the Genoese seem to have given good terms to their own big ships. The distance of a voyage was not generally relevant to the assessment of a premium. Rather the seaworthiness of the vessel and danger from piracy were decisive. Thus the Genoese would often require a premium on a short voyage past the Provençal coast to Spain at a greater rate than would be demanded for the long voyage eastwards into Turkish waters, even after the fall of Con-stantinople. Insurance techniques related to shipping became so much a part of Genoese life that set formulas were often used and notarial assistance dispensed with. Objects of insurance extended far beyond the limits of maritime commerce: the life of a ruler or a person whose death might have important repercussions on trade would often be insured as would that of a slave approaching her confinement; and insurance was taken out against plagues and epidemics. If a spirit of capitalistic enterprise animated the commercial centres of Italy, it was a shrewd spirit that did not invite unnecessary risk.

The Medici bank declined from a flourishing business reinvesting its profits in the time of Cosimo to one that was drawing heavily upon its capital under Lorenzo. Owing to the exceptional position that the Medici held in Florence as the ruling family its fate should not be taken as necessarily typical. One of the governing principles of Cosimo had been never to lend to princes. He had the fate of the Bardi and the Peruzzi in the fourteenth century as a warning example, for their bankruptcies had been largely due to the irretrievable loans they had made to Edward III of England and to Robert of Naples. But even he had not been able to adhere wholly to his rule: in order to obtain licences to export wool from England, he had to agree towards the end of his life to make loans to Edward IV. Much the same pressures were later placed on the Medici in Bruges, when in order to enforce the alum monopoly Tommaso Portinari, the branch manager, lent lavishly to Charles the Bold. Lorenzo, educated as a prince rather than as a merchant-banker, lacked the interest and the knowledge to control the business in the way his grandfather had done before him. Accordingly, no control was exercised over the too lavish loans to Charles that Portinari made. Nevertheless, it was a time when investment possibilities were becoming limited in Flanders and elsewhere and the Medici were committed to the alum monopoly. The loan appeared the only alternative to drawing out of Bruges altogether. In fact, another rich Florentine banking concern, that of Giovanni Rucellai, closed down altogether in 1470, because of the growing limitations on banking. But Rucellai had not the same commitments in the Low Countries as the Medici, nor had he the same reputation to maintain. The Medici position in Florence rested greatly on their success and the ability to hold the confidence of the people. With restricted investment possibilities in many areas they had previously dominated, the Medici were virtually forced into these precarious loans to princes. They could not afford to reject deposits from investors, for instance, as this would have given rise to suspicions about the shaky position of their finances, and so they accepted money they could not safely invest in the way they had done in the past. Political considerations were consequently a potent factor in the general decline of the Medici business.

Banking interests were not necessarily disastrous to all: the Capponi bank was flourishing in 1470, and the whole complex of the interests of the Strozzi, who had prospered even during a long period of exile, was yielding large returns. Nevertheless, Florence shared in the general difficulties common to Italian bankers in the second half of the fifteenth century. The blow to trade caused by the outbreak of the Venetian-Turkish war in 1463 precipitated the bankruptcy of several Florentine firms. In 1471 there were 33 Florentine banks; in 1520 there were only seven. Yet by 1530, although there were still only a small number of banks, those such as the revived Medici bank and the Guadagni, Albizzi and Salviati banks controlled vast fortunes; on the other hand Florentine bankers were owed 600,000 ducats by Francis I in 1533. Venetian banks too were affected and there was an unparalleled spate of bankruptcies in 1499. These were due largely to the demands of the republic at the outbreak of another Turkish war. Yet the Chigi and the Spannocchi in Siena were strong, and the former had the capital to make a going concern of papal alum by storing it in order to slow down sales and create a demand that would produce high prices. Likewise Genoese bankers with their spread of interests, the Centurioni chief amongst them with close commercial links with Spain, remained strong enough to become the biggest lenders to Charles V, even exceeding their rivals from south Germany. Moreover, from about 1530 they monopolised papal business for most of the remainder of the century. Banking during the period from 1464 to 1534 had certainly not a history of undiluted success. Deposit banking, reflecting hard times and political unrest, suffered most. However, by 1575 it was certainly well established again, particularly in Naples and Palermo in the Spanish south and the old commercial cities of Venice and Genoa. Loans to princes such as Maximilian I, who as ruler of Burgundy borrowed heavily from the Genoese in 1487 and again in 1492 from the Frescobaldi and Gualterotti of Florence, from the Doria of Genoa and the Balbani of Lucca, were clearly responsible for the difficulties in which some bankers found themselves. It is clear that the advantages secured by the Grimaldi and Centurioni of Genoa against loans to the Hapsburg rulers of Spain in the sixteenth century were very largely responsible for the revival of Genoese prosperity.

In the republics of Florence, Genoa and Venice an important element of state finances in the middle of the fifteenth century was the public debt. In the monarchies such as Naples, Sicily and Milan, where a ruling class did not exist to govern state finances to their own least disadvantage, this was not the case. Taxation was preferred to the loan. Rome in its dual rôle used its own special opportunities for a unique solution. In Genoa in 1407 an association of state creditors, known as the *Casa di San Giorgio*, was formed to administer the public debt. Until 1444 and later, after the end of this period, it also acted as a bank. The *Casa* developed a variety of functions such as administering several Genoese territories: the Black Sea territories from 1453, Lerici from 1479, Corsica from 1482 and Sarzana from 1484. Only its financial functions will be dealt with now. From 1454 it ran the salt monopoly. It collected taxes, and controlled the mint and monetary regulations in Genoa. From 1450 it also controlled the customs. It farmed out the collection of indirect taxes, to which Genoa under its auspices went over wholly. This of course was favourable to the powerful *alberghi* or associations of families such as the aristocratic Doria, Spinola, Lomellini or the popular Giustiniani or Franchi, who in fact exercised considerable control over the direction of the affairs of the *Casa*. Investment in the *Casa di San Giorgio* was not usually made for profit. There was some speculation in shares, but on an average they were generally held for about 20 years. The great business families of Genoa looked elsewhere for profitable investment, and their shares in the *Casa* were not comparable to their enormous wealth. The *Casa* commended itself to the small investor because above all it was safe, and this is the point that perhaps should be most emphasised in comparison with the public debts of Florence and Venice. Thus poor clerics, nuns, freed slaves, artisans and ordinary working men, the wives of nobles and especially people living at a distance from Genoa had shares in the *Casa*. Woad merchants from Lombardy and businessmen of Asti and Chieri, nobles of Montferrat and Piedmont, people from Marseilles and Spain, and Genoese colonials from Pera, Chios or even Cyprus, all figured among the investors. Also dowries, pensions, bequests to institutions for good works or endowments of chapels were made in the form of shares in the *Casa di San Giorgio*. No Catalan, Florentine or Venetian, important competitors of the Genoese, seems to have had shares in it, at least for the period around the middle of the fifteenth century. By acquiring such great powers within the state the *Casa* clearly did not shift power from one set of people to another; roughly the same set of *alberghi* predominated both in the constitutional organs of government, despite the formal supremacy of a popular *doggato*, and in the direction of the *Casa*. Its usefulness lay rather in the fact that it managed to wed to the success of its operations the personal interests of a wide range of the population and of important citizens of some of the neighbouring states whose friendliness was vital to Genoa.

Direct taxation was also in the hands of the *Casa di San Giorgio*. The most notable direct tax was the *avaria mobili*, which was assessed by special committees. In practice assessable amounts often hammered out very heatedly had little relation to the capital or revenues of the taxed person. Two-thirds of it was collected in Genoa and only a third in the two Rivieras. Because it was in some way linked to a person's moveable assets, the tax fell heavily on those with commercial interests, especially in Genoa. Thus, when it was abolished in 1490 and replaced by a five per cent increase in indirect taxes, this was to the advantage of the important Genoese business-men, whether they were members of aristocratic *alberghi* or *popolani grassi*, technically a sort of upper bourgeoisie, but often socially not always really distinguishable from the aristocrat. The customs were another important source of revenue. The duties were collected for the *Casa* by contractors and were farmed out every year. It was important therefore for the tax-farmer that shipping arrived before 2 February, the day the farm changed hands. This explains the volume of shipping returning to Genoa about this time, for a ship's captain could play the new farmer off against the old, thus managing to gain a reduction in his dues. Salt, wine and other sales taxes were also an important part of the Genoese revenues, which passed through the hands of the *Casa*. By now the only major item of expenditure of the governing council was on the maintenance of armed forces and other military matters. Even here the war of Pietrasanta against the Florence of Lorenzo was waged by the *Casa* rather than by the doge and his government, so that the finances of the state had by then passed almost completely within the province of the *Casa*.

During its long wars with the Visconti of Milan Venice had relied in-creasingly on voluntary and forced loans. Since after the Peace of Lodi Venice was undergoing the economic consequences of the fall of Con-stantinople and from 1463 found herself at war with the Turks for the next 16 years, there was no let up in the situation and the republic was faced with a growing difficulty in meeting the interest payments on these loans. In 1453 payments were eight years in arrears, in 1463 ten, and by 1480 the republic was as many as 21 years behind. The forced loan had virtually become a direct tax, since shares in the public debt were by now being offered for sale at less than 25 per cent of their original price. In 1463, a *catasto* or register of taxable properties and revenues was drawn up covering the city and the territories of Venice, mills, rents of houses, ecclesiastical as well as private possessions. The *decime* or tenths levied on this basis were technically to be returned. They were loans. But in fact it was clear that this was direct taxation and that there would be no restitution of these taxes and soon all pretence was dropped. Over the next

20 years these tenths were collected with growing frequency, often many times a year. Later in the century, in 1482, forced interest loans were exacted along these lines as an addition to the *decime*. These were known as *decime da retituirsi*. Venice had learnt the harsh lesson that government was not an object of profit; on the contrary, it was a service that had to be paid for. The hardening of Venetian attitudes was reflected also in the treatment of its Terraferma possessions. In the first instance Venice had let off its new possessions with a light tribute and a large measure of control over their own affairs. With the sixteenth century direct control of these possessions and severer taxation were enforced.

Customs duties, dues on foreign merchants and their trade, ferry licences and indirect taxation of many sorts were all parts of the republic's revenues. Venice also made heavy demands on her own bankers, such as those leading to the crash of 1499. But perhaps the most important source of revenue—loans and direct taxation apart—was the salt monopoly. The Venetian inroads into Romagna and the acquisition of Cervia were in large measure governed by her policy of acquiring the sources of salt. She developed Larnaka in Cyprus as a salt port and acquired salt from wherever possible, importing it from Sicily and the ports of Apulia. She also exploited her own large supplies at Chioggia. Much of the conflict between Genoa and Venice stemmed from their competition over the salt markets of the Po Valley; Ferrara and Mantua especially were given hard terms by the Venetians, for although the Genoese proved it to be possible to carry salt over the difficult route from the Riviera di Levante to Ferrara, Venice's better position gave her the upper hand. This was not necessarily so with Milan, to where Francesco Sforza for example imported large and regular supplies from Genoa. Yet, when Venetian-Milanese relations were not strained, it proved better for the duchy to use Venetian salt brought by the waterways. But Venice was not only interested in the export of salt; she exploited her home markets ruthlessly with the aid of legislation. Fixed quotas of preserving salt were foisted on all her subjects and, over and above this, salt for culinary uses and seasoning brought in more profits.

Government finance at Florence was inextricably confused with the finances of the Medici in the first 30 years of this period. If Lorenzo used public funds for his private purposes, he also used Medici funds for public purposes. This was only too clear at the time of the invasion of Alfonso of Calabria after the Pazzi conspiracy, when not only his own dwindling resources but those of his reluctant relatives were employed in financing the Florentine defence. In so far as one regards the Medici as the rulers of Florence, one must view the decline of the Medici businesses in London and Bruges, Lyons, Milan and elsewhere as failures in the Florentine financial system. As Ludovico Sforza had to buy the acquiescence of his people with pageants and festivities, so had Lorenzo for his government to function smoothly. If this was a precondition of good Medici government, then such funds that were used to this effect were used on government purposes. Consequently it is hard to draw a line between government and private expenditure. Certainly the Medici by any criterion used less out of public funds purely for their own ends than did any fully recognised ruler amongst their contemporaries.

Like Venice, Florence met extraordinary expenditure by raising voluntary and forced loans. Like Venice, too, her ability to meet the interest payments on these loans progressively decreased. The public debt, known as the *Monte Comune*, was thus pressed by an overwhelming burden of arrears, and its stock had fallen to 60 per cent by 1427, when a tax reorganisation was forced on the Florentine government. Despite the attempt to relieve the burden on the *Monte*, by 1458 stock had dropped further to 20 per cent. Whereas the *Monte* offered five per cent on loans at the end of the fourteenth century, interest had dropped to one per cent by 1490. Another device had been used to raise voluntary loans, which only made matters worse: twice, even three times, as much stock was offered for the price of one unit, which amounted to doubling and trebling the interest. Venice, in similar desperation, had also resorted to much the same methods. The *catasto*, introduced in 1427, was Florence's attempt to solve the financial difficulties with which the *Monte* could no longer cope. The *catasto* was assessed on all property, except the tax-payer's dwelling, and on income from investments. Unlike previous methods of assessing taxation and loans in Florence the *catasto* was based on the tax-payer's ability to pay. That is why a third of the Florentine population was classed for the purposes of the *catasto* as paupers and was completely exempted. The tax was opposed by businessmen and by those who argued that the prosperity of Florence depended on its big business. It worked out at about seven per cent of a man's income and half of one per cent of the value of his property, but this was not necessarily collected only once a year, so that its apparently moderate rates should be multiplied several times to gain a true idea of its magnitude during some years.

Just prior to the introduction of the *catasto* another form of loan, the *Monte delle Doti*, was put into practice in 1425. This was to enable Florentine fathers to provide their daughters with dowries. It was much a case of the salesman creating a need: for dowries became progressively more a condition of marriage for a wider section of the population as a result of this new financial device. Thus the *Monte delle Doti* was able to outstrip the *Monte Comune* by the 1460s. In 1465 Piero de' Medici began to employ the funds of the *Doti* for wider purposes, and in 1467 they were used to defray part of the expenses of the war with Venice, the Papacy and Ferrara. Dowry payments began to fall into arrears and several devices to delay payments with promises of further interest were employed. The Pazzi war provoked an important stage in this evolution. The sum payable by the *Doti* on the instance of Pagolantonio Soderini was reduced by half in 1478; the remainder was to go towards defence. Soon after, the cash payments of the *Doti* were lowered to a fraction of what was due, the rest being converted into seven per cent bonds. This led to an immediate rise in investments to the extent that a limit had to be placed on the amount of stock issued. For a few years these seven per cent bonds were honoured; but, inevitably, interest rates had to be modified before long and payments deferred.

By 1480 the financial difficulties of the republic precipitated constitutional reform that gave power over the purse very largely into the hands of the rich business families of Florence; and the officials of the *Monte Comune* from 1482 to 1494 were drawn from only 26 powerful families such as the Acciaiuoli, Guicciardini, Soderini and Salviati. At the time of the war of Ferrara and the war for Pietrasanta, the *Monte* officials raised huge war loans at interests of 12 per cent and more, largely out of their own resources. The payments of the *Doti*, especially, were sacrificed to those of these men who lent on the grand scale. Meanwhile, from 1481 a new, scaled tax based principally on landed property assessments replaced the *catasto* and lightened the burden of taxation on commerce and industry. Tax increases from a different quarter were also enacted: in 1477 the excise on wine was raised, while in 1490 an attempt to eliminate corruption in the collection of customs dues was made. When the efforts of 1480 and 1490 aiming at the stimulation of trade, in particular the importation of raw materials for industry, are considered within the framework of the government's financial expedients of these years, it becomes clear how the interests of the big businessmen were placed first in the last years of the early Medicean predominance in Florence. At the same time it should be remembered that the greatness of Florence had rested on the achievements of this group and that many held that it was therefore in the interests of the republic that the leading families should prosper. Nevertheless, there was much resentment at the widening gulf that was appearing between the position of these families and the majority of the population whose small investments were growing ever less profitable. With the Savonarolan republic, there was certainly a struggle between more popular elements and the big families or *primati*, who continued to control the *Monte Comune* owing to their unique knowledge and experience of financial procedures and techniques. The ultimate solution was to use a scaled land tax, a modified form of what had been introduced in 1480, as the basis of Florentine revenues. This protected the mobile capital of the business magnate, whilst falling heavily upon him in so far as he had invested in lands. This arrangement was effective in times of peace or of comparatively ordinary expenditure, and it lasted to become part of the government machinery of ducal Florence.

Naples, Sicily and Milan did not develop the same sophisticated, if desperate, types of financial solutions as the republics. They rested far more on traditional monarchical forms of revenue. Revenues from crown property, feudal services and subsidies, taxes levied on communes, customs, licences, gabelles, fines, tolls on transhumance and the use of canals were all important elements in royal or ducal finances. Milan had built up a thoroughgoing bureaucracy, which was allied to the Sforzas against the pressures of baronial independence. But, although the administration tended to fall into routines and operate by force of habit, decisions still had to be made and ultimately the responsibility for such decisions lay with the duke. There was no question, as with the republics, of a political *élite* running the finances of the state to their own advantage. The state was only a source of profit in so far as it was the bestower of office and favours or sponsored public works of financial benefit to private citizens. Moreover, as the new landowners became less speculative as the fifteenth century advanced and began to settle their lands, they were granted enfeoffments by the dukes similar to those of the old feudal nobility. As Milan settled into an economy of landowners and developed a feudal mentality under Charles V, bureaucratic attitudes became partly submerged: an older idea of a class with the right and duty to take part in government and, when necessary, to bear its burdens was revived. Spanish advisers who, like Granvelle, advocated the annexation of Milan believed that the duchy was not only able to pay its own way but that it might also help Spain pay hers. The position was soon found to be different. Precious metals of America were pledged in advance against loans from Genoese bankers in order to pay for the government and defence of the duchy. Not only was Milan itself taxed heavily, but revenues from Sicily and Naples were brought to maintain this new possession of Spain in a state of bare survival during its involvement in the rivalry between the two great European houses of Hapsburg and Valois. Only after the Peace of Cateau-Cambrésis did the duchy of Milan find some relief in a partial industrial revival. But the character of Milan and its financial apparatus continued to be predominantly monarchical.

The papal revenues fell drastically during the great schism, although this drop was in part redressed by the renewed papal ability to profit from the states. However, with the growth of nepotism in the Papacy, particularly under Sixtus IV and Alexander VI, much of the funds from this new source was squandered; and, as the life in the Curia became more sumptuous and gay, demands on the purse often outstripped increases in revenue. Rome itself was exempted from direct taxation, but indirect taxes were collected there, and in the greater part of the Papal States. The salt monopoly in Rome and its surrounding district was extended to Ancona and Romagna in the time of Sixtus IV. Customs on transhumance, licences on the export of grain and the wine tax from Bologna were prominent items of the papal income. The *census* for papal vicariates provided a further important source of revenue after the return of the Papacy from Avignon, but it was not always easy to collect. Roberto Malatesta found it increasingly impossible to foot the bill of 1,000 ducats as the fortunes of Rimini declined. Only Paul II had any great success in getting tribute out of Giovanni Bentivoglio in Bologna. This inability to collect papal revenues with certainty was one of the driving forces behind the reconquest of the Papal States by Julius II. Similar attempts of Sixtus IV and Alexander VI were motivated rather by the desire for personal and family gain. The alum revenues were another source of papal funds, although these fell away by half between the time of Sixtus IV and Clement VII. The Curia, of course, had a wider source of revenues: incomes from vacant benefices, annates, the cost of bulls for varied purposes including the appointment to bishoprics, and profits from a variety of other ecclesiastical functions. Amongst these the sale of indulgences and dispensations were increasingly exploited during this period; and rights over the control of the Church were often partially surrendered to at least the immediate profit of the Papacy in terms of money, although often this led to a long term loss in revenues. Such was the case with the Concordat of Bologna of 1516, the agreement between Leo X and Francis I that determined the future development of the Gallican Church in France. The sale of offices was first used in the beginning of the fifteenth century as an emergency source of funds. The great growth in this form of income occurred towards the end of the century and by 1521 there were over

2,000 venal offices. These offices, whose average return was about 11 per cent of the purchase price a year, were largely a device to overcome the church's usury laws. They were in effect annuities, although the position was not clarified until Clement VII made the distinction between venal offices and proper administrative offices, so that the way was left clear to reform the latter.

The papal revenues were struck at by the Reformation, which closed up large sources of exploitation to the Church. This was especially felt at a time when curial expenditure was at its height with the costly projects of Leo X. The loss was in part offset by population growth not only throughout Christendom, but also in Rome itself. As a result revenues from customs, indirect taxes and the salt monopoly, all rose. But papal expenses had increased throughout the period. New taxes were collected through the offices of the expanding papal bureaucracy such as the Datary. The maintenance of such offices incurred considerable expense. The popes contributed also in no small degree to subsidies to those states engaged in war with the Turks. The Papacy itself was continually at war from the time of Paul II, and as its interests were becoming increasingly involved in the international politics of Europe the costs of papal diplomacy increased rapidly. The growing commitments of the Papacy together with a great loss in the sources of revenues were hardly balanced by the greater efficiency that was developed in revenue collection at about the same time.

The development of private and public financial techniques was obviously in response to needs of commerce, industry and government; but it is equally clear that they were used as money-making activities in themselves. There was a great growth of speculation in shares in the public debts, in insurance and in the exchange market. Land in Lombardy became an object of speculation for a while and its development was purely coincidental to the financial manipulations connected with it. In Florence war was felt at times by the rich to be almost desirable as a way to multiplying their riches. The Medici provide a beautiful illustration of a firm which exploited the profitable monetary manipulations of capitalism, while it almost lost sight of the industry and trade that was its foundation. But it was the primary object that these techniques served that formed the basis of Italy's strength—the trade and industry that as citizens the Medici might have ignored, but that as rulers they could not forget. The remarkable fertility of Italian inventiveness would not have overcome the doctrine of usury simply for the sake of money-lending. Finance was not primarily an end; it was a means. Moreover, these techniques were not simply limited to the cities where they were evolved. The

Pisans and Genoese took them to Palermo; the Strozzi and the Medici to Naples. Rome was a centre that attracted the bankers of Florence, of Genoa, of Siena. Venetians took their methods to Apulia. Bruges, Antwerp, London, Lisbon, Barcelona and Lyons all learnt from the Italians, who were sometimes too far ahead of their customers: they had to use salt for currency in the Balkans, sugar in North Africa, and cloth made out of English wool in parts of the Ottoman empire. If speculation played a large part in their dealings, it was the speculation of the level-headed. Although risk was an element that might soothe usurious consciences, it was reduced to a minimum. Even insurers insured themselves. Merchants had long lines of communication to bring information about the state of markets. They frequently shipped a variety of wares, so that if one commodity did not sell, another might repair the losses; and they diversified their interests as much as they diversified the cargoes of their ships. The businessman also was often able to control his government, or at least win the ear of his ruler. What he could not control was the growing might of his competitors beyond the limits of Italy.

The tendency of the period was perhaps for business to become more aristocratic. The *primati* in Florence certainly maintained the strong position they secured in the last days of Lorenzo, even if they had to survive the republicanism of 1494 and 1527. The Venetians, always dominated by their patricians, now saw their patricians tighten their grasp on the mainland. The Genoese aristocracy, strong in the government and in the *Casa di San Giorgio*, had their position confirmed by Andrea Doria in 1528. But with the growth of aristocracy—Genoa apart, for it had no Terraferma—landed interests assumed a more important rôle. This was true of Milan as well; and one has to look south to Naples to discern something of an opposite tendency. There the big landowner had his power reduced; and imported notions of bureaucracy, especially under Philip II, gained a hold.

With all her ingenuity, in one respect Italy was slow. In the republics and in Rome the idea that government was for private exploitation was hard to shake. The loan was acceptable, for it held promise of returns. But it was taxation that was necessary if Italians were really to foot their bills. Venetian and Florentine finances were in a disastrous state before the lesson went home. Rome had not learnt this lesson and launched out on a reckless sale of offices. Genoa alone had the caution to make her public debt less a source of private profit than a convenient apparatus for carrying on daily affairs. It was the gift of Charles V to Milan to foster the notion that government was service and not the source of individual gain. If this entailed a loss of freedom, it filled the gap left by the passing of a period of exuberant speculation. It was not only the Counter-Reformation that made Italy a staider place, nor simply the presence of Spain. Italy had sifted her rich from the aspirants to riches, and much of the hope and vigour had been drained from her world of business. The very real revival that occurred throughout the sixteenth century was based on the experience and techniques of the past; but it was the work of more settled societies, less fluid and therefore less competitive in structure.

5
External Relations

The Treaty of Lodi of 1454 between Venice, Milan and Florence, to which Rome and Naples adhered in the following year, was an agreement to recognise and maintain the position of the major Italian states as they were then arranged, and to protect each other against aggression from elsewhere. The League, thus formed, was renewed for another 25 years in 1470. In fact up to 1494, when Charles VIII of France invaded Italy, the peninsula was comparatively free from war. Certainly it did not suffer from continual strife such as it had experienced during the long struggle in the first half of the century between Milan and Venice, with Florence first supporting the latter and afterwards the former, and with Naples eventually throwing in its weight against Florence. There were wars enough: the war of Rimini over the succession of Roberto Malatesta; the Pazzi war in which Sixtus IV was trying to carve out a principality for his nephew, Girolamo Riario, at the expense of Florence, and in which the son of Ferrante of Naples, Alfonso of Calabria, tried to secure Siena and Florentine territories for himself; the brief but terrifying Turkish occupation of Otranto; the Ferrarese war in which Sixtus IV and Venice attempted to divide up Ferrara between them; the conspiracy of the Neapolitan barons when Pope Innocent VIII tried to profit at the expense of King Ferrante of Naples; and the limited war between Genoa and Florence over Pietrasanta and Sarzana. From 1463 and 1479 Venice was also at war with the Turks. However, the Turkish war apart, these wars did not occupy ten of the 30 years between 1464 and 1494, and the scale of the fighting, the losses incurred and the damage done never compared with the conflict earlier in the century between Venice and Milan or with the wars that came later with the French and Spanish invasions of Italy. Nevertheless, the struggles between the Italian states are evidence enough that limits must be set to any claims, that are made for the success of the Italian League of 1455. Relations between the Italian powers with few exceptions were constantly strained, and it was with glee that one state watched a rival involved in difficulties.

The reaction to the fall of Constantinople and Fokia to the Turks is a cogent example of the utter inability of the Italian states to apprehend their common interests. Pope Nicholas V offered impossible terms to the Orthodox Christians in the Balkans in return for papal help: that they should adhere to the union of Florence and thereby recognise the pope himself as their head. The Greeks preferred even the sultan to the surrender of their independence to Rome. Papal action was thus stultified until Nicholas had gone. The next pope, the first Borgia pope, Calixtus III, although pledged to the reconquest of Constantinople, as a Spanish pope got little help from the Italian states. He looked for help therefore with the fanciful imagination of the desperate to Ethiopia, the Syrian Christians, the prince of the Turcomans, Persia and Georgia. If he encouraged the Hungarians with some success to resist the Turks in the Balkans, and if a papal fleet under the command of Cardinal Scarampo made considerable gains in the Aegean islands, the Italians did not rally. Likewise with Pius II. The crusading council at Mantua in 1459 was boycotted by Cosimo de' Medici. When Pius II finally went ahead with his plans for a crusade only the duke of Burgundy and the republic of Venice, already at war with the Turks, supported him. To the relief of all but Venice, Pius died at Ancona in 1464 before the crusading fleet set sail. No one was ready to fight Venice's wars for her, for such was the Italian view of the whole crusade. The year before, Cosimo de' Medici had been asked to stop Florentine trade with the Turks while Venice was at war with them. Cosimo had refused: after all it had been Florence that had been in part responsible for the outbreak of the war, by feeding the sultan with intercepted Venetian mail compromising to Venetian-Turkish good relations. But rivalries between the Italian trading states were fiercer still; for Cosimo had quickly seen the chance to profit after the fall of Constantinople and sent ambassadors to Mehemmed II, while at the fall of Fokia Venice jumped in to capture the old Genoese alum monopoly. Genoa replied in kind: after 1463 she supplied the sultan from Caffa with Ukrainean wheat, German arms, slaves for his forces and Caucasian timber for his fleet. It is true that Genoa was excluded from the Italian League; but the fierce rivalry between Venice and Florence, which came to open conflict in the war of Rimini, is evidence enough that the terms of Lodi were not the result of a change of heart This severe economic competition between the commercial republics was at least one of the major factors underlying Italian disunity.

Economic rivalries continued so long as these states counted commerce as a dominant element in their economies. At the beginning of this period they had some justification for regarding themselves as pivotal to the economy of Europe and beyond, the heart of the world. Despite the growth of the great Hapsburg empire of Charles V and the emergent nation of France the small Italian states retained considerable importance in the provisioning of foreign parts. They accordingly felt themselves to be independent of each other, rivals competing for markets and business within and outside Italy. They were in no way able to see that, as Italians, their greatness was dependent on cooperation if it was to survive. Keen rivalry to control the distribution of Tolfa alum thus continued to keep Florence and Genoa in bitter opposition throughout the sixteenth century. Even when in the first decade of that century Genoa was under French control and Soderini's republic clung fatefully to the friendship of France, the Genoese conspired with the rebellious Pisans to accept their territory as a gift, so that Florence would be cut off from the Ligurian and Tyrrhenian seas. If France would not allow this addition to their subject territory, neither would she help Florence reconquer Pisa. In this way the French were able to keep these two Italian powers weak. Moreover, Venice, who also clung to the hope of gaining from a French alliance, poured ducats into Pisa by the hundred thousand. All three Italian trading republics, therefore, played into the hands of Valois aggression.

The conflicts between Italian states were not confined to these three commercial states dominated by considerations of their economies. These regarded the world as a network of alternative routes competing for predominance. They thought internationally and not nationally. Their concern was a long line of communication and not a block of territory to be expanded and exploited. If they had expansionist designs, the driving force was the protection or development of a route rather than the enhancement of territorial power. Venice and Florence underwent a change in attitude during the sixteenth century, and their motives were not entirely unmixed even earlier; but the emphasis of their foreign policies during this period was overwhelmingly commercial. This could not be said of Rome or Naples, nor unconditionally of Milan, which certainly had such motives underlying its repeated and often partly successful attempts to dominate Genoa as an outlet to the sea in an effort to overcome commercial dependence on Venice. Yet, for various reasons, these other states were equally embroiled in the shifting rivalries of the peninsula. Before the policies of the Italian states are further analysed, the curious fact that they identified themselves as Italian should be examined.

The Italian League of 1455 recognised the fact that there were common Italian interests that might be defended by joint action. 'Italy' was a current notion, but it was applied to an Italy regarded as a permanently divided whole. This was in part due to the fact that Italy was a geographical entity defined by the Alps and the sea. It would be difficult to say how far the people of Corsica and Sardinia thought themselves to be Italian; but isolated as they were, they had not this unifying condition to lead them to identify themselves with Italy. Another element of unity stemmed from the broad division between the south and the north, which by their complementary functions formed a unit of interdependency: the granary of Sicily and the south; the industrial, commercial and financial activities in advance of the world which that granary to no little extent allowed the north to develop. This identity was due, too, to linguistic, cultural and historical traditions. The 'descendants' of Rome distinguished themselves from the barbarians of the rest of Christendom; and, despite the obstacles of dialect, common ideas spread through the Italian-speaking states more freely than they surmounted the Alps or crossed the sea. Even Latin was more easily acquired by the Italian than by most; but it must be remembered that ideas permeated more freely by word of mouth than through writings, at least until printing was well advanced. Being Italian was a consciously recognised state. Petrarch in France had yearned for Italy, not for any precise location, and writers after him influenced by the literature of Rome felt that this was their Italian heritage. Beyond the peninsula, Italy was also regarded as a single unit. The Carthusian, Jakob von Jüterbogk, asserted that there was no nation in Christendom that offered such opposition to the reform of the Church and monasteries as did Italy, owing to her fear of losing privileges and her love of worldly gain. The idea that non-Italians were foreigners was also well developed. In the papal conclave that elected Calixtus III, Cardinal Bessarion was rejected as a Greek, and Alonso Borja himself was only elected as an old man who would stop the gap for a time. Even so, as a Spaniard he was fiercely resented; and Rome, right through to the election of his nephew, Rodrigo Borgia, resented the presence of the Spaniards, whom Calixtus had encouraged to come to Rome. After Alexander VI, only Adrian VI has been a non-Italian pope. There was no similar objection to a Venetian like Paul II, a Genoese like Sixtus IV, a Florentine like Leo X or a Sienese like Pius II becoming pope, although these might tend to be regarded as assets to the particular group of states to which their own belonged or with which their private interests corresponded. In fact, both Pius II and Julius II framed their policies in terms of Italy. Pius II was the Italian candidate who was elected in opposition to the French cardinal, Estouteville, and an important factor in his policy was to keep foreign powers out of Italy. It was still a divided Italy, for he was conscious that for Rome to remain an important Italian power there had to be a strong coast-to-coast block of papal territories. This would give Rome contacts in all directions and at the same time make it more difficult for another power to expand to gain preponderance in the peninsula. Julius II in his reconquest of the Papal States had similar aims. Furthermore, he was described by the Venetian diarist, Priuli, as being strongly Italian in sympathies, desiring the welfare of Italy, although his allies were foreigners determined to make themselves masters of Italy. Another Venetian, Antonio Giustiniani, an ambassador at Rome, represented Julius as believing that the French and Spaniards should stay at home and leave Italy to the Italians. The idea of *la libertà d'Italia* dominated papal foreign policy in so far as the Italian peninsula was concerned from Alexander VI to Paul IV, although in all but name it was a considerably earlier factor in the policy of Pius II. It had gained cogency from the invasion of Charles VIII in 1494–95 and the subsequent French and Spanish influence in the peninsula. With the Reformation in northern Europe and the increasing identity of the Church in France and Spain with the crowns of Francis I and Charles V, the popes looked more and more to the solidarity of the Church in Italy, so that Guicciardini could close his sad *Storia d'Italia* in 1534 by identifying his slight hopes for the peninsula with the Rome of Paul III.

But Rome did not monopolise the concept of Italy. Giovanni Bentivoglio suggested to a Milanese envoy in 1494 that 'we Italians should not allow barbarian peoples to come between us, especially as their claws and teeth are long'. Francesco Gonzaga had a coin struck after the withdrawal of Charles VIII with the legend *ob restitutam Italiae libertatem*. In 1509 it was reported to be the hope of Prospero Colonna that Italians and not barbarians should rule in Italy; and in 1513 Francesco Guicciardini advocated that the English should divert France from Italy, but that France should not be made so weak as to leave Italy a prey to the Spanish, so that neither should have *la monarchia d'Italia*. After the battle of Pavia in 1525, Machiavelli regarded the presence of the Spanish as ruinous to the *libertà d'Italia*, but at the same time he deplored the fact that Louis XII and Maximilian I had not put an end to Venice once and for all. The Venetians were later to justify their possession of Friuli and their hold on the patriarchate of Aquileia as vital to the security not only of themselves but of the whole of Italy. If Machiavelli apparently made a serious call

to the Medici to lead Italians to their emancipation from foreign occupation in his enigmatic little work, *Il Principe*, there is no suggestion that
this should be an Italy united under a single political system. Nor was a
programme for a politically united Italy ever seriously entertained in this
period. Even when it was suspected that Ferrante intended to rule Italy
from Naples or later that Venice had ideas of dominating the peninsula,
it was never a part of the policies of either to dominate by forging a political
entity. Had their lesser ambitions succeeded, this may well have been a later
step; but such long range policies were never formulated. On the contrary,
it was the policy of the Italian states as a whole to preserve Italian independence in disunity. But at the very time when the Italian states sang
loudest, *la libertà d'Italia*, they were most busy in inviting foreign powers
to intervene.

The power outside Italy which first became greatly involved in the
affairs of the peninsula during this period was France. The Angevin rulers
of Naples had been expelled by Alfonso V of Aragon in 1442 after more
than 150 years of rule; but, because Alfonso left the kingdom to Ferrante
and so separated it distinctly from the Aragonese lands in Spain, the
Balearics, Sardinia and Sicily, Naples was no longer so closely linked with
the Iberian peninsula. The French, on the other hand, were constantly
considering their claims to the south of Italy, while in the north they were
in occupation of Genoa from 1402–11 and 1458–61. The fact that the
Sforzas were usurpers left the duchy of Milan open to rival claimants, and
the legitimisation of their régime by the imperial investiture of Ludovico in
1495 did not bring a great change in this respect. France had her particular
claim based on the issue of an old marriage alliance between the Visconti
and the French royal house, which made the future Louis XII a descendant of Giangaleazzo Visconti. Any Italian state which allied itself with
France was playing dangerously; for if the French were invited into Italy,
they might well take it into their heads to revive one of their claims and
stay. Florence in view of her trading interests in France established close
relations with the French in 1452; thereby she gave them some confidence
of support in the peninsula. Louis XI, indeed, more than once considered
making good his claims in Italy; but it was not until Charles VIII that
things came to a head. With dreams of empire, heroic crusade and victory in war, imagining himself a second Charlemagne, he reversed the
development of France towards nationhood, in order to be free to follow
his whimsy in Italy. Encouraged by Ludovico Sforza he bargained away
lands which might properly be thought of as French: Rousillon and Cerdagne to Spain, Franche-Comté and Artois to Burgundy. Venice stood

aside in watchful neutrality, but Pietro de' Medici at first had thoughts of opposing Charles in alliance with Naples. Under pressure from the people of Florence and with mounting fear as the French advanced, he changed his mind. But too late; for already Savonarola, the popular preacher, had taken the initiative, since Florentine interests in France corresponded with the divine punishment he had prophesied. The friar succeeded in coming to terms with the French, who passed on towards Rome. Alexander VI likewise vacillated. At first he thought that the French should be opposed; but their evident might made him think again. The French entered Rome without resistance and proceeded to Naples. Naples without allies could no more resist the French than did the Italian states to the north; but the behaviour of the invaders caused hostility everywhere, and it was not difficult for outside help to be enlisted to expel them. This was directed by Ferdinand of Aragon from whose territory in Sicily the young Neapolitan king, Ferrantino, helped by local insurrection initiated the resistance. The Spanish under Gonzalo de Córdoba followed up; and Rome, Milan, Venice and smaller Italian powers joined what was known as the League of Venice, to which Ferdinand had persuaded Maximilian I to lend his support by the offer of a double marriage alliance that ultimately led to the uniting of Spanish, Imperial and Burgundian interests in the person of Charles V. The League under the generalship of Francesco Gonzaga drove the retreating French from Fornovo, although the Italians lost heavily. Louis of Orleans, who during the invasion had remained at Asti, a possession of his own in north-eastern Italy, decided to establish his claims to the duchy of Milan, and occupied Novara. Charles VIII did not support him. Instead he came to terms with Ludovico Sforza, who promised to back a second invasion. But before he had had time to strike again the French king died. Meanwhile, Ferrantino had completed a mopping-up action against those French forces left in Naples. Thus Italian rulers in league— for Ferdinand of Aragon was king of Sicily and Maximilian, a member of the League, if an inactive one, was nominally Imperial overlord of much of northern Italy—had thrown back the French invader by themselves.

A disastrous process of opening up Italy to the imperialistic ambitions of the west as a means of solving her own internal problems had been set under way. The blame is not simply to be laid on Ludovico Sforza, who invited the French to invade. Neapolitan exiles in France had equally urged the Angevin cause at the French court in order that they might return to Naples in a privileged position. Cardinal Giuliano della Rovere, who had been defeated by Alexander VI in the last papal conclave, had also made his way to the French court and it was feared at the Curia that

Charles' purpose might be deflected into conciliarist channels with the object of deposing the pope. Certainly della Rovere did much to confirm Charles in his plan to invade Italy. Even Venice was in large part responsible, for when a League of Italian states was formed in 1493 to resist what were represented as designs of Ferrante of Naples on part of the papal territories, Venice insisted that France should be asked to join the League, although the republic was fully aware of the implications of the Angevin claims to Naples. The League of 1495—for which Venice has too often been held mainly responsible, as it was largely the work of Ferdinand of Aragon—certainly originated the revival of an Imperial policy in Italy under Maximilian I, who had in the first instance been reluctant to involve himself. Thus within a short space of time, French, Spanish and Imperial ambitions became fiercely directed towards the peninsula; and it appeared that the only practical defence left open to a chronically divided Italy was to maintain a careful balance between these giant interlopers.

It was not the Sforzas who invited Louis XII to return to Italy: Milan was his primary object. But Cesare Borgia, the Pope's son, worked hand-in-hand with the king; and, while Louis with the cooperation of Milanese generals alienated by Ludovico Sforza took Milan, Cesare Borgia occupied the Papal States of Romagna. Venice also working with the king occupied Cremona and the Ghiaradadda. Milan taken, Louis XII conspired with Ferdinand to partition the kingdom of Naples. Still convinced that the French would help her recover Pisa, Florence encouraged the enterprise; and Federigo, the king of Naples, in the belief that Ferdinand had come to assist him against the French, offered no resistance to the Spanish in the south. When he realised he had been betrayed, he put himself in the hands of the French. The allied invaders then turned against each other, and on 1 January, 1504 the French lost their last hold in Naples at Gaeta. However, they still held Milan and Genoa, which they had occupied in 1499. Once again therefore Italians—Venice, the Papacy, Florence and Naples—had been involved in the instigation of foreign intervention in the peninsula. This time the foreigners had come to stay.

Even then the dangerous game of enlisting the aid of the greater powers was continued by the Italian states. With the deaths of Alexander VI and Cesare Borgia in 1503, the hold of the papacy over the Papal States was weakened. Venice occupied the northern towns of Romagna; and Giuliano della Rovere, who became pope after the short reign of Pius III, determined to subject the States once and for all. In 1506 the Baglioni succumbed to his advancing forces at Perugia and Giovanni Bentivoglio was driven out of Bologna. The Venetians held fast. Julius had already looked to foreign help to win back his remaining territories; and Louis XII, Maximilian I and Ferdinand the Catholic had explored the possibilities of sharing out the greater part of Italy between them with the complicity of the Pope who was to have his lands restored. Julius believed that the mere threat of such common action would bring about the submission of Venice; but Venice clung to the hope that Louis XII, who as late as 1506 reaffirmed the Venetian alliance of 1499, would stand by her. She therefore called, as she thought, the Pope's bluff with disastrous consequences; for Julius, although preferring a peaceful solution, did not shrink from seeing the might of Europe meddle in the affairs of Italy to help him achieve his aims. Consequently in 1509 and 1510 the Terraferma was occupied by French and Imperial troops. When Julius II had completed his conquest of Romagna, he changed sides in an attempt to minimise the damage his policy had already inflicted on Italy, whose liberty he claimed was his one concern. Ferdinand having seized the Venetian-held ports of Apulia joined him in opposition to the French; but the latter, supported by Ferrara which the Pope aimed at bringing under his control, defeated the combined forces of the Papacy and Spain at Ravenna in 1512. However, the Swiss, also members of the Holy League, descended upon Milan and the French were forced to withdraw. Massimiliano Sforza was thereupon set up as the puppet of the Swiss in Milan in 1513. Meanwhile, the Florentine republic of Piero Soderini which had pinned its hopes on the French found itself deserted, and Spanish troops were easily able to restore the Medici to Florence. Venice, still suffering from the occupation of much of the Terraferma by Imperial troops, turned once again to a French alliance, despite the utter betrayal she had experienced at the hands of Louis. No longer was it thinkable that Italian states could join together to resist foreign control by themselves. Those which had retained their independence could only protect themselves by skilful manipulation of foreign alliances. Fortunately for them, there was no longer any question of a partition of Italy: the great powers angled for complete control.

In 1515 Francis I succeeded Louis XII as king of France. He immediately mounted an attack on Milan and drove out the Swiss, while the Venetians held off the Spanish. Giovanni de' Medici, now Pope Leo X, in control of both the Papal States and Florence, eventually threw in his lot with Ferdinand, but lost Parma and Piacenza which had been occupied by papal troops in 1512. The French, again ascendant, forced Maximilian to restore most of the Terraferma to Venice. Thus Italy was reduced largely to the dominance of two great powers: Spain in the south and

France in the north-west. However, so long as there was a Medici pope, central Italy was entirely in the hands of that family and the north-east was again controlled by Venice. A few small states such as Mantua could only survive in the shadow of the great. When Charles V was elected emperor the whole character of foreign rivalry in Italy changed again. The Hapsburg emperor sought a connection through Genoa and Milan between Spain and his territories in Austria, the Franche-Comté and the Netherlands, while continuing to dominate the western Mediterranean by his hold on southern Italy and the islands. France on the other hand feared a strangling encirclement and sought to break through Charles' grip on the territories around her. The Papacy supported Charles in expelling the French from Milan in 1521, and in the following year Genoa also fell to the emperor; so that in 1524 Clement VII, alarmed at the Imperial successes, joined Venice and Florence in secret alliance with France. Through inferior tactics rather than from inferior force the French were defeated at Pavia in 1525. Again France, Rome and Venice joined forces in the League of Cognac of 1526 and Florence and Francesco II Sforza, the nominal ruler of Milan, lent their support. While a leaderless Imperial army marched on Rome and sacked the Holy City, Francis I once more invaded Milan, and marched south on Naples, backed by the fleet of Andrea Doria. However, Doria changed sides, re-uniting Genoa against the French, but the French army was weakened by disease, and the two sides came to terms. Milan was given back to Francesco Sforza; the Medici, who had been expelled from Florence in 1527, were restored and Genoa surrendered the control of its foreign affairs for a favourable relationship with Spain. The struggle did not end there, but continued with varying intensity until the Treaty of Cateau-Cambrésis in 1559, and perhaps for a hundred years more to the Treaty of the Pyrenees. Milan fell virtually under control of Spain in 1535 with Prince Philip eventually becoming its duke, and the French occupied Piedmont from 1536 to the Treaty of Cateau-Cambrésis. Only the Papacy and Venice survived as both considerable and independent Italian powers, although it will be seen later that other Italian states did not allow themselves to be completely moulded by their conquerors.

Before 1493 the relations of Italian states with non-Italian powers were not aimed at bringing the forces of these powers into Italy. They were mainly economic alliances reflecting the clash of trading and financial interests within the peninsula itself. By the sixteenth century the alignment of Italian states with foreign governments was largely governed by considerations of countering the dominance of one great power in Italy or conversely by making sure of being on the winning side. Yet economic factors were still of considerable importance. For instance, the Venetian persistence in clinging to a pro-French policy, even after the duplicity of Louis XII, was due to a recognition of her spice interests at Lyons. A French-held Lombardy would be safer for the transportation of goods than a Lombardy in the hands of Spain; this would also link Savoy indissolubly to a pro-French policy and leave her in a better position to act independently of France. Thus Venice depended greatly on a friendly France, unrestricted by Spanish encirclement, in order to meet the challenge of the Portuguese spice trade. With the uniting of Spanish and Austrian interests in the person of Charles V, Venetian opposition to the Spanish in Italy only increased; for, from the revival of the Italian policies of the Hapsburg emperors by Maximilian in 1496, Venice's supremacy in the Adriatic was threatened. The Hapsburgs had for long possessed a small Adriatic coastline, but now it was their policy to develop it and so put themselves in a position to dispense with the intermediary function of Venice in their trade. Thus her northern frontiers became a ceaseless object of contention not only with the Turks, who more than once advanced south to the Piave, but also with the emperor, who after 1519 as king of Spain already had control of the long Apulian shores on the Adriatic. Venice was saved by the internal divisions of the Empire, stemming from the particularist policies of the German states and emphasised by the splits caused by the Reformation. The French policy to encourage the internal divisions of Germany played into the hands of Venice and became a powerful factor in the alignment of the republic with France.

The maintenance of Florentine adherence to France at a time when Florentines were only too conscious of the possibility of the French embroiling Florence in a peninsula-wide hostility to themselves was, of course, to some degree due to the hope that the French would help them win back Pisa. But even after 1509, when Pisa was recovered, except for the two occasions when the Spanish helped restore the Medici, the policy of Florence was generally directed towards friendship with France. But Florence tried to keep a foot in both camps, as when marriage alliances were made with both Hapsburg and Valois: Catherine de' Medici married Prince Henry of France, and Alessandro de' Medici married the natural daughter of the emperor, Margaret of Austria. However the silk market of Lyons, which was dominated by the Florentines together with the Lucchesi for most of the sixteenth century, was an important consideration underlying the adherence of Florence to the alliances of France, the Papacy and Venice against the Spanish. Conversely it was the failure of the silk and jewellery interests of Genoa at Lyons in the 1520s which ultimately decided the break between the Ligurian republic and France, so that Genoa finally threw in her lot with Spain—indeed to her great profit—under the leadership of Andrea Doria. Thus, when questions of power became dominant with the struggle between a great new empire and a great new nation, economic considerations to no small degree still governed the attitudes of the Italian republics.

Military might is always a major factor in the external relations of states. So long as the Italians were only concerned with each other the *condottieri* system proved perfectly satisfactory, although it was by no means consistently used throughout Italy and it varied from state to state. In Naples a great emphasis was placed on baronial service in war, although as is clear from the revolts of 1459 and 1485–87 the barons were never completely to be trusted; and those who were supporters of the régime were those most likely to be killed in battle, since it was they whom the kings were most ready to employ. For example, in 1480–81 a significant group of faithful barons fell at Otranto. *Condottieri* were, however, employed by Naples. Amongst them was Gentile Virginio Orsini, the captain-general of Ferrante, an independent and undisciplined papal baron and a close kinsman of the Medici. When the Spanish acquired Naples at the beginning of the sixteenth century, the barons were discouraged from military pursuits and the tendency was for Naples to rely heavily on Spanish arms and men for its defence. Florence under the Medici avoided as far as possible the dangers and expense of maintaining permanent *condotte*, although, when the republic was at war, *condottieri* were always hired. The Medici policy was to make an annual payment to the Sforzas of Milan to hold troops in readiness to be used on behalf of Florence should they be called upon. Under the republic of Piero Soderini, Machiavelli was entrusted with the task of forming a militia on the grounds that the most effective troops were those consisting of men defending their own country. The militia was a complete failure, partly because it was drawn from the *contado* for fear of having armed citizens within Florence itself. Genoa, many of whose noble *alberghi* produced mercenary captains—the Fieschi could call upon 4,000 men from their own lands in the Lunigiana—used mercenaries from outside. On the other hand, she employed the fleets of native mercenary sea-captains such as those of the Grimaldi and the Doria. Venice employed mercenary captains and her troops consisted largely of the *stratiotti*—Albanians, Dalmatians, Greeks and

Cretans, mountain peoples who, like the Swiss, sought riches in the field. But Venice, too, like Genoa, used her own shipping, both public and private, for naval purposes; and her own patrician families provided the admirals and captains of her fleets.

There were broadly speaking two types of *condottieri*, those who had acquired states for themselves and those who had not. Of these the latter were distinctly more disturbing to the equilibrium of Italy. Their profession was purely that of war; so that if a period of peace seemed to be in the offing, as for instance after the Peace of Lodi, the livelihood of the professional soldier was threatened. Thus the *condottieri* and their men became an armed, restless and frustrated section of the population looking for opportunities to make good their losses. They might live off the land to the extreme discomfort of the local populations; they might stir up trouble with the hope of renewed employment; or they might, envious of the greater security of their fellow *condottieri* who had small territories of their own, try to secure such territories for themselves. The supreme example of this last course was the conduct of Jacopo Piccinino after the Peace of Lodi. He ravaged central Italy trying to provide himself with a sizeable principality. He had his eyes on Bologna and Siena; and, although failing to acquire either, was not seriously opposed by those *condottieri* hired to hound him out. They too were feeling the pinch of a warless Italy. Finally, he was invited into the service of Ferrante, who treacherously had him murdered in order to rid himself and Italy of this disruptive element. Another aspect of the mercenary system was that it was not to the advantage of these captains to bring a war to a speedy end. It was also their habit to avoid dangerous engagements, for war was a career not a patriotic gesture of self-sacrifice. If this was not always the case, it was often the general presumption and as a result their activities attracted suspicion. Finally, a paid soldier of this sort might receive a better offer from an enemy of his employers. The Vitelli, hired by the Florentine republic in its war against Pisa, were perhaps guilty of all these faults. They certainly took their time before making any serious attempt to invest Pisa, and they missed an obvious opportunity to realise an advantage they had won by breaching the wall of the beleaguered city. They were suspected, with good grounds, of working for the return of Piero de' Medici to Florence; and they certainly received a large offer from Venice, who had liberally financed the Pisans.

The *condottieri*, who were also substantial rulers of territories of their own or of semi-independent papal territories, were in a rather different position. One reason for employing them was so that they should not take their resources to an opponent. Another reason was that their territories could then be used as a passage for troops, while being denied to the enemy. Friendship with such *condottieri* might also be desirable for the security of trade routes. Finally the Milanese and the Florentines regarded friendly *condottieri* in the Papal States as an extension of their spheres of influence, which at the same time prevented the amalgamation of the Papal States into a strong, neighbouring power. Giovanni Bentivoglio of Bologna was such a *condottiere*. He was employed for 30 years, but was rarely seen in the field. For one thing he seldom dared leave Bologna for fear that rival families might gain influence during his absence. When he entered battle he generally lost. His own aim was to preserve the independence of the various Romagna princelings so that papal power did not grow to threaten his own. Bologna itself was on the main route south from France, Switzerland and Austria to Florence, Rome or the kingdom of Naples. Its strategic and commercial importance was therefore inestimable. Sante Bentivoglio, by playing on the Milanese fear of both Venice and Florence, forged strong links with the Sforzas which lasted throughout the second half of the fifteenth century. Brought up in Florence, he also maintained a firm friendship with the Medici. Yet, while Milan and Florence were at war with Venice before Lodi, he managed to remain strictly neutral, denying passage to the forces of all three states. Giovanni Bentivoglio on the other hand, when the Papacy and Venice were opposing the accession of Roberto Malatesta at Rimini, joined Naples, Florence and Milan because the disunity of the Romagna seemed to be in jeopardy.

The remarkable complexity of Romagnol *condottiere* politics can be seen from the negotiations that took place after the realignment of Italian states at the end of the Pazzi war, in which the Papacy and Naples had opposed Florence, ineffectively allied to Milan and Venice. In April, 1480, the Papacy and Venice joined in alliance; and Naples in July aligned herself with the Sforza-Medici block, which was supporting both Ferrara, threatened by Venetian expansionist ambitions, and the Romagna lordships, unsettled by the attempts of the Pope's nephew, Girolamo Riario, to add to his territories at their expense. Things did not augur well for the second of these alliances; for Ferrante had already granted Riario a free hand to seize Pesaro from its lord, Costanzo Sforza. The situation was made more complicated by the fact that Riario was married to Caterina Sforza. To make the situation worse, Florence and Milan had already decided that the *condottieri* they wished to employ were Galeotto Manfredi and Costanzo Sforza. For Naples, with its understanding with Girolamo Riario, the employment of Sforza was out of the question. But there were also difficulties concerning Galeotto Manfredi. With the help of Ludovico Sforza, Galeotto had overthrown his brother, Carlo, as lord of Faenza. Ferrante claimed that to give him the *condotta* would simply make Carlo a strong ally of those in Venice who were urging the conquest of Ferrara. If the Venetians attacked the duchy, then Naples, Florence and Milan would be involved in war. Ferrante insisted therefore that Carlo should be restored to Faenza as a condition of the employment of Galeotto. Milan and Florence opposed this on the grounds that the restoration of Carlo would alienate the people of Faenza, who would then welcome the Venetians as liberators. There was another reason, however; Galeotto had been married to Francesca Bentivoglio on the instance of Lorenzo de' Medici as part of his policy of securing the goodwill of the rulers of Romagna and of uniting their interests. Clearly the Neapolitan policies were breaking down this system established in cooperation with the Sforzas. The situation was only saved by the Turkish occupation of Otranto, which redirected the efforts of Ferrante to the south. Thus Galeotto Manfredi was confirmed in the *condotta* of the alliance between Milan, Florence and Naples only with great difficulty and some good fortune.

Francesco Gonzaga, duke of Mantua and *condottiere*, provides perhaps the best example of the problems that these small soldier-rulers had to face. Mantua was an imperial fief, although the emperors for long had been unable to exercise any real control over their nominal territories in Italy. Just as the lords of Romagna pursued policies to keep the Papacy weak so that they could enjoy freedom from control, so Mantua was always watchful of Maximilian gaining power in Italy. Mantuan territories had been diminished by the expansion of the Venetian Terraferma. It was therefore a policy of Francesco Gonzaga to regain his lost lands around Peschiera, Lonato and Asola. He could not at the same time alienate Venice without extremely strong backing from other powers for fear of provoking her to encroach even further into his lands. A further consideration in his policy was the marriage tie between himself and Ludovico Sforza, for they had married the sisters Isabella and Beatrice d'Este respectively. Thus the policy of Mantua was also tied to that of Milan and the Estes of Ferrara. Finally, Francesco Gonzaga had to frame his policy in terms of a possible success of the French under Charles VIII and Louis XII in their designs on Italy. Such a complex of considerations and allegiances could not fail to involve Mantua in conflict and suspicion. Nevertheless, by adopting evasive policies and ambivalent and non-committal attitudes Francesco Gonzaga managed to save Mantua from the aggressive designs of greater powers. He had accepted a *condotta* from Venice in 1489, and as Charles prepared to invade Italy this was renewed, for he was never certain which way Ludovico Sforza was likely to turn. However, he continued to keep on terms with Milan and made covert and tentative overtures to Ludovico while in the pay of Venice. The French, too, offered him a command, which tempted him but which he turned down for fear of alienating Venice. Such a key position did he hold that even Alfonso II of Naples sought his help. After the French had passed south, the duke even explored the possibility of opening up relationships with the Emperor Maximilian, while at the same time still showing open signs of friendship towards Venice.

With the fall of Naples, the Venetians quickly reconfirmed Gonzaga's *condotta*. Both he and Sforza, impressed by the ease of the French invasion, were afraid that the returning French troops might occupy their territories. Accordingly, they both moved closer to Venice, and adhered to the League that Ferdinand of Aragon had inspired against the French. Gonzaga received a large sum of money from Venice for undertaking the express task of cutting off the French retreat. He achieved this with only partial success, for the French extricated themselves at Fornovo, although with big losses of equipment, because of the lack of discipline shown by the Venetian *stratiotti*. Francesco Gonzaga was immediately made captain-general of the Venetian forces with increased pay. After the defeat of Charles, Gonzaga paid him a visit which gave rise at Venice to grave suspicions of the duke's trustworthiness. Gonzaga's *condotta* was withdrawn as a consequence in 1497 after a long period of hesitation. With the succession of Louis XII to the French throne Francesco, who had been in negotiation with Milan for a *condotta*, turned again to Venice and threatened an alliance with Milan if the republic would not employ him. By now Venice herself was negotiating the Treaty of Angers with France in which she was promised Cremona and the Ghiaradadda, which threatened to increase Venetian influence over Mantua. Accordingly the Venetians turned Gonzaga away, and he completed his negotiations with Sforza. At the same time he made it quite clear to Venice that he would place himself at her disposal. When Louis entered Milan, Gonzaga was in the official party to welcome him and he received the French order of St Michael; yet he did not commit himself to the French, partly because of pressure from his wife. Instead, he waited to see the outcome of Ludovico's attempt to win back Milan. This hesitancy annoyed Louis, who demanded Francesco's son, Federico Gonzaga, as a hostage. Francesco Gonzaga resisted this and was ultimately able to pacify the king. With

Maxmilian considering an Italian invasion, Gonzaga had to accept the position of captain-general of the imperial armies in 1501. Despite this he met Louis XII at Lyons; and even began negotiations for a Florentine *condotta*. Although the French apparently maintained a stronger influence over him than their rivals and ordered him to Parma to join up with Ercole d'Este, Gonzaga contrived to become ill and soon returned to Mantua. Eventually he took part in the crossing of the Garigliano, but extricated himself from too great an involvement in the French campaign by a further timely illness.

Francesco continued to be caught up in the struggle for power in Italy. In 1506 he was made lieutenant-general of the papal forces which aimed at driving the Venetians out of Romagna. He was hoping for the return of Asola, Lonato and Peschiera. As the alliances that led to the League of Cambrai hardened, he saw his interests lay with the success of the French in the Terraferma; for the last thing he desired was the restoration of imperial power in northern Italy. Venice, meanwhile, made frantic overtures to Mantua; and the duchy of Milan was held out as a possible prize for his assistance. Gonzaga, of course, did not accept the Venetian offers. Instead, he tried to gain favour with Louis XII by giving him a full account of them. In the ensuing war, Venice attacked the duchy and Francesco was taken prisoner. Mantua gained nothing, whereas in due course Venice won back all her territories but Cremona and Ghiaradadda, which she had only recently acquired. If Francesco Gonzaga did not gain anything, neither did he lose. His skilful manipulation of greater powers, his accurate assessment of their intentions, his ability to measure the place of his duchy in their plans, enabled him to see Mantua through a period of extreme crisis without significant loss.

Something has already been said about the external relations of the Papacy. However, so special an institution as the Church was bound to develop methods appropriate to itself, as has been seen in relation to its alum policy. Its peculiar weapons were excommunication and the interdict, neither of which were in any way products of this period. In one respect, these were part of the formal procedure of freeing the Church to go to war. For instance, Florence was placed under interdict and Lorenzo and the *gonfaloniere* and *priori*, the leading members of the government, were excommunicated by Sixtus IV before he entered the Pazzi war. Julius II treated the Venetians similarly before embarking on the war of the League of Cambrai. But this was more than a formality. Those who incurred the Church's censure in this way did not regard it lightly. Especially was the possibility of dying outside the bosom of the Church a terrifying prospect for most people. Therefore the popes could strike a blow at the morale of their opponents in war before an engagement took place. Yet, clearly such moral pressure was not enough to deter states from proceeding with their policies. However, an interdict immediately endangered the merchandise and other possessions of the people who were censured and the Florentines, for example, in 1478 were particularly concerned for their interests and goods in Naples, England and, above all, in Rome. If goods were seldom permanently confiscated, these were awkward moments for the opponents of the popes: at the very least they lost trade on account of such measures.

There were counter-moves that might be taken against the Papacy. During this period the most important of these was the threat to call a council of the Church. Such a threat was used by Lorenzo de' Medici with the backing of Louis XI during the Pazzi war. When the League of Cambrai was broken up by Julius II and the Holy League was formed in opposition to Louis XII, the French king actually assembled a council at Pisa, censoriously referred to as the *conciliabulum*. In the event the council was poorly attended. When Louis proposed moving it to Lyons, Julius II issued a bull re-establishing the fairs at Geneva. The interests of the merchants of Italy and Germany, however, were too powerfully entrenched at Lyons, and this move was not successful. The negotiations of the Venetians with the sultan of Egypt in 1503 and 1505 illustrate the care governments might take to avoid a clash with the Papacy and its consequent disadvantages. The Venetian ambassadors implied obliquely, yet with absolute clarity, that the Egyptians might profitably attack the Portuguese in the Indian Ocean. They could not endanger themselves by incurring spiritual sanctions for asking outright that Muslims should attack Christians. There was perhaps no deeply held religious principle involved in the attitude of either side. Certainly Popes Innocent VIII and Alexander VI had earlier come to a profitable understanding with Sultan Bāyazīd to confine his brother and rival, Djem, in Rome; and the Venetians had had an active alliance with Uzun Hasan, the shah of Persia, against Mehemmed II. Neither of these alliances, however, encouraged Muslims to use force against Christians. The first successful instance of such an occurrence was to wait until Francis I and Sultan Suleiman were to unite in war against the Emperor Charles V.

The development of permanent and semi-permanent diplomatic representation in other states was a striking feature of Italian inter-state and international relations in the fifteenth century. The previous century had seen Visconti Milan and Mantua experiment with the possibilities of such ambassadors. With the return of the Papacy to Rome and a general feeling of apprehension towards the growth of the temporal power in central Italy, ten Italian states had permanent ambassadors at the Curia by 1455. They were the three great commercial republics: the duchies of Milan, Mantua, Savoy and Ferrara; the kingdom of Naples; and the republics of Lucca and Siena. Some of the Papal States also kept permanent representatives at Rome with the futile hope that they might gain full ambassadorial status. Rome consequently became the clearing-house for Italian political information and a centre of political intrigue. A message generally took about four days to cover the 400 miles between Venice and Rome; but it was not unknown for urgent information to be transmitted between the two cities in a day and a half. As a redistribution point of Italian news, therefore, Rome served to keep the rest of Italy up to date with what was going on elsewhere in the peninsula. Permanent ambassadors were not limited to Rome. Milan had a resident ambassador in France from 1463 for a dozen years; for a long period during the Medici-Sforza friendship, she exchanged ambassadors with Florence; and after the disasters inflicted on the Burgundy of Charles the Bold by Louis XI, both Milan and Naples sent permanent orators to the Burgundian court to foster a friendship which might be useful should French expansionist designs turn southwards against Italy. On the other hand, Venice had an embassy there which she withdrew in 1475, sending instead an ambassador to France two years later. Florence, especially under the Medici, tended to rely on resident businessmen to carry out the functions for which other states were using ambassadors. This was perhaps due to the constitutional situation that made it impossible for an ambassador to represent the Medici. The difficulty was not so great for foreign ambassadors in Florence; for, although they were officially accredited to the Signoria, they had no difficulty in maintaining close contact with the Medici with whom they were able to have private interviews. There was also some advantage in using merchants as quasi-ambassadors: much of the purpose of maintaining an embassy was to keep well informed about affairs that might affect trade. If the merchant could not always tap official channels of information, he often had greater contact with less guarded and therefore more useful sources. A typical example of this was the use made by Venice of Giovanni Francesco Affaitadi at Lisbon: he was able to gain important information about Portuguese spice shipping in a way that an ambassador attached to the court of the king would have found difficult. This important element in diplomacy of gaining commercial information had its prototype in the practice of the Italian states of keeping consuls in the Levant; and the

Venetian *bailo*, at Constantinople, whose office was a development of this old consular system, was half an ambassador, half the protector of Venetian commercial interests in the Ottoman empire.

The permanent ambassadors were not usually employed to carry out major negotiations. Special embassies, often consisting of two or more ambassadors, freshly briefed by the home government, were normally entrusted with such duties. Such embassies might be given full powers to negotiate; or they might be used as part of delaying tactics, so that time was wasted by frequent references back to their government. Ambassadorial diplomacy had its disadvantages. In its early stages the presence of an ambassador in one state might be construed as a hostile gesture by a third government. This caused the Florentines great embarrassment when they were debating in 1507 whether to send an embassy to the Emperor Maximilian I; for it was feared that the French, to whom Florence was closely allied, might regard such a move as an overture to the empire of anti-French significance. The effectiveness of these early embassies was not always very great. Both Venice and Florence had ambassadors at the French court in the first decade of the sixteenth century, and Florence after some hesitation decided to send Francesco Vettori to Maximilian. Nevertheless, these two republics were perhaps the least well informed of all the major states involved in the frantic period of negotiations preceding the formation of the League of Cambrai. Florence as late as April 1508— the main lines of the anti-Venetian coalition had long been decided— feared an alliance between Maximilian, Venice and France; whereas the Venetians were not well enough informed to realise that their hopes of a continued alliance with France were quite unrealistic. Apart from the legitimate functions of ambassadors, most states had developed at least rudimentary systems of espionage. This has already been seen in the case of Florentines intercepting Venetian mail. During the Turkish occupation of Otranto, Ferrante was able to intercept letters between Mehemmed II and the pasha of Valona, the commander of the Turkish forces. It was such occurrences as this that made it necessary to send all messages by two separate messengers. Important items were for the same reason in cipher.

The external relations of the Italian states, subtle, complex and evolving new techniques, fall into two distinct patterns during this period. From 1464 to the earlier invasions of the French, inter-state relations were dominant. The Italian powers, according to their nature—commercial republic, territorial monarchy, petty tyrant or papal temporality—angled constantly for position within the peninsula itself. Only Venice was distracted in any major fashion further afield with her long struggle with the

Ottoman empire. The Papal States in Romagna constantly presented an area for disagreement. Their weakness and division invited intervention, and intervention invited counter-intervention. Papal nepotism, which offered a further challenge to the equilibrium that was in the main uneasily upheld, added further complications to the complexity of alignments: the other powers were not only trying to prevent too great an accretion of papal power, they were also concerned up to the time of Julius II with controlling the family policies of the popes (Sixtus IV and Alexander VI), which they feared might outlast a papal reign. The patent illegitimacy of the positions of Girolamo Riario and Cesare Borgia meant that on the deaths of their papal protectors an outcry of rival claims was bound to offer opportunities for the meddling of the greater Italian powers, although they did not always wait for such occasions. The duchy of Milan, despite its rulers' illegitimacy up to 1495, was on the whole stable and prosperous, and Florence under the Medici for the most part stayed in close alignment with the Sforzas. Venice, concerned to dominate the Adriatic and police the entrance to the Po, expanded to the loss of Ferrara into the Polesine di Rovigo and snatched an Apulian port or two from Naples, whenever possible. She tended to ally herself with the popes with the hope of sharing the Papal States in return for helping in their recovery. This was a goal which Florence and Milan, who had satisfactory relations with the tyrants of Romagna, were bound to oppose. Only if Naples threw in her weight on the side of the Papacy did Venice realign herself with Milan and Florence, as she did, for instance, during the Pazzi war when it was clear that Riario's gains in the Romagna might eliminate the opportunity of Venice herself to expand there. Genoa was in the hands of the dukes of Milan between 1464 and 1478 and again from 1488 to the French occupation of 1499. This relieved Milan's dependence on Venice as an entrance and an outlet for her trade. It did not limit Genoa carrying on her own affairs: good relations with Milan were to her commercial advantage; foreign occupation always gave Genoa a greater internal tranquillity than otherwise she had; and the Sforzas' easygoing dominance allowed the Genoese to proceed with their business freely. Naples intrigued constantly under the scheming direction of Ferrante. She was friendless and therefore deserted when the pasha of Valona led his forces into Otranto; and, even when she was innocent, she was suspected of conspiring treacherously. During these years she neither gained nor lost, but expended endless energy on her fruitless ambitions. During the same period relations with non-Italian powers were principally governed by trading interests. This accounted for the deference of the Genoese and the hostility of the Venetians towards the Turks. That Florence remained largely aloof in this respect was the result of Lorenzo's indifference and ineptitude.

The French invasions ushered in a period when old policies died hard, but new conditions required basic changes in the external relations of the Italian states. The successful conquest of the Papal States by Julius II certainly filled in the dangerous vacuum of Romagna. Milan succumbed first to France and then to imperial Spain: the duchy was a focal point of conflicts in a new dimension for which Italy was ill-prepared. Naples likewise fell to Spain and assumed the new rôle of Castilian outpost in a holy mission against the Moor and Turk. Genoa, experienced in leading her masters, finally learnt that Spain, less businesslike than France, offered her better opportunities to exploit her skills. The greatness of Florence shrank before the appearance of enormous powers in western Europe; but, maintaining her trade with France, she survived with the help of two Medici popes through 20 crucial years and emerged politically much less significant, as a small but independent duchy. Venice alone remained something of a force: even late in the seventeenth century, Jan Sobieski regarded her as a useful ally for a sacred crusade against the Turk; while young Tsar Peter, in his perambulations about Europe, believing she still had something to teach, had planned to visit her and learn. But the world had changed. If Italy showed a resilience in economic matters, she was no longer the centre of great events. Politically she had become a prey.

6

Internal Affairs

The tenacious particularism of the Italian states gave rise to a wide variety of constitutional solutions and class structures throughout Italy. Even conquered territories and those swallowed up by bigger neighbouring powers often managed to retain much of their internal organisation as it had been. If power changed hands, the instruments and forms of power usually remained the same. Since the economic needs of such territories did not suddenly alter with a change of government or master, those classes which had been important before the change tended to continue to be important afterwards as well. Only when the nature of the change was economic and social might there have been a reversal in the relationships of classes; but even in this there was no sudden revolution in the structure of classes.

Because of the strength of the towns and communal government in the Middle Ages, feudalism in Italy has often been written off as negligible; yet even in fifteenth-century Italy there were still centres where feudal relationships were strong. In the islands of Corsica and Sardinia the land was dominated by feudal lords. In Sicily and Naples, outside those towns which were seats of government such as Naples, Palermo and Messina, feudal lordships predominated, as they did in the lands around Rome. In the Ligurian territories of Genoa, throughout the Milanese countryside, around Modena, and in the countryside surrounding towns like Perugia and Bologna in the papal states, feudal ties were still common. Sometimes, especially in north and central Italy, the relationships between overlord, feudatory and peasant had undergone changes. Because of the growth of the mercenary system feudal military service was not always exacted, and the services of the serf had often been commuted into money-payments or *mezzadria* agreements. Because of the example of the towns, where mobility of labour was characteristic, it was also not generally the case that the peasant was legally tied to the land, although this was often so in practice. If the spectacular exercise of power lay with the mediaeval commune in Italy, nevertheless there had survived, especially in the south and in the islands, a numerous and unprivileged peasantry that rendered services to an overlord and was subject to seigneurial jurisdiction. At times the relationship between urban and rural populations in some parts of Italy was such that the former outnumbered the latter, but at most times and in most places there were at least two country dwellers to one inhabitant of a town. Since many of the rural workers fell in some way under a form of feudal dominance, the importance of Italian feudalism should not be underestimated.

In the kingdom of Naples Alfonso of Aragon built up a form of bureaucracy and the Aragonese kings were often at odds with their barons; but these feudal lords were strong enough to shake from time to time the stability of the realm and to cling to their privileges and their independence until the régime of Pedro de Toledo, who became the viceroy of Charles V in 1532, brought them more under control. The extension of the fortifications of Naples, begun by Alfonso di Calabria in 1481 and continued by Federico of Aragon in 1499, was in the first case wholly and in the second case partly due to the fear of internal, feudal disruption. Even when Toledo tamed the barons by attracting them to the comforts and delights of Naples the position of the peasants scarcely changed, although they now had a refuge from seigneurial oppression in the brilliant capital where they might find employment in domestic service or public works. Naples indeed expanded vastly at this time with such incentives. Nevertheless of over two million inhabitants in the kingdom more than seven-eighths lived outside the capital. Further north in the country around Rome, independent lords had their castles in the hills, ruled their peasantry without restraint and exercised seigneurial jurisdiction. Great families like the Orsini, Savelli and Colonna fought each other or split and fought amongst themselves, and especially during papal *interregna* they profited from the indiscipline of Rome. At times they were strong enough to form alliances with another Italian power, the kingdom of Naples for instance, and to intrigue against papal rule. Alexander VI brought these recalcitrant elements into line and the papal hold over them was tightened by Julius II; but in the first half of this period baronial independence was one of the many factors that destroyed the countryside of the Roman Campagna. A further feudal hang-over was the practice whereby counties within the *contado* of a papal vicariate were held from the pope himself. Thus the popes might enfeoff citizens who were rivals of the *de facto* rulers. A similar situation sometimes obtained in imperial feoffs. For instance, in the *contado* of Modena there was a continual struggle during this period between the counts of Cesi of Gombola and the commune, the first deriving their claims from the emperor, the second resting on the support of the Este dukes of Ferrara. Although in this area feudal ties had been weakening during the fifteenth century through the traditional practices of manumission, the commutation of services for money-payments, the spread of crop-sharing, wage-earning and long or perpetual leases, a halt to the process had occurred towards the end of the century. Woods and common had been encroached upon, and the counts Cesi had supported outsiders who were responsible for this against the intervention of the commune. Peasants lost their land on account of, for example, the indebtedness they incurred through the non-payment of dowries; and there was generally a tendency to reimpose serfdom. However, this tendency was modified by the support given to commune and peasants by the dukes of Ferrara, in whose interests it was to keep weak relationships between feudal lords and emperor, as in their other territories around Ferrara it was their aim to ward off papal pretensions to overlordship.

In the duchy of Milan the process which had weakened the Church as a landed power did not affect the old feudal lordships. On the contrary they often increased their power by accumulating, during the great turnover of landed property, huge consolidated blocks. Thus apart from his scattered possessions the Count dal Verme controlled a huge stretch of territory from the Po near Castel San Giovanni south to near Bobbio. Such feudal lords were numerous during the period of the Sforzas. If the dukes did much to control the unruliness of these lords by improved communications, they nevertheless treated them with indulgence. The communes of the duchy, therefore, were often faced with the task of opposing feudal arrogance, as armed barons entered the streets of perhaps Piacenza, terrifying the populace and threatening the peaceful pursuance of trade. If there was a strong growth of bureaucratic influence about the court, further afield the old disruptive power of feudal lordship with its immunities and jurisdiction survived; and although new ideas about land tenure evolved along with a riot of speculation, the older forms of feudal tenure continued to exist. With the introduction of Spanish influence under the viceroys of Charles V, an atmosphere was created which was more in sympathy with the older feudal ideas; bureaucratic office-holders were challenged by those who believed a share in government was their right and their responsibility. Whereas Spanish Naples tamed the feudal lords, Spanish Milan offered them and the new landowners who imitated them a fresh lease of life.

The tendency towards a revival of feudal power also occurred in Piedmont in the sixteenth century; whereas in Tuscany and the Venetian mainland the increasing interest in the land, although it did not encourage a society which might properly be called feudal, at least led to serious limitations on the opportunities and freedom of the peasantry. The most interesting case of the strengthening of feudal power is that which took place in the republic of Genoa. In this region, outside the communes, the most influential of which was Savona, and outside the city and suburbs of Genoa itself, feudal relationships were constantly strong during this period. What occurred was not a hardening of feudal relationships so much as an increase in the political power of the aristocrats, among them the great feudatories. The Doria and the Spinola di Luccoli, the Grimaldi, Fieschi and Malaspina were always strong in their feoffs. They had fortresses, power and jurisdiction over the local populace, armed bands to ravage the countryside and to enforce their will. They exploited rights over fulling mills, tolls, forges; the land in so far as it was productive was used mainly to their profit. If small fortified villages were built to counter their influence, these were not always successful in their purpose. The feudatories kept their agents in Genoa to look after the businesses many of them ran both in competition and in association with the urban aristocracy and the great popular families. Some of them, those of the ducal families of Fregosi and Adorni, were technically *popolani* and not aristocrats.

Genoese offices during the fifteenth century were divided between aristocrats and *popolani* equally; and the share of the *popolani* was divided, half among the *popolo grasso* and half among the *popolo minuto*. This was so for positions in the *Casa di San Giorgio* as well as within the governmental institutions of the state. Only the doge from the first, fourteenth-century, popular *doggato* of Simone Boccanegra had always to be a *popolano*. Within each of these classes, individuals were either whites (ghibellines) or blacks (guelfs). These distinctions had no longer any reference to their original meaning of support for the emperor or the pope; yet, of both the aristocratic and the popular representation in offices, half had to be black, half white. As there were more white than black nobles, individual blacks had a greater chance of influence than their white counterparts. Class and party labels were almost meaningless, except for these constitutional procedures. It has been seen that there were great popular feudatories, those of the ducal families. There were also urban aristocrats who held no feoffs, such as the Centurioni. Popular *alberghi* like the Giustiniani were only differentiated from the noble Centurioni, for instance, in this constitutional process whereby they might take office through different channels. The following list, giving the number of times the various, most-represented *alberghi* provided members of

133

the Council of Ancients during the period 1447–67, together with their class and party, should throw light on this complex situation: 26 Fieschi—black, aristocratic feudatories; 24 Spinola—white nobles, mainly feudatories, but some of them urban aristocrats; 23 Lomellini—black, urban aristocrats; 22 Grimaldi—black, aristocratic feudatories; 18 Doria—white, aristocratic feudatories; 18 Giustiniani—black and white, urban *popolani*; 13 Cattaneo—white, urban aristocrats; 12 Franchi—white, urban *popolani*; 7 Vivaldi—white, urban aristocrats. Feudal interests were accordingly well represented in the major council of the republic, which played an important part in the appointment of other offices. It should be remembered, however, that the interests of the aristocrats were by no means always feudal: the aristocratic Vivaldi and the popular Franchi would have had more in common than either had with the Grimaldi; and the business interests of the Doria would have brought them closer to, say, the Giustiniani than to the feudatory Malaspina or to the popular ducal families with their feudal interests. When, however, Louis XII of France occupied Genoa in 1499 the one important distinction that he and his governors understood was that between aristocrat and *popolano*: and it was from this moment that conflict between these nominal classes became significant, for the king turned naturally to the nobles. The unreality of the situation can be seen from the fluidity of classes brought about by the system of *alberghi*. New *alberghi* were continually being formed or new members were being incorporated in them, especially when the number of members of an *albergo* appeared to be declining. Old *alberghi* also very often were dissolved, their members usually regrouping themselves into new aggregations or joining other, already existing *alberghi*. By this means *popolani*, when they became sufficiently wealthy, often found it possible to become members of an aristocratic *albergo*. This fluidity was much more pronounced among the urban aristocracy, but it was certainly not rare among the great feudal *alberghi* as well.

French occupation was not altogether unwelcome to the mercantile interests of Genoa; it meant that Genoese business at Lyons was allowed to develop its interests, and having the French in north-western Italy brought the routes across the Alps into the hands of a friendly power. The most significant limitation it placed on the Genoese was that they were forced to rely on Provençal instead of Sicilian and Neapolitan grain. In addition to this, the anti-Turkish policy of Louis XII made trading conditions with the Levant more difficult. The French régime, however, was very different from the casual dominance of the Sforzas. The governors' main concern was to harness the resources of Genoa to the French policy in Italy. This required heavy taxation; and to carry out such a policy the French looked to aristocratic support. In this way the aristocracy was associated with a policy of extortion, which fell especially heavily on the *popolo minuto*. But by 1505 the French began to recognise the importance of the *popolo grasso*, who under the aristocratic French policy had come to realise a solidarity of interests with the *popolo minuto* that had not existed previously. It was an accident that Genoese Levantine interests, which were suffering under French dominance, were mainly the concern of two important popular *alberghi*, the Giustiniani and the Sauli. Had this not been the case, it would have been far easier for a reconciliation of aristocratic and popular interests. As it was, the *popoli grassi* and *minuti* joined forces in a big demonstration in Genoa in June 1506. This was the prelude to the popular revolt led by Paolo de Novi, who himself became doge for the winter until the French were able to re-establish control in Genoa. In the revolt the Sauli and the Giustiniani figured prominently; but, as the lowliest working-man was seen to be involved actively in the revolt, the *popolo grasso* for the main part stood aside in disdain. As a result the alliance between the aristocracy and the French finally triumphed, and the non-committal, big popular families compromised their position. A class-consciousness had crystallised, and the *popolani* never completely regained their influence in Genoese affairs. With the reorganisation of the *alberghi* by Andrea Doria in 1528, the popular *alberghi* were limited to four and doges were elected for only two-year periods from aristocratic families. It is true that the Sauli, for instance, again rose to prominence, especially as papal alum farmers; but the popular names of the Adorni and the Fregosi were suppressed, and the great aristocratic Grimaldi, Spinola, Doria (all feudatories) and Centurioni amongst others emerged as dominant in Genoese affairs. Thus the triumph of aristocracy in sixteenth-century Genoa brought with it additional power to the great feoffs.

One of the characteristic features of Italy in the fifteenth century was the large number of states that retained their communal forms of government, although at the same time individuals emerged as virtual rulers of the states. In such circumstances there was often tension between the ruler and his supporters on the one hand and the class or classes that felt themselves to have been deprived of their rightful place in the government on the other. The Baglioni of Perugia gained influence in the country around that city by means of successive papal grants, starting from that of the lordship of Spello given in feoff to Malatesta Baglioni by Martin V. This produced factionalism in Perugia and embittered the rivalry between the Baglioni and their adherents and an opposing group led by the degli Oddi. By 1488 the Baglioni had secured a complete hold over the leading magistracy of the city, the *Dieci dell'Arbitrio*, in which Guido and Ridolfo Baglioni together with eight of their supporters were the members. Soon after, the Baglioni family membership of that council had risen to as many as six. By 1494 a list was made of 48 families, all firmly attached to the Baglioni régime: from this the captains of the *contado* had to be selected. This system did not last long: in the first place the Baglioni split amongst themselves; and then Julius II conquered Perugia during his campaign to subjugate the Papal States. The Baglioni fortunes vacillated over the following decades until, in 1540, Paul III destroyed the last trace of Baglioni power by dismantling their houses in Perugia and replacing them by a papal fortress. The Baglioni had gained power by acquiring control of the old communal machinery of government and packing the important positions with supporters. This veneer of constitutionalism was even more pronounced in Bologna, where the council of the *Riformatori dello stato di Libertà* was the magistracy through which the Bentivoglio exercised power. In the capitulations of 1447, designating the relationship between Bologna and the Papacy, the papal legate and the *Sedici Riformatori* were to become the twin rulers of the state, but after a trial of strength papal influence progressively declined. Nicholas V agreed that the legate should be chosen from three or four names presented to him by the *Riformatori*. After the departure in 1467 of the legate, Cardinal Capranica, it was no longer usual for legates to reside in Bolognese territory. Then some years later Innocent VIII agreed that appeals to Rome could only be made with the consent of both the legate and the *Riformatori*. Finally Bologna was strong enough to resist the appointment by Alexander VI of Cardinal Federico San Severino as legate. Thus, until the reconquest of Bologna by Julius II, the city enjoyed a very large measure of independence of the Papacy. Meanwhile, the dominance of the Bentivoglio over the *Riformatori* steadily increased. This was particularly marked by a constitutional alteration made in 1467, when the *Sedici* were increased to 21, with Giovanni Bentivoglio to hold office without interruption, while the other 20 members took their place in the council for six months in alternating groups of ten. The Bentivoglio, like the Baglioni in Perugia, met a great deal of opposition from rival citizens such as the Malvezzi; but, with their armed force and a strong group who found it profitable to throw in their lot with the Bentivoglio, they were able to dominate the state and control its constitutional apparatus. Neither the Baglioni nor the Bentivoglio relied wholly on these methods: the Baglioni were propped up by Lorenzo de' Medici, and both the Medici and the Sforzas worked closely with the Bentivoglio in Bologna. Giovanni Bentivoglio also forged close links by marriage with some of the other Romagna despots. Moreover, the people of these states found it safer and more to their liking to be ruled by a man on the spot with local interests than from Rome. The point has already been made of the Malatesta at Rimini; it was equally true of the Bentivoglio in Bologna. With their careful maintenance of the forms of the constitution the Bentivoglio looked after the interests of the city as well as their own. In such instances those who were deprived of their traditional rights to influence government and exploit society sought a revival of the systems their rulers had overthrown.

The same elements of armed force, outside support and a skilful control of the established machinery of government, lay behind the rise to power of Pandolfo Petrucci in Siena. For the great part of the fifteenth century Siena had been run by a coalition of the different interests within the state: the city-dwelling, feudal nobility; the great merchant-bankers like the Spannocchi and the Chigi; those whose families had risen to high prominence through the guilds. From the time when the republic was shaken during the Pazzi war by the occupation of the Neapolitan troops of Alfonso di Calabria, this equilibrium was destroyed and ultimately the rich merchant class emerged dominant, although by 1495 some compromise was made between the merchants and their rivals. In this year Petrucci became a member of the *Balia*, which was controlled by the business magnates and had supreme legislative and executive powers. It was by now the governing body of Siena, and had assumed the power of the old *signoria* and other councils of the republic. At the same time, the French had just withdrawn from Naples, and so Milan and Venice were free to lend their support to the rebellious Pisans against Florence. Lodovico Sforza had accordingly established an embassy at Siena to exacerbate the position of Florence by persuading the Sienese also to support Pisa. The Sienese responded by sending several loads of grain to the rebels. In this situation Petrucci, a *condottiere* with a band of troops of his own, was of great potential use to the Milanese and so Lodovico sent money to help him pay his soldiers. Thus Petrucci was able to maintain himself as a potent factor in Sienese politics. When, therefore, new elections to the *Balia* were held in November 1497, after a struggle with the peace party backed by Florence, he was elected with a majority of supporters. Like most *condottieri* he was not anxious to engage in an active war of uncertain outcome. He was therefore in favour of negotiating peace with Florence and, by carrying out the negotiations himself, became recognised as the Sienese spokesman on foreign affairs. He thus followed Milan back into a pro-Florentine policy. At the same time he had freed himself of opposition within the *Balia*, because he carried his supporters with him in this change of policy, while satisfying his pro-Florentine opponents. Once again a *condottiere* had managed to dominate a state with the help of military power and with foreign support, but mainly by taking control of the existing constitutional machinery. The concern of these men was to create a strong semblance of legitimacy for their thoroughly illegitimate régimes.

The best example of such a régime was that of the early Medici. Yet they were not military men, they had no armed backing, and they did not establish themselves with the support of foreign powers. Once their position as virtual rulers had been obtained, their continued supremacy in Florence depended on a sustained manipulation of the governing councils so that they were dominated by their supporters, and on the general success of their policies so that opposition was kept to a minimum. Cosimo, who started the Medici régime in 1434, was invited to return to Florence from exile to assume the position of leading citizen, lending his prestige, wealth and experience to the government of the republic. However, his ultimate, unique position within the republic was the result of his own adroit scheming and management. The return of Cosimo was marked by only one constitutional change, the substitution of nomination to the two-monthly office of prior by a committee of ten *accoppiatori* for the old system of election by lot. A *parlamento*, an assembly of artisans in the Piazza della Signoria, was called to institute a *balia*, a commission with plenary powers, to choose the ten *accoppiatori* to serve for a period of five years. These *accoppiatori* were re-elected after their term had expired. This new system of choosing the *priori*, the leading officers of the republic, was one of the two elements of Cosimo's rule that were crucial to his success. Although he himself was not made one of the *accoppiatori*, the ten men who filled this powerful position were all members of the new oligarchy, which had overthrown Cosimo's predecessor Rinaldo degli Albizzi and his supporters from older families. Thus the *priori* were certain to be named from members of the newly dominant group. Moreover, new names were from time to time added to those eligible for election; so that Cosimo gained further support from those thus favoured, and at the same time the ruling class acquired a revitalising fluidity. A further advantage of this system was that no longer did the chance of the ballot place in powerful positions those who were incompetent to fulfil their office adequately. The other method, whereby Cosimo assured himself of powerful support and was at the same time able to strike at his opponents, was the manipulation of the *catasto*.

By regularly failing to modify the *catasto* returns, he let off his supporters with a lighter incidence of taxation, since it was they who generally prospered under his régime and they were taxed according to old assessments. Likewise the tax commissioners, estimating the taxable incomes of the Florentines, dealt harshly with Cosimo's opponents and indulgently with his followers with the result that opposition was weakened and support was made more profitable.

Nevertheless, there was always an important element of rich and discontented businessmen, jealous of Cosimo's power and spurning his favours; and under pressure from these he abandoned for a while in the last decade of his life the system of *accoppiatori*, reverting to election by lot from the carefully vetted names that were put into the electoral bags. The change did not in any way weaken Cosimo's power, and it was these very opponents who pressed him to revert to the system of *accoppiatori*, which he did in 1458. In that year a new council, the council of 100, was created. This was a stronghold of oligarchic, if pro-Medicean, interests, and it gradually encroached upon many of the spheres of the old *consiglio del popolo* and *consiglio comune*, the first originally the representation of the guilds, the second representing the four quarters of Florence, the consent of both being required for the passing of legislation. The other big organ of government was the *parlamento*, whose approval was given by acclamation and was sometimes assured by a display of mercenary force. By the death of Cosimo, the Florentine big business interests were clearly preponderant in the government of Florence. The only question was whether the Medici could continue to command their support or whether they might not be able to branch out after Cosimo's death in an attempt to establish a more direct control of affairs. In the event, the succession of Piero de' Medici to his father was not altogether unchallenged. An oligarchic opposition led by Niccolò Soderini again secured a hollow victory in the form of a return to election by lot, hollow because the pro-Medicean electoral bags of 1458 were still being used. However, chance threw up Niccolò Soderini as *Gonfaloniere di Giustizia* at the end of 1465 and he was able to force through a much broader-based electoral list which now included some small merchants and artisans. The democratic turn of events forced many of Soderini's supporters led by Luca Pitti to go over to the side of the pro-Mediceans. Thus a programme of constitutional reform envisaged by Soderini to restrain the power of the Medici lost the necessary support it needed to be put into practice. Piero was able therefore to maintain the Medici dominance.

Piero's son, Lorenzo the Magnificent, certainly expected to take over his father's position. Whether he was confident about his 'succession' is a different matter. He corresponded with the Sforzas before his father's death, assuring them that he would continue the Medici-Sforza friendship. Such evidence is two-edged; if there was assurance in his tone, his purpose might well have been to enlist powerful support for his cause. However, it was a Soderini, Tommaso, who took the initiative in leading the oligarchs to recognise Lorenzo in the curious ruling position of his predecessors. But already the Medici position had changed: as Cosimo had laid down the principle that his firm should not lend to rulers, so he was insistent that they should not ally themselves by marriage to ruling houses. Cosimo's policy was to remain in the background, avoiding glamorous but dangerous undertakings. Power satisfied him without its trappings; success was enough without its display. Lorenzo's marriage to Clarice Orsini was a break with this tradition. It may have been out of a desire not to alienate the Florentine *primati* by forging a close alliance with one of them; but marriage connections had been and were being forged with members of this powerful class. Lorenzo's mother was a Tornabuoni; other relations married members of these families—the Soderini and the Pazzi; the Ridolfi, Salviati, Rucellai and Rossi. On the other hand, the Capponi, for instance, might well have felt themselves shut out. Lorenzo by his marriage began a long sequence of prestigious alliances: his daughter married the bastard son of Pope Innocent VIII; Piero married another Orsini. Eventually the Medici struck up alliances with the great European families of the Valois and the Hapsburgs. Such marriages were only symptoms of an imperceptibly changing attitude whereby the Medici were considered and considered themselves rulers and openly began to behave as such. It was not Lorenzo's initiative that brought a cardinalate to his son, Giovanni; but it became appropriate that the Medici, like the Sforzas, Gonzagas and Estes, should have a cardinal in the family and access to papal ears. It was the Medici too, who would entertain important foreign visitors; like the Sforzas, put on carnivals for the people; stand first in ostentatious display. Yet, the resentment of the other members of their class was never entirely overcome. The Pazzi conspiracy, in which Lorenzo narrowly escaped with his life and his brother, Giuliano, was assassinated, showed the lengths to which such opposition could run. It is true that the Pazzi were an old noble family; but Cosimo had exempted them from the disabilities to which the nobility had been subjected. Their wealth came from banking and trade, and they had political rights like any of the great business families. To all intents and purposes they numbered amongst the *ottimati*. The failure of their plot only brought sympathy to Lorenzo and strengthened his position; but the war that ensued was costly. It was only a dramatic personal mission to the court of Ferrante that retrieved his position. That the mission was rigged did not matter, for at the time this was not known and Lorenzo had, it seemed, brought peace and safety to Florence. But even these heroics were short-lived in their influence: the oligarchs were beginning to control and profit from the main financial organs of the state and a new council, the *Settanta*, was set up, dominated by this class and especially concerned with Florentine finances. It was now as much a case of the oligarchy controlling the Medici, as the Medici manipulating the machinery of the constitution to their own advantage; for the Medici were now staggering under financial difficulties. A string of blunders by the weak, unintelligent and pretentious son of Lorenzo, Piero de' Medici, was enough to ensure the downfall of his family.

The opposition to the Medici was in the first place led by rich *primati* such as Piero Capponi, and the *Signoria* which brought about the constitutional changes at the end of 1494 was constituted just as it had been under Piero's régime. It was not until its second month in office that Savonarola was able to influence its policy. The initial stages of the post-Medicean republic were therefore carried out entirely by the representatives of the financial oligarchy which had gained so much ground in the years following the Pazzi war. If they had to take account of public opinion, they were nevertheless at the tiller guiding the new situation to their own best advantage. This was even so during the vital days around Christmas when the new *Consiglio Maggiore* and council of 80 were instituted. One reason why the former of these two bodies became acceptable to the *primati* and to Savonarola's followers, the *frateschi*, at one and the same time, was that the Venetian constitution was taken as an ambiguous model. The *primati* saw this model as an expression of the interests of the Venetian patriciate and their business activities; the *frateschi* saw it as the embodiment of a wide and varied range of interests, a government with a broad basis. In fact, it was to give members of the lesser guilds their first opportunity for 60 years to influence significantly through constitutional channels the policies of the republic. Somebody's hopes were bound to be frustrated, and the stage was arranged for certain conflict. Each side, however, had high hopes of a return to an idealised pre-Medicean past: a dream of free exploitation of their business interests through an unfettered control of the policies of the state by the *primati*; vague notions of liberty and limited democracy, not necessarily tempered by the puritanical teachings of Savonarola, on the part of a less opulent section of the population.

The *Consiglio Maggiore* elected officers to the main positions in the government of Florence and voted on legislation, but it did not hold discussions. As a result it was not easy for it to come to a concerted policy and it could never thresh out issues itself. The *Ottanta* and the *Dieci di Balia*, a small body directing foreign relations and war, were more important in taking a lead, and the *Consiglio Maggiore* assumed the function rather of blocking unpalatable policies, as on the occasion of the proposed increase in the salt gabelle. But, even so, the smaller councils were starved of a supply of experienced men. This was partly due to the fact that appointments were often made from the newly enfranchised group of citizens; but it was also because many of the *ottimati* had withdrawn from public life. Some, like Bernardo Rucellai, went into voluntary exile; others purposely disqualified themselves from office by falling into arrears with their tax payments, a course also taken by Rucellai after his return to Florence. Accordingly, the *Dieci* and the *Ottanta* developed the system whereby a group of influential and experienced citizens, usually *ottimati*—Bernardo Rucellai after he had returned to Florence, Pagolantonio Soderini, Piero Guicciardini, the historian's father, amongst them—were invited to discuss vital questions concerning the republic and advise these councils. So, through the sheer necessity of using the best informed and most experienced men available, the broadly-based republic was forced to lean heavily on this class, which within the limits of Medicean control had dominated Florence since 1434. When Piero Soderini was made *Gonfaloniere a Vita* in 1502, as the Florentine approximation to the Venetian doge, it was expected by the *ottimati* that he would introduce policies more favourable to their interests; for he was one of them and came from a family that had defended the interests of that class against the monarchical ambitions of the Medici. They were disappointed; and as the republic went from one problem to another—the Pisan war, what attitude to take towards the French, how to establish a satisfactory military force—the *ottimati* forged greater unity of purpose and managed to rally the increasing numbers of the dissatisfied behind them. Their obvious solution was the return of the Medici, who after the death of the unpopular Piero had gained enormously in popularity. Florence was thinking more and more in terms of the good old days, and had to a great extent prepared itself for a Medicean restoration by the time the Spanish forces conveniently presented this as an alternative to their own foreign occupation.

The new Medici régime was not a revival of the old. In the first place Italy had changed so fundamentally that the physical survival of Florence, and not only its economic prosperity, required unequal alliance with and almost direct dependence upon one foreign power or another. The Medici from the very start relied on Spanish assistance for their return, even though there were strong elements in Florence which were glad to have them back. Then in the following year, 1513, Cardinal Giovanni de' Medici, the head of the family, was elected pope. As Leo X he virtually ruled Florence from Rome. After a short gap during the pontificate of Adrian VI, the second Medici pope, Clement VII, although he became less influential as the Italian power of Charles V increased, continued to carry Florence in the train of the Papacy. But during this period the dissatisfaction of the *ottimati* progressively revived. They had not been instrumental in the restoration of the Medici only to see all their power filched by a family whose interests were not indivisibly tied to Florence and whose ambitions were clearly assuming a dynastic hue. As in 1494 so in 1527 it was a Capponi, Niccolò, who was prominent in the overthrow of a family whose policies had become unsubtle and arrogant. As in 1494, too, the *ottimati* soon lost a direct grip on events to more extreme republican elements. The new republic, redolent of the fervour of Savonarola and dedicating itself to Christ, was doomed in unequal competition. Its business aristocracy could not commit itself to the principles of equality; neither could it, disunited, resist the return of the Medici backed by the armies of Spain. This time there was no great pretence at constitutionalism. The Medici were frankly dynastic. Their perfunctory nod to the republican traditions—in 1532 Alessandro styled himself *duca della repubblica fiorentina*—was not even thin disguise. The grand duchy was not far off. Yet, when it came the great families of the *primati*, although they no longer held out hopes for the direct political control of Florence, were still rich and prospering in their many-sided interests, as land-owners, bankers, merchants and industrialists. It was a far cry from the days of old Cosimo, who had to manœuvre the organs of government in order to keep the *ottimati* in line.

Whereas the government of Florence was fluid, reacting to successive tensions within the city; the stability of the Venetian government was proverbial. Such stability became the envy of all: not only did the Savonarolan republic frame itself, with local variations, on the Venetian model; but years before Venice had been the example in the mind of Niccolò Soderini, when he led the opposition to Piero in the 1460s. If Venice occasioned envy, she also gave rise to jealousy. The Florentines might learn from her trading organisation and her constitution; they were also jubilant when she suffered reverses. There will be no attempt made here to describe the massive structure of the Venetian constitution: the principles underlying it are more important. The Venetian government had come to be monopolised by the patriciate, a class that comprehended a big range of economic levels amongst its members. Some patricians were almost poor and certainly were unable to live the lives of noblemen. Others owned considerable riches which they derived from the commercial life of the republic. Both rich and poor patricians had equal rights to all positions in the government, but it was the rich who usually occupied the key places—the Gritti, Grimani, Loredano, Malipiero, Vendramin, Pisani, Giustiniani, Contarini. Often service was costly: if it was service at home, it meant time away from profitable business; if it was service abroad, the expenses of an embassy might often outrun the grant of money allotted by the government. But the ideal of service had grown strong in Venice, and seldom was it possible for a patrician to refuse an office he was appointed to. If the government thought a man might serve the republic well by accepting a position in the Church even, little could be done to resist it. On the other hand, if a pope appointed a Venetian to a high position in the Church within Venetian territories without the permission of the republic, such a man would most certainly be banished. Because of unhappy experiences with their doges in the past, by this period the highest place in the republic had been reduced to something of a decorative function. The doges officiated over affairs of state; they met important visitors; their signatures were sometimes needed for documents of state. But the *dogado* was rather an office that outsiders might understand; a veneer of monarchy for other monarchs who were disconcerted when faced with dealing with committees or councils. It was the major councils, the Senate and the *Dieci* in particular, that governed Venice—not the doge at the head of the *Signoria* with its imposing array of members, nor the huge *Gran Consiglio*, to which belonged those of the patriciate who were qualified by age, provided they were not members of the clergy, together with a few younger men. But these councils, together with others set up for special purposes of perhaps advising on or organising trade, of administering the criminal law, of supervising the activities of the guilds, the ferries and the canals, were seldom given an absolutely free hand. There was usually cross-checking of functions and the possibility of one council delaying the actions of another. As a consequence, it had become almost impossible for a clique or an individual to gain excessive influence, and the opportunities of a man to support unpopular policies were protected by the careful preservation of secret voting in the councils. The whole system produced a responsible governing class, which usually presented a face of unanimity once issues were decided and which often resolved problems in an unpopular way to the good of the community and the maintenance of the privileged position of the patriciate. Other classes in Venice were the citizens, often tremendously rich and earning their money in similar ways to the patriciate, but disqualified from the highest offices; and the populace, not privileged in any way, working as artisans or less. If the government was stable, it was not unchanging. A crop of new magistracies arose in the sixteenth century to tackle the problems to which the changing economy, the Reformation and other new phenomena gave rise. Certainly until the seventeenth century adaptability went hand in hand with stability. But by then the ruling class was becoming ingrown; for, although there were means of revitalising the patriciate with new blood, it seems they were seldom used during this period. Yet, even so, English writers during the reign of Elizabeth, such as Lewes Lewkenor who translated Gasparo Contarini's *The Commonwealth and Government of Venice*, and the versifiers he quotes, were impressed by the justice, the lack of corruption and the freedom of Venice; and the republic remained as a constitutional exemplar for the Whig thinkers of the English Restoration.

Local government was also an important feature of this period, although with the sixteenth century it tended to undergo significant changes. In the duchy of Milan the communes still enjoyed a considerable amount of autonomy in the fifteenth century; Pavia or Cremona could be fairly said to have had internal policies of their own. Modena under the dukes of Ferrara has already been seen to have had a protracted struggle with the counts of Cesi. Aquila in Naples, Arezzo in Florence, Savona in Genoa, almost every small town in Italy had local constitutional machinery, which dealt with everyday affairs, offered office to the local citizens, decided on the overall development and organisation of the towns themselves and to varying extents of the *contado* surrounding them. It was, for example, Lodi and Parma which had called upon the Milanese government to initiate programmes of irrigation and canal-building in the local countryside. In the Venetian Terraferma, the subject cities such as Verona, Vicenza and Padua all retained in the fifteenth century a large measure of autonomy. It has already been described how Verona was still in a position to negotiate with Venice as late as 1550 regarding the quota of its meat supply to the metropolis. Indeed, it would have been impossible for the capital cities to control these often flourishing outlying towns without the use of the traditional forms of local government. The changes that took place were more in the nature of greater demands being made by the central governments in such matters as levies of taxation and supplies, than a retrenchment of the control traditional groups exercised over their own local populace. In regard to Venice, however, the sixteenth century with its great problems and challenges brought about an increase in direct control by officials sent out from the capital. The Venetian government in the fifteenth century had tended to strike up alliances with the communes of its conquered territories in order to be able to dominate the countryside with their help. This was the case with Brescia, which was allowed to send officials throughout the Bresciano much to the profit of the commune. The commune was also given certain tax exemptions and the conditions of citizenship were made stricter so that immigrants from the countryside could not easily gain the privileges of the city. As a result a close dependency between the interests of the ruling classes of Venice and Brescia was established. Such relationships between the capital and its conquered cities were important for the stability of the Terraferma during the greater part of a hundred years; but they were not strong enough always to survive the united power of the League of Cambrai. Even then, after instances of treachery amongst some of the ruling communal families, these cities generally welcomed at all levels of society a return to Venetian rule; although stronger direction was imposed from Venice itself, and plum jobs in the Terraferma began to be increasingly recognised as the perquisite of able patricians. By this time there was little alternative, for it was not to be envisaged that these cities might play off the ambitions of Milan against the dominance of Venice, a possibility that had always lent a certain moderation to the Venetian rule. Under the indirect and later the direct control of Charles V, Milan no longer offered a thinkable alternative to the rule of the most serene republic, while the Venetian exploitation of the Terraferma brought with it some of the advantages of the equitable and scrupulous rule with which patrician virtues had endowed the city of Venice itself.

One problem which faced all governments alike, monarchy or republic, state or commune, was that of the corn supply. The people had always to be at least minimally provided for; and on occasions they might well present an angry and threatening face, if a government had failed in or ignored so elementary a task. On the other hand, to fulfil such a need might be taken as tantamount to legitimising a ruler with no other claim to government but success. Thus as early as the fourteenth century a lawyer, Bartolo di Sassoferrato, could write that a ruler with a defective title might acquire sanction for his authority by exercising it for the benefit of the community. It was indeed the conscious policy of many governments during the fifteenth century increasingly to foster the gratitude of the humbler elements in their states. Government had grown introspective, less a matter of custom and routine than perhaps it had been in the past. In an age of illegitimacy, as Machiavelli was well aware, rulers had consciously to justify their position to the ruled: they could not sit back and trust to the claims of custom and of blood. Power was based on the support of other men. Lorenzo and later the Medici popes wooed the support of the Florentine *contado*; and even the humble folk of the Terraferma in the countryside, or for example at Padua during the siege of Maximilian I, appreciated the good government of Venice and were loyal during the troubled years of foreign invasion. The popes were careful to protect the people of Rome from the burdens of direct taxation and were indulgent towards their traditional acquisitiveness at the change of papal reigns. In 1459 Sante Bentivoglio could write to Francesco Sforza that it was often necessary to treat the people as one treats children and to act for their good in a way that they dislike. By 1495 Isabella d'Este, writing to Ludovico and her sister, Beatrice Sforza, had shed this paternalistic attitude. She realised it was important that the people should be aware of the advantages a ruler bestowed upon them: 'Every ruler should set greater value on the hearts of his subjects than on fortresses, money, or men-at-arms, for the discontent of the citizens is a more serious cause of war than the enemy at the gate.' The most direct way to do this was to see that all were protected from hunger. The grain policies of governments were all important, and where they failed danger was never far. Sixtus IV, who seldom found much time for the welfare of the people of Rome, took the precaution to import grain from Sicily when supplies were low, although it turned out on one occasion that he was able to preserve the grain untouched and resell it to the Genoese. Lorenzo de' Medici always tried to take good care that there was a reserve supply of good corn to cope with the periods following crop failures. Venice was a haven for the inhabitants of the Terraferma in times of food shortage, and when the commerce of Venice fell off in the sixteenth century one of the prime concerns of the government was to promote the growing of wheat. The ducal policy of supporting irrigation projects in the duchy of Milan was in large part associated with the regular supply of food. Even the communes in the duchy, such as Pavia, saw their primary task as ensuring that the grain stores of the city were always well-stocked. The rich would look after themselves with their own stocks; it was the populace at large that was the concern of governments; and schools, monasteries and hospitals were often partly taken over as places in which to store food supplies against emergencies.

The fertility of Italian constitutional ideas is strikingly similar to the resourcefulness of Italians in overcoming obstacles to the capitalistic economies of the towns. It was also a manifestation of urban needs, closely connected with the business interests of the capitalists. Ideas of liberty, notions of civic rights, although they spread downwards to the lesser citizens, were effectively restricted to financial oligarchies whenever they were practised on a major scale. This is not to say that they had no wider influence. The remaining feudal elements in Italy, for instance, especially in the north, were clearly affected by the examples of town bourgeoisies. Nobles sought to gain the privileges of the upper strata of the towns and often joined in their business activities. Places of varying importance were also found in the constitutions of the cities for members of lesser guilds and artisans. But the dominant class in the various republican and communal governments was undoubtedly that which had obtained economic eminence in the commercial activities in which Italians had learnt to excel. When this economic activity declined in relation to that of western Europe, influence tended to move back into the hands of the owners of the land. This did not always involve a change in the personnel who were powerful. As has been shown, the Venetian patrician and the capitalistic speculator of Milan both ended up as country gentlemen. Likewise members of the Florentine oligarchy had provided themselves with landed estates and were the forebears of the grand ducal, country property-owners. The Genoese, who had not the land to develop, on the other hand remained a race of businessmen, although even for Liguria the tendency was for the old feudatories to increase their share of power. Where the land began to predominate again, it was only in Venice that the landowner and patrician retained direct political power, for the pattern elsewhere was for the growth of autocratic rule: Spanish rule in Milan and Naples, Savoyard rule in Piedmont, the grand dukes in Florence, the popes in the Papal States—all, with or without important bureaucratic elements, asserted a more or less absolute control over their territories. Political liberty had been to a great extent liberty to exploit a capitalistic economy. When this was no longer virile the pressure for constitutional power waned, and Italy tended to retreat into a period of ambitionless submission to the authority of individuals.

7
History, Political Thought and Language

Much of the literary energy of the fifteenth century was directed towards the rediscovery of classical literature, not only in the sense of finding hitherto lost works but also of purifying the texts of works known only in a corrupt version during the Middle Ages. Up to the middle of the century most of this work was concerned with the Latin classics; whereas, later, Greek literature played at least an equally prominent part in these scholarly activities. Hence two exciting new cultures broadened vastly and almost suddenly the field of learning and the range of intellectual stimuli with which men were confronted. Furthermore, the collation of texts with a view to finding the best reading sharpened the tools of criticism, so that they could be used in other spheres. That these newly revealed literatures were in the main secular in spirit gave them the power to appeal to wider audiences and so led to a quantitative development—almost a popularisation—in reading, even before the impact of the press was felt. In such a situation—where there was hardly the time to digest so great a mass of unfamiliar material—misjudgment, misunderstanding and prejudice were bound to occur; yet, in the process of eliminating these misconceptions, a great deal that was entirely new and rewarding emerged. Often it seemed that the achievements of the classical civilisations were so great that nothing greater could be attained: Cicero had written Latin perfectly; Plato's philosophy, reinterpreted in the light of Christian revelation, said all. This could not but have a slowing-up effect on original thinking and creative activity; but in another way it led, often surprisingly for those concerned, to discovery and advances beyond the limits of classical knowledge and achievements, when faults or limitations in a sacrosanct authority were stumbled upon and reluctantly admitted. This was especially so in the fields of scientific inquiry and the visual arts, which will be dealt with in later chapters; but it also occurred in other areas of interest.

Petrarch is usually taken as the starting-point in the revival of classical literature, in the Ciceronianism of the stylists and in the enthusiasm for

Plato. As a superb poet in the vernacular, with Dante and Boccaccio, he was certainly influential in the development of a vernacular, literary language. There was a vast body of classical literature, especially Latin, known and read widely during the Middle Ages. What occurred with Petrarch was the emergence of a new attitude towards it. The treatment of the *Metamorphoses* by the author of the *Ovide Moralisée* draws out the story of Theseus and Ariadne, for instance, with long, inessential trivialities, and contemporary, mediaeval values such as *cortoisie*, *hardiesce* or *valour* are read into the character of Theseus. Added to this, there is the inevitable allegorical interpretation: the labyrinth becomes a symbol of hell; the minotaur is the devil; the tribute the loss of spiritual immortality, which is not regained until Theseus (Christ) makes his voyage from Athens to Crete. Ariadne and Phaedra become the Jews and the Gentiles respectively; the unions of the sisters with Theseus represent the Chosen People and their desertion, when Ariadne falls asleep, and the foundation of the Church amongst the Gentiles. Ariadne's reawakening by Bacchus (God) is projected into the future: the Jews could regain immortality by a reconciliation with the true God and true religion. Petrarch's attitude to the classics could not be further from this. Whereas mediaeval writers read Ovid as though he lived and wrote in the same world of ideas as their own, Petrarch was poignantly aware, for example in his letter to Livy, of the distance of time that separated him from the Roman historian, a distance filled by a deep cultural gloom. Petrarch was also conscious of his cultural kinship with the classical world and his distance in another sense therefore from his contemporaries. The revelation of classical literature did not, however, lead Petrarch in any way to a complete surrender to classical culture. He believed that the personality of the individual should emerge from all writings, and openly condemned imitators, even imitators of Cicero. 'I do not imitate Cicero. I rather try to do the contrary, not wanting to be an imitator of anybody and fearing to become what I disapprove in others.' Foremost he was a Christian, and if he was influenced by any writer more than another it was St Augustine, whose writings infused the Middle Ages with sadness and despair, with the conviction of the transitory and doomful nature of worldly existence. Yet he did not always share this aspect of the Augustinian mentality, or he was rescued from it by his musings on the survival of the classics: the notion of fame such as had been brought to Livy or Cicero through their literary achievement gave him a consciousness of the future into which his own—more serious—Latin writings might survive. The laurel, the poet's laurel he himself wore—lightning-proof, evergreen, its leaves preserving books from decay—symbolised an immortality he hoped to achieve and which would have been meaningless to those sharing the chiliastic notions of the Middle Ages. On the other hand, Petrarch could assert: 'Happier by far is one of those feeble ones who believe in Thee, than Plato, Aristotle, Varro and Cicero, who with all their knowledge knew not Thee'; or: 'any pious old woman was—I will not say more subtle but happier in her recognition of true happiness' than Aristotle. Petrarch was selective in his admiration of the classics; and Aristotle, who had influenced so deeply the scholastics Petrarch attacked, and of course his own Averroist critics, was not included among his chosen. Plato and Cicero crowned his list, and he quoted Seneca, not a Christian, to make the point: 'A man of letters! Let us be content with a more rustic title: a good man.' But Petrarch himself was primarily a man of letters, and this explains the lack of system and the lack of consistency in his thought. His contribution to the world of ideas was in the nature of insights, the full significance of which he did not himself work out.

The work in the tradition of Petrarch of men like Poggio Bracciolini, seeking out forgotten texts in the monastic libraries of Europe, and Leonardo Bruni or Lorenzo Valla, with their critical approach to variant readings in corrupt copies of classical texts, had important implications in the study of history. Chroniclers had written mainly to illustrate the working out of the divine will or, in the case of Florence especially, to glorify their commune. They were criticised by Giovanni da Prato at the end of the fourteenth century—not altogether justly—for not making use of contemporary documents and reliable sources. Later, Leonardo Bruni in his account of the history of Florence certainly was aware of the pitfalls of accepting popular traditions and legends too easily: he used critically a mass of sources for his own times and, even in his account of the origins of Florence, he was sound in his treatment of popular and generally accepted notions. Petrarch, by his contrast between the greatness of classical culture and the long ensuing periods of cultural barbarism, also struck at the teleological periodisation of the Christian chroniclers. Bruni agreed that his own times were in 'a state of darkness and ignorance', but worked out a five-period schema of his own. The Florentines, as their own state was a republic, looked to the republican period of Rome, its days of liberty, as their example. Thus the first period was that of the Roman Republic. This was followed by the Roman Empire, the period of the barbarian invasions, the empire of Charlemagne and, finally, the age of factions and division within the communes. The importance of such a view of history was that it arose out of a close scrutiny of the facts and was not a superimposed pattern to which events were made to conform. It was a step towards accepting the lessons of history and towards a more objective view of the past.

The growth of an attitude towards classical antiquity which aimed at understanding it in its own terms, and of a view of the post-classical period as a barbaric age of darkness, opened up new possibilities of periodisation. Boccaccio regarded Dante as the first great poet after the classical period, and Filippo Villani claimed that there was no poetry between Claudian and Dante. The Florentine sculptor, Ghiberti, believed that the destruction of antique art had accompanied the spread of Christianity, and that Giotto had rediscovered methods buried for some 600 years enabling him to abandon the crudeness of the 'Greeks', that is of Byzantine art. Bruni himself asserted that Petrarch with his classical, literary style had shown the way to overcome barbarism and now after 700 years men were about to emerge from darkness. Poggio felt himself standing on the brink of a brilliant future as he and others enjoyed the enlightened patronage of Nicholas V; while Matteo Palmieri, yet another Florentine writer, saw Giotto, Bruni and representatives of the other arts as having effected a transformation so that the thoughtful should be thankful to God 'to be born in this new age, so full of hope and promise, which already rejoices in a greater array of nobly-gifted souls than the world has seen in the thousand years that have preceded it'. Leon Battista Alberti's judgment was: 'As learning was lacking in Italy, people became vulgar in speech and ignorant of Latin and a crude era ensued. It was only fifty or perhaps sixty years ago that men's minds were sharpened and awakened.' All these judgments were related to developments in the arts and literature, in which there was a conscious renascence of classical culture or an ending of the barbarities of past Christian culture. There was no indication that a new age in any political sense had begun or was about to begin. Even Machiavelli in the sixteenth century (although later his position will be shown to have been ambivalent) believed recent history to be contemptible, whilst the ancients ought to be imitated. The term, *Medium Aevum*, did not emerge until its use by Christoph Keller in the later part of the seventeenth century, when he used the periods of antiquity, the Middle Ages and modernity explicitly for the first time. This is easy to explain: the new age was not the age of Italy, even less that of Florence. Italians might dream of a political greatness, emulating that of Rome; but beyond the limits of literature, the arts and, maybe, science they could never think it had arrived. The political future of Europe lay outside Italy and it was therefore developments elsewhere, especially in the France of Louis XIV, that gave rise to an attitude of confident modernity which politically could detach itself from a mediaeval past.

The idea that history served as a source of examples upon which present actions might be based, especially when this was applied to the exemplary events of classical history, came very close to the growing habit of citing the classical authors as authorities. What Cicero wrote and what Brutus did were both equally taken to be admirable and therefore to be imitated. In the world of action the sphere of the exemplary was ethical and the great men who did good won immortality from their fame in history. 'Good' in republican Florence was usually connected with the successful leaders of republican Rome, whereas in the monarchical duchy of Milan it was related to the great figures of imperial Rome. This is partly true of the Florentine chancellor, Coluccio Salutati, who took the study of the history of the Roman republic to be a foundation upon which a theory of political action could be built. He applauded the republican virtues of Rome; and, if he justified Dante consigning Brutus to the lowest pit of hell with that other traitor to his master, Judas, he also blamed Caesar for introducing cruelty to Rome. Salutati's view of what was admirable in the past was perhaps not so limited as that of his successors as chancellor, Bruni and Bracciolini: 'examples of kings, nations, and illustrious men can either be equalled or exceeded by imitating them'. Clearly the past had not achieved insurmountable perfection either: the virtues of its great could be surpassed. Rome had not therefore achieved the ideal. Bruni was less equivocal concerning the greatness of republican Rome and defended the claims to greatness of Scipio and the republic against those of Caesar and the empire; but in setting up the former as an example to be followed he made no allowance for the historical differences between the societies of Rome and Florence. Nor did Poggio Bracciolini, who also defended Scipio, on this occasion against the attack of Guarino da Verona, who at Ferrara under the mantle of the ruling family of Este had no particular penchant towards republicanism. Poggio illustrates well the parallelism between the authority of classical example in action and thought: man was ennobled through the imitation of antique virtues; he won fame and prestige through immersing himself in classical culture. Yet, with Poggio, the republicanism of the Florentine writers was already becoming rather shallow: he praised Cosimo as the bulwark of democracy and dedicated a work to King Alfonso of Aragon. Cosimo himself tolerated this literary republicanism, but after his death in 1464 political writings virtually ceased in Florence until their revival at the turn of the century.

Certainly it was unrealistic in the Laurentian period for writers to turn too enthusiastically towards republican ideals if they hoped to enjoy the favours of Lorenzo. Moreover, the growing popularity of Plato diverted the interests of the intellectuals towards very different ideas and ideals from those of writers who had cherished the works of Cicero and Livy above all. Political thinking became more the concern of men of affairs. Recalcitrant members of the *ottimati* looked to more recent history in order to contemplate their lost influence and to justify their demands for its return with notions of equality and liberty drawn from pre-Medicean days. Their ideals were aristocratic rather than republican in emphasis, and above all they desired stability. Venice therefore became more relevant than Rome. But the whole of history was by now fair game, for what had happened was a development in the idea of taking history as an example. In the early fifteenth century the view was held that examples of great men might inspire emulation, examples of great political systems, imitated, might lead to the achievement of similar successes. By 1500 a new, more sophisticated view of history was emerging: history was scrutinised in order to discern the laws underlying human action, to find out what consequences would follow different courses of action. After the disturbances, the setbacks, the instability of the Savonarolan republic, the *primati* continued to look to Venice as an ideal; but they also turned back to the days of Lorenzo with a nostalgic yearning and they even revived the old glorification of Rome. At the same time they were no longer simply prepared to imitate; they tried to analyse why certain types of government, at certain times and in certain places, had been successful. They also tried to analyse why others had failed. In so doing they opened up all history as a useful study and not simply that which had produced societies and governments worthy of imitation. In the *pratiche*, which have already been mentioned, the speakers constantly referred to history, pointing out that various steps had been taken in the past—especially the more recent past— and they had led to this or that outcome. These Florentine *ottimati* were feeling their way towards a notion of historical causality. However, they also believed in the distilled wisdom of authorities: they cited the Bible; classical authors, especially Aristotle's *Politics*; and the customary saws of common speech. Again the twin processes of learning from the past examples of action and from the authoritative statements of the wise were employed, and in this instance they were employed by men engaged in the serious business of advising on policies to be pursued by a government.

This new view of history and its relationship to the practicalities of political action found its first mature and self-conscious expression in the works of Machiavelli. Machiavelli normally set up republican Rome as exemplary and recent events in Italy and especially in Florence as examples from which it was possible to discern what not to do. Clearly a detailed scrutiny of history would not bear so bald a distinction. Accordingly Machiavelli brought in other elements to modify this view such as the necessity of the times, the whims of fortune, the inevitable processes of history. ∮The weakness of the first two of these concepts in particular was that they were open to completely arbitrary use: if some event was seen to be inconsistent with and inexplicable by the broad interpretative apparatus of Machiavelli, it was simple enough to assert that fortune had intervened. Machiavelli openly stated that half our actions were determined by such intervention. This was no more than to say that half of the consequences of our actions were inexplicable. So, wherever success was achieved by non-classical methods or failure was brought about by adherence to a classical prototype, fortune was invoked to explain away the discrepancy. This was the method Machiavelli used to account for the successful outcome of the impetuous policies of Julius II. Conversely, fortune conspired against Cesare Borgia with remarkable malignity and brought about his downfall. The necessity of the times was also used to explain away inconsistencies. Machiavelli believed that similar actions taking place in similar conditions would bring about similar results: what had been successful in the past, if the conditions were re-created, could be brought about again. He justified his use of the example of Rome on such grounds. Roman methods were more appropriate for Italians than for others, because the greatness of Rome originated in Italy. They were appropriate to Florence, because Florence was also a republic, with a tradition of what Machiavelli called equality. But conditions in his own Italy hardly reflected those of republican Rome. Methods had therefore to be used to alter them so that eventually modern Italy might emulate ancient Rome. The necessity of the times limited the possible field of effective action. Machiavelli's desperate solution was the emergence of a tyrannical law-giver, who would be prepared to adopt extreme measures such as those of Cesare Borgia in order to force his will on Italy, and, having done so, would be willing to hand on his dictatorially-ordered state to a republican government based on the example of the Roman republic. With the Papacy and Florence under the control of the Medici, he looked to that family for such a leader, especially to Leo X; but he did not believe that any man could be so bad as to be able to carry out such harsh policies as were needed to impose his will in this way and, yet, at the same time be so good as to pass on his achievements to a republican organisation. The time's necessity had thus brought about an impasse which led Machiavelli to believe that the destiny of Italy was to become submerged in foreign occupation.

The third method Machiavelli used to extricate himself from the difficulties presented by the intractable facts of history, and which was closely associated with his notion of the necessity of the times, was the theory of Polybius concerning historical cycles. There was a process whereby each political situation held within it the elements of its own corruption and would lead to the point where there was only one possible solution. The new solution would ultimately be undermined, and so on, until the cycle returned to its original position, when the process would begin all over again. Kingship would decline into tyranny and be replaced by the government of the best, which would become divided, corrupted and then overthrown. A democracy would be set up in its place and become corrupted in turn into a state of popular licence, which was only ended by a return to monarchy. The cycle in Machiavelli's view was seldom completed, for states were not usually strong enough to survive the successive turmoils that such processes involved. This was a further reason for Machiavelli believing that in the long run it was more likely for Italy to succumb to foreign invasion than emerge in a state of Roman greatness. Rome itself had possessed this quality of being able to survive changes of fortune and internal conflicts and still become great. These historical processes were irreversible: all human effort could achieve was the slowing down or speeding up of the stages of the cycle. Those who understood correctly the necessity of the times could intervene to do this, but they could do no more. This dynamic view of history contrasts strikingly with the static ideals of Florentine *ottimati* such as Bernardo Rucellai.

Rucellai was responsible for founding meetings of Florentine intellectuals in the gardens, the *Orti Oricellari*, which he put at their disposal. These meetings discussed literary, philosophical, political and historical problems and ideas, and in their early days they idealised the Laurentian era, while deploring Medicean tendencies towards absolutism. The members of these gatherings were also particularly interested in the workings of the Venetian constitution. Theirs were in fact the same ideas as were often expounded in the *pratiche*, which is not surprising since some of the members took part in both. Machiavelli could not, even had he been so disposed, have shared the hope to return to the situation as it was in Lorenzo's time. His acceptance of inevitable destinies in history would have at least made, in his terms, such an immediate hope vain. Yet there is much to be said for the views put forward in the gardens, especially in relation to Venice. Venice had remained comparatively stable through many centuries; its political organisation could therefore claim to have been successful, and it did not appear to be subject to dynamic forces or corruption and subsequent change in the way Machiavelli claimed all states were. This had also been true of Sparta. Machiavelli, who hated Venice, blinded himself to all the evidence before him and, by making expansion one of the criteria of success and claiming that Venice and Sparta could not expand, ruled out these republics from having anything positive to teach. But the average Florentine citizens, even the *primati*, were not particularly interested in expansion. They wanted a stable and unmolested government under which they could carry on their businesses and enjoy the responsibilities and privileges of office. In the second decade of the sixteenth century, when the *Orti Oricellari* enjoyed the patronage of Cosimo Rucellai, Machiavelli was himself one of its members, and during this period the members held a greater variety of views than before. Under the restored Medici they were frankly opposed to the power of that family; but there were still members such as Antonio Brucioli who had strong sympathies towards a Venetian-type constitution. It was probably also at this time that Machiavelli by way of one of the members, Janus Lascaris, first met the cyclical theory of Polybius contained in his sixth book, so that the static view of history generally adhered to in the gardens met a challenge. Also in 1522 a plot to overthrow the Medici was hatched from within this group. One member, Zanobi Buondelmonte, was executed and another, the poet Luigi Alamanni, was forced into exile. The common element of the group was therefore its anti-Medicean sympathies or its republicanism; but even here Machiavelli does not quite fit in, with his hope that perhaps the Medici might cast themselves in the rôle of saviours of Italy by establishing a tyranny and handing over a peaceful state to republican institutions.

The other great Florentine political thinker and historian of the period was Francesco Guicciardini. Himself of the *ottimati*, he was more in sympathy with the general views expressed in the *Orti Oricellari*, of which he was not a member, than was Machiavelli, a citizen not of the rank of the great *ottimati*. Where Machiavelli saw necessity and inevitable processes in history, Guicciardini saw less stringent, natural tendencies. Machiavelli believed that the historic forces should be consciously used; Guicciardini counselled submission to the tendencies of history. So, whereas Machiavelli would wish great leaders to steer the forces of history and aim at ultimately establishing their ideals, Guicciardini, believing change to be the result of human action (able or stupid), as well as of mere accident and fate, wished his leaders to accept the *status quo*, whatever it may have been, and within its limits work for the best. Too often were the results of action irrational and unpredictable for great ideals to be achieved. Perhaps this made Guicciardini the abler historian and the sounder thinker. Whilst Machiavelli related history to broad, general principles of interpretation, Guicciardini was careful in detail and subtle and complicated in its explanation. Machiavelli was impatient for great men to execute great programmes, whilst sad in frustration at nothing being achieved. Guicciardini, also sadly aware of the failure of Italy, limited himself to the possible and worked for smaller adjustments that might at least render her position more bearable. Yet most Florentine thinkers of this period, when they turned their minds to history and politics—despite a great divergence of opinion in other respects—held in common the belief that history had lessons to teach the politician; and practising politicians looked to history with great diligence that they might become wiser in their craft.

It is pertinent to ask how seriously a man like Machiavelli took the examples of history, whether he searched history in order to derive from it sound principles of political action; or was it that he simply sought illustrations to give authority to ideas he had gained through other means? The answer, like most answers to such questions, would lie somewhere between the extremes. It is hard to believe that Machiavelli really thought that lessons could be learnt from mythical figures such as Romulus and Numa; yet he makes great play with their stories. On the other hand Machiavelli would have had no such doubts about Cesare Borgia, whom he had met personally, nor of many other figures and events from contemporary history and from Livy's account of republican Rome. One might therefore take his use of most history as a serious attempt to derive laws from the experience of the past. At the same time his prejudices obtruded. This has already been noticed in the modern examples of Julius II and Cesare Borgia; it is no less apparent when he discussed the events narrated by Livy. A case in point is his discussion of the relative merits of the generals, Manlius Torquatus and Valerius Corvinus. Machiavelli agreed that both generals had equal success under the same conditions, Manlius employing the harshest of methods, Valerius on the contrary being friendly, polite, almost gentle with his men. This was too much for the Florentine, and he went on to make further distinctions which had nothing to do with the ethic of success implied in his use of history. Manlius' methods, Machiavelli asserted, were suited to the interests of a republic; for his harshness would not give rise to partisanship and his actions could not be interpreted in any way as furthering his own cause—he even killed his own son in order to gain respect and discipline from his troops. Valerius, on the other hand, by securing the goodwill of his troops might well have put himself in such a position that he would have overthrown the republican institutions and set up a tyranny. His actions were therefore potentially prejudicial to a republic but suited to a prince, whereas the converse was true of those of Manlius. But it is clear that these conclusions were not the lessons of history: on Machiavelli's admission the conduct of Valerius and Manlius turned out to be equally valuable to the Roman republic. Machiavelli had gone beyond history and imposed upon it his own views about human nature, drawn from his experience of contemporary events, in order to modify an unacceptable lesson that in his own terms history clearly taught.

The growth in the interest of history was by no means confined to the Florentines, although it was in Florence that most of the new and fruitful ideas emerged. Vespasiano da Bisticci, the Florentine scribe, bookseller and librarian, who wrote the lives of the famous people of his time, suggested that many potentially famous men of the past were not known, simply because the stories of their lives or the histories of their states had not been written. Much history was written in Italy from the middle of the fifteenth century in order to glorify the deeds of the states concerned, and there emerged the habit of commissioning official histories. Thus Lodovico Sforza commissioned Corio's history, and there was a series of Venetian official histories in the sixteenth century including those of Pietro Bembo and Paolo Paruta. History also became apologetics: Simonetta's account of the achievements of Francesco Sforza or Poliziano's version of the Pazzi conspiracy fall into this category. Platina's *Lives of the Popes* on the other hand was in some respects exactly the opposite, an anti-papal document in which he especially enjoyed releasing his spleen on Paul II, at whose hands he had suffered imprisonment. Fame, propaganda and obloquy were thus commonly accepted functions of history; and historical fame became so cherished that an ambassador could seriously offer it as an enticement to a government to follow a particular policy. Such was the case with Pietro Pasqualigo, when he recounted the fame Manuel I of Portugal might win should he help the Venetians in their war against the Turks.

Fame implied merit, merit a rationality underlying human actions; therefore one of the central problems of historical thinkers at the time was to gauge to what extent man could influence events by his own rational action, or to decide how far he was subjected to intangible forces. By and large, belief in the efficacy of reason was common before the foreign invasions of Italy. Thereafter, there was an increasing recognition of the intractability of historical forces, although these were often conceived in a very naïve manner. The notion that civic virtue went hand in hand with the healthy life of a city-state was central to the judgments of Leonardo Bruni, who was very much under the influence of Aristotle's *Politics*. Bruni claimed that promotion to office under republican Rome was based on such virtue or merit. He therefore deplored the intermittent Florentine practice of election by lot, whereby selection according to merit was replaced by a process of chance. Virtue was a product of reason and experience, just like the Aristotelian notion of prudence, the quality of being able to bring actions successfully to a required conclusion; and experience was given another dimension by adding to it the store of experience in history. This faith in the power of man to control his own affairs was widespread. Gianozzo Manetti believed that man could improve upon the crudity of nature in all walks of life; and Leon Battista Alberti asserted man's power to govern his own destiny, to re-create the greatness of the past, to exceed it, even, by being original and using his ingenuity. The Greeks, however, brought into Italy a fatalistic strain: Michaelos Apostolis, stunned by the events he had witnessed in his homeland, introduced the notion of cycles in history, believing that Greece was at the lowest point, but that Italy was about to reach a peak. But the Florentine Platonists did not accept such causal determinism and a belief in the inflexibility of fate in its entirety. Ficino, for instance, admitted that the body was subject to the forces of destiny; but he allowed complete freedom to the spirit, so that it could overcome such pressures. He described man 'as if born to rule' and claimed that he might even make the heavens if only he had the materials and the tools. This almost limitless power of man was also emphasised by Pico della Mirandola, who claimed man could become 'as though God', although the process he described for achieving this was a variety of sympathetic magic. Nevertheless, the point to be made is that these writers of the fifteenth century had generally an overwhelming confidence in the potential achievements of man, and those who had a political turn of mind believed that men of ability could and should be allowed to use their powers for the good government of their state.

But just after the invasion of Charles VIII the Neapolitan writer, Giovanni Pontano, emphasised the forces that limited man's power to organise his own future: the unpredictability of war, the intervention of disease or bad weather, the unaccountable behaviour of individuals. Reason could not cope with such impalpable factors and so, remembering the practices of ancient Rome related by Livy, he counselled that presages, oracles, visions and sacrifices might make up for man's deficiencies. At the same time the Christian view of providence tended to regain currency, especially with the prophesyings and admonitions of Savonarola. When Charles VIII descended into Italy, a predicted scourge, many were convinced that there was little men could do to deflect such forces beyond looking after their personal salvation. Optimism tended to give way to pessimism, confidence in man to a feeling that he was inadequate. Even the cultured and level-headed *ottimati* of the *pratiche* admitted the limits of reason and began to speak freely of necessity, fortune and providence. Machiavelli and Guicciardini refined these views; and the former, more hopeful, if with the hope of desperation, developed his description of *virtù*—the quality of a relentless resolution to put into effect rational calculations based upon experience and historical example—as a human attribute that might at least be employed to modify the forces of destiny. It was only in Venice that Italians continued to have full confidence in the efficacy of rational political action. There, with the Aristotelianism of the university at Padua to influence them, they still felt a deep respect for the quality of prudence they examined in the *Nichomachean Ethics*. The Venetians were perhaps justified, because theirs alone of all the secular states of Italy came through the foreign invasions to retain any reality of independence and importance.

The political ideals of liberty and equality in Italy dated back especially to the mediaeval days of the communes, but they were intensified by wide reading of the history of republican Rome. Liberty, according to the varying histories of the region, signified some form of popular or fairly broadly based government. It was not envisaged that it implied a significant participation by the masses in government, but it was rather restricted to a more or less middle-class citizenship. Even in this office-holding rather than policy-making was the general aim, and offices tended to be scaled in suitability according to class. Where there was general admission to the rights of citizenship for the whole, male, native population, as in Genoa, there was seldom a suggestion that all citizens should have equal political rights. Except for the brief success of the 1506 revolt, the *cappette*, the working-class as opposed to the artisans and small traders, had no direct influence on the government whatsoever. Equality applied to the same limited section of the population. It meant equality under the laws and freedom from oppression. Yet these words, especially in Florence where political concepts were most keenly examined and refined, had highly emotive overtones and appealed beyond the limits of those who might reasonably expect to profit from their realisation. Philippe de Commynes, a French envoy in Italy on several occasions, was amazed at the effect the cry '*libertà e popolo*' had on the general populace. It could become a powerful weapon, as Savonarola demonstrated when he worked up animus against the Medici and helped to launch a broader-based régime. But politically the ordinary person did not profit; and in practice it often happened that the Machiavellian dictum that a tyrant must satisfy the people, when put into effect as often it was, proved to be to greater popular advantage than more liberal régimes. Guicciardini discerned the cant behind these exciting ideals: 'Amongst the enemies of tyranny there are few who act merely out of love of the liberty of their country. To these the highest praise is due, the more so as it is the rarer.' Guicciardini in this sceptical mood suggested that no realisation of equality could be maintained. In a state of equality the stronger or more able would come to the top, office-holders would become greedy for more offices and power, corruption would lead to inequality. This was a dynamic view of human affairs close to the mechanism of Machiavelli's Polybian cycles, a defeatism and pessimism that is far from the attitude of the old Florentine chancellors, Salutati and Bruni, who made almost a theme-song of their limited concepts of liberty and equality.

Republicanism that looked back to the example of ancient Rome was common also in the Holy City, but after the temporary success that forced Eugenius IV into a few years' exile it became largely a matter of intellectual fashion. There seems to have been little chance that the conspiracy of Stefano Porcari against Nicholas V might have succeeded; and Paul II was excessive in his punishment of the puerile plotting and threats of Platina and Pomponio Leto. Another side of such political idealism was the growth and practice of tyrannicide. Brutus was the classic example, and it was his example that inspired the successful assassination of Galeazzo Maria Sforza in 1476. But murder was generally a political expedient rather than an ideal. For instance, the deaths of Galeotto Manfredi and Girolamo Riario in 1488 were connected with the struggle for power in Romagna amongst the petty tyrants, backed up by powerful sympathies from the larger Italian states. They were not the result of popular ambition or of the romantic idealism of the admirers of the classics. Again it was Venice where an Italian idea survived in the sixteenth century. But new conditions gave a new connotation to the word 'liberty'. Liberty came to mean freedom from outside interference, from the invading foreigners and from the long arm of the Church. As the Venetian constitution and its stability were admired by foreigners, so was the religious liberty of Venice, especially by those who sought a place of refuge from persecution as in the case of Jews and Protestants, or from foreign invasion as in the case of the Greek Orthodox. This liberty was in the

main a result of economic necessity, especially after the Lutheran reformation had begun, when Venice's commercial interests lay predominantly outside the Catholic world—with Muslims, Orthodox and
Protestants. Venice was able to provide an atmosphere of partial tolerance
in a Christendom that was accepting increasingly the view that not more
than one church could exist within the borders of any state. In this respect
the Venetian notion of liberty was more modern than that cherished by the
Florentine chancellors and about which Guicciardini was so sceptical.

A much-discussed question during this period was whether it was better
to take an active part in political life or to withdraw into a life of study or,
as the question was sometimes posed, a life of religious contemplation. The
disputes took the form of a discussion about the superiority of *otium* or
negotium, the *vita contemplativa* or the *vita attiva*. While Petrarch, who
discussed this like so many other problems that occupied his successors,
came down on the side of *otium*, the Florentine chancellors, as would be
expected from the nature of their employment, strongly opposed withdrawal from active affairs, despite their conviction of the desirability of
studying classical letters. It has been from time to time suggested that
investment in landed property and the building of country houses by the
urban rich was related to the triumph of the *otium* ideal. Enough has been
said concerning this process to show that in Milan it developed out of an
economic trend related to highly profitable speculative possibilities and
that in Venice it was the result of an enforced change in the economy. In
Genoa the development never really occurred: the rich simply had
suburban homes which were in particular healthy retreats for the summer
months. But in Florence there might well have been some element of this
sort of idealism attached to landed investment. It should always be
remembered, however, that although investment in land did not yield a
great profit it was generally regarded as safe and it largely coincided with a
period of decreasing investment opportunities. The Florentine liked to
diversify his interests, and there was no reason why land should not have
been one element in such diversification. Finally, while the Neo-Platonists
of Florence were pointing out the aristocratic nature of their culture and
the need for wealth and leisure to be able to pursue contemplation to its
highest perfection, the men who bought up land tended to be actively
engaged in office and, if anything, opposed to the cession of political power
to the Medici. Connected with this dispute were the educational ideals
which emerged from the schools of Guarino da Verona and Vittorino da
Feltre who taught at Ferrara and Mantua respectively. They both aimed
at producing men who, by developing their minds and their bodies equally,

were fit for carrying out the social duties their state might require of them. The *vita attiva* was clearly their aim; but they saw no conflict between the refinement of the intellect and service to the state. This had already been practically recognised in Florence by the choice of her chancellors from Salutati onwards; and the typical Italian ambassador was to be drawn from men of such qualities. The supreme statement of this educational ideal was to be made by Castiglione in *Il Cortegiano*. Men should develop their great variety of potentialities in harmony, not only to use them in serving their governments, but also because they were desirable accomplishments in themselves. This recognition of an education—valuable in itself, yet at the same time of service to the state—was perhaps nowhere more accepted than amongst the Venetian patriciate, which was generally educated at Padua from the 1460s onwards as a preparation to a career of service. Here the distinguished patricians would gather together in academies or in private palaces and discuss Aristotle, art, mathematics or questions of principle underlying political problems, never regarding their own education as ending, enjoying their culture and believing it to be useful. They did not, however, give up the debate concerning the active and the contemplative life. Two notable dialogues on the subject were produced by Sperone Speroni and Paolo Paruta, both of whom chose well-known ecclesiastics of their time, Gasparo Contarini and Daniele Barbaro, to defend subtly and without overemphasis the supremacy of the active life to which both had been devoted as Venetian ambassadors, before—as an act of service to their state—they entered the Church. A complete embodiment of the educational ideals of a century of Italian thought was thus accomplished in the Venetian ruling circles by the middle of the sixteenth century.

Lay educational ideals such as these obviously grew out of the expanding interest in the literature of the classical world; but, if they were largely imitative in origin, they had become infinitely more complex and original by the time Padua and Venice won a position of leadership in western culture in the middle years of the sixteenth century. Even the slavish Ciceronianism of some fifteenth-century writers was not altogether sterile; for it drew scholarly minds to a minute study of texts, which led in turn to the refinement of the techniques of textual criticism. Petrarch himself had been greatly concerned to discover the exact words that Cicero had used, and the effort to establish correct readings not only of Cicero but also of other Latin authors became increasingly the preoccupation of writers and scholars. Such historico-philological advances led to a fruitful re-evaluation of Latin literature and was even transferred to other spheres as, for instance, with the brilliant criticism of the Donation of Constantine by Lorenzo Valla. Perhaps the most significant development in this period was the tremendous growth of a knowledge of classical Greek and the opening up of a huge, almost dormant literature to a wide public by men already highly equipped in the critical techniques of their time.

Greek literature was mainly known to the mediaeval scholar through Latin translations and summaries and through its influence on Arab thinkers whose works had been translated into Latin. There was some knowledge of classical Greek in the Latin world during the Middle Ages not only in Italy, but in France, England and elsewhere. The exact extent of this is uncertain; but it is clear that, in so far as Greek writers were a force in shaping the dominant thought of the Catholic world, it was by way of corrupt versions of their work acquired often by a devious route through the mediation of the Muslims. Petrarch, who honoured Plato from a position of ignorance, made a lame attempt to acquire Greek, and in Florence Greek was taught at the university by the Calabrian, Leontius Pilatus, as early as 1360 and later in the century by Manuel Chrysoloras. Traditional views about the revival of Greek still hold good; and the most significant steps forward clearly came with the Council of Florence, when Greek scholars came to Italy to discuss the union of the Greek and Latin churches, and with the Turkish advances in south-eastern Europe, which led to the refuge of several Greek scholars in Italy. It was Florence again that took the lead with the formation of the Platonic Academy which was founded under the patronage of Cosimo de' Medici and guided by his protégé, Marsilio Ficino. This initiated a period in which the study of Plato and the Neo-Platonists became the primary activity of the leading Florentine thinkers. The old problems associated with Cicero and Livy, although they survived as influences in the thinking of practical politicians, no longer played a central part in the interests of the intelligentsia. This was in part due to the Medicean patronage of learning; for, especially under Lorenzo, it was hardly prudent to theorise freely about forms of government, liberty, equality and other matters, which might in some way be taken as a criticism of the prevailing régime. It was also due to the need to assimilate an attitude to the world which was fresh, revealing and fully worked out in a great and hitherto virtually unknown literature. Much of the intellectual effort of the time was therefore expended in exploring the implications of Platonism for Christian thought and in establishing the relationship between the philosophies of Plato and Aristotle.

Florence did not have a monopoly of Greek studies. Cardinal Bessarion, one of the Greeks who had come to Italy for the Council of Florence and remained at Rome after it was clear that the union of the churches was not going to work, gathered around him a number of the refugees from the Turk. These included Argyropoulos, who held the Florentine chair of Greek from 1456, Theodore of Gaza, Michaelos Apostolis and George of Trebizond. But Eugenius IV, who had been in exile in Florence and had got to know the circle of Florentine writers of the time, and Nicholas V, who had also stayed in Florence and mixed with similar circles, both encouraged Italians as well to popularise the writings of the Greeks, especially by translation into Latin. Thus Italians, like Bruni, Bracciolini, Valla, Platina and Manetti were brought into contact with the Greek exiles; and, although the Greeks criticised the Greek of the Italians, and the Italians the Latin of the Greeks, the contact was clearly of advantage to both groups. There was not, however, a continuous development of Greek studies at Rome as there was in Florence for the rest of the century; and Rome had to wait for a Florentine pope, Leo X, before Greek studies became really dominant there. In 1514, three of the 80 chairs at Rome were for the Greek language. In 1516 a Greek school was set up in Rome under Janus Lascaris, and a plan was developed by Leo and Lascaris to set up similar schools at Florence and Milan. Meanwhile in Padua a chair of Greek was founded in 1463 and was first occupied by Demetrius Chalcon-dyles, who later held the chair at Florence. By 1497 a chair for the study of Aristotle in Greek was established at Padua, reflecting the Venetian tendency to marry to its own traditions the developments that were taking place elsewhere in Italy. By 1534, when Florence had lost its pretensions to political greatness, and when Rome had lost many of its scholars to the north after the sack of the city by Imperial troops in 1527, Padua had clearly emerged as the leading centre of Italian scholarship. Not only was Greek taught in the university, but small private classes of Greek studies were run by Benedetto Lampridio for the sons of Venetian noblemen and other important or outstanding young men who gathered there. Giovanni della Casa, Lodovico Beccadelli (both later to become papal legates to Venice) and young members of the Contarini, Morosini, Bembo and other Venetian families numbered amongst Lampridio's students, before he moved to Mantua to tutor the ducal family there.

The development of an interest in Greek literature at Venice and Padua was facilitated and encouraged by shipping contacts between the Venetian possession of Crete and Venice herself. Both Cretan scholars and those Greek scholars who sought refuge on the island from the Turkish expansion in south-eastern Europe, went into the copying trade and sold Greek texts which were taken to Venice by trading vessels. Frequently these scholars boarded the ships themselves to try their luck in Venice, and from Venice they often found their way eventually to other parts of Italy, especially to Rome and Florence. Amongst these Cretan and Cretan-based scholars was Michaelos Apostolis, who had studied under Argyropoulos at Constantinople and Plethon either there or at Mistra. He spent the greater part of his life teaching Greek and copying Greek texts on the island. Amongst his pupils were Laonikos, a pioneer in publishing Greek texts in Venice, and Adramyttenos, who taught Greek to Aldo Manuzio. Apostolis had a short stay in Padua, where he taught some Greek to the Florentine exile, Palla Strozzi. Perhaps the most outstanding of a succession of Greeks from Crete was Marcus Musurus. He was at first attracted by the Florence of Lorenzo, when Ficino, Chalcondyles and Janus Lascaris, under whom he studied, were directing the interests of the Florentine intellectuals. Eventually he found his way back to Venice and Padua, which were growing in attraction as, with the death of Lorenzo, Florence became a less important centre for Greek studies. In 1503 he became professor of Greek at Padua and later he taught mainly in Venice until he moved south to join Lascaris again, probably to teach at the Greek school at Rome. In Venice Musurus was one of the chief Greek editors of Aldo Manuzio, and he helped the latter form the *Neakademia* or Aldine Academy. As an editor he brought out the first Greek edition of Pindar, which led to an important development in Venetian poetic fashions, for the Pindaric ode became a popular exercise among vernacular writers in the literary circles of Venice and Padua, and especially for the old pupils of Lampridio. As a prominent member of the *Neakademia* Musurus met, taught or influenced a great variety of important and interesting people including Linacre and Erasmus, Pietro Bembo, the historian Marin Sanudo, Demetrius Ducas, who later helped Cardinal Ximenes with the Greek section of the Polyglot Bible, and Girolamo Aleandro, who was sent to Germany by Leo X to cope with the difficulties the Church faced from Martin Luther. Aleandro was also one of his students at the university together with such important personages as Gasparo Contarini and another well-known Venetian ambassador, the historian Andrea Navagero. The influence of such men as these Greeks, who found their way to Italy through Crete and Venice, was therefore incalculable; and, if they made their way to Florence during the life of Lorenzo and to Rome during the period of the Medici popes, between 1492 and 1512 and again after the sack of Rome in 1527, Venice was especially the centre that attracted them. But Venice, Rome and Florence were never the sole centres of Greek studies. Especially under Charles V an important group of writers with a good knowledge of Greek congregated at Naples. Janus Lascaris himself was for a while at Milan and Pavia under the French and served Louis XII as an ambassador at Venice. Earlier Constantine Lascaris had taught Greek at the court of Francesco Sforza. Mantua and Ferrara were always interested in attracting leading scholars. Even at Savona as early as 1458, well outside the main cultural stream, the merchant Antonio Grillo owned a collection of 40 books written in Greek. Throughout this development, the Greek-speaking communities of the south in the kingdoms of Naples and Sicily seem to have played little part, although at Bari for instance Greek was spoken as a first language as late as the eighteenth century.

The interest in the historic languages of Rome and Greece led inevitably to an interest in other languages. The new tool of Greek, for instance, focussed attention on the earliest manuscripts of the Scriptures and scholars turned to Hebrew as well as to Biblical Greek. Nicholas V commissioned Giannozzo Manetti to translate the Bible from such manuscripts into the classical Latin of his times. Manetti achieved a translation of the New Testament and the Psalms, and the search for Hebrew texts was consequently added to that of the texts of the classical authors. Lorenzo de' Medici himself included Hebrew amongst the languages that were capable of being the vehicle of important literature; and Pico della Mirandola made the case that truth expressed in any language was valuable. An avid student of languages himself, Pico drew his ideas from the literature of several languages and therefore was in a particularly strong position to combat the view that only the Latin and Greek of the classics were refined and subtle enough to express the loftiest thoughts and the deepest truths. This was just what Flavio Biondo had asserted, writing off the vulgar tongue as a barbarous language, 'an adulterated speech mixed with outlandish usage'. On the other hand, in Florence there was particularly strong reason for believing that at least Tuscan, or for a local patriot like Machiavelli Florentine, was a language which could be used sublimely; for there were the tangible examples of the works of Dante, Petrarch and Boccaccio to support them. Bruni suggested, even, that 'every language has its own true perfection, a tone of its own, and a peculiar way of refined and scientific expression'. Manetti and Landino after him both cited the works of Petrarch and Dante to make this point. Tuscan or Florentine, according to the writer, was the third language; and Lorenzo, as has been pointed out, made Hebrew a fourth. He, too, referred to the three great Florentines to illustrate the powers of 'sweet, harmonious Tuscan', and used it for his own, not inconsiderable, poetic compositions. The inevitable occurred: just as a section of the Latinists had set up Cicero as their sole linguistic authority and would not use a word, a case even, that he had not used, so some apologists of the vernacular would not go beyond Dante, Petrarch and Boccaccio. When Pietro Bembo suggested that Latin was a vernacular of the past and that Italian was therefore appropriate as a vehicle of literary expression, he was thinking in terms of the literary language of the fourteenth century. Francesco Alunno claimed that one could express all of man's concepts with the vocabulary of Dante, Petrarch, Boccaccio and a few other writers. Such vernacular ciceronianism, as it were, met fierce criticism at the end of this period. Before this is discussed the prestige which the *Volgare* had by then attained will be examined.

Giovanbattista Gelli confidently stated that 'the Florentine tongue' was 'most apt for expression of all philosophical conceits . . . and as good as Latin or even the Greek tongue about which they make so much ado.' Italian under one or other of its names had gained this position for various reasons. In the first place it was the language of Mediterranean trade, the international language of the Mediterranean. The attitude of the little Adriatic republic of Ragusa is revealing. This Slavonic state was so impressed by the Italians that its official business was largely carried on in their language; rich Ragusans sent their sons to Bologna or Florence for their education as the fashionable and snobbish thing to do; they employed the Florentine architect, Michelozzo, to build their Palace of Rectors; their documents even, when they were not in Latin, were written in Italian. The rest of the Dalmatian coast was under the influence of Venetian trade and, to some extent, of the Roman Church. It was thus also influenced by Italian dialects which were often popularly spoken, especially during the course of business. In Ragusa, however, there was a conscious adoption of Florentinism, which went far beyond the day to day needs of a commercial language and was a reflection of the prestige and influence that Florence, as a seminal centre of a new Italian culture, had attained. The vernacular also gained popularity with the growing realisation of the potentialities of the press. Writers like the Genoese historian, Agostino Giustiniani, deliberately set out to exploit the situation: 'It seems to me', he wrote, 'right to take account of the multitude and to write with the ordinary people in mind, in order that those who do not know Latin do not remain ignorant of what has befallen in the past, so that through a knowledge of such things they might acquire prudence and work for the public good, since the ways of virtue are open to all.' Publishers, of course, cooperated, only too pleased at their expanding sales, and translations into the Italian from the Greek and Latin became numerous. Lodovico Dolce,

a copious translator of the mid-sixteenth century, justified his activities by
pointing out how translations made available whole literatures to those
who were ignorant of languages other than their own and that even the
Romans often got their knowledge of the Greek authors through translations into their own vernacular, Latin. Pietro Lauro, a fellow translator,
used similar arguments to defend his translations of writers such as
Plutarch and Columella, Erasmus and Vives. By the middle of the century
such arguments about the vernacular had spread beyond the Italian
peninsula. In France in 1549 Joachim du Bellay, for example, wrote: 'all
branches of knowledge can be faithfully and fully treated in the vernacular'; and William Thomas made similar claims for English in the
introduction to his translation of John of Holywood's *de Sphaera*. The
cogent example of the great Florentines had, of course, already crossed the
Alps and English poets, for instance, were assimilating the lessons of
Petrarch's songs and sonnets. But du Bellay and Thomas were making
greater claims: science and philosophy, not only the various forms of
creative and imaginative literature, could be adequately dealt with in their
mother tongues.

What has been called vernacular ciceronianism was criticised by
Castiglione, who was perfectly satisfied that had Petrarch and Boccaccio
been living in his times they would not in fact have used many of the words
that appeared in their writings. Alberto degli Accarigi in his *Grammatica
Volgare* made the same point: 'Avoid those antiquated words that if they
were living today they would not use', he said of the vocabulary of Petrarch,
Boccaccio and Dante. Claudio Tolomei, a Sienese ambassador and lecturer
at Padua, asked with disarming relevancy what one would have done had
not Petrarch written his verses or Boccaccio the *Decameron*—'Kept quiet
perhaps, or written nothing?' The liveliest defence of the use of a living
Italian was made by Alessandro Citolini in his *Lettera in difesa de la lingua
volgare* in 1540, and he supported his thesis by actually lecturing in Italian
to the highly-cultured and classically-trained members of the Paduan
Accademia degli Infiammati, such as Sperone Speroni, Luigi Alamanni,
Pietro Aretino, Benedetto Varchi and Giovanbattista Montano. He suggested that learning medicine or law in Greek or Latin was like making the
journey from Rome to Venice by way of Egypt and Syria: it might be a
delightful journey, but it retarded one's arrival. Modern languages were
more suitable for the transmission of modern ideas; the dead languages
were framed for a different set of circumstances. He urged that his contemporaries should 'leave the obstinate in the damaging poverty of Latin
and search for the most useful riches of the vernacular'. 'Nothing new has

come to light', he claimed, 'such as from day to day we might see appear, but that it is provided with a word in the vernacular while remaining without a Latin or Greek expression to convey it, nothing new but that the lowest artisan or most miserable peasant is not better furnished with words to describe it than can be found in the whole Latin language.' He did not limit his claims to Italian, but was one of those who urged Robert Peterson to translate Giovanni della Casa's *Galateo* into English. But his main concern was with Italian. Latin was a dried-up woman of over 50. Italian was a young woman so that 'we, if we are virile men, would be able to produce beautiful sons and daughters with her such as would bring us honour and immortality'. Although Citolini's letter is important as a defence of the suitability of vernacular languages for teaching purposes and literary compositions, the implication of his argument—that modern thought and learning was going beyond the achievements of the ancients— is even more interesting. The claim will be seen to have substance, when the science and art of the period are discussed.

8

Science, Medicine and Technology

The period between the fourteenth-century contributions of Paris and Oxford to concepts of motion and the publication of the important works of Copernicus, Vesalius and Tartalgia in the 1540s has often been written off as a sterile and retrogressive period in the history of science. Such judgments might concede that the backward trend was in some measure checked by the contribution of the artists to the theory of perspective and a knowledge of anatomy. The charge of sterility, although sometimes still repeated, can no longer be maintained, particularly when it is related to the years after the middle of the fifteenth century. The developments that then took place were to a considerable extent connected with Italy. Several factors converged to bring these advances about. The revival of an interest in Greek scientific literature, coupled with the more scholarly study of the texts, restored much that had been lost of classical science. Navigational problems, the need for calendar reform and, curiously enough, an urgent but unscientific interest in judicial astrology gave rise to the recognition that a close observation of the heavens was desirable, and consequent developments in astronomy occurred. There was also an expansion in the interests of scholars from a study predominantly of problems of the spirit to one that also embraced the physical world. This accompanied the growth of a lay culture inherent in the revival of antiquity. The belief that there was a numerical simplicity underlying the created universe, derived mainly from a study of Neo-Platonic writings, also opened up a new line of investigation for the physical sciences, which found useful tools in the revived understanding of Euclid and in the methods of Archimedes. New attitudes were therefore evolved and in the event they produced significant scientific achievements.

The fourteenth-century theories of motion reached a remarkable degree of sophistication. Up to that time and for two centuries to come Aristotle's ideas about moving bodies dominated thought upon the subject.

A body sought its natural place according to its composition of elements, that is, according to whether it was predominantly made of fire, air, water or earth. Thus objects naturally settled into their appropriate strata, unless some external force were supplied that disarranged the natural order of things. Such a force, in Aristotle's opinion, had always to be applied by physical contact. The problem of why a projectile continued to move after it had become separated from the agent exerting the initial force was explained by the notion that nature abhors a vacuum: the space vacated by the moving object was thus immediately filled by an inrush of air, the force of which pushed the object along its course. Jean Buridan in Paris produced a detailed criticism of these views, and put forward the highly precocious suggestion that it was not motion, but a change of motion, that needed explanation. Ockham had pointed to the example of the magnet to show that mechanical contact was not a necessary part of movement. Buridan added the example of the circular spinning top and showed that the rush of air to fill the vacuum left by the moving object was not the cause of its continued movement, for in this instance there was no space vacated. He also suggested that a javelin pointed at both ends was not inferior to one with only one point, although the postulated pushing power of the rush of air would have been considerably less. Buridan formulated his impetus theory to explain the continued movement of a projectile. This assumed that the agent imparted an impetus to a projectile that was slowed down by the resistance of the air and came to rest at its natural place, as with the Aristotelian theory of the elements. Without the interposition of a resistance or contrary force the impetus would continue undiminished and the projectile would continue indefinitely. In connection with the acceleration of falling bodies he posited the theory that this was due to the fact that the gravity of the body, which caused it to begin to fall, combined with the impetus it gained from falling. Thus the further it fell the greater the impetus accrued from the previous section of the fall. Nicole Oresme later carefully distinguished the notion of impetus from that of heaviness on the grounds that impetus could be exercised in an upwards direction; he gave the examples of a bouncing ball and a pendulum, successively decreasing their upwards thrusts as weight worked against the impetus of the rising movement and thus reduced the amount of the next fall. Oresme also worked out the notion of the parallelogram of forces. Meanwhile in England the concepts of velocity and acceleration were extensively explored by men like William Heytesbury and in the *pseudo-Swineshead*, probably written by a William Collingham. The latter came to the conclusion that a uniformly accelerating body would cover a quarter of the distance it travelled altogether in the first half of the period of travel.

These ideas were first introduced into Italy by Biagio Pelacani da Parma in the first decade of the fifteenth century, and it was in Italy that they were kept alive. It is true that those thinkers at Padua, who were mainly occupied with the Averroist interpretation of Aristotle, often either ignored or rejected these theories of movement and the quantitative treatment of motion. Alessandro Achellini at Bologna for example—a figure of considerable importance in the scientific developments of his time—was strongly opposed to the introduction of any quantitative elements, such as those of Heytesbury, into the arena of natural philosophy. On the other hand, there were those like Gaetano da Thiene, who taught at Padua and died there in 1465, or like Bernardo Torni, a Florentine physician of the end of the fifteenth century, both of whom kept alive an interest in the kinematics of the fourteenth century. In Milan, Giovanni Marliani went so far as to carry out practical experiments with pendulums and rolled balls down ramps in order to explore the quantitative behaviour of falling bodies, notions of velocity and acceleration; while Francesco di Giorgio Martini, a military engineer at the *condottiere* court of Urbino, experimented with the relationships between amounts of powder and weights of projectiles, bore lengths and the diameters of gun barrels. Amongst the spate of publications issuing from the Venetian presses in the late fifteenth century, moreover, the works of the fourteenth-century theorists of motion figured prominently.

Leonardo da Vinci, who exercised his ingenuity in so many directions, had his contributions to make in this sphere as well. His importance to the development of scientific ideas has often been written off, since he did not publish the copious insights he recorded in his notebooks, which were not read by his contemporaries and were also very difficult to handle owing to the curious mirror writing that he employed. It would be unhistorical to take such a view. Because influences are not easily traced it does not follow that they were not present. Leonardo was in constant contact with the intellectual circles of many cities, especially Milan and Florence. He worked closely with the mathematician, Luca Pacioli, and with the anatomist, Marcantonio della Torre; and he frequented circles in which the works of the fourteenth-century theorists of motion seem to have been easily accessible to him. Vasari, moreover, claims that he was a great talker. The presumption is, therefore, that his ideas were familiar to the scientific environment in which he found himself, and it would be no greater assumption to assert his influence than to deny it. From the similarity of thought evinced in several later writers the likelihood is that Leonardo's thought was an important landmark in the development of scientific ideas. At least, it would be fair to say that a similar intellectual environment gave rise to similar insights, as, for instance, in the classic case of Darwin and Wallace. Leonardo came to the conclusion that there was an exact equation between the force of the agent and the reaction of the object submitted to a blow; but the transferred force was not necessarily complete, the amount of transference being dependent upon the elasticity or inelasticity of the two objects concerned. His interest in flight led him to a concern about the behaviour of falling bodies, a subject made familiar to him by the works of the fourteenth-century Parisian and Oxford thinkers. He saw falling as the excess of power exerted downwards over resistance the falling body met. The problem of flight was, therefore, a problem of exploiting such resistance. He also had something to say on the connected subject of the behaviour of projectiles. The orthodox view about motion was that violent and natural motion could not be mixed: thus a projectile should have continued—to apply this belief consistently—in a straight line in the direction thrown, until the natural motion of gravity took over, when the object would have fallen vertically. Leonardo believed this to be only partly true. A missile would start on a straight course and finish with a vertical drop, but there was an intermediate section which was circular—he saw that there was no abrupt angle in the course of a projected object—and during this circular section of the course a mixed motion took place, that is to say, a mixture of violent and natural motion. Oddly, for a man with such acute powers of observation and with explicit faith in the evidence of the unerring senses, Leonardo cited the example that an arrow fell perpendicularly to the ground, as evidence of the complete way natural motion replaced violent motion during the course of flight. The power of preconceptions to blur the evidence of the senses can nowhere be better illustrated.

Niccolò Tartaglia's work carried out mainly in the second quarter of the sixteenth century provided the next important contribution to the knowledge and theory of the behaviour of missiles. His interest, like Martini's, was largely governed by problems of artillery, and like Leonardo he combined original observation with an examination of the traditional explanation of kinematic behaviour. He emphasised the value of experience, suggesting that a person who had never shot a gun was not likely to know how shot from guns behaved. The eye, to him, was the source of true testimony. He agreed that more than the senses was necessary for the understanding of universals and that sight contributed no more than a knowledge of particulars; but his attitude was that universals were derived from an experience of particulars, even if universals were understood and not sensed. His senses, however, were in the event not always reliable. If he ultimately corrected several misconceptions, he nevertheless believed that a second cannon shot would travel further than the first, and he explained this putative phenomenon by the theory that the air had been divided by the first shot, leaving less air resistance for the second to encounter. For a long while he also clung to the idea that natural and violent motion could not be mixed, although he attributed to a projectile a similar course to that which Leonardo outlined: a straight upwards movement at an angle, followed by an arc of a circle, until a vertical, downward movement took over. However, he deserted the notion of the incompatibility of violent and natural motions in a work published in 1546, when he came to the conclusion that the flight of a missile was curved throughout its flight, the violent and natural movements being mixed all the way. Another popular notion that he finally rejected was that a projectile accelerated during the early stages of its flight, so that it was more devastating to shoot at some distance than at point blank. Initial acceleration of this nature had been universally accepted and it was a great revolutionary step to reject it. Finally by trial and error he stumbled on the fact that to project a missile furthest with a given force, it should be initially aimed at an angle of 45 degrees. He went on to suggest that having measured the elevation of a shot and the distance a particular weapon had projected it, the distances at different elevations for a similar shot from the same weapon were calculable. At about the same time, the Spaniard, Domingo de Soto, who was a considerable time in Italy and played an important part as a theologian at the Council of Trent, arrived at accurate conclusions concerning vertically projected and falling bodies. He accepted the impetus theory, but believed that the force imparted remained constant; and suggested that the body thrown upwards was uniformly decelerated by its gravity or attraction to its natural place, whereas the dropping body was similarly uniformly accelerated. He also refined the conclusion of the *pseudo-Swineshead* by noting that a body accelerating uniformly along a given course from a still position to a given speed would cover exactly the same distance as an object travelling along the same course at half the maximum speed of the first object. Thus by the middle of the sixteenth century a great deal had been discovered by Italians or by men closely connected with Italy concerning the behaviour of projectiles and falling bodies. Even the theory of inertia, which was implicit in de Soto's description of vertical motion and in Tartaglia's final view concerning the course of a projectile, had gained much ground since its early adumbration at Paris.

The growing interest in first-hand observation and the consequent willingness to question works that had previously been held as unquestionable authorities were perhaps most noticeable in the sphere of the medical sciences. As has already been indicated, this was a characteristic development of the period in most regions of thought, even if it was not unanimously held. If the individuality of writers was often expressed freely and their use of language became personal, there was always a slavish ciceronianism working in the opposite direction. With the rediscovery of classical writings on science the initial effort had usually been to understand and accept, and inaccuracies in the classical authorities were generally only reluctantly admitted. But once complete faith in an authority had been undermined by the discovery of demonstrably false statements, there tended to follow a new attitude which placed greater confidence in the evidence of the senses and the exercise of reason. The authorities were not generally overthrown entirely: they remained the starting point of investigation, the basic textbooks for teaching; but at the same time they were beginning to be considered as something to be fallen back upon when no better information or explanations were available. Alessandro Piccolomini, the bishop of Siena, who had spent much of his time in the intellectual circles and academies of Padua and Venice, put the position clearly in 1558: 'Just as, for example, in the doctrine of primary matter, of movement, of time, of the sensitive soul and of many other natural phenomena, owing to the lack of demonstrative reason or experience of the senses to prove the contrary, I have approved and followed Aristotle and his arguments; so, on the contrary, in treating of the void, the milky way and certain other things, seeing the force of reason and demonstration to be different from what he writes, I have departed from the side of Aristotle himself. Likewise concerning habitation below the equator and in other matters besides I have preferred to believe in experience that has been undergone rather than in Aristotle himself, prince of the peripatetics, whose weighty authority for lack of actual experiences and necessary and vital reasons before all other authorities I have elected as least wrong and least false in philosophy.' Not all thinkers were so articulate about their positions in this matter as was Piccolomini, but his statement describes substantially the attitude of many scientific thinkers of the middle of the sixteenth century. Yet even by the end of the century Galileo's predecessor at Padua, Giacomo Zabarella, felt it incumbent upon himself to justify why he did not accept the teachings of Aristotle in their entirety.

The willingness to accept the evidence of the senses, which underlies the attitudes of those scientists who have so far been mentioned, was a hard-won way of looking at things. It should also be noted from the start that this seldom, if ever, implied the superiority of the senses over reason or other faculties. It was connected with theories of universals. A too distinct contraposition of the theories of Plato and Aristotle is not tenable, simply because their thoughts on a knowledge of universals were not always consistent; but, by and large, Plato's view was aprioristic, whereas Aristotle's was inductive. For Plato the universal was known through a disengagement from the world of material things, where the simple, pre-existent ideas of his rational and numerical universe had become corrupted in their material realisations. For Aristotle, on the other hand, it was only through abstraction from the knowledge brought to us by our senses that we had any idea of the rational principles underlying the universe. Thus at a time when the views of Plato were becoming increasingly popular with scholars and writers in Italy, it was a singular achievement that the Aristotelian tradition should have given rise to an empirical attitude towards the sciences. This is not to say that there was not also a continuous section of opinion that rejected the importance of experience and experiment. Salutati in 1399 suggested that medicine was inferior to law because of its fundamentally experimental nature; while Daniele Barbaro in 1556 evinced a lack of confidence in the *Harmonics* of Aristoxenus on the grounds that the Greek attributed the whole theory of music to the ears, conceding nothing to reason. In the light of the text of Aristoxenus, if Barbaro's statement is to be taken as meaningful, it can only be an attack on an empirical approach which involved rational discourse only after sense experiences had been assembled. Even Galileo tried to disclaim the necessity for experience and experiment, contending that he only devised his experiments as demonstrations to convince his Aristotelian opponents; but it is clear that much of his positive achievement was very closely tied to experiment and observation.

Niccolò da Lonigo, the original occupant of the Paduan chair for the study of Aristotle in Greek, which dated from 1497, was one of the first to concentrate his attention on the scientific errors of classical writers, especially those of Pliny; and Iacopo Berengario da Carpi and Alessandro Achellini, although they both used Galen as an anatomical authority, by their own observations from comparing the results of dissections with the classical textbook were able to correct Galen and make original contributions of their own. Galen was not their sole authority. The mediaeval anatomist, Mondino, was also closely studied, and Berengario noticed that Mondino had already corrected some of the Galenic errors. This would suggest that there was nothing new in the rejection of authorities. This is partly true. The challenge of men like Berengario was at a time when classical learning had reached a high point in prestige. His effort in rejecting some of Galen's findings was, therefore, so much greater than Mondino's; for the latter had not the same predispositions to overcome. More important, in the time of Mondino there was never the same realisation of the importance of sense data: his corrections were more haphazard and did not reflect a conscious doctrine of the paramountcy of the sense world as a starting-point for scientific investigation. However, it was in the Aristotelian circles of the university of Padua that there had been a systematic and critical examination of a classical authority throughout the fifteenth century.

Aristotle up to this time, although his writings had profoundly influenced the thought and the modes of thought of the later mediaeval world, had never been as a pagan philosopher absolutely accepted as a final authority. Differences between his own thought and, for instance, that of Arab commentators like Averroes had generally encouraged discussion rather than acceptance. Later with the emergence of the Italian Neo-Platonists a vociferous school of anti-Aristotelians came on the scene; although, as a result, some thinkers tried to show the essential conformity between the views of Aristotle and Plato. However, the Paduan school had already developed before there was a diffusion of the works of Plato and his followers. This school or tradition of studies predates the fifteenth century, but there is an unbroken thread running from Paolo da Venezia at the beginning of the fifteenth century to, at least, Zabarella two centuries later. The importance of this school was that through centuries of painstaking study and criticism it produced a methodology which on his own admission was of extreme importance to Galileo, although it was not the only element behind the unparalleled fertility of his work. What is most striking about this school of methodologists is that they never questioned the assumption that correct scientific procedure should begin from a study of the material facts. They believed that these facts, the effect, should give rise to a knowledge of the cause and that then one should be able to demonstrate by rational discourse how the effect rose from the cause. Thus one started with an irrational knowledge of the sense world and ended up by having a rational explanation of it through a knowledge of its causes. Greater sophistications were added to this simple scheme, such as the introduction of the stage of a rational exploration of the possible causes; and Agostino Nifo at the beginning of the sixteenth century produced what was tantamount to the concept of a hypothesis. Most of the thinkers connected with this development in scientific thought did not themselves take part in the active research that their method implied; in their studies rather than in laboratories they had hammered out a programme which, when it was put into practice in the seventeenth century, produced unprecedented advances in the field of scientific knowledge.

If Aristotelianism provided a method, Platonism produced an inspiration. The frequently made assertion that Aristotle, by dominating the minds of the later Middle Ages, held up scientific progress by his insistence on quality rather than quantity is without doubt correct. His persistent categorising, the construction of qualitative hierarchies, tended to make his world a static world of values. His vast mediaeval influence, therefore, made it difficult for thinkers like Ockham and Oresme to enlist enthusiasm for their mathematical treatment of motion. It was the Platonic and Pythagorean tradition which ultimately led men to think of the physical world in terms of mathematical relationships, and it is because of this that the Florentine Platonists might be said to have contributed indirectly to the emergence of a new and fruitful science, although they themselves showed no interest in mathematics or a scientific investigation into the physical world. They were not to remain alone in this: both Erasmus and Vives satirised discussions on accelerative motions, falling bodies and the like; whereas Pietro Pomponazzi, in the centre of productive scientific enquiry at Bologna and Padua, condemned the Ockhamite departure from qualitative physics. However, the study of Plato and the Neo-Platonists, such as Plotinus and Proclus, popularised the view that there was a structural simplicity underlying the universe and that this was intelligible in mathematical terms. It was the Pythagorean elements of the Platonic tradition that were clearly important in this respect; and they included both those elements that were mathematically and scientifically sound and those which were rather the wild and uncontrolled products of a fantastic world of assumptions. For instance, the simple proportionality of musical harmonies and the curious, sometimes magical properties attributed to various numbers could both be taken as significant of the numerical basis of the universe. Such ideas had not been lost to the Middle Ages: the survival of a few Platonic works such as the *Timaeus*, if in a corrupt and mutilated form, is evidence that these ideas were never entirely forgotten; but from the fifteenth century they gained new significance and wider popularity with the growth of Greek studies. At the same time the texts were more accurate, fuller and more plentiful, as Greek scholarship gained momentum; and, as efforts like Ficino's to square Plato's thought with Christianity became more convincing, they also became more respectable and more acceptable.

But Neo-Platonism was only one of several streams that converged to develop this view that the universe was created according to certain mathematical relationships, beautiful in their simplicity. The work done by the artists on perspective was a telling confirmation of the notion. The study of Euclid, of Ptolemy, of Archimedes and of other Greek scientists not only seemed to prove the view by actually revealing some of the mathematical secrets of the universe, but it also provided valuable tools and methods with which further investigations might take place. Bessarion is known to have possessed a Greek version of the *Elements* in the middle of the fifteenth century. A Latin translation from the Arab version was published at Venice in 1482. Thence there were successive republications, retranslations, sometimes partly, sometimes wholly from the Greek, into Latin. By 1510 Euclid was widely diffused in printed works. The *Almagest* of Ptolemy was possibly translated by George of Trebizond as early as the mid-fifteenth century, although this text was not published until 1528 at Venice. A Latin version of the *Almagest* had already been published there in 1515, while the complete Greek text did not appear until 1538 at Basle. Meanwhile Archimedes had been printed in part as early as 1503. Tartaglia brought out a Latin version in 1543, while Commandino's Greek version was published only in 1575. Nevertheless, enough has been said concerning the popularity of these three most influential Greek works to indicate the increasing emphasis on a view of the universe which concentrated on underlying numerical principles.

Nicholas of Cusa, because he spent so much of his life in the papal curia in the circles of Cardinal Bessarion, must be considered as essentially a part of the development of Italian intellectual attitudes. His contribution belongs to the quarter of a century before he died in 1464, that is to say, to the period of Cosimo de' Medici and Francesco Sforza, of Brunelleschi, Valla and Alberti, to the time when the laicisation of culture and Greek studies were spreading throughout Italy in depth. That he was an important ecclesiastic and devoted to his religious ideals was not uncharacteristic of those who made the great contributions to the widening culture of the age. So was Copernicus, to give another example. In fact, Cusa's insights, which helped to show the way to a revaluation of the universe and the place of the earth in it, were primarily conceived by him as an enrichment of the Christian's ideas of creation, in the way that the introduction of principles of pagan architecture into the churches of the time was sometimes felt to glorify God by reflecting the principles of his creative act. It was his religious concept of the infinite, his unwillingness to limit God and his creation, that led him to challenge the basis of the Aristotelian cosmology that held sway in the later Middle Ages. That he was not primarily concerned with a new physics does not in any way restrict his importance in that field. Many of his most fruitful ideas in that respect were thrown off casually rather than as a matter of central concern to him, and he often later developed ideas in conflict with earlier cosmological insights. But this is unimportant for the history of the development of new scientific attitudes; for the fact remains that he had these ideas, he wrote them down, and they were read by others. They were the first great challenge for many years to traditional views of the world, and they bore their fruit.

With Plato, Cusa believed that mathematics alone allowed the mind to reach an absolute degree of certainty. There was no element of empiricism in this aspect of his thought. Matter was corrupt and therefore the materialisation of principles only blurred them. They were not therefore to be abstracted from the material world; only when the mind disengaged itself from matter was it likely to arrive at truths. But since God was unlimited it was the mathematics of the infinite that was pertinent to the highest truths. His view therefore of the indefinite extension of the universe, as God's creation, suggested that its centre was everywhere and that its circumference was nowhere. Thus the earth could not be regarded as the centre of the universe, nor could the eighth sphere of the fixed stars be rightly thought of as the outward limit of the universe, its circumference. The concept of geocentricity underlying Aristotle's elemental theory of natural place and of the quintessence, which explained the stars' immunity from the gravitational mechanism of the elements, were thus completely undermined for those who thought like Cusa. The stars, the sun, the earth, none of them had pride of place in the universe, for none of them had more claim than the others to be regarded as central. This was the mathematical consequence of an infinite God. The earth was thus no longer the hub of creation as for the Aristotelians, nor simply the corrupt recipient of the materialised ideas as for the Platonists, including Cusa himself in other contexts. In a sense it was relegated to become just one of the heavenly bodies; in another sense it was elevated to equality with the stars. No longer was the distinction between the sublunary and the celestial valid: the sun could be treated as if it were made of the same elements as the earth and subject to the same forces. The earth needed no longer to be a centre of corruption: it took its place equally with the rest of creation. If there was an ambivalence within such thinking, it was nevertheless the beginning of a great break-through, opening up new possibilities to the understanding of the universe, its movements and its physical composition. It even inspired some to re-examine the data upon which the old assumptions had been based; to observe the heavens anew, critical of what previously had been thought to have been seen.

The geometry of the infinite led Cusa to other significant conclusions., The circle, for instance, he understood as an infinitely-sided polygon; an infinite circle was indistinguishable from an infinitely-extended straight line; the maximum of greatness must meet the minimum of minuteness in infinity. The infinite implied the continuous: for example, there must be an infinite number of circles between the infinitely small and the infinitely great circle. Therefore every area must be able to be incorporated into a circular figure. If one had a square inscribed between two concentric circles, by the continuous enlargement of the smaller circle to the size of the larger circle the area of the square must be passed through and so be able to be represented in a circular form. Thus in principle it was possible to square the circle. This, of course, was a demonstration of what was already known: the Greeks had already arrived at several mechanical solutions to the construction of a squared circle. What they could not find was a purely mathematical solution. What is important about Cusa's point is that it illustrates a development in the conceptual world, which derives from the Christian penchant for the infinite, as opposed to the preponderantly finite world of classical Greece and Rome; and it was this aspect of Christian thought that was in part responsible for the emergence of new, scientifically productive ways of looking at the universe. Cusa had a more practical side to his interest in mathematics and mathematical relationships in the physical world. Although he himself did not experiment, he devised programmes for possible experimentation, involving calculation or measurement. He proposed that it could be fruitful to compare the weights of equal quantities of blood or urine of the diseased and the healthy, the old and the young, and to time pulse and respiratory rates with a clepsydra. He suggested that the weight of similar amounts of wool on different days would be a gauge to the humidity in the air; and that a comparison of the weights of blown-up and deflated bags would indicate the weight of the air. Another experiment for measuring the weight of air, as he called it, was to time similar weights falling from the top of a tower at different times. One could measure depths of water by the time taken for a light object to emerge from the bottom and one could measure the speed of a ship by seeing how long an object dropped at the bows would take to reach the stern. These experiments were perhaps not original, but they illustrate Cusa's great interest in phenomena which were amenable to one form or another of mathematical treatment.

The assumption of geocentricity had been questioned both in the classical era and in the mediaeval period. In the later period Albert of Saxony and Nicole Oresme had indicated the possibility of the eighth sphere of the fixed stars being motionless and the earth revolving on an axis. This involved a notion of the relativity of movement, which they accepted in a purely scientific context; for questions of faith forced them to admit the fact of an earth-centred universe in which the earth was motionless. This concept, however, was challenged not only by Cusa but by an Italian contemporary of his, Celio Calcagnini. Calcagnini argued that the stars were weightless and therefore could not move, movement only being a property of matter which had weight. Moreover, the heavens were perfect and therefore immutable. What is immutable is immobile. On the other hand the earth was imperfect; it therefore changed and accordingly had movement. Thus it was more appropriate to regard the earth as rotating within a fixed sphere of the stars than to regard the stars revolving about a fixed and motionless earth. If such aprioristic ramblings were in themselves nonsensical, they at least opened up possibilities of viewing the universe from a different angle, so that old, deeply-ingrained assumptions were challenged.

The same might be said of the influence of the putative works of Hermes Trismegistus, which were believed to date back to the Egypt of the time of Moses and to have been a precursor to Greek philosophy. In fact, they belonged to the second or third century A.D., and thus what was thought to be remarkable about them—that they foreshadowed Christian and Neo-Platonic thought—was illusory. As this was not known at the time, their apparently inspired insights into future Christian revelations gave them the greatest authority. Cosimo had Ficino break off his work on the translation of Plato to translate the *Corpus Hermeticum*, and Ficino's own thought was profoundly influenced by Trismegistus. So was Pico's, who also used the *Cabala* which was similarly misdated and thus gained a similarly misplaced reputation. If the *Corpus* had no importance scientifically in Florence, at Bologna it was influential in the circles of Domenico Maria da Novara, who was greatly influenced by Florentine Neo-Platonism, styled himself a Pythagorean and so came to the view that the universe was created according to the principles of mathematical harmony. With this Platonic faith, he combined a strong belief in the need for astronomical observation and was, in fact, able to criticise the Ptolemaic view of the universe on observational grounds. He was helped in his observations by Copernicus. Already Demetrios Kavakes, a Greek scribe at Rome at the time of Paul II, had referred to Trismegistus in relation to his views that the universe revolved around the sun. But Copernicus did not follow this view to a logical conclusion: although he related the earth's orbit to the sun, he described the movements of the other planets in reference to the earth's orbit. But Copernicus himself explicitly referred to Trismegistus and was profoundly influenced by the Neo-Platonic concepts he met in the circles of Domenico Maria. He also mixed with Girolamo Fracastoro, while he studied at Padua; and Fracastoro is known to have entertained the aim of getting rid of the eccentrics and epicycles of Ptolemy and establishing homocentric circular movements in their place.

Like Cusa's, Copernicus' achievement can therefore be partly attributed to his stay in Italy. When he wrote that the book of the universe was 'written in the language of mathematics and its characters are triangles, circles, and other geometrical figures' he was evincing an attitude, a faith, which had permeated through to him from the work of the Greek scholars in Italy and the Florentine disciples of Plato and the Neo-Platonists. His aim was mathematical simplicity, to explain the heavenly movements with 'fewer and much simpler constructions'. This involved a belief in the harmonic arrangement of the universe, its essentially mathematical structure. His solution involved also a universe, not infinite like Cusa's, but enormously large, in order to account for the absence of astral parallaxes. This was an act of faith in the supremacy of reason over the senses, as was his denial that the sun circled the earth. In 1533 his ideas were explained to Pope Clement VII and were received without censure. By then they had been circulating for more than 20 years; and, although they were not generally accepted as superior to Ptolemy's they were at least thought worthy of consideration. Through fear of ecclesiastical censure, Copernicus did not have his work published until 1543, the year of his death; and then they received a preface emphasising the hypothetical nature of the system and its usefulness for calculation. In 1561 he was listed by Girolamo Ruscelli indifferently with both Gemma Frisius, the first to accept his system publicly, and some Ptolemaic astronomers, as amongst the most important astronomical observers of the time. Perhaps the use of the term 'observer' denoted a lack of understanding; for Copernicus, although perhaps his first questioning of Ptolemy arose from the observations he carried out with Domenico Maria, based his theory on a reinterpretation of the data used by Ptolemy himself.

Italy's contribution to mathematics as such was very much more limited and largely related to the revival of Greek mathematics and the introduction of Arab arithmetic and algebra. In the fifteenth century, especially at Nuremberg, a beginning was made to the drawing up of trigonometrical tables by men like Peurbach and Regiomontanus. Both these men came to Italy—Cusa met them at Rome. But they did not receive their inspiration there, and their influence was perhaps to confirm a reverence for the idea of mathematics rather than to produce any original Italian contribution. Thus it was that Sixtus IV called upon Regiomontanus and not an Italian, when he attempted to tackle the problem of the reform of the calendar. That no reform occurred was due largely to the fact that observational data were inadequate. Later the Council of Trent set up a committee to investigate the problem under the chairmanship of Daniele Barbaro. This too produced no results, and it was not until towards the end of the sixteenth century that reform took place under Pope Gregory XIII. In France Chuquet was responsible for the beginnings of logarithmic calculation and this was carried over into the work of Luca Pacioli. Pacioli was typical of the practical bias that Italian mathematics tended to have: he produced a work on double-entry book-keeping and, deeply influenced by Piero della Francesca's investigations into perspective, he worked closely with Leonardo da Vinci when he wrote his work, *De Divina Proportione*. But he was also interested in such problems as that presented by the chances of winning in unfinished games and therefore began that pedigree of the study of probability which passed through Girolamo Cardano, Fermat and Pascal. Even the restoration of Euclid, largely carried out by Italian scholarship, received a great practical impetus. Federigo Commandino, a great sixteenth-century Euclidean editor, rested heavily upon the geometer in his sophisticated methods for calibrating sundials; and Euclid became an important tool in the exploration of mechanical principles employed in the reconstruction, for example, of some of the old machines described by Heron.

Italy's great contribution to mathematics during this period was the solution of third degree equations. The achievement was based on a study of Arab sources but was none the less a considerable intellectual accomplishment, especially when the clumsy notational equipment of the time is considered. Scipione del Ferro, who taught at Bologna, and Tartaglia made significant contributions, and later in the century, Lodovico Ferrari produced a solution to fourth degree equations. The exact allocation of credit for the third degree solutions is impossible to disentangle from a series of charges and counter-charges concerning plagiarism, which involved most of the leading figures concerned including Cardano, who seems to have published Tartaglia's results as his own in the *Ars Magna* of

1545. The important point is that in Italy from the early part of the six-teenth century there was a widespread interest leading to positive achieve-ments of considerable merit in the solution of algebraic problems. If this was immediately less useful than the rediscovery of Euclid, it showed that Italians at the time were able to carry their interest in mathematics beyond the point where it was simply a storehouse of symbols of the world's numerical order or at most an inspiration to development in the physical sciences. For Tartaglia and others it was a viable discipline, which could lead to new discoveries within the limits of its own field.

The contributions to medicine and anatomy, perhaps surgery, of this period were in some ways equal to the important changes that took place in attitudes towards the physical universe; but the fruits of the latter matured earlier. Kepler, Galileo and Newton in the seventeenth century were able to utilise the insights and the clearing away of dead wood that had taken place in the preceding decades or even centuries. But when, for instance, William Harvey came out with his theory of the circulation of the blood, none of his practices as an active physician were in any way modified. So it was with many of the earlier achievements in the history of medicine. During the period of this book it is possible that it became rather worse to be a patient, since new diseases or more virulent strains of old diseases seem to have been introduced into Europe. This is probable of malaria and syphilis. It is also true to say that not only doctors but at least one government, that of Venice, became increasingly conscious of the inefficacy of medicine and the need to tackle the problem systematically. But whatever the advances in medical science during the period, their effect was not felt for perhaps centuries.

As with other fields of learning, the revival of antique medicine played a prominent part in modifying the outlook of the time. Galen's anatomy had been central to mediaeval thought on the subject, although his views, as has been seen already, were modified by the practical investigations of men like Mondino. In the later decades of the fifteenth century, Hippo-crates, Theophrastus, Dioscorides, Pliny and Galen himself became the accepted authorities on medical treatment and the properties of herbs: but, as was normal, authority became modified into the object of critical inquiry. The desire to ascertain exactly which plants were being referred to by a classical text led to the effort to assemble such plants together. One of the aims of the members of the *Orti Oricellari*, for instance, was to gather together all the plants mentioned in the classics. Gherardo Cibo, about 1532, developed the technique of gumming dried specimens to paper. The private gardens of Venetian patricians, such as those of Lorenzo

187

Priuli at Padua and Giovanbattista Contarini at Dolo, had great collections of plants imported from other parts of Italy or from the Levant. Scientific interest urged men like Niccolò Comasco to travel to Greece and Crete in search of herbs mentioned and described in the classics; and Luigi Anguillara travelled throughout Italy on a similar mission. Venetian ambassadors abroad were instructed to keep their eyes open for rare plants and send them back to Venice; and the Venetian Senate instituted a chair of simples at Padua in 1533. At the instance of the first professor, Francesco Bonafede, a professor of medicine, Giovanbattista Montano, and other members of the university and influential people in their circles, the Venetian government was persuaded to establish the famous herb garden at Padua in 1545, under the direction of Anguillara. The Senate's grounds for doing this are revealing: it wished to facilitate the study and development of medicine by providing ready materials for demonstration and investigation for the teachers and students of the university. A dispensary was also to be built in the gardens. The driving necessity underlying the Senate's decision was that the apothecaries in Venetian territories were producing medicines which were not leading to cures, but instead were tending to be poisonous themselves. This was blamed on the linguistic deficiencies of the apothecaries; but there was also wide recognition by then that the classical authorities were often in conflict, and there was accordingly a need for active research into the appropriate medicines to prescribe. At the time, practical approaches to even the teaching of medicine were evolved, and Giovanbattista Montano seems to have developed a clinic where he took his students round the beds of patients to examine symptoms and to watch the effects of treatments. Theory and authority were giving way to practice and research; words were being supplemented by things. This is not to say that Montano and his contemporaries were completely original in this: it is known, for instance, that Fracastoro's insistence on bedside observation was derived from Hippocrates. Moreover, the *consilia*, casebooks in which the symptoms and results of treatment were recorded, date back to the thirteenth century. Already there was a long tradition of empirical medicine. What was especially creditable about the early sixteenth-century doctors was that they overcame the strong pressure of current cultural habits to follow slavishly the authority of antiquity, while at the same time profiting from what antiquity had to teach.

The period was beset by numerous summer diseases and by typhus plagues in the winters. Typhus itself was especially serious in Milan in 1477. It was again prevalent in Italy in 1492–93, and during the Hapsburg-

Valois wars in Italy it was particularly virulent. In Brescia in 1528–29 it followed a serious food shortage of the previous year. Its connection with lice was not discerned until the beginning of the seventeenth century, but Fracastoro had already noted that its incidence was greatest in times of war and famine. Malaria was a disease with a long history back to classical times. In Italy it was most acute in the kingdom of Naples at Brindisi and Aquila and from the district around Rome south into the Pontine Marshes and north into the Maremma. Pola on the Istrian peninsula and Ravenna both suffered badly from the disease which was also common in the intervening marshlands around the Venetian lagoon and in the rice-growing areas of the Po Valley. There was a pronounced increase in its virulence at the turn of the century, which suggests that perhaps a more virulent strain was introduced from America. Plagues were the common fear of all, especially town-dwellers. That is why those blessed with riches left the cities during the summer months for country palaces and villas. Patricians of Venice, businessmen of Florence or Genoa, cardinals of Rome, all developed the habit. The nature of these plagues is not always identifiable. Often they were bubonic plagues; perhaps sometimes they were plagues of diphtheria, influenza or other diseases. Whatever their nature, these great epidemics repeatedly devastated populations. Perugia had plague continuously from 1460 to 1468. Naples suffered terribly in 1527–28. At Venice there were 11 outbreaks of plague during the 50 years from 1478. Plague at Mantua followed the floods of 1478, a year when Brescia was also hit badly by an epidemic.

Of all diseases perhaps syphilis made the greatest impression on Italy during this period. It was a disease well known to the American Indian and his animals, the alpaca and the llama, already in pre-Columbian days. The Indians had developed mercurial treatments for it, salves and internal medicines, and they had their own words for the disease. It was also probably known in Japan and perhaps China in less virulent forms. The high and terrifying incidence of the disease in Europe, including Italy, after Columbus had returned from his first voyage almost certainly indicates that the disease was brought back from Hispaniola. It is also highly likely that French and Spanish soldiers brought it into Italy. Most early Italian writings on the subject suggest that it was a previously unknown malady there. It is possible that the disease was not entirely new to Europe, or even to Italy. A work of the twelfth-century physician, Ruggiero Frugardi da Palermo, which was re-edited in the next century by Rolando Capelluti da Parma, described an infection that may well be syphilis and which was treated by mercurial salves. There are other such descriptions dating back to the later Middle Ages in English and French medical works. There is also the tenuous evidence of bone lesions found on pre-Columbian Europeans, which could have been caused by syphilis, although other explanations are equally tenable. Whatever the case for the disease existing in Europe before the discovery of America, it is clear that it was a widespread problem only after Columbus' return, when it spread through Europe at an alarming rate. The external application of mercurial ointments was used from the very first, but the guaiac treatment that Paracelsus was so strongly to condemn was also learnt from the Indians and was known in Europe by 1508. Ulrich von Hutten, who suffered from the disease, was to devote much of his time to advocating the use of this treatment, while Pietro Mattioli, the commentator on Dioscorides, was one of the first in Europe to recommend the internal use of mercury. Niccolò da Lonigo began the spate of literature on the subject in Italy, and the Genoese surgeon of Julius II, Giovanni da Vigo, gave the most accurate of the early descriptions. Berengario da Carpi, Girolamo Fracastoro, who invented the name, and Niccolò Massa, who mentioned cases of supposed contagion through bed-linen, were amongst others of the early writers on the disease. The authorities quickly took prophylactic measures. In 1496 the prostitutes were expelled from Bologna and Ferrara, and in 1505 a confraternity was licensed by Alfonso I d'Este to collect contributions for a hospital for syphilitics. From 1507 prostitutes at Faenza were examined before a magistracy before they were allowed to practice their trade, and the Church preached chastity as a preventative. But as late as Pius V measures to outlaw prostitution were energetically resisted by the populace and efforts to control the disease were frustrated.

State intervention to prevent disease is as old as history. It occurs in the laws of Hammurabi, the Mosaic Law, the organisation of sanitation in ancient Rome. Emperor Frederick II went a step further in his insistence on adequate standards at the medical school of Salerno. Taddeo Alderotti before 1300 strongly urged the imposition of hygiene regulations, while he was professor at Bologna; and in the fatal year of 1348 the Venetian government set up the magistracy of three guardians of public health. When there was plague in the Mediterranean in 1394, Venice excluded all suspect ships from the port, and quarantine facilities were instituted in 1403. When there was a plague there in 1448, the Genoese government immediately took precautions, since their shipping was likely to frequent the same areas as those of the Venetians. The Florentines set up a *lazaretto* at Pisa for quarantine purposes in 1464; and there was widespread activity in hospital building during the fifteenth and sixteenth century in most

Italian towns with the governments playing a leading part in it. Sometimes the authorities fought a losing battle against vested interests, as in the case of the Venetian government's attempts to keep the ricefields at a distance from city walls; but the Italian cities were generally more conscious of the needs of public health and more active in their efforts to achieve it than elsewhere in Europe or even in the Mediterranean. Leonardi Bruni could write proudly of the cleanliness of Florence; and Publio Fausto Andrelini da Forli was impressed by the filth he encountered in the streets at Paris, which suggests that it was noticeably worse than what he was used to in Italy. The public works in Rome under Nicholas V, Sixtus IV and Leo X must certainly have made the Holy City a less unhygienic place to live in; but the rapid growth of Italian cities during the sixteenth century presented greater problems than the authorities could keep up with, so that the plagues of the mid-seventeenth century took their vast toll of human lives.

It is clear that the relationship between filth and disease was a recognised principle upon which public action was based. It was equally recognised that diseases were passed from one person to another, which accounts for the establishment of quarantine centres and the habit of deserting the towns by those who could afford to in times when disease was prevalent. These connections were by no means newly perceived, but during this period they became increasingly the basis for action. By 1546 Girolamo Fracastoro produced his theory of the three forms of contagion: by simple contact, by the agency of infected articles and by transmission at a distance. The last he explained by the supposition that there were minute, unseen bodies with the power of reproduction, carrying disease from one person to another through the air. The notion of such *seminaria*, adumbrating the concept of a germ, thus challenged the view of the spontaneous generation of diseases; and the idea of material agents, which were controllable, took the place of the classical notion of miasmata, a general corruption of the air about which nothing could be done. Such an advance in theory was not necessary to impress upon people the need for cleanliness and public hygiene, which has already been seen to have been well understood. In the fifteenth century there had been a flourishing literature both for lay readers and for doctors on the advantages of personal hygiene by such writers as Ugo Benzi, Antonio Cernisone and Bartolomeo da Montagnana. The growth of the soap industry during the period is perhaps testimony of its success, although much of the soap was exported to the Levant. Fracastoro's theory was nevertheless a notable step forward in the knowledge of the nature of disease.

Anatomy, perhaps of all sciences, most encouraged close observational techniques. Autopsies were carried out frequently, especially at Bologna, from the thirteenth century. They were used for post-mortem diagnosis, for anatomical research and for demonstrations to students being taught surgery. During the Middle Ages knowledge of the human body had advanced far, but owing to an inability to employ this knowledge effectively in medicine and surgery old ideas were often revived to replace more accurate ones. For instance, Guglielmo da Saliceto in the thirteenth century was convinced of the superiority of the knife over the cautery and Rolando Capelluti in the same century was advocating ligatures instead of cauteries to prevent haemorrhages. They were right principally because cauteries often produced grave burns. Yet throughout the fifteenth and sixteenth centuries the same battle had to be waged. Thus much of the achievement of these centuries was a matter of the revival of ideas which had been advocated in the mediaeval period, and sometimes with little more lasting success. Yet there were very real achievements during this period which, if again they did not produce very great therapeutic results, nevertheless represented a considerable advancement in learning and in method.

An anatomical theatre for demonstrations, for instance, was built at Padua in 1446, and in ensuing years a change in methods of demonstration marked a profound change in attitude. The professor had originally sat apart reading and commenting on Galen or some other authority, while an *ostensor* pointed to the relevant parts of the body and a *demonstrator* did the actual dissecting. The students simply sat around and watched. By the end of this period some professors had got rid of their helpers and their books, and lectured and did their own dissections, whilst the students handled bits of the bodies. This was the method used by Vesalius, the Belgian commentator on Galen, who did most of his productive research at Padua. It reflects the same spirit that underlay the foundation of the gardens at Padua and the clinical methods of Girolamo Fracastoro and Giovanbattista Montano. First-hand knowledge from close observation and from handling materials was replacing the bookish aloofness of traditional methods. The same attitude is perhaps discernible in the authorisation of anatomy on the dead body by Sixtus IV, an example that was confirmed by Clement VII. Previously the Church's attitude had not been cooperative. In 1311 edicts had forbidden priests to engage in medical work and the fourth Lateran Council in 1215 had reaffirmed that priests should not practise surgery. Dissections had always run the danger of incurring the censure of the Church and thus the ruling of Sixtus IV represents a considerable advance in the liberalisation of anatomical research, although anatomies were still very strictly regulated by local authorities.

Alessandro Achellini, who worked most of his life at Bologna but spent some time after Julius II took that city at Padua, was one of the most successful anatomists of the period, although his main concern as a professor of philosophy was in expounding the commentaries of Averroes. Among his discoveries were the hammer and stapes of the middle ear and the fourth cranial nerve. He was one of the first conscious correctors of Galen; although it was Berengario da Carpi who formulated the principle that Galen should be accepted as the anatomical authority, but only where his assertions were not at variance with observation. Berengario made his contribution to the emergence of a knowledge of the circulatory systems of the blood by noticing the valves of the heart regulating and directing the flow of blood. His work began a long series of investigations into the arteries, veins and capillaries, modifying and overthrowing the work of Galen: the reluctant but major attack on Galen by Vesalius, who amongst other achievements showed how an animal could be kept alive by artificial respiration after the thorax had been opened; Canano's discovery of the valves in the veins; Colombo's theory of the lesser circulation of the blood; Fallopio's work on the cerebral arteries and the *arteria profunda* of the penis; Fabrizio's accurate description of the valves of the veins; the account of the circulation of the blood by his pupil, Harvey; and with the aid of the microscope Malpighi's observation of the hitherto hypothetical capillaries. Unlike the mediaeval achievements, many of those of the late fifteenth and early sixteenth century became part of a continuous process of discovery and theoretical refinement. It should be emphasised, however, that these advances did not immediately avail the patient. There was a tendency towards simplicity in the treatment of wounds such as had already been advocated in the Middle Ages, just as the battle over the cautery was largely won again. There were also experiments in new techniques. Innocent VIII, who it is said was fed on women's milk during his last days, received transfusions of blood from three ten-year-old boys, who took their ducat in payment and died. Jewish doctors are reputed to have carried out the desperate experiment. Caesarian sections were attempted in the middle of the sixteenth century by Pietro Franco, who also avoided castration in the cure of hernias. It was in France that surgical midwifery met some success: Guillemeau and Paré were able to induce premature labour in cases of haemorrhages and they successfully accomplished podalic versions. But Guillemeau was unsuccessful in his efforts to achieve a Caesarian birth.

Before leaving the subject of anatomy and dissections, the achievement of the artists of the period should be noted. By their desire to present the natural world accurately they developed the habit of close observation. For those who, influenced by the Neo-Platonic doctrines of the time, sought to understand the underlying structure of the natural world rather than its superficial appearances, there was the incentive to probe the skeletal and muscular structure of bodies beneath the surface of the skin. Michelangelo went so far as to study with Realdo Colombo; Leonardo earlier had carried out as many as 30 dissections of his own, and cooperated for a while with Marcantonio della Torre, an anatomist from Verona. Leonardo himself made the first accurate representation of the uterus and asserted that the heart was a muscle, contrary to Galen's authority. Amongst his innumerable insights was the observation that the size of the pupil varied inversely with the degree of light, and he demonstrated his contention by moving a lighted candle towards the eye in the dark; moreover, he pointed to the fact that nocturnal animals are wider-eyed than animals that move by day. Leonardo also experimented with injections into veins and cavities; and he found by the inflation of lungs that he could not drive air into the heart, concluding that the branches of the air tubes in the lungs had no direct connection with the blood. Thus Galen was wrong in asserting that the pulmonary vein conveyed air to the heart.

The Middle Ages were by no means backward in their technological achievements: towering Gothic cathedrals, canal building in the Netherlands and Lombardy, dykes against the sea, windmills, watermills, machinery for the textile industries, military and naval architecture, metalwork, woodwork, the manufacture of glass and ceramics. Such a list could be prolonged indefinitely. Yet the fifteenth century began a period of technological development and invention at a rate previously unknown, and Italy was in the forefront of this activity. If she was not always responsible for the advances herself, she was generally quick to use those of others. Some of these achievements have already been noticed: the introduction of pound gates and later mitred lock gates in Milan; the diversion of the course of rivers in Venice; the development of shipbuilding and sailing techniques; large-scale irrigation and drainage undertakings; the exploitation of the printing-press; mass production glass-making equipment at Murano. The development of patent laws in fifteenth-century Venice and their very considerable use are witness to the close association between the inventiveness of the period and the profit-making incentives underlying it. Most of these patents in so far as they were connected with technological advances related to new designs of mills of various types and protected the inventor's sole right of manufacturing them over a limited period of years. But if they reflected money interests, they also proclaimed the glory of the inventor's genius: fame was not the monopoly of political, artistic and literary success. That full-scale legislation was employed, such as the Venetian patent laws of 1474, suggests that already a future of technological advance was foreseen and that the developments that had already occurred were only regarded as a beginning.

The leading part played by the architect and artist in the technology of the period was due largely to the popularity of Vitruvius' *De architectura*. A complete manuscript of this work, which had been an intermittent influence on architectural theory throughout the Middle Ages, was unearthed in a monastery in Switzerland in 1414. It profoundly influenced the thought of Leon Battista Alberti and the form of his book, the *De re aedificatoria*. The *De architectura* was first published in 1486; thence it had a long history of publication with a variety of searching commentaries and left its mark on the work of every significant architect of the time from Alberti, through Bramante to Palladio and beyond. The feature of Vitruvius' work, which is at the moment most relevant, was its comprehensiveness: the architect not only built temples, basilicas and villas, he was also a civil engineer, a mechanical engineer, a town-planner, a military architect, an expert in acoustics for theatre-building, a musical theorist, a climatologist, a philosopher. It may well be that Vitruvius therefore had a strong influence on the development of the educational ideal of the many-sided man; it is certain that he inspired the architect to challenge specialisation in constructional technology. Thus Alberti was interested in canal-building and Leonardo was actually employed to build canals in Milan and Florence. Michelangelo was called in to see to the defensive walling of Florence. Giuliano Sangallo and Antonio Marchesi da Settignano fortified Naples; Antonio Sangallo the Elder built the fortress at Leghorn; his nephew, Antonio the Younger, built defence works at Civitavecchia. This Vitruvian amateurism in the construction of fortifications was eventually attacked by Giovan Tommaso da Venezia, who was a military engineer of the Emperor Charles V in the middle of the sixteenth century. He attributed the fact that few fortresses could withstand a well-organised attack to the fact that they were built by architects who had studied Vitruvius and Alberti. They never came to grips with current problems, as would a soldier, who would have a shrewd insight into the tactics of possible enemy attacks. Nor did one learn these skills from the universities, at Bologna, Padua or Perugia, but through lifelong experience in the field. This was why the defences of Piacenza, constructed by soldiers, were superior to those of Florence, which were built by architects. Yet, of course, architects were able to contribute vastly to technological advancement during this period. Already Brunelleschi had made a remarkable step forward in the construction of the cathedral dome at Florence, but it was under the stimulus of Vitruvius that architects and architectural theorists looked to the works of Archimedes and Heron, for instance, to explore the mechanical achievements of the Greeks and involved themselves in town-planning, as did Alberti. This all-embracing rôle of the architect gave rise to the notion of God the Architect; and it was up to the architect therefore to reflect God's all-embracing, creative activity.

9
Religion

Italy during this period has often been characterised as a land of ir-religion, paganism and ecclesiastical corruption. Machiavelli's passage on the superiority of Roman paganism over Christianity, because the former bred the sort of warlike citizen who would be able to dedicate his life more effectively to the interests of the state, is a clear piece of evidence of the small hold traditional Christianity might have on the men of those times. Pietro Aretino, who used his acid pen to blackmail princes and the rich when they failed to favour him with tangible gifts, was one of several self-confessed atheists. There were never more corrupt leaders of the Church than Sixtus IV and Alexander VI; and pagan values certainly permeated Italian society at several levels with varying degrees of intensity. The Church was in no very good shape with widespread abuses and often an ignorant, immoral or uninterested clergy. But, paganism apart, most of the failings of the Church in Italy were no different nor worse than those found elsewhere or at other times in the Latin Church in Europe. Yet, however limited was the spiritual provender offered by the Church, the flocks were there ready to receive it, from the ordinary folk of town and country to the great and powerful figures of the time like Cosimo de' Medici, Francesco Sforza and Isabella d'Este, to mention a few most notable examples. The legislation of the commercial republics was circumscribed by the teachings of the Church, and it must be remem-bered too that even the popes were Christians. With the growth of Spanish influence in Italy from the beginning of the sixteenth century there was administered a powerful thrust towards conformity, which gained further momentum with the decrees of the Council of Trent; but conformity is a cloak and it need not go hand in hand with religion. The fifteenth-century tendency in Italy to give play to individuality was little, if at all, less religi-ous than what generally followed.

It would be special pleading to exaggerate the religious character of the period from 1464 to 1534. A quick glance at the popes would be enough to suggest that the Church at least left much to be desired. Yet one particular achievement stands out: their success in establishing the primacy of the Papacy over rival aspirants to power within the framework of the Roman Church; and it was largely the triumph of this monarchical principle that enabled the Church to preserve itself from utter decimation and to present a reasonably united front against the challenges of the protestant Reformation. The chief threat to papal supremacy came from the conciliarists, who after a period of schism saw the Papacy as a vulnerable and unstable element in Church government, open to rival claims that tended to divide Christendom. Only general councils of the whole Church, they believed, could bring order and stability and prevent factionalism. Little less challenging to the popes were the claims of the cardinals. Overweeningly ambitious as a rule, most with their sights on the papal throne, they were ever reluctant in conclave to grant to one of themselves powers whereby the office of pope could be carried out effectively. Before proceeding to elections they would impose upon the future incumbent conditions or capitulations limiting his powers and preserving an influence for themselves. A policy was set down that reform should be undertaken in the head and in the members of the Church; that such reform should take place only with the consent of the cardinals; that councils could not be called without their consent or conversely, in the conclave that led to the election of Pius III, that a council should be called every three years; that the pope should not promote more than one relative to the cardinalate; that the cardinalate should not become too numerous so that they themselves would not lose their power in numbers; that crusades should be undertaken only with their consent or on occasions that they should not be undertaken without it. Such preconditions threatened to make of the Papacy an empty office, prestigious, ceremonial, but without power. As early as 1460 Pius II countered the tendency with a firm statement of papal absolutism in his bull *Execrabilis*. If the bull was explicitly directed against the conciliarists, of which he himself had been one in his younger days, by implication the cardinals were hit at, too, in their attempts to shackle the popes. In 1509 Julius II confirmed the bull. None of the popes stood by their promises as laid down by such capitulations and perhaps it was a comfort to them that a bull of Innocent VI, dating from 1353, made such conditions void if they turned out to be in any way harmful to the welfare of the Church. Thus Paul II felt himself free to promote three nephews to the cardinalate; and Sixtus IV, Alexander VI, Julius II, Leo X, Paul III promoted sons, grandsons, cousins and nephews in abundance. Innocent VIII paid lip-service to the capitulations by assembling a few ships at

Civitavecchia in a half-hearted attempt to launch a crusade; but Alexander VI created an unprecedented number of cardinals, many of them Spaniards, and Julius II partly bought French aid for recovering Bologna with cardinalates to three relations of the Cardinal d'Amboise.

Poor quality popes were bound to arise from election by a college of cardinals, itself appointed for reasons extraneous to the welfare of the Church. The circle was vicious. Often inability to agree led the cardinals to appoint a pope, ailing or old and therefore not expected to live long. Stop-gap popes were not expected to have policies and therefore reform above all was not seriously envisaged in such cases. Their function was to provide time for a rallying of forces behind one particular aspirant or another. This had been the case with the election of Alonso de Borja, Calixtus III, who for three years confounded the Curia with crusading fervour and alienated Rome with unwanted Spaniards. Innocent VIII survived eight unexpected years before his squalid death in 1492. Pius III, on the other hand, died too soon for the opponents of Giuliano della Rovere and perhaps for the spiritual good of the Church. The Papacy tended to be regarded more and more as a prerogative of the Italians. The French Cardinal d'Estouteville and the Greek, Bessarion, were both voted out on racial grounds. The cardinals were particularly cautious in this respect, looking back to the Avignon Papacy with fear and distaste. An Italian was less likely to move the Curia from Rome, but the precaution was sometimes taken to write into the capitulations that this should not occur without the cardinals' consent. After the stop-gap Calixtus III, only Alexander VI and Adrian VI have been non-Italian popes. Alexander was elected on the grounds that he had of all the cardinals the most offices to vacate and share amongst the others. By well-placed promises he won the Italians over. Adrian was successful with the help of the enormous influence the Emperor Charles V was able to bring to bear. In the middle of the sixteenth century the Englishman Reginald Pole was almost elected, but since then foreigners have scarcely been in the running for the Papacy. Elections also reflected political or factional divisions: Colonnas and Orsinis often rallied their current supporters behind opposing candidates, and the failure of Giuliano della Rovere to win votes in 1492 was a direct reaction against his pro-French associations. It is odd that with all their power to pack the cardinalate with their supporters the popes of this period were never immediately followed by a pope of the same colour. Even Adrian VI came briefly between the two Medici popes. In all cases a pronounced reversal in policy, especially temporal policy, accompanied a change of popes.

Papal policy at this time tended to reflect the interests of the place of origin of the popes themselves. This was obvious with the Medici popes, who were largely responsible for the government of Florence as well as that of Rome. Adrian VI, a Dutchman of Utrecht, who had been Charles' tutor and had later served him as his regent in Spain, granted the Spanish king the right to appoint to bishoprics in Spain in 1523. The della Rovere popes supported Genoese interests: Sixtus IV gave a large part of the alum trade to Genoese merchants; Julius II supported the anti-French elements in Genoa against French domination, especially when Louis XII embarked upon a conciliarist programme at Pisa and thereby linked Genoese and papal interests more obviously. Alexander VI, like his uncle, did much to increase Spanish influence in Rome, and Paul II gave the Venetians a big cut in the alum trade and to some extent subsidised Venice's war against the Turks as a crusade. Although the private ambitions of Paul II sometimes conflicted with Venetian interests and much the same could be said of the relations of the other popes with their homelands, by and large a state would find it advantageous to have one of its own people as pope. The converse was equally true. The opposition of Alexander VI to Savonarolan Florence and that of Clement VII to Spanish Naples were both based on political considerations connected with the respective attitudes of the native government of the two popes to French intervention in Italian affairs. Alexander had a Spanish point of view; Clement eventually acquired the traditionally pro-French, Florentine point of view. Alexander would apparently have been willing to relax his attitude towards Savonarola, if Florence had joined the Holy League of 1495 against France; Clement was even glad to throw in his lot with Venice in order to preserve papal and Florentine integrity against a Spanish influence that was characterised by crusading zeal.

Family policies were also characteristic of these popes. Nepotism was by no means limited to this time, but it reached a previously unimagined degree of intensity. The preferment of papal families was perhaps most common within the sphere of the spiritual offices of the church. Nevertheless, Sixtus IV and Alexander VI in particular distributed the temporal offices of the Church lavishly among their relatives, and aimed to carve out small principalities from the papal territories with which to enrich their kin. The two most blatant examples of such misuse of power were those of Girolamo Riario and Cesare Borgia. Important towns of northern Romagna fell to Riario, who with the connivance of his uncle had aimed also at gaining control of Florence. Cesare Borgia's success in dominating the greater part of the papal territories was eventually achieved independently of papal approval, but in origin his efforts were due to his father's sponsorship. Riario and Borgia paved the way for the reconquest of the papal territories by Julius II and in this sense served the Papacy well; but service was far from their thoughts or, for that matter, from those of the popes who abetted them. Their main object had been to prolong the power and wealth of themselves and their families beyond the lives of the incumbents of the elective, papal monarchy, and their methods were murder, bribery, force, every kind of corruption.

The popes of this period were worldly men, unattractively self-indulgent, and harmful to the reputation of the Church. Paul II, in private life, had his concubines and was particularly avaricious in his collection of jewels, perhaps a reflection of his earlier life as a merchant. Sixtus IV, in the unrestrained pursuit of the interests of his numerous nephews, was callous of the welfare of others. If he showed some horror at the brutal way Lorenzo de' Medici waged the Volterra war, he had no such scruples about the way Girolamo Riario furthered his interests. Innocent VIII made justice venal for even the most heinous of criminal acts, but sought to safeguard his family interests more legitimately by marriage rather than by plundering the papal territories. Alexander VI kept a mistress for whom he found a convenient cuckold for the sake of appearances, countenanced murder that forwarded his own ends, and patronised sexual orgies at the Curia. Julius II lost all sense of justice and humanity when it came to the reconquest of the papal temporalities. Leo X, milder in every respect, was dedicated to the hunt and to luxury to the detriment of the Church's welfare, until slowly the importance of Luther began to dawn on him and reluctantly he turned to the problems of the Reformation, but with no real understanding of the needs of the situation. Clement VII could not afford to ignore the challenges the Church faced; but, as the virtual ruler of Florence, he saw greater danger from Catholic Spain and imperial domination in Italy than from a Protestant Germany, which helped to keep the emperor weak.

Despite the general depravity and ineptitude of the Papacy three points by way of mitigating circumstances might be made in respect of some of the papal failings. Firstly, the Papacy was hard put to it to pay its way, as has previously been shown; next, it was generally believed that the popes required a large and inviolate temporality in order to maintain themselves free from undue influence from other powers; lastly, the distinction could always be made between the pope as a man and the pope as pope. The first point does not free the popes from charges of personal or family greed; it does, however, explain to a great extent their considerable preoccupation with material wealth. On the whole, they succeeded in putting Rome on a sounder economic footing: by developing the city as a centre both of pilgrimage and ecclesiastical business, they stimulated population growth, industry and trade; and by subduing the Papal States they not only increased tributary revenues, but they also increased their income from inland customs. The importance of this can be seen from the setback to revenues that followed the sack of Rome in 1527. The sack of Rome also gives some substance to the second of these points: Clement VII was taken prisoner by the imperial forces and his policies were consequently placed very much under the direction of the emperor. Perhaps the most striking example of this was the fateful part played by Charles V in opposing the divorce of his aunt, Catherine of Aragon, by Henry VIII. The last point was invoked by Alexander VI in justifying his authority against the challenge of Savonarola. Used in the context of the enormities of this pope the argument no doubt has a hollow ring; yet it is an argument that any Catholic priest might use with some justification, when accused of human failings. It is only in very special situations that he is in some way an inspired and privileged person, a vehicle of the divine workings.

These popes in fact carried out a great deal of work of consequence. Bulls of Sixtus IV and Alexander VI defined the spheres of influence of the new colonial powers, Portugal and Castile, and thereby deferred colonial rivalry for many years, before new powers came on the scene. Another bull of Sixtus founded the Spanish Inquisition, which, if with its uncompromising nature it was terrifying in its effects, was nevertheless a powerful instrument in the maintenance of the Church's influence over a large number of people. Julius II assembled and Leo X continued the fifth Lateran Council, which condemned fashionable pantheistic doctrines, and followed the bulls of Pius II and Julius II by stressing the principle that the convocation, removal and dissolution of general councils were papal prerogatives. A bull against simony was also published by Julius II in 1505. Alexander VI introduced the principle of the censorship of printed publications and the Lateran Council forbade printing without the sanction of the ecclesiastical authorities. Thus the Church interested itself early in the control of this new instrument of the propagation of ideas long before the Pauline and Tridentine indexes proclaimed their formidable lists of forbidden reading. In this it had the full concurrence of governments, whose censorship laws combined the suppression of matter that was heretical with forbidding the publication of writings contrary to the interests of princes or governments. This identity of the interests of Church and state was incorporated in the censorship duties of the *Riformatori dello Studio di Padova*, who supervised Venetian publications. It was also the principle underlying much of the discussion of censorship at the Council of Trent.

In one important respect the popes relinquished much of the power of the Church. Julius II ceded to Louis XII, as duke of Milan, the right to appoint to benefices in the duchy, as a further concession whereby the pope enlisted French support for his conquest of Bologna. The right was later transferred to Charles V. Leo X, by the Concordat of Bologna in 1516, virtually gave similar powers to Francis I to fill French bishoprics, although in this instance the chapters rather than the pope lost influence. Then in 1523 Adrian VI granted parallel rights to the Spanish crown in Spain. But papal power over appointments had never been complete and to represent such grants as the surrender of complete powers would certainly be to overstate the case. Not even in Rome had the pope a free hand; for it had become traditional that local benefices should be filled by members of local families and the first act of a newly elected pope was to confirm this principle. In Florence Lorenzo was able to resist the appointment by Sixtus IV of Francesco Salviati to the archbishopric of Florence and, when the pope nominated Salviati to the archbishopric of Pisa instead, Lorenzo refused to allow him to take over the see on the grounds that no see should be filled in Florentine territory without the permission of the Signoria. The ensuing *impasse* was only settled when Salviati was hanged for his part in the Pazzi conspiracy. The tension between Church and state over ecclesiastical appointments is perhaps best illustrated by the example of Venice. In 1451 Nicholas V established the patriarchate of Venice to replace that of Grado and the bishopric of Castello. Thus all the lagoon dioceses together with those of Venetian Dalmatia were brought under an administration centred on the capital. This left to the patriarchate of Aquileia a large ecclesiastical province spreading beyond the confines of the Terraferma as the other important centre of Venetian ecclesiastical interests. The history of Venice's attempt to dominate these two patriarchates throws considerable light on the problems involved in the struggle for the right to appoint bishops and the factors that influenced the papal policy.

The patriarchs of Venice were from the beginning appointed by the Venetian senate with papal approval. Up to 1492 candidates could put forward their own applications; but in that year the council of ten prohibited applications and the initiative was left entirely to the senate, which by the middle of the sixteenth century even appointed laymen to the position on more than one occasion. Normally there was no conflict over an appointment owing to the recognition by the Papacy of the supreme importance for the republic to have a loyal and trusted person as the patriarch. However, Paul II held out for a year against the appointment of Maffeo Girardi in 1466–67. Later, Julius II refused to agree to the appointment of Antonio Contarini for some months in 1508, ostensibly on the grounds that Venice was placing obstacles in the way of a papal appointment to the bishopric of Vicenza. There had been a series of such disputes going back to 1505 when the Venetians had resisted the appointment of a relative of Julius II to the see of Cremona, a stand that only proved successful on the payment of a considerable sum of money to the disappointed candidate. The matter was further complicated by the demands that Julius II was making on Venice to surrender her recent territorial gains in northern Romagna, while at the same time he was conspiring to unite the great powers of Europe to force her to do so. In 1513 the right of the Venetian government to fill vacant sees was officially limited to those of the patriarchate of Venice and the archbishopric of Candia. This might have done much to clear up a rather fluid situation, had it not from the Venetian point of view been quite so sweeping in its limitations.

Meanwhile, the Venetian government was concerned to secure similar privileges in relation to the election of the patriarchs of Aquileia. In 1420–1421 Venice seized Friuli from the temporal control of the patriarchs; and in 1445, after a long period of rivalry in that region, an agreement was made whereby the Venetians were ceded the right to rule Friuli with a lieutenant based at Udine, while the patriarch maintained the feudal lordship over a limited area around Aquileia itself. The ecclesiastical powers of the patriarchate, spreading from Como in the west to Mantua in the south and throughout the main part of the Terraferma north-east as far as Styria and Laibach, were left under the authority of non-Venetian patriarchs. Within the next few decades some outlying dioceses such as those of Laibach and Mantua were detached from the province; but Aquileia, whose administrative seat was moved to Udine, continued to hold ecclesiastical authority over the Austrian territories of Carniola, Carinthia and Styria until 1751, when its influence was confined to those Venetian territories not directly under the patriarchate of Venice. Appointments by Eugenius IV and Paul II, both Venetian popes, began a long and unbroken occupancy of the patriarchate by Venetian patricians. The appointment of Ermalao Barbaro by Innocent VIII in 1491 without the approval of the republic prompted Venice to exclude Barbaro from her territories, although he was a Venetian nobleman. Thus, unless the popes agreed to appoint patriarchs acceptable to the republic, Church government in a large area was likely to be neglected. Consequently Venice virtually secured rights regarding the nomination to Aquileia similar to those she already had to the patriarchate of Venice itself. With the invasions of Venetian territory by Maximilian I and the League of Cambrai, Venice lost temporarily most of the province and her right to appoint to the patriarchate and the bishoprics within the province was denied. Yet, although Venice did not receive recognition of her possession of much of Friuli and Istria until the Diet of Worms of 1521, in 1517 she was able to make her control of the patriarchate surer by the employment of the procedure of the *renuncia cum regressu*. This took various forms in detail, but its basic features were these: the patriarch renounced his spiritual and ecclesiastical powers to a patriarch elect, maintaining the title of patriarch for himself together with the main revenues of the metropolitan see; if the patriarch elect should die first, the full powers of the patriarch would revert to himself, otherwise the patriarch elect would replace him and another *renuncia* would be required; one of the two patriarchs, except on very unusual and rare occasions, would be required to reside in Venice, while the other would generally do so; vicars at Udine would carry out the normal spiritual and administrative functions of the patriarch. The patriarchs were thus considered very much as political appointments; and although it was sometimes difficult to get the popes to sanction a new *renuncia* on the death of a patriarch—especially after 1549 when the Council of Trent ruled that the process was only valid for cardinals required to reside at Rome—the Venetian government in the end always managed to get its own way. This was not always so for the appointments to sees within the province, and there were continual disputes between Venice and the Papacy over the distribution of benefices in the Terraferma. In the middle of the sixteenth century the republic won the right to nominate four candidates from which the bishop of Verona was to be chosen, a system that was used with appointments in Cyprus and sometimes in the case of Aquileia itself. But each individual bishopric was regarded separately, and no overall principles emerged; although, if the lists of bishops of Terraferma sees are scanned, it becomes immediately clear that loyal Venetian patricians as a rule were appointed. In the beginning of the century the diarist, Lorenzo Priuli, had written that a result of the Portuguese discovery of the Cape route was that Venetian patricians turned from their traditional merchant activities to a tranquil life in possession of ecclesiastical benefices. There was something in his observation; but at the same time it is clear that the Venetians aimed at exercising political power through control of the administration of the Church in and beyond their own territories. They explicitly stated from time to time that to function effectively against inroads from the Hapsburgs or the Turks such control was necessary, and it served not only Venice but the security of all Italy. Thus their claims over the control of the Church were directly related to the two main enemies of the Papacy, the Hapsburg and the Ottoman empires.

Venice accordingly was able to maintain a reasonable independence in the ecclesiastical affairs of her territories. The fruits of benefices were largely the perquisite of her ruling class, and incumbents had freedom of action, except where the interests of the state were involved. From the beginning of the sixteenth century much the same could be said of Milan. The rulers had considerable control over ecclesiastical appointments and therefore the Church could be used as an important instrument of government policy. It became an essential part of ducal patronage, and preferment could be used to buy support and reward service. In Florence the position was rather different for the last two decades of this period, for the government there was identified for most of that time with the Papacy itself. Thus Medici government had for the greater part a compliant clergy, especially in its higher ranks, while there was no question of conflict between these and the Papacy itself, as was sometimes the case at Venice. In the Roman territories also the position was reasonably stable, with the great local families usually being granted the profitable benefices and often a cardinalate as well. Once Julius II had reunited the temporalities under papal control, there was little chance of these high ecclesiastics becoming involved in the type of arrogant independence that had characterised the behaviour of their families in previous centuries. In Genoa the rich fruits of the Church had traditionally been the monopoly of the great landed feudatories. When aristocracy, especially landed aristocracy, emerged predominant from the popular revolt of 1506–07, the Church was very largely identified with the ruling class in the Ligurian republic. Ferdinand of Aragon was successful in introducing the Spanish Inquisition into Sicily as early as 1487 and therefore his government was able to exercise over the Church in the island the tight control it had in the Iberian peninsula. He failed, however, to bring the Inquisition to Naples, where similar efforts by Charles V were also resisted. Nevertheless, Spanish political power in Naples was sufficiently strong both to control heterodox tendencies and to assure the cooperation of the dignatories of the Church in Naples. Likewise in the duchies of Mantua and Ferrara the ruling families, who invariably had a cardinal in the family, managed to keep a profitable control of the affairs of the Church. If Renée of France, the duchess of Ferrara, presided over a small protestant cell at the court of the Estes, her husband, Ercole II, frowned upon her conduct and severely limited its effects. Italy was therefore in the main controlled by rulers who were in no way inclined to support any movement towards a protestant Reformation either on grounds of the profitability of such a move or because it might lead to an increase in their own power. The Church in these respects was already a ductile instrument, a source of power and wealth to Italian rulers sufficient to make the attractions of a reformation not worth the attendant risks. There was also no pressure for the secularisation of Church lands. The families which would have gained from such a process were already largely in possession of the revenues of ecclesiastical property. In Lombardy, as has already been shown, such lands had dwindled so much as to be no longer a primary object of covetousness. It was only with the full effects of the Counter-Reformation that the Church again began to accumulate large amounts of landed property.

This is not to say that the Reformation left Italy untouched. Apart from Ferrara there were early appearances of reformed ideas in Lucca, Venice, Cremona and Piedmont, and views of dubious orthodoxy were held in every part of Italy. But by the middle of the sixteenth century those individuals who made a decisive break with the Church, under pressure from the Roman Inquisition, the Jesuits and the growing concern for orthodoxy that accompanied the Council of Trent, tended to emigrate to more receptive areas in the north, where it was possible to live under the protection of less hostile régimes. Notable examples were Pietro Paolo Vergerio, Bernardino Ochino and Peter Martyr Vermigli. There were also those Italian businessmen who carried on their business in centres of Reform, and often accepted the local religious forms; but generally, if they returned to Italy, they reverted easily to Catholicism. Of all Italian governments, Venice's was the most tolerant of the reformers. This was in large part due to her trading interests, as has been said already. Greek Orthodox were therefore given as much latitude as German Protestants in Venice; and in order not to alienate her business associates Venice tended to tread warily in putting down protestantism amongst her own subjects, until it became clear that by supporting the Council of Trent—Venetian bishops were generally discouraged from attending before 1562—she would strengthen her claims over the patriarchate of Aquileia against those of the Austrians, whose problems with protestantism led them to support a policy of partial concession.

Italy's contribution to the reformation of the Church was almost entirely directed towards changes within its traditional structure. Its main field was moral reform, a problem very near at hand. Sometimes criticism was directed at the Christian population at large; sometimes it was aimed at the clergy itself, from the pope down to parish priest. The most immediately effective of the critics were the popular, itinerant preachers and others who used the sermon, especially in Lent and Advent, to stir up a mass sense of guilt and a wave of repentance and self-abnegation so intense and intolerable that it had no chance of producing an enduring change. In the first part of the fifteenth century San Bernardino of Siena was the most moving example, plunging cities—faction-ridden Perugia or Genoa with its hard-headed merchant morality—into a state of uncompromising, puritanical gloom. There was much for such preachers to inveigh against: the tyrannical misuse of power, the concubinage of the great, sodomy, idolatry, magic, gambling, usury, the preference of pagan literature and culture to the sacred literature and traditional culture of Christianity. Amongst these preachers were Roberto da Lecce; San Giovanni Capistrano, although his greatest activity was in Germany; Girolamo da Siena. But it was Savonarola who had not only the greatest direct effect on the people who heard him, but also the most enduring influence.

The main instrument of Savonarola's influence was, like that of the other great preachers of the time, his ability as an orator to arouse a sense of righteousness and outraged justice in all classes of people; and of course the pulpit and the *piazza* gave him the widest and most immediate of publics. But fearlessness was also an integral part of his technique; for he attacked rulers, popes and vested interests of all kinds with equal vigour. His courage came from two sources. Firstly, he believed himself to be under the direct orders of both the Father and the Son: 'God has told us to prophesy; we will therefore obey God and not men', or 'I am ordered by Christ to defend this truth.' Secondly, he was consumed with the desire for martyrdom: 'O Lord, grant me then this martyrdom and quickly let me die for Thee, even as Thou hast died for me.' With such assurance it was not difficult to make an attack on tyrants, which everyone knew to be levelled against Lorenzo. 'Tyrants are incorrigible, because they are proud, because they love flattery, and because they will not restore ill-gotten gains. They leave all in the hands of bad ministers; they succumb to flattery; they hearken not unto the poor, and neither do they condemn the rich; they expect the poor and the peasantry to work for them without reward, or suffer their ministers to expect this; they corrupt voters, and farm out the taxes to aggravate the people.' His defiance of Alexander VI was no less. But in each case there was a certain practical caution: he condemned tyrants and not Lorenzo explicitly; and likewise he always suggested the pope was misinformed or that he would oppose him under certain conditions, which he did not suggest had already been fulfilled. Yet he certainly attacked the unerring authority of the popes and by implication that of Alexander himself. 'Thou art mad to say that a pope cannot err, when there have been so many wicked popes who have erred. . . . Read how many decrees have been made by one pope and revoked by the next; and how many opinions held by some popes are contradicted by those of others.' There was another strongly implied criticism of Alexander in Savonarola's description of the way the clergy conducted themselves at Rome. 'Wouldst thou hold them to be pillars of the Church or temporal lords? Have they not courtiers and grooms, and horses and dogs; are their mansions not full of tapestries and silks, of perfumes and lackeys? . . . They do all things for gold, and they ring their bells because of their greed. . . . They sell benefices, sell the sacraments, sell marriage services, sell all things.' He accused the prelates of the Church of ignoring the scriptures and of reading only Virgil, Horace and Cicero; and he ridiculed and abhorred their reliance on astrologers. If he criticised the great, he criticised all. His sermons in Florence continually harangued the congregation to reform their ways, to replace their material and cultural values with the mean and narrow puritanism he advocated. When the Medici were expelled and a more radical republican régime was instituted, the people—although they had been thrilled with the enthusiastic devoutness of the friar—soon recalled the gayer days of Lorenzo's Florence with yearning. With the thrill of Savonarola's oratory they had burnt their vanities—carnival dress, ornaments, cosmetics, games of chance, non-religious paintings, poetry books and musical instruments; but it was not long before most realised that they had sacrificed the things that made life exciting, desirable or even just tolerable.

Yet Savonarola had given the people of Florence, the citizens at least, one valuable gift, an opportunity to share more widely in the direction of their state. It was unfortunate that the choice should have presented itself so simply between Medicean authority and Savonarolan liberty; but, when the revolt of 1527 took place, the example of 1494 came quickly to mind. There had been a considerable following of the friar over the intervening decades, the *Piagnoni*; although their aspirations had been largely stifled after the restoration of the Medici in 1512. Their frustrated aspirations were suddenly released by the renewed expulsion of Medicean rule and the city was quickly dedicated to Christ, King of Florence. But even had the new republic managed its political and administrative affairs better, the influence of Savonarola must have killed it; for Savonarolan Christianity had no independent organisation, whereas a puritanical régime needed, as with Calvin's Geneva, free scope to enforce its narrow will. The republic of Savonarola and that of Soderini after him had already demonstrated that such a state could not endure indefinitely the Florentine desire for more light-hearted days of pageant, carnival and magnificence.

A comparison between Savonarola and Luther is revealing, for it helps to show the nature of the friar's stand against the Church. Although Luther recognised Savonarola as a forerunner to the protestant Reformation, there is very little point of contact between the two. Most obviously they agreed in the need for a revitalisation of the Church, the uprooting of the corruption they saw to have permeated its whole structure. They shared a deep revulsion especially at what went on at Rome, its centre. But Luther was haunted by a sense of guilt, whereas Savonarola was inflated with his own indignant righteousness. Luther therefore came to the conclusion that merit was of no avail in the process of salvation and emphasised the paramountcy of faith, which could only be granted to the helpless human being by the unmerited grace of God. Savonarola on the other hand relegated faith with law as inferior to charity. It was through charity that man could win the favour of God and thus by his own merits play a part in his own salvation. In a sense this did away with the need for the mediation of the priesthood, but for Savonarola merit was still only ultimately attained through the sacraments of the Church. In contrast Luther's *sola fide* doctrine of justification established a direct personal relationship between God and man; the priest had no essential function in the operation of salvation, nor was he in any way a privileged person standing above other men by virtue of his holy orders. If Savonarola recognised a personal God it was for himself. He did not advocate that his hearers should or could reproduce his own private communion with the Almighty. Whereas for Luther the problem of salvation was central to his thinking and social problems were only dealt with reluctantly as peripheral, for Savonarola the whole problem of human conduct from private morality to the organisation of government and society was the main concern, and so he readily became involved in the politics of Florence. This concern with morality was the source of Savonarola's harsh puritanism. If Luther shared the friar's revulsion at the corrupt lives of the leaders of the Church and made this a basis of his attack on Rome, he nevertheless despaired of man's power to be good. He was thus more indulgent towards men's failings. Moreover, temperamentally Luther was more inclined to enjoyment, and did not despise the good things in life. But the basic difference between the two men was in their attitudes towards the doctrines of the Church. Theologically Savonarola was very much a Thomist and therefore ultimately influenced by Aristotle and his methods of approach. Luther was vehemently opposed to scholasticism and its Aristotelian influences, and with his final break with Rome was free to think independently towards a new theology. It is this revolutionary nature of the Lutheran Reformation that makes it above all inappropriate to regard Savonarola, a rigid conservative, as a precursor of the essential work of Luther.

The most lasting achievements in reform of the Church did not come from powerful preachers such as Savonarola, whose effects were very much limited to their own personal exhortations, even if they persuaded many of their followers to forsake this world and to take monastic vows. A more enduring Catholic reform was begun by prominent ecclesiastics in Venetian territory, whose work—mainly in the pastoral sphere—had continuity and by the time of the Lutheran Reformation was already spreading to other parts of Italy. The pioneer of this movement was San Lorenzo Giustiniani, the bishop of Castello who became the first patriarch of Venice. Giustiniani instituted a mode of electing priests by parishioners; but the latter were not given a free choice: the elected priest had already to have taken holy orders and had to be unimpeachable in doctrine, and the election had always to be ratified by Giustiniani himself. Nevertheless, this was an interesting attempt to draw the people into an active interest in the running of their church. He also made a small beginning to instituting a college for the education of priests, enforced the residence of canons and insisted on the clergy paying their debts. He set about reforming monasteries and convents, requiring strict observance of rules. The clergy was forbidden to wear habits of gay colours and Giustiniani had some success in imposing sumptuary regulations throughout his diocese, although this met with powerful opposition from some of the leading ladies of the patriciate.

An important propagator of this new movement within the Church in Venetian territories was Pietro Barozzi, a nephew of Paul II, who was successively bishop of Belluno and bishop of Padua over a period of nearly 40 years. One aim of this movement was to bring the clergy from the bishops down into active contact with the people, by preaching themselves rather than leaving it to the friars, and by taking a regular part in the rites of the Church and fulfilling punctiliously the duties implied by a cure of souls. Pietro Barozzi himself celebrated mass every morning as bishop. Gasparo Contarini based his *De officio episcopi* on the example of Barozzi and although the account of the bishop's attitude might be somewhat idealised it certainly gives some idea of what this Venetian episcopal tradition was aiming to achieve. The bishop should take divine service, administer his diocese scrupulously, take an active part in the cure of souls, be an example of virtue in his own life and see that revenues were properly collected and employed. To accomplish the many facets of his duty an ordered life was necessary, but he should not limit himself by a strict rule. He should reside and therefore could not be a pluralist, but he should be able to take a holiday outside his diocese each year. He should also supervise his clergy personally, preserve the youth of his diocese from corrupting influences and employ surplus revenues on works of charity for the sick and poor.

Perhaps the outstanding figure in this movement was Matteo Giberti. Before his appointment to the bishopric of Verona in 1524, he was as datary an important curial official and persuaded Clement VII to foster a French alliance against the emperor. He was thus well grounded in practical affairs before he went to Verona. The first thing he did as bishop was to renounce his other benefices apparently on the grounds that, now he was no longer tied by curial duties, his benefice should represent a cure of souls, and he maintained the principle of residence scrupulously throughout his diocese. He set up a seminary for the instruction of priests and conducted an examination of all candidates for holy orders within his diocese. If a priest were transferred to Verona from elsewhere, his suitability was ascertained before he was allowed to undertake his duties. Priests in the diocese were required to attend weekly classes even after they were ordained, and the clergy of Verona as a whole were assembled for fortnightly discussions. Giberti also encouraged the publication of works helpful to priests in their pastoral duties. He was interested in the whole work of the diocese and made it his duty to come into personal contact with as many people as possible, drawing laymen into the work of the Church by giving them an active rôle in cooperation with the clergy in the administration of charitable works and institutions. By instituting baptismal registers and having lists of parishioners drawn up, he was able to check on church attendance and make sure that no one was omitted from the watchful surveillance of the Church. Although he did not preach himself on account of a feeble voice that was hardly audible from the pulpit, he took an active part in all the other duties of the Church and instituted reforms in the convents, placing a special emphasis on enforcing enclosure.

Gasparo Contarini was another great figure in this Venetian movement to revitalise the Church. A Venetian patrician, he spent the greater part of his life serving the republic in various offices, which culminated in the ambassadorship at the Roman Curia. However, his overriding interest had always been his religion. As a young man he had mixed in the circles of Vincenzo Querini and Paolo Giustiniani, who joined the Camaldolese order and did much to revive its original ideals. A small work dedicated to Leo X, the *Libellus ad Leonem X*, gives some idea of the religious interests of Contarini's friends. They suggested that it was not effective to legislate for reform, which came rather from a spiritual renovation, and they sought a lead in this in the example of the pope. But they had a tangible programme to recommend. They deplored the ignorance of the clergy, whom they contended were unable to read the Latin of the liturgical texts. Besides advocating clerical education, the authors of the *Libellus* believed that a translation of the Bible would overcome some of the problems of religious ignorance. They also wanted a new codification of canon law and were perturbed about the influence of classical literature—pagan fables, they called it—on the education of the young. They were equally opposed to the scholastic traditions, preferring a study of the scriptures, the early fathers of the Church and the councils as a basis for education. Their vision spread to the Orient and the New World; and they suggested that the Christians of the East should be brought under the rule of Rome and that the natives of America should be converted, not mainly by European missionaries, but by training natives to carry out the missionary work themselves. Contarini did not agree with all their ideas and rejected their call to him to join the Camaldolese order, but he was extremely moved by their example and continued to be preoccupied by movements aiming at the renovation of the Church. Thus he was closely connected with the group that called itself the Oratory of Divine Love, amongst whose early members were Giberti, Gaetano da Thiene and Gian Pietro Carafa. This group of priests and laymen was dedicated to the renewal of the Church. It had no rule, but aimed by the austere life of its members to set an example that might lead the way to a purification of religious life. In 1521 Contarini was the Venetian ambassador at the Diet of Worms. Already as early as 1511 he had come to believe that penitence alone was not adequate for salvation and had emphasised the importance of faith in Christ, which was dependent on the grace of God. Later in 1541 he was sent by Paul III to the Diet of Regensburg, where he negotiated with Melanchthon unsuccessfully for a reunion of the Church. In these negotiations he went so far towards a compromise that he was suspected of heresy by a powerful section at Rome, and lost the favour of the pope. However, although he insisted on the rôle of God-given faith in the process of salvation, he never deserted the view that justification was inseparable also from merit and the sacrament of penance. If at Worms he might have had some sympathy with the reformers, he did not accept their extreme emphasis on faith. Although at the end of his life he was in some danger of being cast out of the Church as a heretic, at the same time it was he above all who had persuaded the pope to recognise the institution of that supreme weapon against heresy that came to be known as the Society of Jesus.

In 1535 Paul III promoted the Venetian ambassador to the cardinalate with a view to enlisting his aid in the reform of the Curia. A commission for this purpose was set up and included, apart from Contarini, Girolamo Aleandro, once a member of the Aldine Academy at Venice and papal nuncio also at the Diet of Worms, and several cardinals such as Carafa, Sadoleto and Pole, who like Contarini had been members of the Oratory of Divine Love. The document the commission produced in 1537 has been regarded as tame and missing the realities of the situation—the spiritual shortcomings and lack of faith and inspiration in the Church. This was not its point, which was to tackle the problem of practices rather than that of attitudes within the Church. Taken as it was intended, it was an outspoken document, attacking many of those abuses in the organisation of the Church that the Venetian reformers had for long been fighting against. It demanded standards in admission to the priesthood, and attacked simony; it insisted on the need for residence, and condemned pluralism; it asked that discipline be re-established in the Church and suggested that the best way to do this was to give power to the men on the spot, the bishops. Every kind of corruption in the administration of the Curia, the dioceses and the monasteries came under the scrutiny of the Contarini commission, and was condemned. Unhappily the trammelling of the freedoms of speech and expression was advocated. But if the members of the commission were conservative in their recommendations, they wished to conserve what they believed to be the true office of the Church and this involved them in recommending changes which for the times were revolutionary. That they were listened to demonstrates a certain liberality in the pope; but, had he been willing to make great sacrifices in the interests of his religion, financial difficulties would have held him back, for the recommendations struck right at the heart of the papal revenues.

The primacy of Venice and its territories in the religious revival of the first part of the sixteenth century was not limited to the circles of Contarini and Giberti, although they were closely connected with all the developments there of that time. One of the most significant sides to this revival was the founding of new orders of clerks regular and new religious associations of women, and nearly all of these had some real connection with Venice. The first of these were the Theatines, an association of priests who lived together and took monastic vows. It was founded in 1524 at Rome by members of the Oratory of Divine Love, including Gaetano da Thiene (St Cajetan), who came from Vicenza, and Gian Pietro Carafa (later Paul IV), a Neapolitan bishop. After the sack of Rome, in which some of its members suffered horribly, the Theatines moved to Venice, where they stayed until 1557 when Paul IV brought them back to Rome. They engaged in the strictest religious life, forsaking all their property, preaching in churches, undertaking with great vigour and self-denial all kinds of charitable works. The Barnabites, founded at Milan in 1533, were a similar order of priests devoted to charitable works. Their leader was Sant' Antonio Maria Zaccaria of Cremona, but their earliest foundations apart from that at Milan were all in Venetian territory at Venice, Vicenza, Padua and Verona. The Somaschi, yet another organisation of the same kind, was founded by San Girolamo Aemiliani in Venetian territory near Bergamo in 1532 with a group of friends who had been active in the recent plagues at Bergamo, Brescia and Verona. Even the foundation of the Jesuits, of which these orders had been forerunners, had important connections with Venice, although none of the founding members were Italians; for it was at Venice that they were forced to desert their original idea of proceeding to Jerusalem, owing to the Venetian-Turkish war that was being fought at the time. Those who were not already priests were ordained there and during a prolonged stay they undertook menial works of charity at Venice, such as working in hospitals. It was also, as has already been mentioned, the Venetian Cardinal Contarini who against the opposition of Carafa finally persuaded Paul III to initiate the order. In 1535 in Brescia, another Venetian town, Sant'Angela Merici founded the Ursulines, in origin a religious association of lay spinsters and widows, but which eventually became strictly enclosed under a rule and like the Jesuits developed a strong emphasis on educational works, although its original purpose was to carry out works of charity of a less specific nature amongst sick and poor. The only important development in this active movement towards spiritual renovation within the Church that had no real connection with Venice was the foundation of the Capuchins, after a while a separate order detached from the Franciscans, having as its aim the primitive simplicity and spirituality of the rule of St Francis.

Much has been said to suggest that Venice was a leader in the reform of the Catholic Church both before and after the beginning of the Lutheran Reformation. Several of her leading ecclesiastics had tackled an array of problems. They tried to enforce residence, starting with their own personal examples—even Cardinal Pietro Bembo, far from a model of spiritual and moral rectitude, refused benefices on the grounds that he could not reside. They opposed pluralism; attempted to restore monasteries and convents to their original objects; took measures to draw congregations into an active participation in the work of the Church; founded seminaries to cope with the acute problem of an uneducated and uninformed clergy; advocated censorship to control heresy; made assaults on venality and gave every encouragement to priests to carry out properly the cure of souls. Yet much remained to be done. If Cardinal Pisani made some attempt to put into practice many of the reforms of the movement, he was still a gross pluralist, as were many of his contemporaries. Nor did it help the reformers that so many of the important ecclesiastical appointments in Venice were principally made for political reasons. But, if everything was not perfect within the Church at Venice, there were parts of Italy where the situation was considerably worse. With the innumerable small dioceses in the south of Italy, there was a great deal of pressure for multiple benefices owing to the comparative poverty of the bishops, but the situation in Corsica was perhaps worst and gives some insight into the depths to which the functioning of the Church could descend. Here, as in Liguria, many of the high positions were reserved for the great Genoese feudatories, who very seldom resided and had no particular qualifications to recommend them. Generally they had not even the general educational and cultural background that was fairly widespread amongst other members of the privileged classes elsewhere in north and central Italy. Sometimes a man like Andrea Bussi, a writer immersed in the classical culture of the times and attached to the papal Curia, was appointed to a Corsican bishopric; but he never visited the island, and his diocese of Aleria was left in the untended state that characterised the rest of Corsica. The priests there were untrained, usually quite illiterate, working on the land and raising poverty-stricken families like any peasant on the island. It was not until the Jesuits made their way to Corsica in the middle of the sixteenth century that any attempt was made to put the situation right. Corsica is an extreme example of the neglect of the pastoral duties of the Church in Italy, but especially in the remoter country areas of the peninsula similar conditions prevailed.

Religious developments in Italy during this period were not confined to questions of morals and the organisation of the Church. On the contrary, there were several doctrinal challenges to orthodox Catholicism. In the middle of the fifteenth century Lorenzo Valla foreshadowed some of the most important features of the protestant Reformation. He emphasised, for example, the irreconcilability of faith and reason, a viewpoint that was inherent in Luther's later attack on the 'whore' philosophy, although it should be remembered that Valla preferred reason, while the protestants came down on the side of faith. He also believed that monastic vows conferred no higher merit on those who took them, an opinion with which the protestants later fully concurred. Perhaps his most direct influence on protestant thought was through his *Dialogue on Free Will*. In this he made a valuable philosophical clarification that was not always accepted afterwards: predestination was in no way caused by God's foreknowledge, but some form of determinism was a necessary condition for absolute foreknowledge to be possible. If there was an omniscient God who knew what was going to occur through time, then no human being was a free agent to do otherwise than what was foreknown. There was either free will and no omniscient God or an omniscient God and no free will. The protestants developed the argument into a proof of predestination, a conclusion that was not inherent in Valla's thought, although as a possibility it was not inconsistent with his argument. What Valla did was to lay bare the untenability of the Catholic views of free will and an all-knowing deity. When one adds his attack on the legality of the temporal possessions of the Church to his revelation of the inherent absurdities of some of its main doctrines, it is clear that he presented a powerful threat to religious unity. Yet many of his ideas had no immediate effect, and after withering attacks on the Papacy he sought successfully a profitable post in the Curia. In the next century his arguments were not forgotten and protestant thinkers owed a great deal to the clarity of Valla's thought.

In the Aristotelian and Averroist circles of the university cities of Padua, Bologna and Pavia a great deal of thought was given to the question of the immortality of the soul. Discussion became so dangerous that the bishop of Padua, Pietro Barozzi, banned in his diocese, which included the university, the subject of the unity of the intellect that was closely connected with the problem. The central argument goes back to the third-century Aristotelian commentator, Alexander of Aphrodisias, whose ideas were elaborated by Averroes, but whose main conclusion was not accepted by him. Alexander developed the distinction of Aristotle between the passive intellect and the active intellect. The passive intellect was the form of the body and lived and died with it. In so far as it realised its potentialities, it participated in the active intellect which activated it. The active intellect was a unified, fully realised intellect, equal to the sum of individual intellects. Nothing of it died with a human being; it was eternal. This eternal, all-pervading intellect was identified by some in the universities with a pantheistic deity; the intellect which was coterminous with the body was the human soul, and as it died with the body so did the soul of the individual. Thus there was no individual immortality; the immortality of the soul was the immortality of that general, all-pervading soul, the active intellect. It was this movement of thought that in part prompted the fifth Lateran Council to condemn pantheism, as Barozzi had tried to ban it from Padua. Both were unsuccessful; for the distinction was made by many thinkers in the universities, including Pietro Pomponazzi, between what was philosophically tenable and what was theologically true. It was behind this doctrine of double truths that some freedom of inquiry was maintained, in just that way that Copernicus made the distinction between what was the best system for the calculation of astral movements, his own, and what might be the truth concerning the movements of the stars, the Ptolemaic system. Others like Nicoletto Vernia and his pupil, Agostino Nifo, in the first place accepted the Alexandrist view of the mortality of the personal soul, but finally renegued under pressure from the orthodox Catholics.

The Florentine Neo-Platonists also developed doctrines of dubious orthodoxy, whilst at the same time countering the thought of the university commentators of Averroes. Whereas, for the latter, man as an individual tended to be regarded as mortal and therefore essentially insignificant; for the former, man only realised his potentialities in an ultimate contemplation of God. But it was, Ficino believed, so rare that this vision of God was achieved on earth, that he regarded it as a proof of an afterlife that the goal of existence would have been barred to too many if there was none. Thus the Neo-Platonists were primarily occupied with the afterlife and the university professors with life on earth. Yet oddly enough it was the circle of Ficino that emphasised the dignity of man just because of this. Man's dignity had been implicitly or explicitly perceived by earlier Florentines such as Bruni and Manetti. This was of a different nature: they showed man his almost unlimited possibilities along lines set by the example of ancient Rome, that is, purely in terms of human achievement within a social context. Ficino, on the other hand, saw man's dignity in a religious context. Man was free to exercise his intellect or submerge himself in his will. If he followed the first course he would free himself from the astrological necessity governing the world of matter and the beasts; if not, he would succumb to such determinism and be in effect no better than the beasts. The first course was similar to that taken by the Platonic philosophers, whereby they freed themselves from the corruption of matter in which the eternal ideas were only imperfectly realised in order to be able to contemplate those ideas in their perfection. The Platonic imagery was given Christian overtones and the process became identified with gaining a knowledge of God. To do this Ficino leaned heavily on the mis-dated Hermetic writings and the Orphic hymns. The world of sympathetic magic and incantations was thus given a Christian meaning, and the virtues of the heavenly bodies were called down to inhabit the material world. Pico della Mirandola did much the same, although he was also strongly influenced by the similarly mis-dated *Cabala*. For Pico man's place in the universe was also a matter of his own choice. God had created the universe, but had left no place for man, nor properties that might be peculiar to him. He created man therefore so that he could 'have joint possession of whatever had been peculiar to each of the different kinds of being . . . with freedom of choice and with honour, as though the maker and moulder of himself'. Thus he could fashion himself in whatever shape he preferred. He had the magic power of marrying the earthly to the heavenly, of becoming almost divine; or he could identify himself with 'the excrementary and filthy parts of the lower world'. Pico, like Ficino, believed that such magic or such philosophy was only accessible to a small circle of initiates: Moses was 'commanded to proclaim the law but not to commit the interpretation of the law to writing or make it common knowledge'. Likewise, the wisdom of Paul, the *Cabala*, the Orphic prophesies and so on, were only for the initiated to share. This goal in life was only gained with difficulty, and Pico claimed to have dedicated himself to it: 'I have relinquished all interest in affairs private and public and given myself over entirely to leisure for contemplation.' Such esoterism became fashionable and hidden meanings in paintings, for instance, divided off a proud *élite* who understood; but this was intellectual snobbery, and Ficino and Pico seem to have been moved by a deep, if heterodox, devoutness.

10

Art and Architecture

The fifteenth and early sixteenth centuries in Italy form a period which perhaps saw the most vigorous and far-reaching changes in the whole history of the arts. By 1464 these changes were already well advanced. The mediaeval artist was thought of as a craftsman. He was a member of a guild; he served an apprenticeship in the workshop of a master in order to learn the foundations of his trade; and, even if his abilities were outstanding, he seldom emerged from the anonymity common to most other craftsmen of the time. As a painter or sculptor, his job was almost exclusively to serve religion; the highest achievement of the architect or builder, although he was employed in all kinds of building, lay in the construction, modification and repair of cathedrals, churches and chapels. Mediaeval art was therefore an expression of an essentially Christian civilisation; its function was to hold before the community a moving and prominent reminder of a lofty and dedicated religious purpose. If such art glorified and exhorted, it was also didactic: a cathedral was a library of devout works for the instruction of a largely illiterate congregation.

In the first half of the fifteenth century a rather obscure Florentine painter, Cennino Cennini, produced a treatise on the art of painting. Although this little work was chiefly concerned with painting as a craft, it also made claims concerning the loftiness of spirit, the theoretical knowledge and the exercise of imagination required of artists, if they were to realise the greatest achievements. A dedication, which avoided more than moderate indulgence in food, wine and women, and involved a thorough study of all the techniques of painting, was also essential to the development of a painter of greatness. Cennini's artist was therefore a man of some education, with pretensions beyond those of a simple craftsman, an individual with the freedom to exercise his imagination, able to rise to exalted heights through work, which was worthy of a single-minded devotion. Cennini was not prophetic; on the contrary he reflected a change that was already beginning to take place at Florence. He wrote in the middle of the long and brilliantly original careers of Ghiberti, Donatello and Brunelleschi, whose works embodied the new attitudes discernible in his treatise. Their work and that of some of their contemporaries, mainly at Florence, certainly added to the intellectual requirements of the artist, made art more of an expression of individuality, partly weaned it from being the fulfilment of a communal and religious need, as they won for it a wider field of patronage, and made themselves sought-after for their own talents to a far greater extent than had been the case with their mediaeval fore-runners.

The activities of these artists reflected the growing interest in Ancient Rome and the new way of looking at it. Rome also lent their works prestige. After Ghiberti won in competition with Brunelleschi, perhaps Donatello, and others the commission for the second baptistery door at Florence, Donatello and Brunelleschi went off to Rome together to study, it seems with deep absorption, remains of classical sculpture and architecture. The result was not a mere imitation of what they saw, but its adaptation to the needs of new art forms they were evolving. Donatello aimed at a vigorous and unromanticised representation of people and things as he saw them. The ability of the Romans to sculpture lifelike human figures no doubt helped him to achieve his aim, influencing his way of looking at things as in the head of the *St John the Baptist* (Florence, Campanile) which has an unmistakably classical mould. His studies also helped him to achieve in his reliefs an atmosphere of historical verisimilitude by incorporating the antique architecture he had seen in Rome into the scenes he depicted. That these finally reached a high degree of representational accuracy through the employment of the rules of linear perspective discovered by Brunelleschi added to his effectiveness. But his real greatness lay in an ability to make his figures express mood, emotion and character through their bearing, their apparent movement, their facial expressions, the hold of their heads. Like Donatello, Brunelleschi assimilated his knowledge of classical buildings into a new and highly original style which owed much also to the eleventh- and twelfth-century Romanesque architecture of Tuscany, at the time accepted as being in the 'good' tradition. Accordingly the architecture of Brunelleschi incorporated classical columns and decorative pilasters, a concern for measurement and simple, proportional relationships, the circular arch of the Romanesque style, the strength of a well-defined entablature borne by the columns and decorated economically by classical motifs. Yet his buildings were Florentine and his churches were in no way pagan temples. Even his columns, which owed so much to his study of classical remains, had a grace and elegance that distinguished them from their classical prototypes. He was an artist of independence and the similarity of his interests with those of Donatello becomes clear, when it is remembered that it was Brunelleschi who, surpassing the achievements of antiquity, revealed the basic secrets of the laws of linear perspective for the first time. His concern was therefore in one aspect closely related to the conquest of nature, and in this he did not limit himself to the imitation of antiquity. His solution to the problem of constructing the great dome of the cathedral at Florence was also essentially unclassical, a development of the techniques of Gothic architecture. Like Pico in his writings, Brunelleschi in his art was willing to draw eclectically from any master who had something of value to teach him; but above this he relied upon his own finely original mind and an exquisite judgment.

Ghiberti too was influenced greatly by the new interest of the time. A comparison of the two baptistery doors, his main work, reveals his openness to new ideas and his willingness to experiment. Like Donatello and Brunelleschi he was not satisfied to employ only the old formulas of his craft, and yet in forging a new style he relied strongly on the Florentine tradition. Not having gone to Rome he was less exposed to the examples of antiquity; but even in his earlier door some detail, such as the representation of columns, was classical in form. The architecture was suggestive rather than representational—a portico or colonnade, a niched throne, a battlemented tower, rather than any attempt to create a naturalistic scene; and in this he was still tied to the fourteenth century. The effect of the recent discovery of perspective on his second door is striking, and that he was deeply interested in this new science is clear from the fact that he attempted to put down in writing a scientific account of its laws. The second door as a result reveals much more than the first the techniques of drawing, a lighter relief increasing the possibilities of grace and movement; and the buildings, though still hardly representational, are on a grander scale, facilitated by some ability in the use of linear perspective. Even then Ghiberti failed to achieve convincing spatial effects and his art lay rather in the rhythmic relationships of his forms. The panels of the first door are simpler in detail and the subject matter is unified, whereas in the later door Ghiberti fell back on the mediaeval technique of incorporating different movements of a narrative into one panel. Where the scenes were occasionally crowded on the first door he created a rhythm of huddled heads, most effective in *The Entry into Jerusalem*, in order to avoid the appearance of chaos. The technique was carried over into the second door and was developed for example in *The Creation and Fall of Man* in the cloud of heads and wings of angels; but the freely 'drawn' figures and the use of landscape and architectural motifs, made this a less obtrusive device. Ghiberti's great achievement was in his handling of the human figure, its movement and especially the expression of the face. In this there was nothing of the deep insight into the human situation of Donatello, but his people were real, appropriate and with characters of their own. The man's head by the top left-hand corner of the St Luke in the first door is a triumph of naturalism; and in the second door the group of the creation of Eve—the tender authority of the Creator, the graceful emergence of Eve herself and the relaxed body of Adam—make a meaningful contrast to the later scenes of the same panel. Imagination was here at work as Cennini would have wished.

Masaccio was perhaps the first painter to apply the new discovery of Brunelleschi. That a painter of such genius did so made even more remarkable the possibilities which were then suddenly revealed. Masaccio was little influenced by classical art, although in the *Holy Trinity* (Santa Maria Novella, Florence), for instance, his architectural setting within the painting was classical in detail, reflecting the style of Brunelleschi. He was the first great exponent of a conception of humanity such as Donatello's in two-dimensional representation. Like the sculptor, he used light with which to mould his forms and aimed at the creation of weight, a graceless realism, the drama of every man, in his figures. No painter before him had planted feet so firmly on the ground, nor achieved so well the illusion of space, for which he did not always rely upon the line but employed also light, moulding and landscape to achieve his effect. This is most convincingly achieved in *The Tribute Money* (Chiesa del Carmine, Florence), a painting of grave dignity and controlled, but fierce, emotion. Nature, with these four Florentines, was therefore largely conquered, not only by their remarkable advances in technique but—Brunelleschi as an architect apart—also by their ability to reveal a deep knowledge of man. They had taken up and perfected what the isolated achievement of Giotto over a century before had begun.

After Masaccio Florentine painting was left with two diverging traditions. Domenico Veneziano, who settled in Florence not long after Masaccio's death, introduced a preoccupation for colour which became a salient element in the art of Fra Angelico. Fra Angelico did not ignore the changed attitudes and techniques of early fifteenth-century Florence, out he tended to borrow from them eclectically. His figures had nothing of the heaviness and natural weight of Masaccio's, but were closer to the slender grace and stylisation of fourteenth-century Siena; yet he incorporated the perspectival skills of the Florentines, sometimes even turning to the classical orders in his buildings. He also developed, as in the *Noli me tangere* (San Marco, Florence), a superb mastery of natural scenery, in this instance incorporating grass and trees in greens that were scarcely known before in painting. Together with such naturalistic representation he could still use the sort of stage scenery suggestive of, rather than representing, a building, recalling the sentry-box type buildings often used by Giotto or the Sienese. His great delight was colour. He ranged from blatant primaries contrasting with an autumnal gloom, as in the *Decapitation of Saints Cosmas and Damian* (Louvre), to the delicate variation of pastel shades, the stone colours of one of the San Marco *Annunciations* or the pale, greenish blues of the *Transfiguration* in another cell of the same monastery. In the *Annunciation* the satin colours of the gowns were colours till then seldom used in painting, and the effect of space through the stone-coloured walls, floor and vaulting was an accomplishment of subtlety and originality.

Paolo Uccello represents the other divergence in its extreme. A friend of Donatello, he lacked the essential humanity of the sculptor, and became wrapped in the techniques of illusion. His vision, so far as it reached, was like that of Gentile da Fabriano or Benozzo Gozzoli, apparently stimulated by the court art of Burgundy. This is particularly clear in *A Hunt* (Ashmolean), but even in the ordered chaos of *The Rout of San Romano* (Uffizi) the backdrop of fields and foliage and scattered movements has something of the same decorative intention. But the obsession with linear perspective triumphs: the converging parallels of the fallen weapons and the foreshortened fallen soldier, together with the ordered pattern of pikes and standards, dominate the viewer. Naturalism is destroyed by a geometricity, only enhanced by the moulded wooden horses and the armour of their riders. This painting is an example of the submergence of art in technique, and its inspiration came perhaps from the desire of the artist to justify his art as intellectually exacting, an aim inherent in the little treatise of Cennini's.

Piero della Francesca, born in the little Tuscan town of Borgo San Sepolcro, gathered within his art the accomplishments of his predecessors and moulded them into an achievement distinctively his own. Something of the heaviness of the figures of Donatello or Masaccio with their unidealised human features returns to his paintings as in the angel of the *Annunciation* (San Francesco, Arezzo) and, indeed, throughout the *Legend of the Cross*, of which it is a part. His ability to show the human body under both physical and emotional strain was great and his scope in this respect was more ambitious than that of any of his predecessors. Like Uccello he too was captivated by the problems of perspective. His architectural settings were often minutely classical in detail and he created space through strict, classical lines. Indeed later in life he gave much of his time to a theoretical study of perspective and this work provided the basis for the theoretical studies of Luca Pacioli. But like Masaccio he also created space through landscape and the play of light on his moulded figures. Aerial perspective with its hazy distances is highly developed too, for example, in the background to his portraits of Federico di Montefeltro and Battista Sforza (Uffizi). Piero was also a master of the whole range of colour—the mauves and blues of the *Annunciation*, the metallic solemnity of the *Pala di Urbino* (Brera, Milan), the wooden colours of the *St Jerome* (Accademia, Venice); but he never over-diversified his colours and thereby he established a harmonising unity for his paintings. Yet, with all his achievements Piero in many ways is less satisfactory as a painter than, for instance, Masaccio. This was partly because his range was so much greater and he attempted things beyond his reach: his animals were never completely successful, as neither were those later of even Leonardo or Raphael, although his horses lost something of the woodenness of Uccello's; and his faces, although they varied considerably from painting to painting, in a group all retained a family likeness that tended to deprive them of individuality. But Piero's art, although he spent so little time in Florence and produced his known work only after he left there, crowned the early fifteenth-century Florentine achievement. Apart from the intrinsic value of his work, his importance lay in extending a taste for the new techniques and visions in painting through a larger part of central Italy; but he did not start a school and, although a few painters such as Signorelli and Perugino came under his influence, he marks the end of, rather than a stage in, a development.

At the same time as Piero was working at Borgo San Sepolcro, Arezzo, Rome, Ferrara and Urbino, Leon Battista Alberti was developing a theory of art which, in tune with the great artists and architects of his time, went beyond the limits of current achievement to embody a great personal vision. An exile from his family's land of Florence from birth through much of his life, Alberti was saved from making the Florentine tradition, as it emerged, the sole criterion of great art; but he was singularly impressed by the Florentines and especially the achievements of Brunelleschi, whom he judged to have become the arbiter of taste in the architecture of his time. Like the Florentines and going beyond them, Alberti also believed in the revival of antiquity. His work on architecture, although he affected not to be able to understand the Graeco-Latin terminology of Vitruvius, was very largely derived from the Roman architect's *de architectura*. In fact, the structure of his work very closely resembled the Vitruvian triad: *venustas, firmitas, utilitas*: Alberti laid it down as a principle that the works of architects 'should not only be strong and useful, but also pleasant to the sight'. Involved in this last element was an aesthetic which derived from a world-view that was to dominate Italian art for more than a century in varying forms and degrees.

Vitruvius himself theorised about architectural perfection from a tradition of Greek theory cast in a Platonico-Pythagorean mould. Underlying the theory was the belief that architecture reflected the constructional principles of the physical world and that, since these were simple and mathematical as in the harmonic proportions of music, so a building should be reduced to simple, mathematical proportions. A characteristic Albertian version of this view was: 'Beauty is a kind of harmony and concord of all the parts to form a whole which is constructed according to a fixed number and a certain relation and order, as symmetry—the highest and most perfect law of nature—demands.' Beauty was not therefore a matter of taste, and art was never a discovery through a process of trial and error; it was rather a construction following the principles inherent in nature as it was created by God. This was a reason why later artists sometimes won the epithet 'divine'. This claim to the God-like activities of the artist was developed further under the influence of the Florentine Neo-Platonists. Alberti was content to show that art was a highly intellectual discipline, as exacting as any liberal art. There was a certain tension, however, in Alberti between the curious, almost Neo-Platonic assumptions in Vitruvian theory and the comfortable, urbane architectural experience he had had from examining the remains of classical Rome. Inherent in Vitruvius' work was the Neo-Platonic view that nature, as it embodied the principles of creation, was beautiful and should be imitated. Since matter was corrupt, the material embodiments of such principles would be imperfect. Therefore it was nature's laws rather than her outward manifestations that should be copied. Alberti believed that one might discern these laws from a study of the most beautiful things in nature, but one did not proceed to choose from nature's most excellent parts to assemble, like Zeuxis, a perfection surpassing nature. This suggestion was left to less original theorists like Filarete. Instead one chose the mean, the normal, what was common; and here Alberti shows himself to be closer to the views of the Florentine *ottimati*, more Aristotelian in temperament than the circle that later surrounded Lorenzo. Indeed his own buildings, which since the architect was an intellectual and not a craftsman he left to others to build according to his plans, moved from the subtle elegance of Brunelleschi to a much greater solidity. This is especially so in the Tempio Malatestiano at Rimini, where a sophisticated system of proportionality echoing simple musical harmonies is clothed in a heavy, unethereal form. Although the unfinished state of the rebuilt church adds to this impression, nevertheless a reconstructed version of Alberti's plans bears it out. One could go too far in concentrating on Alberti's theory of beauty, for almost as essential an element in his work was a governing notion of the function of a building. Indeed, with Vitruvius he made this something of an aesthetic principle. Thus, because his Rucellai palace was for a Florentine business family, it remained fundamentally a traditional building. The ground floor was principally for business purposes, cut off by a firm line from the main floor above it. The palace was conceived to front the city streets and was accordingly inward-looking in conception; and, although it was embellished by a clever use of the motifs of the classical orders, nothing like it could have been found in Greece or Rome. Even the windows were just a simplification of a traditional Gothic style, reduced to basic geometrical shapes, Romanised rather than Roman. Yet this was the model from which the great urban domestic architecture of Italy's future spread and developed, as building in Italy for long stemmed largely from principles first enunciated, at least since antiquity, in Alberti's book. With a greater emphasis placed on the courtyard as in Michelozzi's Palazzo Medici the inward-looking quality of much urban architecture was complete.

Despite the travels of Florentines through north and central Italy and the dispersal of theory through books such as those of Alberti, art in Italy was still to some extent regional in character. Perhaps Siena and Ferrara provide the outstanding examples of this stylistic parochialism, although even in these cities there were to be found examples of works by strangers such as Donatello and Piero della Francesca. In Siena fifteenth-century art lay still very much in the local traditions of the past 200 years, and perhaps it had largely exhausted them. The gold ground, for example, was common with painters like Matteo di Giovanni, while the scientific perspective of the Florentines was practically ignored. At most, like Giotto, the Sienese felt their way towards some idea of converging lines. Giovanni di Paolo's *The Birth of St John the Baptist* (National Gallery) by using such pragmatic techniques in fact created a considerable illusion of recession: tiled floors, reinforced by the lines of a fireplace and bed-head, lead one back into a succession of doorways and ultimately into shadow in a way reminiscent of what occurs when one looks through facing mirrors. The foot of the bed on the other hand converges into the foreground, a contrary rhythm forcing the eye towards the central theme of the painting and thrusting St Elizabeth forward into the rather undistinguished scene. Another example of the same painter running with some success contrary to the rules of perspective can be seen in his *St John the Baptist Entering the Wilderness* (National Gallery). Here the civilised foreground spreads cultivated into a distance brought close by maintaining the size of St John amongst the stylised mountains, so that he towers over a distant homestead. Although it is two pictures in one, features in both merge to give the whole a unity and therefore to maintain the striking effect of an inverted perspective. Children draw like this to highlight their main characters: their perspectives are dramatic and not visual. A more scientific, representational art of the Florentines on the other hand, by losing the freedom to employ such devices, made for itself problems—both of creating dramatic intensity and simply of filling up a space—such as were unknown to Giovanni di Paolo. The figures in the Sienese art of the time likewise owed little to what had occurred in Florence. They represent a curious contrast between the stylised faces of the Virgins and holy women with graceful rhythms to their robes and peasant-like persons, awkward and real and mostly men, who have brought life and its troubles to their Byzantine forbears. Perhaps the most disturbing and at the same time the most careless of reality amongst these Sienese painters was Francesco di Giorgio. His *Annunciation* (Pinacoteca, Siena) is dominated by a set of Corinthian columns—the column in Florentine art had long divided off the Virgin from the archangel; but these columns have more the proportions of a telegraph pole than anything that would have been built of marble. Perspective is absent except as a piece of wild guesswork, and the painting is therefore rocking with instability. Yet the movement of the two disproportioned figures is perhaps enhanced by the movement of their surroundings and the Virgin jerks backwards with surprise as the angel appears. It has been said that fifteenth-century Sienese art is decorative in intent, but clearly it has effects that, if not always successful, go beyond so limited a goal. Siena was to a large extent isolated politically and therefore culturally from Florence by a lasting antipathy; it was cut off from the main developments of fifteenth-century art; but it nevertheless succeeded in making a contribution of its own until eventually it was submerged in the Tuscany of the grand dukes.

Less need be said of the Ferrarese, not because they were in any way less interesting than the Sienese nor because their achievements were less, but because they assimilated much of the technical development that had occurred elsewhere in Italy. Yet they created a distinctively regional style. Their scenes were often full of swirling activity as in *The Life of St*

Vincent Ferrer (Vatican) of Ercole de' Roberti, and rich detail could crowd their works (*Madonna Enthroned with Four Saints* by the same painter, Kaiser Friedrich Museum, Berlin). They experimented with the eye level to give impressions of height as in the last painting or in the *Crucifixion* of Francesco del Cossa (Washington) and in his *St Vincent Ferrer* (National Gallery). Their realism was often ghoulish as in Cosmè Tura's *St Sebastian* and detail was at times full of curious, sometimes frightening symbols (Tura's *Allegory of Spring* or Cossa's *St Lucy*, Washington). They used light and colour with dramatic atmospheric effects (Tura's *St Jerome*, Roberti's *Last Supper*, both in the National Gallery), which in some ways foreshadowed Giorgione's *Tempest* (Accademia, Venice). By the third decade of the sixteenth century Dosso Dossi was painting atmospheric scenes that certainly derive from Giorgione, whom he knew; yet these were at the same time very much in tune with the work of his Ferrarese predecessors.

With its openness to ideas as a meeting-point of international trade and its mixture of traditions southern Italy, and especially Sicily, had become accustomed to the reception of influences from foreign cultures perhaps even more than in the centre and north of Italy. Antonello da Messina, the greatest of Sicilian painters, as a product of this environment, wedded a Flemish concern for detail and the new powers of representation granted by the Florentine conquest of perspective (both of which he learnt at Naples) into a highly individual art, recipient of a succession of further influences as he moved through Italy. At the same time he himself left his mark on others, even on Giovanni Bellini for a while; and the complex of stylistic and technical interactions, which had gone on for long in Italy with the travels of Giotto, Donatello, Piero and others, became during the later part of the fifteenth century so intricate that regional styles, such as have just been dealt with, were largely becoming submerged in what might be more properly called an Italian style. Although this is most obvious in Antonello, his artistic career was only symptomatic of what was emerging as a general tendency of his time. Each new contribution to the skills and insights of art was now influencing artists over a far wider area than before. The growth of patronage to be discussed later was perhaps the prime mover in this process; but the travels of artists such as Antonello, independent of the summons of a patron, also helped considerably to blur regional distinctions. Schools rather than regions perhaps retained more meaning; but where this was so, it was largely a matter of the great and their less talented followers. The great themselves broke new ground in a context of Italian painting rather than the painting of their native locality;

if they were associated with regions, it was usually the region of the prevailing boom in patronage and not so much that of the artist's home. This is not to say that the process was completed then, or that it was ever completed; but a decided change of emphasis had taken place. Mantegna perhaps defines the extent of this process; Bellini, its limits.

Mantegna began his career as a painter at Padua where he was influenced by works of the most seminal of Florentine artists, the sculptor Donatello. Perhaps this would explain why his figures were almost metallic, certainly statuesque and monumental. They had weight, but were without the ruggedness or tenderness, the humanity and naturalness that Donatello could capture. They were deployed carefully like over-directed actors on a stage, rather stilted and somewhat self-conscious. Mantegna's use of architectural settings likewise was carefully staged, drawing upon and developing the subtleties of linear perspective to dwarf or magnify his figures, to separate them or to frame them. It was probably he who showed the way to the Ferrarese in lifting the figures in the foreground by employing a low eye-level, as for instance in the main panels of the San Zeno polyptych (Verona) or even more subtly in the San Luca polyptych (Brera), where there were no background figures to aid the effect. Here it is the audience and not other figures in the painting that is in a sense dwarfed, despite the comparative smallness of the figures themselves. *The Adoration of the Shepherds* (New York), on the contrary, raises the eye-level to display the Christ Child on the ground. Mantegna, although thrilled by the possibilities new techniques had opened up, never went so far as Uccello in their exploitation. Even in *The Dead Christ* (New York) the extreme foreshortening, if experimental, was an experiment in using an artistic device to serve an emotional purpose. Perhaps here Mantegna failed to make a convincing dramatic statement in much the same way as he failed to infuse his sculptured figures with life; yet he had dramatic intentions where, it seems, Uccello had not.

Much of the landscape painting of Mantegna was also sculptural, perhaps architectural, in conception. The great rocks, symbolic of mountains, were built up layer by layer carefully moulded by the play of light on a single colour. These symbolic features contrast discordantly with more natural scenes in, for example, *The Adoration* and they illustrate how far Mantegna had strayed from the naturalistic aims of the earlier Florentines, while his monochromatic tendencies further exemplify his debt to sculpture. Finally, Mantegna was perhaps the earliest of Italian painters to tackle the wide range of varied subjects that became the hallmark of the ensuing period: if his Bible was largely limited to the New Testament, with a feeling for history he set his early saints in the settings of the Roman Empire. To paint his patrons he did not feel impelled to put them by the side of a Mother and Child or kneeling before a crucifixion, but portrayed them in a courtly group—posed, it is true, but in a historically possible situation. If he painted the classical gods with allegorical overtones of a highly unclassical nature, nevertheless like Bruni he attempted to re-create a historic reality and did not ignore all sense of time in the manner of the *Ovide Moralisée*.

Bellini like Mantegna drew upon much of the repertoire of Italian art. He was at home with linear perspective; and he knew the vocabulary of classical motifs with which he sometimes embellished the architectural furniture of his paintings. He moulded the contours of his landscapes and figures with a masterly play of light and shadow, experimented with the change of colours with distance, and produced landscapes than which none have been more natural nor more enchanting. As a truly great artist many elements of his paintings were of course entirely his own; but in a sense some were Venetian too, not in so far as they borrowed from a Venetian tradition, but rather because they owed their origin to a Venetian environment and in fact led to future developments in Italian art that were most happily pursued by Venetian painters. This is particularly true of his use of light, which suffused his landscapes and figures, as in *The Agony in the Garden* (National Gallery), bringing them into a single, atmospheric unity. It was so also with his use of shade: he saw through shadows to apprehend that substantially the same colour remained in them, darkened and subdued, as would be present in full light. It was delight and interest in colour such as this that led to the amazing atmospheric effects of Giorgione. They led also to Titian's bold use of colour, at times to replace form and subject-matter as the main element in achieving compositional balance. With their long contact with the art of Byzantium and the East through their trading empire, Venetians were perhaps the most suited of all Italians to develop these interests and, although he had colourist fore-runners such as Domenico Veneziano, it was Bellini who showed them how.

If Bellini unified his paintings atmospherically, he was still too much within the Christian tradition to merge his New Testament scenes in every respect into a modern landscape of the Terraferma with its modern, not even classical architecture. Invariably the superb naturalism of the setting was divided from the stage of the sacred action. In *The Agony in the Garden*, for example, a stream separates a formalised foreground bearing a stylised rock for the kneeling Christ from the Italian countryside, the linear rhythms of the one part directly countering those of the other; or in

The Madonna of the Pear at Bergamo there is a neutral panelling to mark off the Mother and Child from the background of scenery peopled with figures wrapped in their own irrelevant concerns. Bellini's *Agony* contrasts strikingly with that of Mantegna (National Gallery), although both were painted at about the same time and were apparently based on a drawing by Bellini's father, Mantegna's father-in-law. Mantegna's countryside is not divided from his main scene, but instead develops the curvilinear rhythms of the foreground. The stylised rock of the kneeling Christ contrasts only with part of the background scenery, the rocks rising above the town being texturally similar. Mantegna's soldiers, moreover, are characteristically clothed in Roman dress, whereas Bellini is unconcerned with historical veracity. Finally Mantegna's saints are grouped together with an over-riding compositional purpose, too chiselled to be relaxed. Bellini's on the other hand are separated, conceived as individuals, a triumph of the artist's power to portray humanity relaxed. The foreshortened Peter has risen completely beyond a technical trick of perspective, as Mantegna would have had *The Dead Christ*, but failed; and the leaning John, with slightly dropped jaw, embodies the essence of absolute relaxation.

The mastery of Bellini over the representation of sleep stretched even to the sleeping child. In *The Virgin and Child Enthroned* (Accademia, Venice) the Child asleep on the Madonna's lap is perhaps the first wholly successful painting of a baby in representational terms. Bellini also solved the problem of how to paint babies awake, a task which quite defeated artists of the stature of Masaccio and Piero della Francesca. It was not realised until Bellini that a baby does not achieve a poised balance of its own, but needs a counter-force beyond that of its own vertical weight. In the *St Christopher* of the altar-piece of SS. Giovanni e Paolo (Venice) he therefore gave the child a sideways motion snuggling into the neck and holding the head of the saint; and most of Bellini's Madonnas really hold the Christ Child, drawing him in towards them like real mothers, instead of being too awed to exert a firm pressure on the holy infant body. When this was not the case the child was usually laid out on some material or propped up against a cushion so that balance was no longer a problem. Bellini went beyond solving the problems of distributing the weight of the body and con-summately expressed character and meaning through the faces of his figures. The idealised authority of the *Doge Leonardo Loredano* (National Gallery), the sensitivity of *A Man with Long Black Hair* (Louvre) or the solicitous concern of the Madonna, caught between maternal grief and inquiring wonderment (*Pietà with St John*, Brera), demonstrate something of the scope of Bellini's powers. A whole range of human understanding was his, and he was able to recreate it in his art with a certainty which has not been surpassed. Yet when he was prompted towards the fashionable painting of classical scenes with allegorical programmes his powers deserted him. As a consequence he usually resisted the pressures of courtly patronage.

The art of Italy dealt with so far was primarily concerned with the conquest of reality. This process certainly did not stop with Bellini or Mantegna and technically perhaps the most imaginative of Italian painters in this respect was their younger contemporary, Leonardo da Vinci. Indeed the problems of representing three-dimensional phenomena on a plane continued to exercise painters right up to the impressionists, who were much concerned with the representation of light and the way people actually saw the world rather than the way they believed they saw it, or even to the period of the cubists who tried to project their shapes forward from the canvas rather than treat the frame as a window opening on a world beyond. In fact both these tendencies had precursors in the fifteenth century. Leonardo's development of the *sfumato* technique, the blurring of outlines as around the eyes of the *Mona Lisa* (Louvre), was very similar in purpose to the blurred and shimmering vision of the impressionists; whilst Mantegna's moulded figures tended to push forward like a relief, although his perspectival lines receded into a distance behind the frames. But the Neo-Platonists of Florence gave a new conception to reality which profoundly influenced its representation in art. Before this is described the emergence of a new set of Florentine artists after the comparatively lean period that followed the deaths of the great early fifteenth-century Florentines should be considered.

Domenico Ghirlandaio was one of several Florentine artists of the time who tended to reduce painting to a comfortable and decorative function, charming and lacking in poetic intensity. *The Last Supper* (Ognissanti, Florence) is a good example of his limitations. The Christ is in no way high-lighted; the disciples, although they mostly take up actions of response to the significance of the moment, fail to indicate the momentousness of the scene. Ghirlandaio could at times arrange his figures effectively in rhythmic groupings; but here he lines them unimaginatively across his picture as was the tradition, with Judas divided off on the near side of the table. The scene is that of a civilised meal in the comfortably opulent surroundings of Florentine bourgeois society. The background of trees, some of them fruit-bearing, of birds and summer skies creates a lazy atmosphere which adds only to the pleasantly decorative effect of the painting. Ghirlandaio was competent in the techniques of the Italian painting of his time; he reflected the easy confidence of a section of pre-Savonarolan society; he could paint classical details with a Roman air of serenity to satisfy the current penchant for antiquity. With one exception he added little to the vocabulary and accomplishments of art. From the time when Giotto experimented with the arrangement of his figures, turning them away from full-face views, even showing their backs, a new possibility of rhythmic composition emerged, the connection of figures with objects and other figures through the direction of their vision. Such rhythms were developed with great effect by Leonardo and Raphael in particular. What Ghirlandaio achieved with the use of such an invisible link was the transmutation of an essentially ugly old man, whose face was covered with morbid protuberances, into a person of sympathy and tenderness by tying his gaze to a reciprocal gaze, oblivious to the unsavoury complexion of the old man, from his grandson (Louvre). In this painting Ghirlandaio lifted himself from the ordinary to attain one of the high achievements of Italian art.

Botticelli, a few years older than Ghirlandaio, was in a sense the decorative artist *par excellence*; but he was original, out of the main stream of Italian art, of the circle of the Neo-Platonists rather than of the Latinists, and later drawn into the enthusiastic and puritanical following of Savonarola. If his art owed much to tradition, it was the tradition of the fourteenth century, and his emphasis on line is closest in his own century to the later Ghiberti and to Fra Angelico. But his refinement of line, so vastly different from the moulded and heavy forms of Masaccio or the blurred outlines of Leonardo, was something entirely his own. The exquisite delicacy of his outlines made him the supreme painter of an ethereal and untouchable feminine beauty, alive with fragile grace; and his men had the smooth bodies of youths. In his painting touch is always gentle and movement deft; hands caress, hair flows, feet trip or glide. His action is mime, and drama is reduced to a form of sweet ballet. This is so as much in the swirling movement of *The Annunciation* (Uffizi), as in the slower rhythms of the Venus or of the Graces in the *Primavera* (Uffizi). The allegories of Botticelli's classical programmes seem to have been devised by Ficino and his circle of Neo-Platonists. They draw eclectically from ancient stories, clothing them with the Christian-Antique synthesis of Ficinian thought. The values inherent in them lead Platonically to higher, purer realms and indicate a dissociation from the corrupt material world, an approximation to the perfection of the Ideas or to the mind of God. But Florentine Neo-Platonism did not touch Botticelli's attitude to his art, unearthly as it was; it only entered the content of his paintings. His techniques, although personally refined, were much in the tradition of Gothic Christianity; his subjects were those of the new Christianity of Lorenzo's Florentine circles. When therefore he fell under the influence of Savonarola, only a certain agitation was needed to dismiss the emotional uninvolvement of his painting and to make it an apt vehicle for the disturbed spirit of a *Piagnone*.

The fifteenth-century architects and artists of Italy had unremittingly rifled nature for her secrets. Brunelleschi and Alberti, Masaccio, Piero della Francesca and Bellini with numerous others had brought so much to light that it seemed hardly possible that much else remained to be discovered. The searching and omnivorous mind of Leonardo da Vinci proved that this was not so. It ranged through a great diversity of sciences, named and yet to be named—geology, hydraulics, anatomy, aeronautics, cartography, optics, ballistics, mechanics—and was fertile with insights into their principles. This consuming activity was directed for the main part towards serving his painting which Leonardo regarded as the loftiest of occupations, the most suited of the arts to do justice to the miracles of nature. Unhappily his wide interests, if ancillary to his work as an artist, left him far too little time to paint. Moreover, painting itself was for Leonardo largely a matter of problem-solving—that was the dignity of his art—and so, the problem solved, he often left the work unfinished, since the routine task of completing a painting seemed not to be able to hold his interest. Perhaps, even, it was too undignified a matter for him, with his high opinion of the nature of his work to carry such routine painting through to an end. In this his attitude is reminiscent of that of Alberti, who believed architecture to be a highly intellectual pursuit and left the supervision of the actual building to others. The smallness and incompleteness of Leonardo's output has been made worse by the fact that his painting techniques were often faulty, and consequently some of his works have not lasted or have survived only in a most degenerated state. To compensate for these losses and shortcomings much of his preliminary work has been carefully preserved, and there are magnificent studies to illustrate the careful thought and ingenious experimentation that preceded his committing himself in paint.

The contribution made by Leonardo to the techniques of painting can easily be seen by comparing his early *Annunciation* (Uffizi) with later works. In the *Annunciation* he had already mastered aerial perspective and its hazy, blue distances. But this was not an entirely new contribution and later perhaps he over-emphasised the technique and painted a blueness that went beyond nature. He was also already feeling his way towards the blurred facial features that created the fluidity of the *Mona Lisa's* expression. Yet here too he went no further than perhaps Bellini independently had gone. Certainly he gave a softness to his figures that was absent in the work of Verrocchio, his master, and was of a different order from the pallid grace of Botticelli's figures. What is most striking is his dependence on line: the detail of the hair, the stark outline of the silhouetted trees, the clear-cut architectural features, the distinct limits of hands and faces. Line was still the main instrument of movement, and like that of Botticelli Leonardo's was graceful, light and contrary to a sense of drama. Masaccio had, of course, achieved in his moulded figures a heavy, lumbering, peasant-like movement; but Leonardo was later to arrive at a solution of his own, avoiding the extremes that till then had alone been mastered. The great example of this is *The Last Supper* (Santa Maria delle Grazie, Milan), a complexity of movements which perhaps can only be explained by its faithfulness to an acute observation of the attitudes of men. Linear effects are almost entirely deserted, even in the architectural furniture of the scene that with its converging, but not always distinct, lines draws the eye to a Christ, framed by the central window. Elsewhere *sfumato* prevails, and yet each figure reacts dramatically to the announcement of the impending betrayal. The movements, although immensely involved in their interactions, are controlled. The scene is not a riot, but an intense drama, the disciples grouped in threes contrasting in their shocked responses (except for the sullen Judas) with the sadly placid Christ. Judas himself is no longer isolated from the scene as in earlier versions like Ghirlandaio's; and, where Ghirlandaio had made a soothing decoration out of the portentous story, Leonardo, sceptical as he was, told it with moving intensity.

Neo-Platonic theories began to influence the fifteenth-century concept of art indirectly through the architectural writings of Vitruvius. More strictly perhaps such theories should be called Pythagorean, for they emphasised, above all, notions of harmony, proportion and the curious mysteries of number such as had intrigued Nicholas of Cusa. It has been shown how Alberti was far removed in attitude from the Florentine Neo-Platonists; yet the words of Ficino suggesting the close parallel between the principles of the creation of the universe and those followed in the construction of a building make it clear that effectively Alberti's and Ficino's ideas about building were of a kind. Of creation, Ficino wrote: 'In this common order of the whole, all things, no matter how diverse, are brought back to the unity according to a single determined harmony and rational plan. Therefore, we conclude that all things are led by one certain orderer who is most full of reason.' Of the process of building he wrote:

'. . . unless the perfect form of an edifice is prescribed by the architect, the different workmen will never be moved to particular tasks which accord with the plan of the whole itself.' Again, of the arts in general: '. . . man imitates all the works of the divine nature, and perfects, corrects and improves the works of lower nature . . . he imitates all the works of the higher nature.' He calls God the artisan of nature, while his friend, Pico, used the well-worn metaphor: 'God the Father, the supreme Architect.' Artistic processes were therefore elevated by the Florentine Neo-Platonists to a God-like activity. Architecture and, indeed, art in general for Ficino was an imitation of nature, not in its appearances, as it had been for the greater part of Italian art up to about the time of Lorenzo, but in its principles, those principles with which God had created the universe. The prestige given to the occupation of the artists was thus inflated by its parallelism with God's creative act and the epithet 'divine' was clearly applicable to art's greatest practitioners. Moreover, as for Alberti, art became an intellectual pursuit, strictly involved in the rational and harmonic order of the universe. Such an attitude led to the emphatic geometricity, the symmetry and proportionality of the works of Giuliano Sangallo or Donato Bramante, and was clearly in tune with their pre-occupation with classical forms. It led them, too, to develop the fashion of the centrally-planned church, built up from the circle, symbol of eternity without beginning or end, and crowned by the dome. For Bramante architecture became almost a pursuit divorced from function, a work of art for its own sake, justified by its reflection of the principles of creation; and appropriately it was he who was commissioned to draw up plans for the new St Peter's at Rome to be man's closest approximation to the work of the supreme Architect. The complete contrast between this attitude, that singled out intuitively the inner principles of nature for imitation, and the attitude of Leonardo, insistent upon the close observation of the physical world through the senses and especially the eye, perhaps becomes most clear in the paintings of Raphael and Michelangelo. But a little more should first be said about developments in architecture.

The development of architectural thought in the sixteenth century relied very much on the twin foundations of Vitruvius and Alberti; but, as in the case of Sangallo and Bramante, the interpretation became increasingly Pythagorean and Neo-Platonic in emphasis. Commentaries on Vitruvius multiplied. In them with the growing interest in the mathematical structure of the universe—made more convincing by a better understanding of Euclid, the incontrovertible evidence of harmonics and perspective, advances in astronomical concepts, mechanics and ballistics—it was the notions of order, symmetry, harmony and proportion that tended to be magnified. Building became almost symphonic in its spatial and surface harmonies; and, although a place was left for the sensibility of the architect (and all the greater architects relied very much on their own taste and judgment in the last analysis), at the same time a predictable and common logic underlay most that was built. Yet this allowed a great variety of effects; and it is clear that this was so when one Vitruvian commentator, Cesariano, could illustrate the principles of the Roman architect from the façade of the Gothic cathedral of Milan. Mathematical relationships did not resolve very much more than the comparative sizes of parts of a building; its shapes, unless they were dictated by mystical notions such as was the case with Bramante's centrally-planned churches, could still retain a great deal of freedom. Tendencies towards uniformity came, not from the metaphysical bases to architectural theories, but from a detailed knowledge of classical forms and from the influence one architect would exert upon another.

Later in the sixteenth century the great variety of Palladio's work, which was consistently based on fundamentally uniform theories of the type described above, is a telling example of the scope such architectural principles left to the imagination of the architect. Three Palladian palaces at Vicenza illustrate this well. The Palazzo Colleoni is very much in the Albertian tradition with its severe ground floor flanking the street. Above, the main floor or *piano nobile* is broken with Ionic half-columns between alternately pedimented and rounded windows. The contrast in rhythms between the two floors is therefore traditional and the detail of the first floor façade is classical, but the arrangement is entirely Palladio's own. The Palazzo Valmarana is in conception again in the tradition of Alberti. A balustrade emphasises the division between ground and first floors; but the severity of the ground floor is minimised by stone reliefs above the plain windows flanked with small Corinthian pilasters and an ornately crowned entrance, while larger pilasters of the same order rise from the bottom of the ground-floor windows to the top of those of the *piano nobile*. It is only below the lower windows that the traditional ground-floor severity remains, and the two main floors are tied by the tall pilasters which make stronger vertical divisions and destroy the Albertian isolation of each floor. The third palace, the Palazzo Chiericati, is different again. The division between the two floors is marked strongly by a Doric entablature, but except for the central block of the *piano nobile* the whole façade is recessed in shadow behind (on the ground floor) Doric and (on the main floor) Ionic colonnades. Thus the façade is divided in such a way as to highlight a decorated surface against shadows that link the two floors, despite the firm division across the building made by the entablature mounted with a balustrade.

The impact of the Platonic idealism in Neo-Platonism was perhaps more obvious and even more fundamental for the representational arts of painting and sculpture than for architecture. It led artists to attempt to perfect the superficial appearances of nature, to transcend them and create a greater approximation to the unmaterialised ideas of which they were imperfect copies. Consequently painters and sculptors sought to represent a generalised beauty, a nature that was based upon and revealed universal principles. Raphael could say, for instance, that 'to paint a beauty I need to see many beauties, but since there is a dearth of beautiful women, I use a certain idea which comes to mind'. This was, of course, a combination of the eclectic procedure of Zeuxis, picking the best features from a range of examples to make a composition that exceeded any one of the originals, and the Platonic notion of the Ideas, which were directly intelligible only to the mind. Both processes would, according to their respective proponents, improve upon nature. The attitude was at the opposite pole to that of Leonardo, who had written of Masaccio: 'his perfect works showed how those who take for their standard any one but nature—the mistresses of all masters—weary themselves in vain'. Even so, Raphael inherited through his master, Perugino, a soft and sweet style which owed much to Leonardo's *sfumato* technique, so that the difference between their philosophical attitudes in so far as it affected their work should not be over-emphasised. Yet when the naturalism of Masaccio or Bellini is compared with the idealism of Raphael, it becomes only too obvious that there was a vast difference between the aims of the earlier painters and those of Raphael. Even the idealised authority of Bellini's *Doge Loredano* was far different from Raphael's treatment of Julius II (National Gallery). In the latter painting there was no pretence at exaggerating qualities which were already latent in the subject; Julius II became altogether another man, full of gentle wisdom and the sympathy of experience. In Raphael's hands he was no longer the impatient warrior and unprincipled diplomatist of reality. He had not even the august serenity of an idealised pope. But Raphael's contribution to art, apart from the obvious, ethereal beauty of his paintings, was a hard-won but apparently easy mastery of balance within his works. His rhythms flow harmoniously, nothing seems out of place, and he was in full control of the movement of his figures. This last point was so whether he relied on line or moulding for his effect. The linear movements of the cupids in the *Galatea* (Farnesina, Rome) are full of grace and buoyancy, while the *Mercury and Psyche* in the same palace push forward with a light but more solid movement towards the viewer. Raphael for the most part had also learnt the lesson of Bellini in the portrayal of babies, giving them the counter-movement they required, if they were to convince, by means of the confident caresses of their lovely mothers.

Like Raphael, Michelangelo was also deeply influenced by Neo-Platonic thinking and, although his career developed through several stages, he consistently strove to disengage himself from external appearances to concentrate on the inner realities of his subjects. This was so with his interest in anatomy and he seemed to build up surfaces to reveal the skeletal formations and muscular behaviour beneath. His towering *David* in Florence was conceived in this way; but it was fashioned also to counter the optical recession of perspective, so that again and in another way surface realities were put aside as the intellect intervened. Later in his life this dissociation of the senses was exaggerated further. He believed art to be in the mind; and, like the Platonised view of creation, the work itself could be no more than a feeble materialisation of a prior mental image. Art did not imitate nature in the ordinary sense; it rather imitated the creation of nature. Consequently art—especially in the mind of the great artist—surpassed nature. This attitude explains to some extent why several of Michelangelo's works were left unfinished, although at times there were other more human reasons too—disagreement with a patron or the feeling that to go further would add nothing to the solution of a problem. It also explains the distortions that entered his later work, the elongated figures, the rough-hewn surfaces, the effort to express the spirit rather than to portray the body. Moreover, he had solved all the problems of the body: the strength and the determination of the *David*, the unmatched loveliness of the Madonna in the first *Pietà* (St Peter's, Rome), the absolute lifelessness of the dead Christ in the same group, the amazing range of attitudes displayed across the Sistine ceiling. The *Pietà* in the Duomo at Florence, for instance, although unfinished and worked on by another hand, reveals the deep spiritual preoccupation of Michelangelo as an old man and shows how far he had travelled in the half century that divided it from the *David*. Unhappily these later tendencies produced a host of imitators who, missing the point of the master's incursions into new realms of expression or at least failing to tread the same path successfully, formed an often sterile movement in Italian art.

Titian, the last of the great artists of the period to be considered here, shared something of the idealising qualities of the Neo-Platonists without feeling impelled to give them the same philosophical justification. Yet no painter had a wider range of powers and interests than he did. He learnt his mastery of colour and its use in giving unity to a painting from Bellini and Giorgione, and he developed it as an instrument of balance. He was at home in a great variety of subject matter: the nude, the classical allegory, the portrait, scenes of contemporary ceremonies and the traditional dramas of religion. He used all the techniques of Italian painting with great sureness and facility and adapted them to highly original applications of his own. Nevertheless, all his work has the stamp of being executed by the same man, although he lived and worked into a very old age. This is not to say he did not develop or change his artistic purpose during his long career. Later in life, for example, he began to paint portraits that laid bare the character of his sitters, sometimes with cruel psychological insight, a less kind approach than he had previously followed. He reflected too the changes that took place in Italian art around the 1530s, the elongation of forms, the tensions of religious uneasiness; and, like Michelangelo, as an old man he evinced a deep religious preoccupation. His vast output defies selection. One could mention the energetic grace of the *Bacchus and Ariadne* (National Gallery), in which the Bacchus catches completely the taut thrill of sexual expectation; or the *Pesaro Madonna* (Frari, Venice), in which the displacement of the Mother and Child, owing to a mastery of colour and perspective, does not destroy their central importance in the painting; or the portrait of Paul III with his grandsons (Naples) with its deep understanding of age. But these only give a glimpse into the ranging versatility of Titian, who could be said to have assimilated the achievements of a century of Italian painting and still have found a place for considerable contributions of his own.

The status of the artist, his relationship to his employer or patron, his attitudes towards his art and consequently the concept of art itself, all changed considerably during the period surveyed in this chapter. It has already been noticed that in the little treatise of Cennini a claim was being laid early both to the independence of artistic imagination and to the intellectuality of art. Art was aspiring to a status comparable to that of the liberal arts. Ghiberti developed these claims and by his achievements certainly gave some justification to them; while the brilliantly original researches of Brunelleschi into the unknown field of perspective and, with Donatello, his study of classical remains, so in tune with current intellectual fashions, gave an added boost to the growing prestige and respectability of artistic activities. The more art had a basis of intellectual principles and was in accord with the current literary apotheosis of antiquity, the more likely was it to rise through the levels of social respectability. In this regard Alberti in his books on painting, sculpture and architecture did more than anyone to add to the prestige and therefore to the commercial value of the arts. Even in the first half of the fifteenth century some of the Florentine artists were already men of some means. Ghiberti owned land and other property, had considerable shares in the Monte di Comune, employed assistants in his workshop. Brunelleschi seems to have had a business turn of mind, being one of the earliest known patent-holders for the enjoyment of profits of one of his own inventions, and he held high office in the government of the Florentine republic. Donatello, however, appears not to have been so interested in his own material prosperity. The relations of these artists and their contemporaries with their patrons was generally governed by hard business principles. There are several records of work being held up because money for buying materials, especially marble, only came in slow instalments, and there was much bickering between patron and artist on this account. Some artists apparently suffered great poverty, or at least were precariously dependent upon a patron's generosity. This was probably true of Fra Lippo Lippi, who of course as a religious was in rather a special position. Nevertheless it would be true to say that most important Florentine artists of this period were men of some substance.

Patronage in early Medicean Florence was ambiguous in motive. Cosimo, it seems, paid out large sums on ecclesiastical architecture partly to salve a conscience worried by the fact that much of his wealth was usuriously gained. He built also for grandeur; but in order to maintain the fiction of his role in Florence he was wary that his schemes did not seem too splendid for an ordinary citizen. Thus he moved slowly, avoiding the appearance of princely lavishness. This may well be the reason behind his preference of Michelozzi over Brunelleschi as the architect of the Medici palace. Another sidelight to Cosimo's patronage is that he controlled his relations with his architects himself, whereas he left to his sons the dealings with painters and sculptors. This might throw some light on the comparative values he attributed to the respective arts, but it more likely reflects the costs involved in these various artistic undertakings. Later Lorenzo, whose architectural interests lay more in the villas of the *contado* than in the city, had less money with which to patronise the arts. He acted as a leader of taste, a field in which he had large pretensions, rather than as one who commissioned artistic works in great quantities like his grandfather. Patronage was left to another branch of his family and to other Florentine *primati*, who nevertheless had to tread carefully for fear of giving the appearance of trying to rival the Medici in magnificence. The difference between the attitudes of Cosimo and Lorenzo has been brought forward to show the emergence of the concept of art under the latter, with the suggestion that patronage of art as such could not predate the concept. In the earlier period the works of art were stamped by the personality of the patron, whom they were to glorify, if tactfully; and paintings often included his portrait, a signature as it were to show his importance for the genesis of the work. Cosimo's son, Piero, certainly had a profound influence on the nature of the works he commissioned. He insisted on the use of gold and he did not like seraphim, old men and corpses. Thus the decorative art of Gozzoli was largely an expression of his requirements. But one could over-emphasise the effects of patrons on artistic style: Popes Nicholas V and Sixtus IV knew the value of the artists they tempted to Rome. Nicholas attracted Alberti, Fra Angelico and Piero della Francesca, while Sixtus used Botticelli, Signorelli, Perugino and Ghirlandaio. In such choices there was clearly a great amount of artistic discernment and, whatever limitations were placed on artists by their patrons, they were wanted because they were artists of great technical accomplishments through which, even if this was not overtly recognised, they expressed their own personalities. The above view, moreover, stresses the importance of the expression of individuality in a work of art; whereas even in the work of the most individualistic of Italian painters during this period, that is to say Michelangelo's, art was also an expression of a civilisation. In so far as this is true, there seems to be no valid reason why a work of art should not bear the mark of more than one mind or hand.

But artists were emerging as individuals elsewhere than in the circles of Lorenzo or at the papal court. The small ducal courts of Mantua, Ferrara and Urbino offered a patronage that freed the artist from the restrictions of the guild and offered a broad scope for initiative and personality. Mantegna was drawn to the court of Ludovico Gonzaga at Mantua, where initially his position was that of a valued servant. Ludovico's sons, however, had grown up with Mantegna in their household, so that when the duke died his successors virtually accepted the painter into their family. Late in his career Mantegna's subjects were often dictated by the learned literary requirements of the duchess, Isabella d'Este, but by then Mantegna himself was well-versed in the appropriate background and contributed something to the preparation of his own artistic programmes. Bellini too enjoyed a great measure of artistic freedom. He was at ease with the religious subjects he was generally commissioned to paint. Even in his early days he painted a great number of small portable paintings which he sold to private patrons, limiting his activities to congenial fields. When he was asked to paint a classical allegory for Isabella according to a strictly detailed programme, he stalled and never carried out the commission, although Alfonso I d'Este succeeded in getting from him such a work at Ferrara. In the instance of Isabella's commission, Pietro Bembo mediated and counselled the duchess that Bellini was unhappy and not at his best with such limiting demands. That the painter held out displays his artistic independence and indicates that his art was primarily an expression of his own insight and personality, although it embodied a dominant facet of the civilisation of his time. Isabella herself came to realise that art could be the independent expression of the artist himself. When Giorgione died prematurely she desperately tried to buy one of his paintings. It was no longer the case that a painting was a piece of exquisite interior decoration ordered to measure: a Giorgione was worth having for itself. Likewise she was willing to accept anything from the hand of Leonardo.

It is true that the notion of art being concerned with the expression of the individual gained currency in the circles of Lorenzo. Ficino combined the concept of *mania* attached by Plato to poets and seers with the Aristotelian notion of melancholy. This was taken over by some of the artists in the Neo-Platonic tradition, the most important of them being Michelangelo. Thus a belief in the inspired vision of the artist developed. This ran counter to the Albertian tradition of intellectualism, education and respectability, to which despite his Neo-Platonism Raphael adhered. Raphael became therefore the type of painter who tended to dominate the artistic world until the nineteenth century, the painter who was decorous and noble in manner, in strong contrast to the bohemian, arrogant and temperamental nature of Michelangelo. Such artists, urbane or extravagant, could as the sixteenth century got under way dictate their terms. They could accept or reject commissions capriciously, and they could command according to their talents large fees. Titian with great business acumen worked to please until he had amassed a sufficient fortune and reputation to act more whimsically. Raphael politely refused the patronage of Alfonso d'Este, which Michelangelo was on the verge of accepting when a tactless messenger of the duke spoke slightingly of the artist's status. The approaches of Federico Gonzaga to Michelangelo in 1527 show the high status and magnificent arrogance of the artist by then. The duke asked for a work of any subject, painting or sculpture, so long as it was by the master's hand. When this was not forthcoming he urgently solicited a slight piece of work, if only a charcoal drawing, while he waited for the more important work to materialise. In the event he got nothing. Lesser men like Cellini took their cue from Michelangelo and treated their patrons with similar bravura, but not always with equal impunity.

During this period art travelled far. From its earlier purpose of conquering nature as it appeared to the senses, it moved to the imitation of the very process whereby nature itself was thought to have been created. From the material world it turned to an idealised, almost divine world of eternal principles. The artist no longer tried to copy things but rather the principles of things. Furthermore the meaning of the word 'invention' shifted from the idea of finding or discovery towards that of making up or imagining. A greater freedom was consequently allowed to the artist. He was no longer tied to the stringent necessities of reality; or perhaps because he acquired a greater freedom he was able to give freer play to his inventiveness. But such changes were irrelevant to the quality of the art: Masaccio or Bellini in the earlier period were perhaps as great as Michelangelo or Titian later. These changes rather reflect changes in social and cultural attitudes. They show a fifteenth-century preoccupation with the observable world that with the impact of Neo-Platonism and a widespread religious uneasiness tended for many to become lost in the first decades of the next century. They echo the scientific interest in the mathematical principles underlying the physical universe, which grew to some extent at the expense of relying on the evidence of the senses and authority. They demonstrate in yet another vast field the widening horizons that accompanied the laicisation of culture throughout this period. Finally they give evidence that it was merit and no longer birthright that often came to be most greatly valued.

11
Conclusion

The years from 1464 to 1534, which have provided the focus rather than the limits of the preceding chapters, in many respects divide in two round about the year 1494. This year saw the alarming descent of King Charles VIII and his army into a split and helpless Italy, which without outside help was unable to cope with the marshalled resources of a strongly governed and recently integrated territory such as France. Spain and the Empire were subsequently brought in, powers soon to merge into one enormous new empire which was to embrace lands and seas, surmised or just known but not yet taken seriously. French policy was also imperialistic rather than nationalistic at the time; for despite the fact that the power of France really lay in her emergent nationhood, Charles and his successors had an eye on the eastern Mediterranean. Italy was therefore caught in the midst of two imperial impulses, both of such magnitude that they gave an entirely new quality to international affairs. No longer could the conflicting states of the peninsula with their uncoordinated resources retain a leading position in European or even Mediterranean politics. Rather was Italy with her attractive riches an object of ambition and plunder, the scene of aggressive rivalry between predatory neighbours. The change was not sudden, not even always to the disadvantage of the people; but it was a harrowing experience to watch foreign armies reveal the inherent weaknesses of the divided land, and a pessimism blighted the spirits, if at times it sharpened the minds, of many Italians. From a self-confident belief in man's power to emulate the greatness of antiquity, to fashion the future along rational principles, to project their fame and glory into posterity, they turned to a more fatalistic view of life. They discerned historical forces; consulted the stars to gain an understanding of the necessity to which they were subjected; and, believing increasingly that the material world was corrupt, they turned without great confidence to a Platonic and Christian idealism whose objects could generally only be fully achieved after death. This is not to say that historical determinism, judicial astrology and Platonic idealism were new phenomena that did not appear before 1494; on the contrary, they were instruments at hand whose usefulness then became more apparent, and as a consequence the number of their adherents grew.

Thus the 1490s formed a critical decade for the Italian states. In 1492 Rodrigo Borgia was elected to the Papacy and set a new low level of papal morality, hardly imaginable even for those who had already experienced the depths of the reigns of Sixtus IV and Innocent VIII. Yet his family policy went far towards ending the centrifugal chaos of petty despotic rule in the Papal States. In Florence the Savonarolan movement gained impetus partly in reaction to the futility of looking for guidance from Rome, partly because of Piero de' Medici's inadequacy and the friar's superior ability to make capital out of the French invasion. The early Medici government fell and a new but labouring Florentine republic was established in 1494. In the same year Ferrante of Naples died, ending a long life of unconstructive intrigue; and the French invasion immediately provided the occasion for the development of Aragonese influence in the south under Ferdinand, the Catholic king. In this decade Milan suffered two French invasions, which finally produced the end of effective Sforza control, while Genoa was also re-occupied by the French and became a central consideration in the nascent rivalry between Hapsburg and Valois. Venice, if she reached a high point in her commercial activities, was too confident in her own powers, ignored too long the twin threats of foreign invasion and Atlantic rivalry to her commerce, and consequently followed a course that almost led to complete disaster. Yet, misguided as was Venetian policy at the time, Venice was the only Italian state in the end to survive the pressures of the great powers and emerge with a significant degree of self-respect and independence. Indeed she became the centre not only of Italian culture, but of the culture of Europe as a whole, attracting scholars and gentlemen from Poland or England, as well as from Naples or Siena, to enjoy the intellectually stimulating circles of her patriciate and to study at the most productive and original of European universities at Padua.

Attempts at strict periodisation will always distort a view of European history. Even revolutions—apparently clean breaks with the past—have recognised and rationalised changes that had already largely taken place rather than effected sudden changes themselves. But, if one is to find in late mediaeval or early modern Italian history (to fall back upon conventional terminology) a convenient point in time which could be taken as most momentous in changing the course of the history of the peninsula, there is none more crucial than when Charles VIII embarked upon his Italian adventure. Events had been working up to this moment: France and Spain had through the century consolidated their territories; Columbus had not long returned from his first voyage, and before that Dias had reached the Cape; commercial interests in Antwerp and Lyons were expanding and south German industries were already significant. The stage was set for a tremendous challenge to the commercial, financial and industrial supremacy and to the political survival of the Italian states. None of them was prepared. As a result the rate of transition under non-Italian pressure accelerated, so that the Italy of 1464 and the Italy of 1534 in many respects present a vigorous contrast. If therefore one should attempt to break down the history of Italy into periods, 1494 would have to be taken as the end of one and the beginning of the next.

The dates 1464 and 1534 are only of incidental significance. The years between are not too many for a manageable study of a land which during the Middle Ages and up to the end of the sixteenth century was of great consequence for what was happening in Europe. These years, moreover, fall within most, perhaps all, definitions of what has come to be accepted as a period of Renaissance, and they cradle nicely the accelerated transition of the 1490s. Yet these dates also stand out to some extent by virtue of their own importance. In August 1464, three men of profound influence died. Pius II was on the verge of launching an old-fashioned crusade against the new occupants of Constantinople. He was ill-supported, for his aggressive, religious motives had little appeal for those in charge of the policies of the time: crusades in future were organised by individual great powers and conceived in terms of defensive military action and tangible political or economic gain. For this reason Pius has been dubbed 'the last of the mediaeval popes'; but his greater blow to the Turks would still have been, even had his quasi-chivalrous campaign materialised, the founding of the Tolfa alum works, which greatly minimised the economic advantages of the sultan's conquests. Cosimo de' Medici's death deprived Florence of the shrewd and tactful guidance he had exercised in a nerve centre of Italy's political and economic life. Subsequent policies in Florence were more pretentious and less sound, although even the level-headedness and subtlety of Cosimo might not have been sufficient to cope with the changing conditions. His influence was more lasting in unexpected fields. His patronage of the arts and letters, for whatever reasons, set an example which was widely followed; while his personal predilection for Plato, and in his last months his urgent request to Ficino to translate the *Corpus Hermeticum*, promoted the movement away from the Latins, with far-reaching consequences for philosophy, religion, art and the sciences. In the same month Nicholas of Cusa died. He was a man of religion with deep reforming zeal, orthodox in all essentials in so far as that religion was concerned. That is perhaps why he did not pursue his insights into a reappraisal of current ideas about the universe. Yet those insights, when developed later by others, were of great importance to the emergence of a new scientific outlook and the development of a new understanding of the physical world. These three were therefore all men of a past which they accepted unchallengingly, and yet at the same time they exercised a strong influence on changes that were to occur not long after their deaths.

But the years around 1464 were much more significant than this. In 1458 Alfonso detached the kingdom of Naples from the rest of his possessions, leaving it to his putative son, Ferrante. As a result Naples was no longer tied so closely to the interests of the rest of the Aragonese territories. In 1463 Venice entered a long and costly conflict with the Turks, a major stage in the loss of her extensive colonial possessions. The next year Louis XI undertook the reorganisation of the Lyons fairs, which led to an important redirection of the flow northwards of Mediterranean trade and eventually swayed the allegiance of some Italian states towards closer alliance with Valois France. In 1465 Florence admitted her failure in trying to compete with the greater seafaring states by removing discriminatory measures against foreign shipping. Then in 1467 the first and only great Sforza duke, Francesco, died; and a stabilising influence on Italian affairs, especially in cooperation with Cosimo, was lost. In art Donatello, the last of the great school of early fifteenth-century Florentines, died in 1466, when the works of northern artists like Bellini and Mantegna were just beginning to attain maturity. Finally, it was Paul II, the first of a long series of self-seeking, self-indulgent and discreditable popes, who succeeded Pius II in 1464. The fact prompted John Addington Symonds to write: 'No fiction contains matter more fantastic, no myth or allegory is more adapted to express a truth in figures of fancy, than the authentic well-attested annals of this period of seventy years, from 1464 to 1534.' Symonds overlooked the devout energy of the Venetian reformers of the Church. He also ignored the positive administrative activity of the Curia during this period. But his general condemnation of the moral depravity of the Papacy is substantially justified, and that he should date it from 1464 is fair. From the days when he took up holy orders, Pius II tired of dalliance and frivolity and dedicated himself to the Church's cause. His predecessors—Eugenius IV, Nicholas V and Calixtus III—although men of human weaknesses, took their position seriously and did much to help the Church recover from the legacies of exile and schism. Little can be said for his successors (apart from Pius III and Adrian VI, whose short reigns rendered them almost insignificant as popes) until Paul III, who although morally very much in the tradition of those he followed, at least made the first effective moves after his election in 1534 to block the Reformation.

1534 and the surrounding years were important in other ways. In 1528 Genoa definitely threw in her lot with the Spanish, and worsening relations with France led in 1535 to the opening of the Besançon fair. Meanwhile, Spanish influence had been steadily increasing in Milan, until in 1535 Charles V virtually took over direct rule (although there was long debate between opposing factions among his advisers as to whether Milan or the Netherlands should be the centre where Spain's European interests should be developed). In 1530 the rebellious Florentines were put down by Spanish intervention, and over the next years the restored Medici began more openly and increasingly to assert themselves as monarchs. In Naples strong but wise Spanish government was enforced from 1532 by Pedro de Toledo. Venice by this time had already extricated herself from the consequences that followed from the blow administered by the League of Cambrai; she was now already well advanced in assuming the rôle of the one Italian state of any independence and was attracting to herself the dispossessed intelligentsia of the peninsula. She was the real centre of an Italian cultural and spiritual revival. But that Rome should have a pope willing to take seriously the problems of the Reformation and tackle them constructively was perhaps the most significant development that occurred in the peninsula at this time. Paul III appointed several cardinals whose primary concern was the religious welfare of the Church; he asked some of them to advise him on how to reform the Curia; he agreed to the foundation of the Jesuits; he set up the Roman Inquisition; he called the Council of Trent and saw its first sessions through. These were more than symptoms of a changed attitude in the Papacy: they led to measures and actions that affected profoundly the future course of the Church's history. Together with the prolonged presence of Spanish rule in Italy and the general emphasis, then emerging, on the priority of landed interest, they were also responsible for the development of important changes in the attitudes and culture of Italians.

If the two dates that roughly define the limits of the period have some place as guide points in the course of Italian history in general, the falsity of rigid division into periods can no more clearly be seen than in the eco-

nomic history of the time. The economies of the Italian states were subjected to diverse pressures that produced a variety of solutions. There were
general pressures such as the Turkish advances in south-eastern Europe,
the overseas discoveries of Portugal and Castile, the growth of big European political units like France and Spain, the foreign inroads into Italy.
But these had differing effects on the economies of the various states. The
commercial states were threatened most, but showed a remarkable adaptability to new conditions. Venice looked landwards more; Genoa eventually played a subtle game within the orbit of Spain; Florence perhaps
lost most, although her economy was already less flexible than those of her
commercial rivals even before Cosimo died. Smaller pressures, whose
effects were only felt by some of the states within the peninsula, were
numerous: there were local wars, political troubles within states such as
Florence and Genoa, keen competition between states for markets, the
challenge of new foreign industries or the appearance of new competing
industries, in other Italian states, and local hazards of poor harvests or
plague. Such recurrent problems required the discovery of imaginative
solutions and the resourcefulness to apply them, and from the grim periods
of depression in the first half of the fourteenth century until well into the
sixteenth century Italians responded with these qualities.

There were general economic changes which were common to most of
Italy. Perhaps the most outstanding of these was the development of silk
industries, in the first place to offset the losses following the growth of
west European woollen manufacture, but later because silk was recognised
to be a highly attractive source of profit. Shipping adapted itself to the
changing trade patterns of the period, until the new ocean routes were
developed. Then Italians were again forced by competition to modify
their habits, and they rationalised land transport. Rising transport costs
probably played some part in the general sixteenth-century tendency of
Italians to specialise in expensive luxury goods, and fine Murano glassware, decorated Milanese iron manufactures, fashionable Neapolitan silks
were developed and became increasingly important for the economy. But
it was the resilience and adaptability of many of the Italian states, enabling
them to ride their own particular difficulties, which is most striking. Rome
capitalised on its privileged spiritual attractions; and if by so doing she
turned many away in revulsion, at the same time others flocked there to
squander their wealth and save their souls or simply to cash in on the trade
created by an expanding administration.

Milan exploited her favourable position by developing the revived carry-
ing-trade overland; and nowhere else was the use of land subjected to so

251

many changes as in Lombardy, where competition, irrigation, financial manœuvres and foresight led to a series of fruitful experiments. Genoa, owing to her shortage of precious metals, developed financial techniques of great sophistication and, when she could no longer sustain herself between two great powers, she made herself indispensable to one to protect herself against the other. Venice in one important respect ran counter to the main trend. With the development of a cheap woollen cloth industry she saw what it took the rest of the world centuries to see: that there was a great market of the common man to exploit. But this only helps to illustrate the uniqueness of each state's solution. What all shared —Naples perhaps apart, as her economy was largely influenced by the formulas of Castile—was the imagination and determination to cope with a succession of changing situations. Instead of succumbing to the dis- heartening realities of a world full of novel forces, Italians had conserved enough of their old dynamism to prolong a losing battle right up to the seventeenth century. This was achieved despite the long, painful and disruptive interval from the 1490s to the 1520s, when foreign intervention had its greatest effects on the economy of Italy. But after this setback most states recovered rapidly and continued to develop imaginatively, much as they had done through the previous century. Towns grew in population; new industries were started and old ones were revived; agriculture responded to a more settled society in which the land- owner predominated; experimentation with new crops was often success- ful; and the Alpine passes bore an increasing trade as Italian shipping declined. Foreign occupation did not cast a pall over the life of Italy— Italy still prospered; but, under the influence of the aristocracy and the land, the mobility of the population grew less and the condition of the ordinary people became correspondingly less free. Italy was prepared for an era of two centuries of popular depression.

The most impressive aspect of Italian economic life during this period is the extent to which capitalistic attitudes and techniques were already employed. Businessmen were dedicated to the pursuit of profit to swell their riches, even when they had already reached fabulous dimensions. If these men manœuvred within the limits imposed upon them by the doc- trines of their Church, they did not need the sanction of new prophets like Luther or Calvin to furnish them with the spirit and justification of capital- ism. Centurioni, Bonvisi, Affaitadi, Vendramin or Rucellai never ceased to take advantage of opportunities to effect a good business deal, although often they spent lavishly on unproductive luxuries. They were not mean- spirited capitalists, although they were cautious and obviated as far as they could elements of risk in their transactions. It was a sane, calculating and careful world of business they inhabited; but in the main they were not narrow men, but rather men of a wide culture who knew how to enjoy their good fortune. The techniques they evolved, like the culture they patronised, spread with their activities through Europe. Men of business at Augsburg or Nuremberg, Antwerp or Seville, Lyons or London, borrowed from their experience and imitated their methods. Their exchange techniques, banking devices such as the use of cheques or endorsement, manufacturing skills, book-keeping, factory organisation, were all eventually copied beyond the Alps. They invented commercial insurance, industrial patents, new manufacturing processes for silks, glassware and paper. They were fertile in expedients to exploit their working staff, often rising above the protective regulations of the guilds, sometimes controlling them through their hold on government, using methods of remuneration unfavourable to the workers, utilising loopholes in the law. Their world of cut-throat competition was enhanced by the political divisions of Italy, whilst governments were often harnessed to their business needs. Foreign policies and domestic legislation were thus often determined by the requirements of capitalism. If capitalism was later dominated by the protestant world, it had its origins deep in pre-Reformation Italy.

It is a great misfortune that the idea of a Renaissance has been attached to a period of history that is presumed to mark the transition from the Middle Ages to modernity. The notion has given rise to a long history of sterile argument and has often directed research along barren paths. Historians have searched for evidence to substantiate their own particular points of view. Some have tried to push the origins of the Renaissance back into periods that clearly have little in common with that which has been dealt with in this book; but their single-mindedness has not allowed them to see the inappropriateness of their activities. Others have written of Renaissance states or Renaissance popes as though this were to say more than that these states or popes existed or lived in a particular time under a prevailing culture. The epithet in any case is so imprecise, has so many subjective meanings, is open to so much controversy, that it can communicate little to the reader. That is why the word has been eschewed in the previous ten chapters of this book. The Renaissance, if it means anything, is a cultural phenomenon, the revival of interest in the classical world in a way that had some inkling of the different assumptions people have at different times. Men tried to understand antiquity in its own terms and not in the terms of the Catholic world. By this definition Petrarch in the fourteenth century might be said to be a 'Renaissance man', but too few of his contemporaries were of the same turn of mind to permit the characterisation of his age by the word 'Renaissance'. By the fifteenth century there was wide enough interest in Florence, by the middle of the century in Rome and Milan, for one to say that by then in these places Renaissance culture was significant. By the end of the century it had spread through most parts of Italy. But this did not replace the already existing culture of the so-called Middle Ages. It rather added a new dimension to what was already there.

The revival of antiquity, the impact of the literary and artistic remains of Rome and Greece, appealed primarily to the educated layman. The business world of Florence in the first place, because of its requirements of literacy and numeracy, was ideally prepared to engender this new enthusiasm. Hitherto there had been a sparsely-filled gulf between the highly subtle but not generally attractive literature of the Church and a rather insignificant popular literature. In between were the professional writings of law and medicine; the Latin Aristotle and the works of the Aristotelians; the chronicles; craft manuals; and a handful of great but exceptional writings like those of Dante, Petrarch and Boccaccio. There was little of general appeal. But once the first small beginnings were made to a critical approach to the classics and an idea of what they had to offer was coming to be realised a ready audience pressed for more. The classics spoke of humanity and its immediate problems, a side of man's interests that the literature of Christian society had never much dwelt upon. They also spoke elegantly, without the involved subtleties of argument found in the scholastics with their tendency towards an exhaustive coverage of every possibility. These were literatures with refreshing insights; easy to read; smooth-flowing; sometimes relaxing, sometimes gripping; such as men with jobs to do could read with profit and delight. There is little more in the impulse that gave rise to the Renaissance than this. Its consequences, however, were great. The classical art and literature turned men's minds more to the world they lived in: artists became intent on conquering the representation of the natural world; thinkers examined the nature of man from new angles and investigated the kind of society he inhabited, comparing it with others they read about; the scientific accomplishments of the classical world were relearnt and, with the emphasis on observing the physical world and humanity that these new interests encouraged, scientists were able to correct and improve upon the classical achievement. In spite of this, the cultural attitudes of the Middle Ages were not lost; they subsisted by the side of what was new or newly discovered. Sometimes they underwent stylistic rather than substantial change; sometimes the old was integrated with the new. But often mediaeval culture still held pride of place in men's minds. Horizons were therefore widened and not changed, and a lay culture with a bias towards this world was added to a primarily religious culture that looked rather to an hereafter.

This new dimension to the culture of Italy was encouraged by the eager patronage of the rich and even by the Church, the seat of the old, subsisting culture. One attempt at explaining this, especially the patronage of the visual arts, suggests that it was due to the narrowing opportunities for investment. There are several answers to such a contention. The first is that the artistic patronage of the Church occurred even in Milan, where the Church was notably hard put to it to raise funds. In the duchy vast church-building projects were undertaken without practical necessity, simply because the new styles were thought to be superior to the old and it was deemed fitting to make the financial sacrifice for the honour of God and the glory of the Church. Much the same could be said of the new St Peter's at Rome. There was no question at the Curia of investing spare cash in the project; on the contrary, the efforts taken to raise the funds were partly responsible for precipitating the Reformation. As far as the Church was concerned, the patronage of the new culture was motivated by a belief in its inherent value. There is no reason to think that it was otherwise with lay patrons. It has already been seen that Cosimo's patronage had various motives: partly it was an act of conscience; partly a tactful instrument of prestige. But his less costly encouragement of letters was clearly carried out in the belief that he was doing something of value in itself. Indeed the wide patronage of writers at the time could hardly be represented in terms of investment, not even of a political nature, for there was little use made of systematic propaganda and most writers were left to indulge with tact their own purely literary interests. Moreover, the expense was often negligible, and Cosimo unlike his successors was not short of profitable opportunities for investment. The reason for his protection and encouragement of writers like Ficino, therefore, probably also explains his attitude towards artists: he believed their work to be worthwhile for itself. The same could be said of patrons all over Italy from the courtly patrons of Mantua, Ferrara or Urbino to the patricians of Venice and the businessmen of Florence. A work of art, once acquired, was not regarded as a salable commodity until the sixteenth century, when for instance Isabella d'Este sought to buy a work of Giorgione's after his death; and the first art dealer of any importance, Giovanni Battista della Palla, did not emerge until the 1520s.

Although the Renaissance was in origin purely a cultural phenomenon, it had one important effect on the conceptual apparatus of political thinking which even affected political action. Italy in many ways, despite its political divisions and rivalries, had for long had some form of underlying unity. Its geographical position and its physical delineation gave its various political parts common and rival interests. In agriculture the south was complementary to the north, a further factor tending to give unity. What Italy included is nevertheless not always easily defined; it depended largely on the influence its closer neighbours were able to exert. Particularly is this the case with Piedmont and the three great islands. With the growth of an interest in Ancient Rome, however, there developed something of a feeling for a common heritage; and as cross-influences in art and literature were felt throughout the peninsula, the Renaissance tended to create an Italian culture to exist by the side of a culture of Latin Christendom, only shared by Italians with the rest of Europe. As the use of a literary vernacular grew the distinction became even clearer. The concept of 'Italy' consequently became more popular. It is one of the great ironies of history that, as Italians became more aware of their common bond, Italy succumbed largely to foreign rule; but the process of self-realisation was in a way accelerated by the resentment caused by this humiliation. The unity, thus learnt in subjection, found an asylum for its expression in the independent republic of Venice, which then became the real seat of Italian culture.

Bibliography

Although not intended to be comprehensive, the following is a list of those publications which I believe will be most helpful to students developing an interest in Renaissance Italy. It also includes those books and articles which I have found of most value in the preparation of this book. The comments after each title are hoped to be a guide to readers who wish to follow up particular aspects of the Italian Renaissance. There are several reference works that could be added. For instance, the great *Enciclopedia Italiana* is full of informative articles by the leading authorities in the field at the time they were written. The *Dizionario Biografico degli Italiani* has hardly got under way; but it will clearly be a mine of most valuable information. I have not yet had the advantage of being able to use in Perth the monumental *Storia di Milano*, a fine work that every student should try to consult. There are vast numbers of historical periodicals—regional, national, international and specialist—some of whose articles I have quoted in the bibliography. These should be used systematically by students intending to make a deeper study of the period. General works, such as Pastor's *History of the Popes* and *The Cambridge Economic History of Europe* have much of interest relevant to some aspect of the period. There are also several important histories of Italian literature. I have given only a few introductory titles relating to the art of the period. There is a vast literature on the subject and, of course, nothing can replace actually going to view the works themselves, some of which are to be found in most great cities of the European world. Works of Renaissance writers are available in several collected selections, the most generally accessible perhaps being the appropriate volumes of *La letteratura italiana : storia e testi*. English translations of works by Machiavelli, della Casa, Vespasiano da Bisticci, Castiglione, Cellini, Vasari, etc., are often to be had in cheap editions, and students would have no better way of getting the flavour of the period than through these. Burckhardt's *The Civilisation of the Renaissance in Italy* is, as I have already said in the preface, indispensable to all students, and English translations are also available in several cheap editions.

General Works, Historiography, Interpretation

ADDARIO, Arnaldo d', 'Il Convegno sulla Storia della Repubblica Veneta nei secoli XV–XVI', in *Archivio Storico Italiano*, CXXI, no. 4, 1963. An interesting report of important general views put forward by leading historians of Venice.

BRAUDEL, Fernand, *La Méditerranée et le Monde méditerranéen à l'époque de Philippe II* (Paris, 1949). One of the great seminal works of modern historiography. It has given rise to an active school of investigators, concerned both with developing Braudel's own immediate interests and with transposing his methods to other historical fields.

DANNENFELDT, Karl H., *The Renaissance: Medieval or Modern?* (Boston, 1959). A volume of the *Problems in European Civilisation* series, bringing together some major interpretations by important historians.

DURANT, Will, *The Renaissance* (New York, 1953). The fifth volume of *The Story of Civilization;* this is good reading, but an expansive work that does not add very much either by presenting a new view of the period or by contributing new facts.

FERGUSON, Wallace K., *Renaissance Studies* (London and Ontario, 1963). A stimulating collection of thoughtful papers on central problems of the Renaissance.

The Renaissance in Historical Thought: Five Centuries of Interpretation (Boston, 1948). An indispensable work for the subject, but also important for the history of historiography in general.

HAY, Denys, 'Italy and Barbarian Europe', in *Italian Renaissance Studies* (London, 1960). Good for the concept of 'Italy'.

The Italian Renaissance in its Historical Background (Cambridge, 1961). Has an interesting historiographical discussion, and a useful consideration of intellectual attitudes during the period.

The Renaissance (London, 1963). A masterly little introduction.

MARINI, Lino, *La Spagna in Italia nell'età di Carlo V* (Bologna, 1961). An examination of the views of other historians setting the history of Naples and Milan in a broader European context.

MARTIN, Alfred von, *Sociology of the Renaissance* (London, 1944). A classic work of interpretative history whose conclusions would be considerably modified by research subsequent to the German edition of 1932.

SYMONDS, J. A., *Renaissance in Italy*, 7 vols (New Edition, London, 1904–9).

TENENTI, Alberto, 'Studi di Storia Veneziana', in *Rivista Storica Italiana*, No. 75, II, 1963.

External Relations, War, Diplomacy

ADY, Cecilia M., 'The Invasions of Italy', in *The New Cambridge Modern History*, Vol. I (Cambridge, 1957). A most competent and lucid exposition of a very complex series of events.

BABINGER, Franz, 'Le vicende veneziane nella lotta contro i Turchi durante il secolo XV', in *La civiltà veneziana del Quattrocento* (Venice, 1957). A useful survey of Venetian policy in the Balkans and Aegean.

'Lorenzo de Medici e la Corte ottomana', in *Archivio Storico Italiano*, CXXI, no. 3, 1963.

CATALANO, Franco, 'Dall' equilibrio alla crisi italiana del Rinascimento', in *Storia d'Italia*, vol. II (Turin, 1959)—gen. ed., Nino Valeri.

CHABOD, Federico, 'Venezia nella politica italiana ed europea del Cinquecento', in *La Civiltà Veneziana del Rinascimento* (Venice, 1958).

CONIGLIO, Giuseppe, 'Francesco Gonzaga e la Lega di Cambrai', in *Archivio Storico Italiano*, 120, 1962. An interesting study of the place of Mantua in the diplomacy of the first decade of the sixteenth century.

'La politica di Francesco Gonzaga nell' opera di un immigrato meridionale: Iacopo Probo d'Atri', in *Archivio Storico Lombardo*, LXXXVIII, 1963. An excellent study of the subtlety of ducal politics and the powers and weaknesses of *condottiere* government.

HALE J. R., 'International Relations in the West: Diplomacy and War', in *The New Cambridge Modern History*, Vol. I (Cambridge, 1957).

'War and Public Opinion in Renaissance Italy', in *Italian Renaissance Studies* (London, 1960). An indispensable article by an imaginative Renaissance military historian of broad interests.

MATTINGLY, Garrett, *Renaissance Diplomacy* (London, 1955). Has many good points to make about Italian embassies, but needs to be used with caution owing to a number of dubious judgments scattered through the book.

MORANDINI, Francesco, 'Il conflitto tra Lorenzo il Magnifico e Sisto IV dopo la congiura de' Pazzi', in *Archivio Storico Italiano*, 107, 1949. Useful information illustrating diplomatic techniques of the time.

MORRALL, John B., 'Pius II: Humanist and Crusader' in *History Today*, VIII, no. 1, 1958. Good account of foreign policy of Pius II.

PASERO, Carlo, *Francia, Spagna, Impero a Brescia, 1509–1516* (Brescia, 1958). A detailed reconstruction of the events of these years, revealing the nature of foreign intervention at the time.

PONTIERI, Ernesto, *Per la storia del Regno di Ferrante I d'Aragona, Re di*

Napoli (Naples, n.d.). Mainly interesting for Ferrante's external relations.

PRATICO, Giovanni, 'Lorenzo il Magnifico e i Gonzaga', in *Archivio Storico Italiano*, 107, 1949.

RUBINSTEIN, Nikolai, 'Firenze e il problema della politica imperiale in Italia al tempo di Massimiliano I', in *Archivio Storico Italiano*, 116, 1958. An illuminating study of attitudes and problems connected with Florentine relations with non-Italian powers.

'The Place of the Empire in Fifteenth-Century Florentine Political Opinion and Diplomacy', in *The Bulletin of the Institute of Historical Research*, 30, 1957. Useful for Florentine attitudes to the Empire.

SASSO, Gennaro, 'L'Italia del Machiavelli e l'Italia del Guicciardini', in *Storia d'Italia*, Vol. II (Turin, 1959)—gen. ed., Nino Valeri.

SENECA, Federico, *Venezia e Papa Giulio II* (Verona, 1962). Deals with a complicated decade of European diplomacy centred upon Venetian-Papal relations.

SPOONER, F. C., 'The Hapsburg-Valois Struggle', in *The New Cambridge Modern History*, Vol. II (Cambridge, 1958).

VALERI, Nino 'Venezia nella crisi italiana del Rinascimento', in *La civiltà veneziana del Quattrocento*, (Venice, 1957). An examination of traditional views of Venetian foreign policy.

WEINSTEIN, Donald, *Ambassador from Venice—Pietro Pasqualigo in Lisbon, 1501* (Minneapolis, 1960). Good for a study of Venetian reactions to the early news of the Portuguese discovery of a sea-route to the east at the time when Venice was embroiled in war with the Turks.

State Histories, Internal Policies

ADY, Cecilia M., *Lorenzo dei Medici and Renaissance Italy* (London, 1955). Well-informed and competent introduction to Florentine history under Lorenzo.

Morals and Manners of the Quattrocento (London, 1942). A useful study of the values of the Italian ruling classes.

The Bentivolgio of Bologna: A Study in Despotism (London, 1937). An admirably presented piece of research on the politics of Romagna.

CAIZZI, Bruno, 'I tempi della decadenza economica di Cremona', in *Studi in onore di Armando Sapori*, 2 vols (Milan, 1957). A revealing analysis of the decline of Cremona.

CHABOD, Federico, *Lo stato di Milano nella prima metà del secolo XVI* (Rome, 1955). Especially good for a study of the impact of Spain on the government, social structure and changing attitudes of the time.

COLES, Paul, 'The Crisis of Renaissance Society: Genoa, 1488–1507', in *Past and Present*, No. 11, 1957. A provocative interpretation by one of the school of gifted over-simplifiers who contribute to this journal.

CONIGLIO, Giuseppe, *Il Regno di Napoli al Tempo di Carlo V* (Naples, 1951). An invaluable work on the economic and administrative history of the kingdom.

DAVIS, James Cushman, *The Decline of the Venetian Nobility as a Ruling Class* (Baltimore 1962). An interesting insight into a reason why a resourceful government lost its vigour after the sixteenth century.

HALE, J. R., *Machiavelli and Renaissance Italy* (London, 1961). A thoughtful work giving a sound and original view of both Machiavelli and High Renaissance Italy, at the same time serving as a good introduction to several general aspects of the period.

HAZLITT, W. Carew, *The Venetian Republic*, esp. Vol. II (London, 1900). Still a useful work through which English readers can familiarise themselves with the basic framework of Venetian political history and acquire some idea about Venetian society.

HEERS, Jacques, *Gênes au XVe siècle* (Paris, 1961). A brilliant and exhaustive work on the economy, government and society of Genoa in the middle of the fifteenth century.

HEYWOOD, William, *A History of Perugia* (London, 1910).

HICKS, David L., 'The Education of a Prince: Lodovico il Moro and the Rise of Pandolfo Petrucci', in *Studies in the Renaissance*, Vol. VIII, 1961. An interesting study of the political techniques of a *condottiere* ruler.

JONES, P. J., 'The End of Malatesta Rule in Rimini', in *Italian Renaissance Studies* (London, 1960). A first-class account and analysis of a process significant for the evolution of papal government.

'The Vicariate of the Malatesta of Rimini', in *English Historical Review*, CCLXIV, 1952. A study of the relations between the Papacy and one of her Italian possessions.

LUZZATTO, Gino, *Il debito pubblico della Repubblica di Venezia dagli ultimi decenni del XII secolo alla fine del XV* (Milano, 1963). Useful for government finance in Venice.

MARKS, L. F., 'La crisi finanziaria a Firenze dal 1494, at 1502', in *Archivio Storico Italiano*, 112, 1954. Interesting, not only for the financial expedients of the republic, but also for class and factional rivalries.

'The Financial Oligarchy in Florence under Lorenzo', in *Italian*

Renaissance Studies (London, 1960). A fine study showing the importance of the *primati* under Lorenzo.

MORRALL, John B., 'Pius II and his Commentaries', in *Historical Studies*, 3, 1961. Useful for Pius II's attitude towards his temporal responsibilities.

PAMPALONI, Guido, 'Fermenti di riforme democratiche nella Firenze medicea del Quattrocento', in *Archivio Storico Italiano*, 119, 1961. A revealing study of the politics of the succession of Piero di Cosimo de' Medici.

PARTNER, Peter, 'The "Budget" of the Roman Church in the Renaissance Period', in *Italian Renaissance Studies* (London, 1960). A good analysis of papal finances at this time, although he interprets the sale of offices in terms of loans rather than annuities.

PASERO, Carlo, 'Dati Statistici e notizie intorno al movimento della popolazione bresciana durante il dominio veneto (1426–1797)', in *Archivio Storico Lombardo*, LXXXVIII, 1963. A revealing demographic study.

PEYRONNET, Georges, 'Il ducato di Milano sotto Francesco Sforza (1450–1466): politica interna, vita economica e sociale', in *Archivio Storico Italiano*, 116, 1958. A convenient general summary of the state of the duchy at this time, although the population figures given are of dubious validity.

RODOLICO, Niccolò, 'Nel quinto centenario di Lorenzo il Magnifico', in *Archivio Storico Italiano*, 107, 1949. A short essay useful as an introduction to some Florentine political problems of the period.

ROTH, Cecil, *The Last Florentine Republic* (London, 1925). A well-told account of the events in Florence from 1527 to 1530.

RUBINSTEIN, Nikolai, 'I primi anni del Consiglio Maggiore di Firenze (1494–99)', in *Archivio Storico Italiano*, 112, 1954. A fine analysis of an important institutional experiment.

'Politics and Constitution in Florence at the end of the 15th Century', in *Italian Renaissance Studies* (London, 1960). Enlightening for Florentine government and 'parties' from 1494 to the end of the century.

SCHEVILL, Ferdinand, *Mediaeval and Renaissance Florence*, 2 vols (rev. ed., available Harper Torchbook, New York and Evanston, 1963). Still the best introduction to Florentine history up to the first part of the sixteenth century.

The Medici (available Harper Torchbook, New York, 1960). Deals with the Medici and their rule in Florence up to Alessandro, duke of Florence.

SORANZO, Giovanni, 'Lorenzo il Magnifico alla morte del padre e il suo primo balzo verso la Signoria', in *Archivio Storico Italiano*, 111, 1953. A useful analysis of conditions at the time of Lorenzo's succession to the Medici leadership of Florence and of the considerations leading to his acceptance by important citizens.

THESEIDER, Eugenio Dupré, 'I papi medicei e la loro politica domestica', in *Studi Fiorentini* (Florence, 1963). A stimulating comparison of Leo X and Clement VII.

ZANETTI, Dante, 'L'Approvisionnement de Pavie au XVIe siècle', in *Annales*, 18, no. 1, 1963. A revealing glimpse into the important governmental problem of the food supply.

General Economic Histories, Business Methods

BARBIERI, Gino, *Origini del Capitalismo Lombardo* (Milan, 1961). A great deal of important information and source material concerning Milanese business activities in the ducal period.

FELLONI, Giuseppe, 'Per la storia della popolazione di Genova nei secoli XVI e XVII', in *Archivio Storico Italiano*, 110, 1952. Includes useful figures that reveal the small population of Genoa compared to Naples, Milan and Venice.

FERGUSON, Wallace K., 'Recent Trends in the Economic Historiography of the Renaissance', in *Studies in the Renaissance*, VII, 1960. A useful survey for English readers.

LUZZATTO, Gino, *An Economic History of Italy from the Fall of the Roman Empire to the Beginning of the Sixteenth Century* (London, 1961). A good and convenient introduction for English readers.
Storia economica dell'età moderna e contemporanea, 2 vols (Padua, 1932–8). The first volume covers much the same ground.
Storia economica di Venezia dall' XI al XVI secolo (Venice, 1961). An invaluable survey.

MANDICH, G., 'Le privative industriali veneziane: 1450–1550', in *Rivista del Diritto Commerciale*, XXXIV, 1936.
'Primi riconoscimenti venezioni di un diritto di privativa agli inventori', in *Rivista di Diritto Industriale*, VII, 1958. Both articles give much information, revealing for attitudes towards business and technological developments.

NUDI, Giacinto, *Storia Urbanistica di Livorno* (Venice, 1959). Useful for the Florentine ports and the difficulties arising from surrounding terrain.

ORIGO, Iris, *The Merchant of Prato* (London, 1957). An enthralling account of society and commerce in a period somewhat earlier than that of this book and centred upon the Datini family.

RENOUARD, Yves, 'Affaires et hommes d'affaires dans l'Italie du moyen âge', in *Annales*, 3, no. 3, 1948.

'Du nouveau sur les hommes d'affaires italiens du moyen âge', in *Annales*, 7, no. 1, 1952.

'Lumières nouvelles sur les hommes d'affaires italiens du moyen âge', in *Annales*, 10, no. 1, 1955: these three articles assemble valuable points concerning the business history of late mediaeval Italy.

'Destin d'une Grande Métropole Médiévale: Pise', in *Annales*, 17, no. 1, 1962. Useful for fate of Pisan business interests in the years around the Florentine conquest of Pisa in 1406.

ROOVER, Florence Edler de, 'Restitution in Renaissance Florence', in *Studi in onore di Armando Sapori*, 2 vols (Milan, 1957). A study of the impact of the Church's doctrine of usury in Florentine business circles.

ROOVER, Raymond de, 'Cambium ad Venetias: Contribution to the History of Foreign Exchange', in *Studi in onore di Armando Sapori*, 2 Vols (Milan, 1957). Interesting as a description of a non-usurious loan, which was in effect interest-bearing.

'Lorenzo il Magnifico e il tramonto del Banco dei Medici', in *Archivio Storico Italiano*, 107, 1949. Discusses some almost contemporary judgments of Lorenzo's business ability in relation to de Roover's own well-known conclusions.

The Medici Bank: Its Organisation, Management, Operations and Decline (New York, 1948). A penetrating analysis based on pioneer research.

The Rise and Decline of The Medici Bank (Cambridge, Mass., 1963). Fills out his earlier little book on the same subject without adding a great deal to his essential conclusions.

SELLA, Domenico, 'Les mouvements longs de l'industrie lainière à Venise aux XVIe et XVIIe siècles', in *Annales*, 12, no. 1, 1957. Important statistics of woollen cloth manufacture at Venice set against figures for other Italian centres of wool production.

Trade

ARGENTI, Philip, *The Occupation of Chios by the Genoese and their Admini-*

stration of the Island, 1346–1566, 3 vols (Cambridge, 1958). An important work for a study of Genoese Levantine interests.

BERGIER, Jean-François, 'Marchands italiens à Genève au dèbut du XVIe siècle (1480–1540)', in *Studi in onore di Armando Sapori*, 2 vols (Milan, 1957). Interesting information together with an enlightening explanation of the fluctuations of Italian trade relations with Geneva.

BRAUDEL, Fernand, 'La vita economica di Venezia nel secolo XVI', in *La civiltà veneziana del Rinascimento* (Venice, 1958).

BRULEZ, Wilfrid, 'L'Exportation des Pays-Bas vers l'Italie per voie de terre au milieu du XVIe siècle', in *Annales*, 14, no. 3, 1959. Interesting detail which throws light on the re-orientation of Italian trade at the time.

COLEMAN, Olive, 'Trade and Prosperity in the Fifteenth Century: Some Aspects of the Trade of Southampton', in *The Economic History Review*, 2nd Series, XVI, No. 1, 1963. Gives interesting details concerning Italian trade at Southampton.

DELUMEAU, Jean, *L'Alun de Rome XVe— XIXe siècle* (Paris, 1962). Excellent detailed description of the wide implications of this commodity, so important in the political and economic relations of European states.

GASCON, R., 'Un siècle de commerce des épices à Lyon: Fin XVe—Fin XVIe siècles', in *Annales*, 15, no. 4, 1960. Useful on the comparative importance of 'Mediterranean' and 'Portuguese' spices in the sixteenth century.

GIOFFRÈ, Domenico, *Gênes et les foires de change—De Lyon a Besançon* (Paris, 1960). Especially useful for the interrelationship between the foreign and economic policies of Genoa.

GOLDENBERG, S., 'Notizie del commercio italiano in Transilvania nel secolo XVI', in *Archivio Storico Italiano*, 121, 1963. Information concerning a little known area of Italian trade.

HEERS, Marie-Louise, 'Les Génois et le Commerce de l'Alun à la fin du Moyen Âge', in *Revue d'Histoire Économique et Sociale*, XXXII, 1954. Useful for the alum trade prior to the fall of Fokia.

HEYD, Wilhelm von, *Histoire du commerce du Levant au Moyen-âge* (Amsterdam, 1959). The translation of a brilliant and comprehensive nineteenth-century German work on a trade in which Italians played a leading rôle.

LANE, Frederic C., 'Fleets and Fairs: The Functions of the Venetian Muda', in *Studi in onore di Armando Sapori*, 2 vols (Milan, 1957). An informative article on the nature of Venetian, state-regulated trade. There are several other important writings on Venetian shipping by Lane that have not been available to me while writing this book.

MALLETT, M. E., 'Anglo-Florentine Commercial Relations, 1465–1491', in *The Economic History Review*, Second Series, Vol. XV, No. 2, Dec. 1962. Interesting details on Florentine trade and an original insight into the economic difficulties of the early Medici, especially after Cosimo.

MORELAND, W. H., *India at the death of Akbar* (Delhi, 1962). Gives a good idea of the nature of the economy of a land which had been, not long before, so important for the success of Italian commerce.

RAU, Virginia, 'A family of Italian Merchants in Portugal in the XVth century: the Lomellini', in *Studi in onore di Armando Sapori*, 2 vols (Milan, 1957). An illustration of the wide dispersal of Genoese business interests.

RICHARDS, G. R. B., *Florentine Merchants in the Age of the Medici* (Cambridge, Mass., 1932). A wealth of interesting detail, translated from the Selfridge Medici MSS, concerning especially trading relations with the Turks.

SAPORI, Armando, 'I primi viaggi di Levante e di Ponente delle Galere Fiorentini', in *Archivio Storico Italiano*, 114, 1956. A useful summary of commercial history of Florence in the fifteenth century and important facts concerning the state trading galleys.

TADIĆ, Jorgo, 'Les archives économiques de Raguse', *Annales*, 16, No. 6, 1961. Useful indications of the scope and nature of Ragusan trade.

TENENTI, Alberto and VIVANTE, Corrado, 'Le film d'un grand système de navigation: Les galères vénitiennes, XIVe—XVIe siècles', in *Annales*, 16, no. 1, 1961. A striking illustration of the fortunes of the various routes of officially sponsored Venetian trade.

THIRIET, Freddy, 'Les lettres commerciales des Bembo et le commerce vénitien dans l'empire ottoman à la fin du XVe siècle', in *Studi in onore di Armando Sapori*, 2 vols (Milan, 1957). Gives a good picture of the way privately organised Venetian trade was carried on after the fall of Constantinople and of the type of factors that influenced it.

VERLINDEN, Charles, 'La colonie italienne de Lisbonne et l'économie portugaise', in *Studi in onore di Armando Sapori*, 2 vols (Milan, 1957). Good for fifteenth-century Florentine and Genoese contacts with Portugal.

VIVANTI, Corrado. *See* TENENTI, Alberto.

WEE, H. van der, *The Growth of the Antwerp Market*, 3 vols (The Hague, 1963). Useful for Italian interests at Antwerp during this period.

Agrarian History, Land Ownership, Classes

BERNADSKAYA, Elena V., 'L'imposizione di tributi ai contadini dell' Italia settentrionale nei secoli XV e XVI (su documenti concernanti il Modenese)', in *Studi in onore di Armando Sapori*, 2 vols (Milan, 1957). An interesting study of the relationship of landlord, peasant, commune and ducal government in the territory of Modena.

BUENO de MESQUITA, D. M., 'Ludovico Sforza and his Vassals', in *Italian Renaissance Studies* (London, 1960). A revealing description of the importance of the old feudal lordships in the duchy of Milan.

CIPOLLA, Carlo M., 'Per la storia delle terre della 'bassa' Lombarda', in *Studi in onore di Armando Sapori*, 2 vols (Milan, 1957). An analysis which develops Cipolla's main thesis concerning the agrarian economy of Lombardy, namely:

'Une crise ignorée. Comment s'est perdue la propriété ecclésiastique dans l'Italie du Nord entre le XIe et le XVIe siècle', in *Annales* 2, no. 3, 1947. The superb study that shows how land speculation influenced profoundly the agrarian economy of northern Italy.

DOWD, Douglas F., 'The Economic Expansion of Lombardy, 1300-1500: A study in Political Stimuli to Economic Change', in *The Journal of Economic History*, XXI, no. 2, 1961. A useful survey of agrarian change in Lombardy.

DUBY, Georges, 'Sur l'histoire agraire de l'Italie', in *Annales*, 18, no. 2, 1963. An assessment of the main agrarian developments in mediaeval Italy based largely on the work of Emilio Sereni (q.v.).

IMBERCIADORI, Ildebrando, 'I due poderi di Bernardo Machiavelli ovvero Mezzadria poderale nel '400', in *Studi in onore di Armando Sapori* 2 vols (Milan, 1957). Of general interest for the agrarian history of the Florentine *contado* besides giving some local colour to Machiavelli's family background.

JONES, P. J., 'Florentine Families and Florentine Diaries in the Fourteenth Century', in *Studies in Mediaeval History presented to Miss E. M. Jamison, Papers of the British School at Rome*, Vol. XXIV (N.S. Vol. XI), 1956. A most revealing article concerning landownership and farming in the *contado*.

'Per la storia agraria italiana nel Medio Evo: Lineamenti e Problemi', in *Rivista Storica Italiana*, No. 76, II, 1964. A brilliant survey of Italian agrarian history up to c.1500, marred only by an ill-concealed tendency to play down the importance of cultural achievements, also shown elsewhere, and implied in the use of the term *il vero rinascimento* for the economic revival in Italy, c. 1000–c.1300.

MADDALENA, Aldo de, 'Il Mondo Rurale Italiano nel Cinque e nel Seicento (Rassegna di studi recenti)', in *Rivista Storica Italiana*, No. 76, II, 1964. An invaluable assemblage and organisation of the findings of recent research.

MIANI, Gemma, 'L'Économie lombarde aux XIVe et XVe siècles: Une exception à la règle?', in *Annales*, 19, no. 3, 1964. An excellent article bringing together critically the results of the most recent research on the subject.

RODOLICO, Francesco, *The Florentine Landscape* (Florence, 1959). Includes a few well-chosen quotations from writers such as Ficino and Giovanni Villani, revealing their attitudes towards the countryside.

SERENI, Emilio, *Storia del Paesaggio Agrario Italiano* (Bari, 1961). A great pioneer work on Italian agrarian history.

SERPIERI, Arrigo, *La Bonifica nella storia e nella dottrina* (Bologna, 1957). Useful information concerning the reclamation of land, irrigation, etc.

STELLA, Aldo, 'La proprietà ecclesiastica nella repubblica di Venezia dal secolo XV al XVII', in *Nuova rivista storica*, 42, 1958. Indicates that the Venetians differed considerably, especially in the fifteenth century, from the Milanese (see Cipolla) in their attitudes towards land speculation and that the Venetian Church was not forced to sell, but on the contrary bought up land.

The Church, Religion

ADY, Cecilia M., *Pius II: Aeneas Silvius Piccolomini, the Humanist Pope* (London, 1913). Still the best account of his life.

AUBENAS, R., 'The Papacy and the Catholic Church', in *The New Cambridge Modern History*, Vol. I (Cambridge, 1957).

CANTIMORI, Delio, 'Italy and the Papacy', in *The New Cambridge Modern History*, Vol. II (Cambridge, 1958). Useful for the turmoil of religious views in Italy in the first half of the sixteenth century.

Prospettive di storia ereticale italiana del Cinquecento (Bari, 1960).

EVENNETT, H. O., 'The New Orders', in *The New Cambridge Modern History*, Vol. II (Cambridge, 1958). A very well-informed survey.

JEDIN, Hubert, 'Gasparo Contarini e il contributo veneziano alla Riforma Cattolica', in *La civiltà veneziana del Rinascimento* (Venice, 1958). Good for Venetian Church reform activities in the sixteenth century.

Il Tipo Ideale di Vescovo secondo la Riforma Cattolica (Brescia, 1950). Interesting for the Church in Venice in the sixteenth century.

NIERO, Antonio, *I patriarchi di Venezia* (Venice, 1961).

PALMAROCCHI, Roberto, 'Lorenzo de' Medici e la nomina cardinalazia di Giovanni', in *Archivio Storico Italiano*, 110, 1952. An account of how the future Leo X came to be nominated to the cardinalate; an insight into the politics of the Renaissance Church.

RIDOLFI, Roberto, *The Life of Girolamo Savonarola* (London, 1959). A curious mixture of sound scholarship and naïve interpretation.

RODOCANACHI, E. P., *Histoire de Rome : Une cour princière au Vatican pendant la Renaissance* (Paris, 1925). Full of interesting facts on Sixtus IV, Innocent VIII and Alexander VI.

Intellectual Trends

BARON, Hans, 'Fifteenth-century Civilisation and the Renaissance', in *The New Cambridge Modern History*, Vol. I (Cambridge, 1957). A good introduction to the culture of the time and Italy's place in it.

'Machiavelli: The Republican Citizen and the Author of *The Prince*', in *The English Historical Review*, Vol. 76, No. 299, 1961. An investigation into Machiavelli's purpose as a writer.

The Crisis of the Early Italian Renaissance (Princeton, 1955). An important work especially for early fifteenth-century Florentine political and historical thought.

BURKE, Peter, *The Renaissance* (London, 1964). A useful selection of passages from important historians and sources for Renaissance culture.

BURROUGHS, Josephine L., 'Translation of Ficino's Platonic Theology', in *Journal of the History of Ideas*, V, 1944. Useful for English readers.

CAMPANA, Augusto, 'The Origin of the Word "Humanist"', in *The Journal of the Warburg and Courtauld Institutes*, IX, 1946. Information revealing the type of writer who first employed the word to describe himself.

CANTIMORI, Delio, 'Rhetoric and Politics in Italian Humanism', in *The Journal of the Warburg and Courtauld Institutes*, I, 1937–38. Particularly interesting for the assumptions underlying the thought of Antonio Brucioli, an important member of the circles of the *Orti Oricellari*.

CASSIRER, Ernst, *The Individual and the Cosmos in Renaissance Philosophy* (Oxford, 1963). An important study of Renaissance concepts, especially interesting for Nicholas of Cusa.

CASSIRER, Ernst, KRISTELLER, Paul Oskar and RANDALL, John Herman, Jnr., *The Renaissance Philosophy of Man* (Chicago, 1948). Translations from key passages from Renaissance thinkers with good introductions by a selection of leading scholars in the field.

CHABOD, Federico, *Machiavelli and the Renaissance* (London, 1958). A brilliant study by a leading Italian scholar of the Renaissance.

COCHRANE, Eric W., 'Machiavelli: 1940–1960', in *The Journal of Modern History*, XXXIII, no. 2, 1961. A survey of recent work.

GARIN, Eugenio, *La cultura filosofica del Rinascimento italiano* (Florence, 1961). Comprises important articles on a wide range of Renaissance ideas and thinkers.

GEANAKOPLOS, Deano John, *Greek Scholars in Venice* (Cambridge, Mass., 1962). A great deal of information showing the importance of Venetian relations with Crete for the furtherance of Greek studies in Italy.

GELDER, H. A. Enno Van, *The Two Reformations of the Sixteenth Century* (The Hague, 1961). A rather far-fetched theory, which is nevertheless illustrated by a great deal of fascinating information connected with the intellectual attitudes of the time.

GILBERT, Felix, 'Bernardo Rucellai and the Orti Oricellari: A study on the Origin of Modern Political Thought', in *The Journal of the Warburg and Courtauld Institutes*, XII, 1949. A good insight into the changing ideas of the Rucellai circles in relation to changing political circumstances.

'Florentine Political Assumptions in the Period of Savonarola and Soderini', in *The Journal of the Warburg and Courtauld Institutes*, XX, 1957. Invaluable for information about the *pratiche* and the opinions expressed in them during this republican period.

Machiavelli and Guicciardini: Politics and History in Sixteenth-Century Florence (Princeton, 1965). A thoughtful work developing much of his earlier published research.

GILMORE, Myron P., *Humanists and Jurists: Six studies in the Renaissance* (Cambridge, Mass., 1963). Includes three articles useful for understanding Italian intellectual developments.

GRAYSON, Cecil, 'The Humanism of Alberti', in *Italian Studies*, XII, 1957. A good description of Alberti's attitudes to life.

HAY, Denys, 'Intellectual Tendencies; 1. Literature: the Printed Book', in *The New Cambridge Modern History*, Vol. II (Cambridge, 1958). Good for a wide range of technical, linguistic and intellectual developments.

KELLER, A., 'Two Byzantine Scholars and their Reception in Italy', in

The Journal of the Warburg and Courtauld Institutes, XX, 1957. Interesting for different outlooks on the world possessed by the Greeks and Italians in the middle of the fifteenth century.

KRISTELLER, Paul Oskar, *Renaissance Thought: The Classic, Scholastic, and Humanist Strains* (New York, 1961). A useful introduction, but through lack of reasonable editing unnecessarily repetitive.

Studies in Renaissance Thought and Letters (Rome, 1956). A most important collection of papers, especially for the Neo-Platonism of Florence.

The Philosophy of Marsilio Ficino (New York, 1943). An excellent presentation of the main aspects of Ficino's thought. *See* also CASSIRER, Ernst.

NARDI, Bruno, *Saggi sull' Aristotelismo Padovano dal Secolo XIV al XVI* (Florence 1958). Important studies of a side of Italian thought which has been largely ignored at the expense of the Florentine Neo-Platonists.

RANDALL, John Herman, Jnr., *The Career of Philosophy from the Middle Ages to the Enlightenment* (New York, 1962). A stimulating and original survey which includes Randall's work on scientific methodology at Padua. *See also* CASSIRER, Ernst.

RENAUDET, Augustin, *Humanisme et Renaissance* (Geneva, 1958). A collection of essays dealing with some major problems concerning especially the thought of the Renaissance.

RIDOLFI, Roberto, *The Life of Niccolo Machiavelli* (London, 1963). A careful account of Machiavelli's life and writings.

ROBB, Nesca A., *Neoplatonism of the Italian Renaissance* (London, 1935). A useful study of Florentine Neo-Platonism.

RUBINSTEIN, Nikolai, 'The Beginnings of Political Thought in Florence: A Study in Mediaeval Historiography', in *The Journal of the Warburg and Courtauld Institutes*, VIII, 1945. An interesting insight into the origins of Florentine, Renaissance political ideas.

SAXL, F., 'A Marsilio Ficino Manuscript written in Bruges in 1475, and the Alum Monopoly of the Popes', in *The Journal of the Warburg and Courtauld Institutes*, I, 1937–38. A revealing note indicating the connection between cultural influences and business interests.

TRINKAUS, Charles, 'A Humanist's Image of Humanism: the Inaugural Orations of Bartolommeo della Fonte', in *Studies in the Renaissance* VII, 1960. A good study of a typical fifteenth-century attitude towards classical culture.

WEINSTEIN, Donald, *The Renaissance and the Reformation, 1300–1600* (New

York, 1965). A source-book which includes a few useful passages from Renaissance literature in translation.

WEISS, Roberto, *The Spread of Italian Humanism* (London, 1964). Deals authoritatively with intellectual and literary aspects to the Renaissance.

WHITFIELD, J. H., 'Discourses on Machiavelli, VII: Gilbert, Hexter and Baron', in *Italian Studies*, XIII, 1958. A critical analysis of the nature and genesis of Machiavelli's *Discorsi*.

ZANETTI, Dante, 'A l'université de Pavie au XVe siècle: les salaires des professeurs', in *Annales*, XVII, no. 3, 1962. Interesting for the place of the scholar in Renaissance society.

Science

BROWN, Harcourt, 'The Renaissance and Historians of Science', in *Studies in the Renaissance*, VII, 1960. Gives an interesting account of the benefits bestowed by the East on European advances in science and technology up to 1500, but lacks an appreciation of pre-Galilean European achievements.

CAPPARONI, Pietro, *Profili bio-bibliografici di medici e naturalisti celebri italiani dal secolo XVo al secolo XVIIIo*, 2 vols (Rome 1925–28). Has some useful biographical information.

CASTIGLIONI, Arturo, *A History of Medicine* (New York, 1941). Full of interesting information and at the same time giving space to a discussion of the main historical problems involved.

DUGAS, René, *A History of Mechanics* (Neuchatel, 1955). Essential for the development of varying outlooks towards the physical world during the Renaissance.

GARRISON, Fielding H., *An Introduction to the History of Medicine* (3rd ed. rev., Philadelphia, 1921).

HALL, A. R., 'Intellectual Tendencies: 2. Science', in *The New Cambridge Modern History*, Vol. II (Cambridge, 1958). A fine chapter on six-teenth-century science which perhaps underestimates the achievements of the previous century. *See also* SINGER, Charles.

HOLMYARD, E. J. *See* SINGER, Charles.

HULL, L. W. H., *History and Philosophy of Science* (London, 1959). Especially good for conceptual developments, but deals little with the Italian scientists of this period.

KING, Lester S., *The Growth of Medical Thought* (Chicago, 1963). Especially interesting on the teaching of anatomy and its significance for changing scientific attitudes.

KLEMM, Friedrich, *A History of Western Technology* (London, 1959). Deals briefly, but interestingly, with some important aspects of the period. Has several original examples and quotations.

KOYRÉ, A., 'La dynamique de Nicolo Tartaglia', in *La Science au Seizième Siècle* (Paris, 1960). A detailed study of Tartaglia's work on trajectories.

MCKENZIE, A. E. E., *The Major Achievements of Science*, 2 vols (Cambridge 1960). Very good on the development of conceptual apparatus and methodological advances.

PANNEKOEK, A. J., *A History of Astronomy* (New York, 1961). A useful introduction, especially good for explaining the stimuli to astronomical interests.

RANDALL, John Herman, Jnr., 'The Development of the Scientific Method in the School of Padua', in *Journal of the History of Ideas*, Vol. I, 1940. Shows the contribution of the Aristotelians to the developments leading up to Galileo.

   The School of Padua and the Emergence of Modern Science (Padua, 1961). Includes Randall's article on scientific method at Padua together with assessments of the importance of Pomponazzi and Leonardo da Vinci in intellectual history.

SIGERIST, Harry E., *On the History of Medicine* (New York, 1960). Brings out a few interesting points of central importance to the developments of the period.

SINGER, Charles J., *A Short History of Medicine* (2nd ed. Oxford, 1962).

SINGER, Charles, HOLMYARD, E. J., HALL, A. R. and WILLIAMS, Trevor I., *History of Technology*, Vols. II and III (Oxford, 1956–57). Presents interesting information especially on ships and canals in Renaissance Italy.

TATON, René (General Editor), *Histoire Générale des Sciences: La Science Moderne* (Paris, 1958). Has illuminating sections, especially by A. Koyré, P. Delaunay, M. Daumas and A. Davy de Virville, on a comprehensive range of scientific developments during this period.

THORNDIKE, Lynn, *Science and Thought in the Fifteenth Century* (New York, 1929). Has some interesting discussion of fifteenth-century attitudes, but discounts too much the contributions of the period that were essential to later advances.

WIGHTMAN, W. P. D., *Science and the Renaissance*, especially Vol. I (Aberdeen, 1962). A most useful and penetrating survey.

WILLIAMS, Trevor I. (*See* SINGER, Charles).

273

Art

BLUNT, Anthony, *Artistic Theory in Italy, 1450–1600* (Oxford Paperbacks, 1962). A good selective treatment of important contributions to art theory, serving as a first-class introduction to the subject.

'The Legend of Raphael in Italy and France', in *Italian Studies*, XIII, 1958. Interesting for how the artist behaved and thought of himself after Raphael.

CHASTEL, André, *Italian Art* (London, 1963). A detailed survey, useful for reference.

FRANCASTEL, Galienne, 'De Giorgione au Titien: L'artiste le public et la commercialisation de l'œuvre d'art', in *Annales*, 16, no. 6, 1960. An account of the growing independence of the artist and the development of the view of a work of art as a salable commodity in the sixteenth century.

GOMBRICH, E. H., 'Botticelli's Mythologies: A Study in the Neoplatonic Symbolism of his Circle', in *The Journal of the Warburg and Courtauld Institutes*, VIII, 1945. A brilliant interpretative essay on the content of Botticelli's paintings with interesting points concerning patronage and the attitudes underlying Renaissance art.

'The Early Medici as Patrons of Art: A Survey of Primary Sources', in *Italian Renaissance Studies* (London, 1960). A study of patronage and the growth of the concept of a work of art.

The Story of Art (London, 1950). The relevant chapters are certainly the best introduction to Renaissance art.

GOULD, Cecil, *An Introduction to Italian Renaissance Painting* (London, 1957). Usefully fulfils its introductory purpose.

HOLT, Elizabeth G., *A Documentary History of Art*, 2 vols (New York, 1957, 1958). A well-chosen selection of translated passages from writings important for the history of art.

MURRAY, Linda (*See* MURRAY, Peter).

MURRAY, Peter and MURRAY, Linda, *The Art of the Renaissance* (London, 1963). A usefully illustrated and highly competent introduction to the European art of the period.

WITTKOWER, Margot (*See* WITTKOWER, Rudolf).

WITTKOWER, Rudolf and WITTKOWER, Margot, *Born under Saturn* (London, 1963). Full of interesting facts that throw light on several aspects of the artistic world.

WITTKOWER, Rudolf, *Architectural Principles in the Age of Humanism* (London, 1949). An indispensable examination of the aesthetics of

Renaissance architecture, especially revealing for Alberti, Bramante and Palladio.

'Individualism in Art and Artists: A Renaissance Problem', in *The Journal of the History of Ideas*, XXII, 1961. A useful article on the nature and genesis of individualism in the art of the period.

'The Arts in Western Europe: 1. Italy', in *The New Cambridge Modern History*, Vol. 1 (Cambridge, 1957). A good survey which suffers from a total lack of pictorial illustration.

WÖLFFLIN, Heinrich, *Classic Art* (2nd ed., London, 1952). An important discussion of Italian Renaissance painting.

Index

Abbiategrosso, 50, 51
Abruzzi, 15, 16, 17, 19
Accarigi, Alberto degli, 170
Acciaiuoli family, 102
Achellini, Alessandro, 174, 178, 193
Acqui, 39
Acre, 70, 71
Adda, River, 24, 51, 59
Aden, 75
Adige, River, 30, 46
Adorno family, 133, 135
    Antoniotto, 42
Adramyttenos, Emmanuel, 167
Adrian VI, Pope, 111, 143, 199, 200, 203, 250
Adrianople, 54, 65, 66
Adriatic, The, 17, 19, 45, 46, 59, 60, 61, 84, 95, 118, 128
Aegean, The, 16, 46, 60, 64, 69, 80, 87, 109
Aemiliani, San Girolamo, 215
Affaitadi family, 64, 252
    Giovanni Francesco, 126
Agnano, 84
Alamanni, Luigi, 157, 170
Albania, 60, 119
Albenga, 31
Albert of Saxony, 184
Alberti, Leon Battista, 23, 48, 51, 152, 160, 181, 195, 196, 225-7, 235-8 passim, 242, 243, 244; 10
Albizzi family, 97
    Rinaldo degli, 138
Alderotti, Taddeo, 190
Aleandro, Girolamo, 167, 214
Aleppo, 40, 41, 60, 63, 64, 67, 71
Aleria, 216
Alessandria, 24, 38, 40, 47
Alexander VI, Pope (Rodrigo Borgia), 49, 71, 104, 111, 112, 114, 115, 125, 128, 131, 136, 197-202 passim, 208-9, 247
Alexander of Aphrodisias, 217-8
Alexandretta, 71
Alexandria, 38, 60, 61, 62, 64, 66-70 passim, 74, 75, 78
Alfonso V of Aragon and I of Naples, 17, 79, 113, 131, 153, 249
Alfonso II of Naples (Alfonso of Calabria), 48, 100, 108, 123, 137
Alghero, 69
Almeria, 77
Alps, The, 29, 31, 32, 89, 110
    Alpine Passes, 23, 59, 85, 87, 134, 252

The Dolomites, 30
Alpes Maritimes, 46
Alum, 43-4, 61, 63, 64, 77, 80-4, 94, 95, 97, 104, 109, 110, 200, 248
Alunno, Francesco, 169
Amalfi, 22
Ambassadors, Diplomacy, etc.: 65, 105, 125-127, 164, 188
Amber, 67, 77
Amboise, Cardinal d', 199
America, 75, 77, 103, 189-90, 213
Anatomy, 172, 187, 192-4
Ancona, 66, 88, 95, 104, 109
    Anconans, 45, 66
Andalusia, 32, 76
Andrelini, Publio Fausto, da Forli, 191
Andria, 16
Angelico, Fra, 223-4, 234, 243; 2
Angers, Treaty of, 78, 123
Anguillara, Luigi, 188
Antwerp, 45, 75, 78, 82, 84, 88, 106, 248, 253
Apennines, The, 19-24 passim, 32, 39, 53, 88
Apostolis, Michaelos, 160, 166, 167
Apulia, 16, 17, 18, 61, 65, 100, 106, 116, 118, 128
Aquila, 16, 43, 145, 189
Aquileia, Patriarchate of, 112, 203-7 passim
Aquinas, St Thomas, 211
Arabia, 67, 68
Archimedes, 172, 181, 196
Arenzano, 46, 52
Aretino, Pietro, 170, 197
Arezzo, 19, 36, 145, 224, 225
Argentario, Monte, 84
Argyropoulos, John, 166, 167
Aristotle, 151, 154, 160, 161, 164, 165, 166, 172-3, 174, 177-80, 182, 211, 217, 226, 244, 254
Aristoxenus, 178
Arles, 46
Arno, River, 78
Artois, 113
Asola, 122, 124
Asti, 27, 85, 98
Astronomy and Astrology, 172, 185, 209, 218, 246-7
Atlantic Islands, 19, 62
Augsburg, 68, 74, 88, 253
Augustine, St, 150
Austria, 82, 83, 87, 88, 117, 118, 121, 204, 207
Averroists, 151, 174, 179, 193, 217, 218
Azov, Sea of, 60

Baber (Moghul Emperor), 75
Baghdad, 67
Baglioni family, 115, 135-6
  Guido, 136
  Malatesta, 135
  Ridolfo, 136
Balbani family, 97
Balearic Islands, 113; see also Ibiza, Majorca
Balkans, 60, 63, 64, 65, 106, 109
Balm, 69
Baltic Sea, 36, 88
Banking, 91-4, 97
Barbarigo family, 71
Barbaro, Daniele, 164, 178, 186
  Ermalao, 204
Barcelona, 106
Bardi family, 35, 96
Bari, 16, 61, 168
Barletta, 16
Barnabites, 215
Barons, 16, 19, 20, 48, 103, 108, 119, 131, 132;
  see also Feudalism
Barozzi, Pietro, 211-12, 217
Basle, 85, 88, 181
Basques, Basque Provinces, 44, 52, 84
Bassano, 88
Bāyazīd I, Sultan, 125
Beccadelli, Lodovico, 166
Beirut, 38, 40, 61, 62, 64, 66, 68, 70, 71, 74,
  75, 78
Bellay, Jaochim du, 170
Bellini, Giovanni, 229, 230, 231-3, 235, 236,
  239, 240, 241, 243-4, 245, 249; 14, 15, 19
  Jacopo, 232
Belluno, 211
Bembo family, 166
  Pietro, 159, 167, 169, 215, 244
Bentivoglio family, 20, 33, 56, 136-7
  Francesca, 122
  Giovanni, 104, 112, 115, 121, 136-7
  Sante, 121, 147
Benzi, Ugo, 191
Bereguardo, 51
Berengario, Iacopo, da Carpi, 178-9, 190, 193
Bergamo, 36, 38, 85, 215
  District, 27, 28, 52
Bernardino, San, of Siena, 208
Besançon, 86, 89
Bessarion, Cardinal, 111, 165-6, 181, 199
Binasco, 50
Biondo, Flavio, 168
Bisagno, River, 31
Bisticci, Vespasiano da, 159
Black Sea, 37, 40, 43, 60, 61, 63, 64, 65, 85, 98
Bobbio, 132
Boccaccio, 150, 152, 168-9, 254
Boccanegra, Simone, 133
Bologna, 20, 21, 41, 56, 88, 115, 184, 190
  State, 20, 21, 33, 104, 120, 121, 136-7, 199,
  203
  District, 21, 130
  Concordat, 104, 203
Bolzano, 88
Bonafede, Francesco, 188
Bonvisi family, 64, 252
Borgia, Cesare, 115, 128, 155, 158, 200-1
Borgo San Sepolcro, 224, 225
Borromei family, 64
Bosporus, 65, 85

Botticelli, Sandro, 234, 236, 243; 16
Brabant, 63, 78, 87
Bracciolini, Poggio, 151, 152, 153
Bramante, Donato, 49, 50, 195, 237-8: 12
Brasov, 85
Bread, 16, 19, 25, 31
  Chestnut, 18, 31
Brenta, River, 46, 50
Brescia, 36, 38, 41, 84, 146, 189, 215
  District, 28, 52, 146
Breslau, 85
Brigandage, 18, 65, 87, 120, 133
Brindisi, 16, 61, 189
Brucioli, Antonio, 157
Bruges, 54, 74, 81-4 passim, 96, 101, 106
Brunelleschi, Filippo, 181, 196, 221-2, 223,
  225, 226, 235, 241, 242
Bruni, Leonardo, 151, 152, 153, 160, 162,
  168, 191, 218
Building Industry, 38, 47-50
Buondelmonte, Zanobi, 157
Burgundy, 109, 113, 126, 224; see also
  Netherlands, Brabant, Flanders, and
  various towns
Buridan, Jean, 173
Bursa, 41, 54, 63, 65, 66, 67
Bussi, Andrea, 216

Cabral, Pedro, 71
Cadiz, 77, 80
Cadore, 46
Caffa, 60, 61, 63, 66, 89, 109
Cairo, 67, 69, 70
Calabria, 16, 17, 21, 33, 41, 42
Calcagnini, Celio, 184
Calendar, The, 172, 186
Calicut, 42, 43, 67, 74
Calixtus III, Pope (Alonso de Borja), 109,
  111, 199, 250
Calvin, John, 210, 252
Camaldolese Order, 213
Cambay, 43, 67
Cambrai, League of, 30, 38, 89, 124, 125,
  127, 146, 205, 250
  Peace of, 37, 58
Camera di Mercanti, 87
Campania, 15-18 passim
Canals, 15, 26, 33, 50-2, 103, 145, 195
  Irrigation canals, 24, 28
  Navigable canals, 21, 32, 59
  Canals at Venice, 47, 144
Canano, Giambattista, 193
Candia, 61, 204
  Candiotes, 56, 62, 66
Cannanore, 67
Cape Route, The, 68, 205
Capelluti, Rolando, da Parma, 189, 192
Capistrano, San Giovanni, 208
Capitalism, 27, 89, 91-9, 101-3, 105-6, 107,
  148, 252-3
  Capitalists, 23, 26, 52, 54-5, 57, 68, 82,
  88, 207
Capponi family, 97, 140
  Niccolò, 143
  Piero, 141
Capranica, Cardinal, 136
Capuchins, 215
Cardano, Girolamo, 186
Carinthia, 204

Carniola, 204
Cartagena, 77
Casa, Giovanni della, 166, 171
Casa di San Giorgio, 98–9, 106, 133
Castellammare, 16
Castel San Giovanni, 132
Castiglione, Baldassare, 164, 170
Castile, 41, 77, 82, 90, 129, 202, 251, 252
Castles, Fortresses, Fortifications, 21, 47, 48,
    49, 60, 65, 131, 133, 147, 195–6
Castro Giovanni di, 81
Catalonia, Catalans, 44, 46, 47, 80, 87, 98
Catania, 19, 47
Cateau-Cambrésis, Peace of, 104, 117
Catherine of Aragon, 202
Cattaneo albergo, 134
Cattle, Dairy farming, 21, 24–8 passim, 31,
    33, 37
Caucasus Mountains, 109
Celebes, 67
Cellini, Benvenuto, 245
Cennini, Cennino, 220, 223, 224, 241
Censorship, 202–3, 214, 215
Centurioni albergo, 64, 81, 83, 86, 97, 133,
    135, 252
Cerdagne, 113
Cernisone, Antonio, 191
Cervia, 100
Cesariano, Cesare, 238
Cesi, Counts, 131–2, 145
Ceylon, 42, 67
Chalcondyles, Demetrius, 166, 167
Charcoal, 52
Charles III of Savoy, 86
Charles V, The Emperor, 17, 39, 41, 51, 52,
    57, 84, 86, 91, 97, 103, 106, 110, 112,
    117, 118, 125, 131, 132, 143, 146, 167,
    195, 199, 220, 202, 203, 206, 250
Charles VIII of France, 108, 112–15 passim,
    122, 123, 160, 161, 246, 248
Charles the Bold, Duke of Burgundy, 79,
    81–2, 83, 126
Cheese, 18, 19, 24, 28, 29, 61, 63, 76
Chiaravalle, 50
Chiavari, 47
Chieri, 27, 39, 98
Chigi family, 97, 137
    Agostino, 83, 84
China, 40, 67, 88, 189
Chioggia, 29, 30, 100
Chios, 41, 43, 46, 60–4 passim, 66, 76, 98
    Maona of, 42, 64
Chrysoloras, Manuel, 165
Chuquet, Nicolas, 186
Church, The, 25, 26, 27, 42, 56, 62, 81, 91,
    92, 103–4, 105, 112, 124, 132, 144, 162,
    165, 169, 190, Chapter 9 passim, 225
    Councils, Florence, 109, 165; IV Lateran,
    192; V Lateran, 202, 218; Mantua,
    109, Pisa, 125, 200; threats of, 125, 198;
    Trent, 176, 186, 197, 203, 205, 207, 250
    Reform, 105, 111, 198, 199, 202, 207–16,
    249, 250
    Seminaries, 211, 212, 215
    Greek Orthodox, 62, 109, 162–3, 207
Cibo, Gherardo, 187
Cicero, 149–50, 151, 153, 154, 164, 165, 168,
    209
Cinque Savi della Mercanzia, 29, 74

Cinqueterre, 31
Citolini, Alessandro, 170–1
Città della Pieve, 19
Civitavecchia, 47, 76, 83, 84, 195
Classics, The,
    Influence on literature, 149–50, 152, 164
    Classical subjects in art, 231, 233, 234, 241
    Imitation of classical example, 151–2, 153,
    155, 158–9, 162, 197, 218, 221, 222,
    223, 225, 238–9, 246
    Appeal to classical authority, 153, 154, 177,
    178–9, 187, 188, 192–4
Claudian, 152
Clement V, Pope, 91
Clement VII, Pope, 20, 21, 49, 83, 84, 104,
    105, 117, 143, 185, 192, 200, 201, 202
Cochin, 67
Cognac, League of, 117
Collingham, William, 173, 176
Cologne, 85, 88
Colombo, Realdo, 193, 194
Colonna family, 131, 199
    Prospero, 112
Columbus, Christopher, 57, 189, 248
Columella, 170
Comasco, Niccolò, 188
Commandino, Federico, 181, 186
Commynes, Philippe de, 161
Como, 36, 38, 40, 50, 204
    Lake, 51
Condottieri, 20, 33, 34, 89, 119–24, 130, 137
Consoli del Mare, 55, 79
Constantinople, 48, 61, 62, 64, 65, 66, 109,
    167, 248
    Fall of, 37, 40, 43, 49, 60, 61, 63, 64, 80, 85,
    95, 99, 109; see also Pera
Contarini family, 71, 144, 166
    Antonio, 204
    Gasparo, 145, 164, 167, 211–14, 215
    Giovanbattista, 188
Copernicus, 172, 181, 185, 218
Copper, 69, 71, 87
Coral, 69
Corfu, 61
Corio, Bernardino, 159
Corner di San Luca family, 62
Corneto (Tarquinia), 76
Coron, 61
Corsica, 16, 18, 46, 79, 98, 111, 130, 216
Corvinus, Matthias, 41
Cossa, Francesco del, 229
Cotton, 17, 19, 61, 62, 69, 70, 77, 84
Counter-Reformation, 27, 107, 207
Country and Suburban Houses, 21, 30, 31,
    34, 50, 189, 242
Cracow, 85
Crema District, 28
Cremona, 24, 28, 36, 39–40, 50, 73, 115, 123,
    124, 145, 204, 207, 215
    District, 24, 28
Crete, 44, 60, 61, 62, 120, 166–7, 188
Crusades, 81, 109, 198–9, 200, 248
Cusa, Nicholas of, 181–4, 185, 186, 236, 249
Customs, 47, 70, 85, 98, 99, 103, 104, 202
Cyprus, 39, 46, 60, 61, 62, 70, 74, 98, 100, 205

Dalmatia, 60, 119, 169, 203
Damascus, 41, 43, 60, 63, 64, 67, 69, 71
Damietta, 67

Dante, 150, 152, 153, 168-9, 254
Danube, River, 65
Danzig, 85
Dardanelles, 65
Dauphiné, 46, 76
Depopulation, 15, 17, 20
Dias, Bartolomeu, 248
Dioscorides, 187, 190
Disease, *see* Plague
Djem, 125
Djerba, 69
Dnieper, River, 32
Dolce, Lodovico, 169-170
Dolo, 188
Don, River, 32
Donatello, 221-4 passim, 227, 229, 230, 241, 242, 249; **6**
Doria albergo, 81, 97, 98, 119, 133, 134, 135
   Andrea, 84, 106, 117, 119, 135
Dossi, Dosso, 229
Drugs, Medicines, 66, 94, 187-8
   Aloes, 19, 67
   Alum, 43
   Cassia, 67, 69
   Guaiac, 190
   Ladanum, 62
   Mercury, 189-90
   Rhubarb, 65, 67, 71
   Saffron, 16
   Senna, 69
   Tragacanth, 71
   Gum, benzoin, Camphor and Zedoary, 67
Ducas, Demetrius, 167
Durazzo, 61, 65
Dutch Republic, 58, 89
Dyestuffs, 15, 42-4, 66, 70, 80, 94
   Alum, q.v.
   Brazil-wood, 42, 43, 67
   Cochineal, 77
   Cramoisy, 43, 54
   Indigo, 19, 42, 43, 54-5, 67
   Lac, 43, 67
   Madder, 24, 43, 80
   Saffron, 16, 22, 25, 43, 94
   Woad, 24-5, 26, 33, 43, 44, 84, 95, 98
   Gall-nut, Ultramarine, Aloes, *Aqua fortis,* Dyer's weed, Potassium, Tartar, 43

East Africa, 67, 68
East Indies, 42, 67, 74
Edward III of England, 96
Edward IV of England, 96
Egypt, 60, 63, 64, 67, 68, 69, 74, 125
Elba, 52, 84
Elizabeth I of England, 66
Emmanuel Philibert of Savoy, 27
Empire, The, 58, 117, 118, 212, 246
   Influence on Italy, 38, 50, 115, 122, 124, 132, 166, 201, 202, 206
England, the English, 17, 24, 35, 36, 44, 58, 63, 66, 77, 82 passim, 88, 89, 90, 96, 106, 125, 145, 165, 247
English Channel, 44, 76, 77
Epirus, 60
Equality, concept of, 154, 161-2, 165
Erasmus, 167, 170, 180
Estates, 22, 30, 148
   Large, 16, 18, 19, 26, 132
   Scattered, 25

Este family, 132, 140, 153
   Alfonso, I d', 190, 244
   Beatrice d', 122, 147
   Borso d', 27
   Ercole I d', 124
   Ercole II d', 27, 207
   Isabella d', 122, 123, 147, 197, 243, 244, 255
Estouteville, Cardinal, 112, 199
Ethiopia, 109
Euclid, 53, 172, 181, 186, 187
Euganei Hills, 22
Eugenius IV, Pope, 162, 166, 204, 250

Fabriano, 53
Fabriano, Gentile da, 224
Fabrizio, Girolamo, 193
Faenza, 122, 190
Fairs, Besançon, 86, 89, 250; Champagne, 35; Geneva, 85-6, 89, 125; Lyons, 41, 86, 89, 249; Salerno, 41
Falcons, 69
Fallopio, Gabriele, 193
Famagusta, 46, 62
Federico of Naples, 48, 115, 131
Feltre, Vittorino da, 163-4
Ferdinand of Aragon, 17, 114, 115, 116, 123, 206, 247
Fermat, Pierre de, 186
Ferrante I of Naples, 16, 48, 82, 108, 113, 114, 119, 120, 121, 122, 127, 128, 141, 247, 249
Ferrantino of Naples, 114
Ferrara, 190, 225, 227-30 passim, 243, 255
   Duchy, 20, 21, 27-8, 100, 102, 108, 116, 121, 122, 126, 128, 132, 145, 153, 163, 168, 206-7
   War of Ferrara, 65, 102, 108
Ferrari, Lodovico, 186
Ferro, Scipione del, 186
Feudalism, Feudal lords, 18, 25, 30, 31, 33, 52, 55, 88, 103, 130-5, 147, 148, 206, 216; *see also* Barons
Ficino, Marsilio, 160, 165, 167, 180, 184, 218-19, 236-7, 244, 248, 255
Fieschi albergo, 18, 119, 133, 134
Filarete, Antonio, 226
Finale Ligure, 31
Fish, salted cod, 32, 43; herring, rock fish, tunny, salted fish and freshwater fish, 32; caviar, 32, 65
Flanders, 35, 36, 44, 59, 63, 65, 78, 80, 81, 82, 87, 90, 229
Flax, 21, 24, 27, 39
Florence, 21, 22, 35, 36, 38, 39, 40, 50, 54, 56, 57, 74, 79, 82, 83, 88, 92, 93, 94, 96, 121, 166-9 passim, 174, 184, 189, 196, 220-5 passim, 228, 240
   Republic and People of, 23, 41, 44, 45, 47, 55, 64, 66, 68, 69, 71, 76, 78-82 passim, 85, 89-90, 95, 97, 98, 99, 101, 102, 103, 105, 106, 108-11 passim, 113-22 passim, 124-9 passim, 137, 138-43, 145, 148, 151, 152, 153, 155, 156, 157, 159, 160, 161, 163, 164, 165, 190, 195, 200, 201, 203, 206, 209-10, 226-7, 229, 230, 233, 235, 242, 247-51 passim, 253, 255
   Duchy of, 23, 90, 103, 143

Florence—*cont.*
  Countryside of, 22–3, 32, 147
  Public debt of, 91, 97, 98, 101–3, 242;
    see also Tuscany
Fodder, 21, 24, 25, 31, 33
Fodri family, 50
Foggia, 17
Fokia, 43, 61, 63, 66, 80, 89, 109
Fondachi, 60, 69, 86–7
Fornovo, Battle of, 123
Fracastoro, Girolamo, 185, 188–92 passim
France, the French, 35, 42, 58, 63, 78, 80,
    82, 85, 86, 87, 90, 104, 108, 110, 111,
    119, 121, 123, 124, 126, 127, 152, 165,
    170, 193, 199, 203, 212, 246, 248–51
    passim
  Influence on Italy, 27, 33, 38, 51, 75, 112,
    113–17, 118, 129, 134–5, 142, 189,
    200, 203, 247
Franche-Comté, 86, 117
Franchi albergo, 98, 134
Francis I of France, 75, 86, 97, 104, 112, 116,
    117, 125, 203
Franco, Pietro, 193
Frangipani family, 81
Frederick II, The Emperor, 190
Fregosi family, 18, 133, 135
Fréjus, 87
Frescobaldi family, 74, 97
Frisius, Gemma, 185
Friuli, 29, 112, 204, 205
Frugardi, Ruggiero, da Palermo, 189
Fruit, 32; Citrus fruits, 19, 31, 64, 94;
    Dried fruits, 31, 77; Raisins, 61, 69, 80;
    Preserved fruits, 71; Figs and Melons,
    31, 33; Gourds, 31; Apples, Oranges,
    Peaches, Pears, Pomegranates and Pump-
    kins, 33
Fugger family, 74, 87, 88
Furs, Hides, 37, 65, 77, 80
Fustian Industry, 24, 27, 39, 57, 71, 77
Future, The concept of, 150–1, 246

Gaeta, 16, 115
Galen, 178–9, 187, 192–3, 194
Galilei, Galileo, 177, 178, 179, 187
Gallipoli, 63, 66
Gallipoli in Apulia, 16, 61
Gama, Vasco da, 57, 71
Garda, Lake, 27, 29
Gargano Mountains, 16
Garigliano, River, 124
Gattilusii family, 60
Gaza, Theodore of, 166
Gelli, Giovanbattista, 169
Geneva, 32, 85, 86, 89, 210
Genoa, 18, 21, 24, 31,32, 36, 37, 40–3 passim,
    47, 48, 52–5 passim, 59, 63, 64, 88, 92,
    93, 97, 98, 99, 117, 133–5, 161, 189, 208
  Republic and People of, 16, 17, 18, 30–1,
    37, 40, 44, 46, 47, 60–6 passim, 68–71
    passim, 76, 77, 80–7 passim, 89, 91, 95,
    97, 99, 100, 106, 108–11 passim, 113,
    115, 117, 119, 120, 126, 128, 129,
    133–5, 145, 147, 148, 163, 190, 200,
    206, 247, 250, 251, 252
  Public debt of, 93, 97–8, 106; *see also*
    Sampierdarena

Gentili albergo, 83
Georgia, 109
Germany, 68–9, 82, 83, 85–9 passim, 97, 109,
    118, 125, 201
  Industries of, 24, 27, 39, 40, 52, 65, 248
Ghiaradadda, 115, 123, 124
Ghiberti, Lorenzo, 152, 221, 222–3, 234, 241,
    242; 1
Ghirlandaio, Domenico, 233–4, 236, 243; 18
Giberti, Matteo, 212, 213
Gibraltar, Straits of, 35
Giorgione, 229, 231, 241, 244, 255
Giotto, 152, 223, 224, 227, 229, 234
Giovanni di Paolo, 227–228; 8, 9
Girardi, Maffeo, 204
Giustiniani albergo, 64, 81, 98, 133, 134
  Agostino, 169
Giustiniani family, 64, 135, 144
  Antonio, 112
  San Lorenzo, 211
  Paolo, 213
Glass, 69, 251, 253
  Industry, 43, 47, 52, 53, 55, 57
Goa, 67, 74
Goats, 32
Gonzaga family, 34, 50, 140
  Federico, 123, 244
  Francesco, 112, 122–4
  Ludovico, 243
Gozzoli, Benozzo, 224, 243
Grado, Patriarchate of, 203
Grain, 15, 17, 19–23 passim, 25, 28, 29, 31,
    32, 84, 88, 104, 111, 134, 137, 146–7
  Barley, 16, 62, 63
  Buckwheat, 16, 18
  Dhurra grass, 16
  Maize, 30
  Millet, 25
  Oats, 27
  Panic grass, 31
  Rice, 18, 24, 25, 27, 28–9, 33, 39, 63, 189,
    190
  Rye, 25, 26
  Spelt, 27
  Wheat, 16, 18, 20, 24, 27, 28, 29, 62, 63,
    65, 109, 147
Granada, Kingdom of, 41, 76, 77, 89
Granvelle, Nicolas Perrenot de, 103
Greece, 43, 188
Greek Language and Literature, 53, 56, 62,
    149, 165–72 passim, 178, 180, 181
  Biblical Greek, 168
Greeks (modern), 62, 111, 119, 160, 165, 166,
    167
Gregory XIII, Pope, 186
Grillo, Antonio, 168
Grimaldi albergo, 87, 97, 132, 134, 135
  Ansaldo, 84
Grimani family, 144
Gritti family, 144
Guadagni family, 97
Gualterotti family, 74, 97
Guicciardini family, 102
  Francesco, 112, 157-8, 161, 162, 163
  Piero, 142
Guilds, 35, 55–6, 91, 139, 141, 144, 148, 220,
    243, 253
Guillemeau, Jacques, 193
Guinea Coast, 77

Hama, 71
Harmony, Concept of, 180, 184, 185, 226, 227, 236, 237–8
Harvey, William, 187, 193
Hebrew, 168
Hemp, 19, 21, 27, 30, 31, 39, 46
Henry II of France, 118
Henry VI of England, 82
Henry VII of England, 79, 80
Henry VIII of England, 66, 80, 202
Heron, 186, 196
Heytesbury, William, 173, 174
Hippocrates, 187, 188
Hirschvogel family, 74
Hispaniola, 189
Historiography, 151–9
    Historical necessity, 154–61 passim, 246–247
Hochstetter family, 74, 87
Holywood, John of, 170
Horace, 209
Horses, 27, 32, 69
Hospitals, 50, 188, 190–91, 215
Hungary, 65, 85, 87, 109
Hutten, Ulrich von, 190

Ibiza, 69, 76
Imhof family, 74
Indo-China, 67
Indus, River, 67
Innocent VI, Pope, 198
Innocent VIII, Pope, 108, 125, 136, 140, 193, 198, 199, 201, 204, 247
Inquisition, Roman, 207, 250; Spanish, 202, 206
Insurance, Marine, 45, 92, 95–6, 106
Ionian Islands, 60
Iron, Iron Industry, 28, 47, 52, 57, 84, 251
Isabella of Castile, 17
Ischia, 44
Istria, 30, 189, 205
Italian Language, 111, 150, 167, 168–71, 256
'Italy', The concept of, 111–13, 256
Ivory, 67

Jacques II of Cyprus, 60
Jaffa, 71
Japan, 189
Java, 67
Jeddah, 67, 70
Jerusalem, 71, 215
Jesuits, 207, 214, 215, 216, 250
Julius II, Pope (Giuliano della Rovere), 20, 21, 34, 49, 83, 104, 111, 112, 114–15, 116, 124, 125, 128, 129, 131, 136, 155, 158, 159, 193, 198–204 passim, 206, 239
Jüterbogk, Jakob von, 111

Kānsūh-al-Ghaurī, 74
Karahissar, 63, 80
Kavakes, Demetrius, 185
Keller, Christoph, 152
Kepler, Johann, 187

Labour, 24, 26, 36, 41, 56; see also Wage-earning
    Shortage, 16, 17
    Domestic manufacture, 54
    Labour movements, migration, 18, 21, 22, 33, 36, 38, 40, 41, 53, 56, 130, 146, 252

Scarcity of work, 18
La Ciotat, 87
Laibach, 204
Lambro, River, 51
Lampridio, Benedetto, 166, 167
Land, see Estates and Small Holdings
    as an investment, 22–3, 25–6, 30, 34, 103, 105, 163
    Reclamation or Improvement of, 29, 30, 49, 50–2; Terraces, 15, 22, 31, 33; Drainage and irrigation, 15, 21, 23, 24, 26, 27, 33, 145, 147; see also Canals
Landino, Cristoforo, 168
Landlords, 22, 25, 27, 28, 30–1, 52, 132, 148, 252
    Absentee, 18, 26, 30
Langhe, The, 27
Laonikos the Cretan, 167
Larnaka, 62, 100
Lascaris, Constantine, 168
    Janus, 157, 166, 167, 168
Latin Language and Literature, 111, 149–50, 152, 164, 166, 168–71 passim, 249
Latium, 19
Lauro, Pietro, 170
Lead, 69, 80
Leather Industry, 43, 53, 55, 57
Lecce, Roberto da, 208
Lecco, 51
Leghorn, 18, 23, 47, 78, 90, 195
Leguminous Crops, 25, 31, 32
Leira, River, 53
Leo X, Pope (Giovanni de' Medici), 21, 38, 41, 47, 48, 49, 104, 105, 111, 116, 140, 143, 155, 166, 167, 191, 198, 201, 202, 203, 213
Lepanto, Battle of, 45, 46, 76
Lerici, 98
Lesbos (Mitilíni), 60, 61, 63
Leto, Pomponio, 162
Levant, The, The Near East, 16, 29, 36, 38, 40, 41, 42, 60, 61, 62, 66, 70, 75, 77, 78, 80, 81, 89, 94, 126, 134, 135, 191
Lewkenor, Lewis, 145
Liberty, The concept of, 141, 147, 148, 154, 161–3, 165, 209
Licata, 18
Liguria, 18, 22, 30–1, 46, 130, 148, 216
Ligurian Sea, 46, 85, 110
Limassol, 62
Linacre, Thomas, 167
Linen, 69, 71
    Bocasin, 62
Lippi, Fra Lippo, 242
Lisbon, 75, 77, 106, 126
Livy, 150, 154, 158, 165
Loans, 91–2, 94, 96, 97, 99, 100, 101, 103, 106
Locks, 51
Lodi, 145
    District, 24, 50
    Treaty of Lodi, 79, 99, 108, 109, 120, 121
Lombardy, 24, 25, 27, 31, 32, 33, 36–41 passim, 43, 44, 50, 59, 65, 76, 77, 83, 84, 87, 98, 105, 118, 130, 194, 207, 252
Lomellina, 24, 50
Lomellini albergo and family, 64, 69, 74, 98, 134
Lonato, 122, 124
London, 54, 80, 101, 106, 253

Lonigo, Niccolò da, 178, 190
Loredano family, 144
  Doge Leonardo, 232, 239
Lorraine, 88
Louis XI of France, 53, 82, 86, 113, 125, 126, 249
Louis XII of France, 37, 58, 112, 113, 115, 116, 118, 122–5 passim, 134, 168, 200, 203
Louis XIV of France, 42, 48, 152
Lucca, 22, 33, 40, 41, 42, 53, 85, 86, 97, 118, 126, 207
Lunigiana, 31, 119
Luther, Martin, 49, 163, 167, 201, 210–11, 217, 252
Luxemburg, 88
Lyons, 41, 53, 54, 75, 85, 86, 89, 101, 106, 118, 119, 124, 125, 134, 248, 253
  Gulf of, 76, 79

Macedonia, 65
Machiavelli, Niccolò, 112–13, 119, 147, 152, 155–9, 161, 162, 168
Madagascar, 88
Maggiore, Lake, 51
Magic, 160, 219
Majorca, 63, 76
Malabar Coast, 42, 67, 68, 74
Malacca, 74
Malaga, 63, 76, 77
Malaspina family, 31, 133
Malatesta family, 20, 137
  Roberto, 104, 108, 121
Malay Peninsula, 67
Malpighi, Marcello, 193
Malvezzi family, 136
Manetti, Gianozzo, 160, 168, 218
Manfredi, Carlo, 122
  Galeotto, 121–2, 162
Mantegna, Andrea, 230-3 passim, 243, 249; 13
Mantua, 36, 50, 109, 189, 204, 243, 255
  Duchy of, 27, 34, 100, 117, 122–6 passim, 163, 166, 168, 206
Manuel I of Portugal, 71, 159
Manuzio, Aldo, 53, 62, 167
Marches, The, 19, 20
Marchesi, Antonio, da Settignano, 195
Marchioni family, 74
Marengo, 24
Margaret of Austria, 118
Maritsa, River, 65
Marliani, Giovanni, 174
Marsala, 18
Marseilles, 47, 53, 75, 98
Marshland, Swamp, 15, 16, 19, 21, 23, 24, 28, 32, 33
  Pontine Marches, 19, 189
  The Maremma, 18–21, 47, 189
Martin V, Pope, 135
Martini, Francesco di Giorgio, 174, 175, 228
Masaccio, 223, 224, 225, 232, 234, 235, 236, 239, 245; 3
Massa, Niccolò, 190
Mastic, 64, 69
Mathematics, 185–7
Matteo di Giovanni, 227
Mattioli, Pietro, 190
Maximilian I, The Emperor, 78, 87, 97, 112,

115, 116, 118, 122, 123, 124, 127, 147, 205
Mazarron, 44, 82
Meat, 17, 18, 21, 24, 28, 32, 145
Medici family, 34, 50, 55, 64, 79, 80, 82, 83, 86, 91, 93, 94, 96, 97, 100, 101, 102, 105, 106, 113, 116–19 passim, 121, 126, 128, 137, 138–43, 156, 157, 162, 163, 165, 206, 209, 243, 250
  Alessandro de', 118, 143
  Catherine de', 118
  Cosimo de', 36, 64, 66, 85, 96, 109, 138–9, 140, 143, 153, 165, 181, 184, 197, 242–3, 248–9, 251, 255
  Francesco de', 91–2
  Giuliano di Giovenco de', 91–2
  Giuliano di Piero de', 140
  Lorenzo de', 56, 66, 83, 86, 96, 99, 100, 101, 106, 122, 124, 125, 129, 136, 139–41, 147, 153–4, 156, 165, 167, 168, 201, 203, 208, 209, 226, 235, 237, 242–3, 244
  Piero di Cosimo de', 102, 139, 143, 243
  Piero di Lorenzo de', 114, 120, 140, 141, 142, 247
Medicine, 187–8, 189–90
  Surgery, 192–3; see also Drugs, Plague, etc.
Mehemmed II, Sultan, 43, 64, 66, 109, 125, 127
Melanchthon, Philip, 213
Mella, River, 28
Mercury, 80
Merici, Sant'Angela, 215
Mers-el-Kharez, 69
Messina, 40, 41, 76, 130
Messina, Antonello da, 229
Mesta, The, 17
Mezzadria, 22, 26, 27, 31, 130, 132
Michelangelo, 195, 237, 240, 241, 243, 244, 245; 7, 24, 25
Michelozzi, Michelozzo, 169, 227, 242
Milan, 32, 36, 38–41 passim, 50–1, 54, 55, 57, 84, 88, 94, 101, 166, 168, 174, 188, 215, 236, 238, 253
  Duchy and People of, 23–7, 28, 29, 33, 37, 41, 51, 52, 79, 84–7 passim, 90, 95, 97, 99, 100, 103, 104, 106, 107, 108, 110, 113, 115, 116, 117, 121–6 passim, 128, 129, 132, 137, 138, 145–8 passim, 153, 163, 195, 203, 206, 247, 250, 251, 255
  Countryside of, 24, 32
Mills, 23, 30, 99, 133, 194–5
Mincio, River, 27
Mistra, 167
Mitilíni, see Lesbos
Modena, 27, 145
  Countryside of, 130–1
Modon, 61
Molgora, River, 51
Moluccas, 67, 88
Monaco, 87
Monasteries, 30, 50, 111, 211, 212, 214, 215
Moncastro, 66, 85
Mondino dei Luzzi, 178–9, 187
Moneglia, 31
Monenvasia, 60
Money, 25, 65, 91, 92, 94, 98
Montagnana, Bartolomeo da, 191

Montano, Giovanbattista, 170, 188, 192
Montefeltro, Federico di, 225
Montferrat, 27, 85, 98
Monza, 36, 39
Moors, 17, 40, 41, 129
Morea, 60, 62
Morosini family, 71, 166
Motion, Theories of, 172–7, 180
Mules, 17, 24, 32
Murano, 47, 52, 55, 69, 251
Murcia, 44
Musk, 65
Musurus, Marcus, 167

Naples, 16, 38, 48, 50, 57, 87, 88, 90, 97, 125,
    130, 131, 168, 189, 195, 229, 247
    Kingdom and People of, 15, 16–18, 20, 31,
        32, 35, 41–2, 44, 45, 57, 61, 79, 82–3,
        94, 97, 103, 106, 108, 110, 113, 114,
        115, 117, 119, 121, 122, 126, 128–32
        passim, 134, 137, 145, 148, 168, 189,
        200, 206, 249–52 passim
Nauplia, 61
Navagero, Andrea, 167
Negropont (Euboea), 60, 82
Neo-Platonism,
    Ancient, 165, 172, 184, 185, 236, 237, 239,
        240–1, 244, 245
    Florentine, 160, 163, 165, 179, 180–1, 184,
        185, 194, 218–19, 226, 233, 234, 236–7
Netherlands, Low Countries etc., 17, 24, 35,
    44, 46, 51, 77, 78, 80, 81, 82, 84, 96,
    117, 194, 250
Newton, Isaac, 187
Nice, 46
Nicholas V, Pope, 48, 49, 109, 136, 152, 162,
    166, 168, 191, 203, 243, 250
Nicosia, 62
Nifo, Agostino, 179–80, 218
Nile, River, 32, 67
North Africa, 17, 36, 76, 77, 106
    Barbary Coast, 60, 64, 82, 84, 87
North Sea, 32, 44, 63, 76, 77, 78, 84
Novara, 40
    District, 50
Novara, Domenico Maria da, 184, 185
Novi, Paolo de, 135
Nuremberg, 39, 52, 74, 88, 186, 253
Nuts, 69

Ochino, Bernardino, 207
Ockham, William of, 173, 180
Oddi, degli, family, 136
Oglio, River, 28
Olive Groves, 21, 31; Oil, 16, 22, 32, 61, 77
Oratory of Divine Love, 213, 214, 215
Orbetello, 84
Oresme, Nicole, 173, 180, 184
Ormuz, 43, 67, 74
Orsini family, 131, 140, 199
    Clarice, 140
    Gentile Virginio, 119
Otranto, 45, 61, 108, 122, 127, 128
    Straits of, 61
Ottoman Empire, The Turks, etc., 28, 37,
    38, 40, 41, 43, 44, 46, 60, 61, 63–7 passim,
    69, 71, 74, 75, 76, 78, 80–1, 83, 84, 87,
    89, 94, 95, 97, 99, 105, 106, 108, 109, 118,
    122, 127, 128, 129, 134, 159, 165, 166,
    200, 206, 215, 248, 249, 251
Ovide Moralisée, 150, 231
Oxen, 17, 32
Pacioli, Luca, 174, 186, 225
Padua, 53, 145, 147, 164, 166, 167, 177, 188,
    211, 215, 217, 230
    District, 79
Palermo, 18, 52, 76, 88, 97, 106, 130
Palla, Giovanni Battista della, 255
Palladio, Andrea, 30, 195, 238–9; 11
Palmieri, Matteo, 152
Pantheism, 202, 218
Papacy, The, 56, 81, 82, 83, 94, 97, 102, 104–
    105, 106, 108, 109, 110, 112, 115, 116,
    117, 119, 121, 122, 124, 125, 126, 136,
    143, 155, 198–203, 206, 217, 249–50
    at Avignon, 19, 104, 199
    Schism of, 19
    Conclaves, 111, 114
    Sale of Offices, 104–6
Papal States, 19, 20, 34, 44, 76, 81, 104, 112,
    114, 115, 116, 121, 126, 128–31 passim,
    136, 148, 200, 201, 202, 206, 247
Paper, 77, 253
    Industry, 43, 53, 54
Paphos, 62
Paracelsus, 190
Paré, Ambroise, 193
Paris, 48, 191
Parma, 24, 51, 116, 124, 145
Paruta, Paolo, 159, 164
Pascal, Blaise, 186
Pasqualigo, Pietro, 71, 159
Pasta, 32
Pasture, 16, 21, 24, 29
Patmos, 46
Patronage of the Arts, 221, 229–30, 241,
    242–5, 248, 255
Paul II, Pope, 49, 81–2, 83, 104, 105, 111,
    159, 162, 185, 198, 200, 201, 204, 211,
    249
Paul III, Pope, 112, 136, 198, 213, 214, 215,
    241, 250
Paul IV, Pope (Gian Pietro Carafa), 112, 213,
    214, 215
Pavia, 37, 38, 40, 41, 50, 145, 147, 168
    Countryside of, 24, 39
    Battle of, 112, 117
Pazzi family, 50, 82, 83, 140
    Conspiracy, 140, 159, 203
    War, 100, 102, 108, 121, 124, 125, 128, 137,
        141
Pearls, 63, 67, 71
Peasantry, 16, 22, 24, 25, 30–1, 130–4
Pelacani, Biagio, da Parma, 174
Pera, 60, 64, 66, 98
Persia, 40, 43, 69, 71, 109, 125
Persian Gulf, 63, 67, 71, 74
Perspective, 172, 181, 184, 221, 222, 224–5,
    227–31 passim, 237, 241
    Aerial, 225
Perugia, 115, 135–6, 189, 208
    Countryside of, 20, 130
Perugino, 225, 239, 243
Peruzzi family, 35, 96
Pesaro, 84, 88, 121
Peschiera, 122, 124
Peter the Great of Russia, 129

Peterson, Robert, 171
Petrarch, 111, 149–51, 152, 163, 164, 165, 168–9, 170, 253, 254
Petrucci, Pandolfo, 137–8
Peurbach, Georg von, 185
Philip II of Spain, 18, 106, 117
Philip the Fair of Burgundy, 84
Philip the Good of Burgundy, 109
Piacenza, 24, 116, 132, 196
Piave, River, 46, 118
Piccinino, Jacopo, 120
Piccolomini family, 50
    Alessandro, 177
Pico, Giovanni, della Mirandola, 160, 168, 184, 219, 222
Piedmont, 27, 39, 59, 85, 86, 98, 117, 132, 148, 207, 256
Piero della Francesca, 186, 224–5, 227, 229, 232, 235, 243; 5
Pietrasanta, 99, 102, 108
Pigs, Bacon, etc., 17, 22, 29
Pilatus, Leontius, 165
Pilgrims, 48, 49, 76, 202
Pindar, 167
Pinerolo, 85
Pioraco, 53
Piracy, 18, 87–8, 95
Pisa, 40, 55, 76, 78–81 passim, 85, 93, 106, 110, 115, 118, 137, 190, 203
    War of, 23, 80, 90, 120, 142
Pisani family, 144
    Cardinal Francesco, 216
Pistoia, 36
Pitch, 46, 64
Pitti family, 50
    Luca, 139
Pius II, Pope, 44, 66, 79, 81, 109, 111–12, 198, 202, 248, 249
Pius III, Pope, 115, 198, 199, 250
Pius V, Pope, 91, 190
Plague, Disease, 21, 39, 188–9, 190–1, 215, 251
    Black Death, 15, 56
    Diphtheria, 189
    Influenza, 189
    Malaria, 23, 187, 189
    Public Health, 28
    Swamp fevers, 21
    Syphilis, 187, 189–90
    Typhus, 188–9
Platina (Bartolomeo Sacchi), 159, 162
Plato, 149, 151, 154, 165, 178, 179, 180, 182, 184, 185, 226, 239, 240, 244, 246–7, 248
Plethon, Gemistos, 167
Pliny the Elder, 178, 187
Plotinus, 180
Plutarch, 170
Po, River, 21, 24, 27, 37, 46, 51, 128, 132
    Valley, 17, 23, 28, 29, 33, 100, 189
Pola, 189
Poland, 247
Pole, Cardinal, 199, 214
Polesine di Rovigo, 30, 128
Poliziano, 159
Polybius, 156, 157, 162
Pomponazzi, Pietro, 180, 218
Pontano, Giovanni, 160
Pontremoli, 31
Population figures, 38, 39, 41, 48, 74, 131

Porcari, Stefano, 162
Portinari, Tommaso, 81–2
Porto Ercole, 84
Porto Pisano, 23, 47, 78
Portugal, the Portuguese, 19, 30, 38, 44, 58, 66, 67, 68, 71, 72–6, 78, 80, 83, 89, 118, 125, 126, 159, 202, 251
Postal Services, 59
Poultry, 22, 30
Pozzuoli, 44
Prato, 36
Prato, Giovanni da, 151
Precious Metals, 68, 69, 75, 77, 93–4, 103, 252
    Goldsmiths, 53
    Silver and Gold Thread, 40, 41, 42
Precious Stones, 69
Printing, 53, 167, 169, 174, 181, 202
Priuli, Lorenzo, 187–8
    Lorenzo (the diarist), 112, 205
Proclus, 180
Provence, Provençal coast, etc., 32, 46, 69, 87, 95, 134
Ptolemy, 53, 181, 184, 185, 218
Pyrenees, The, 59
    Treaty of, 117
Pythagoras, Pythagoreans, 180, 184, 226, 236, 237

Quirini family, 71
    Vincenzo, 213

Ragusa, 66
    Republic and People of, 44, 45, 66, 95, 169
Raimondi family, 50
Rapallo, 31
Raphael, 225, 234, 237, 239–40, 244; 20, 22
Ravenna, 21, 116, 189
Red Sea, 63, 67, 74, 75
Reformation, The, 89, 105, 112, 118, 145, 163, 201, 207, 210–11, 213–14, 215, 217, 250, 255
Regensburg, Diet of, 213
Reggio Calabria, 40
Regiomontanus (Johannes Müller), 185
René of Anjou, 69
Renée of France, 206–7
Rhône, River, 46, 69
Riario, Girolamo, 108, 121, 128, 162, 200–1
Richard III of England, 80
Ridolfi family, 140
Rimini, 20, 137, 227
    Lordship and District of, 20, 104, 108, 109, 121
Roads, Routes, Land Transport, etc., 20, 24, 26, 32, 40, 51, 52, 59, 63, 65, 66, 69, 85–9, 100, 121, 251
Robert of Naples, 96
Roberti, Ercole de', 229
Romagna, 19, 20, 21, 82, 100, 104, 11⁻, 116, 121, 122, 124, 128, 129, 137, 162, 200, 204
Rome, 18, 19, 21, 38, 48–50, 55, 57, 82, 88, 90, 94, 104, 105, 114, 121, 125, 126, 131, 147, 162, 166, 167, 186, 189, 191, 200–3 passim, 205, 209, 210, 213, 215, 221, 225, 237, 243, 251, 253, 255
    Countryside of, 19, 20, 33, 104, 130, 131, 189

Rossi family, 140
Rousillon, 113
Rucellai family, 50, 140, 227, 252
  Bernardo, 142, 156
  Cosimo, 157
  Giovanni, 96
  Paolo, 83
  Orti Oricellari, 156–7, 187
Ruscelli, Girolamo, 185

Sadoleto, Cardinal Giacomo, 214
Saint-Florent, 18
Salerno, 16, 41
Saliceto, Guglielmo da, 192
Salonika, 31, 63, 65
Salt, 19, 32, 62, 64, 69, 76, 84, 98, 99, 100, 104, 106
Salutati, Coluccio, 153, 162, 164, 178
Salviati family, 97, 102
  Francesco, 203
Salzburg, 88
Samarkand, 40
Sampierdarena, 46, 50
Sangallo, Antonio the Elder, 195
  Antonio, the Younger, 195
  Giuliano da, 195, 237
San Severino, Cardinal Federico, 136
Sanudo, Marin, 167
Sardinia, 16, 18, 69, 76, 87, 111, 113, 130
Sarzana, 31, 98, 108
Sassoferrato, Bartolo di, 146
Sauli albergo, 135
Savelli family, 131
Savona, 31, 46, 47, 133, 145, 168
Savonarola, Girolamo, 86, 103, 114, 141, 143, 154, 161, 162, 200, 202, 208–11, 234, 235, 247
Savoy, 27, 85, 118, 126, 148
Saxony, 68
Scarampo, Cardinal, 109
Scholasticism, 151, 254
Scientific Method, 172, 174, 178–83 passim, 249
  Experience, Experimentation, Observation in Science, 174, 175, 177–9, 183–5, 188, 192, 193, 194
Scutari, 63
Seneca, 151
Sestri Levante, 31
Seville, 77, 253
Sforza family, 26, 33, 51–2, 103, 113, 115, 119, 121, 122, 126, 128, 134, 137, 140, 247
  Battista, 225
  Caterina, 121
  Costanzo, 121
  Francesco I, 25, 41, 50, 51, 79, 85, 100, 147, 159, 168, 181, 197, 249
  Francesco II, 117
  Galeazzo Maria, 24, 162
  Ludovico, 50, 51, 56, 101, 113, 114, 115, 122, 123, 137, 147, 159
  Massimiliano, 116
Sheep, 16, 27, 29, 33, 37
  for milk, 17, 32
  Transhumance, 15, 17, 18, 28
Shipping Industry, 18, 30, 44–7, 52, 57–8, 61, 64
Ships, 16, 18, 44–6, 63, 76, 77, 79, 95
Sibiu, 85

Sicily, 16–20 passim, 22, 31, 32, 33, 40–3 passim, 62, 97, 100, 103, 111, 113, 114, 130, 134, 147, 168, 206, 229
Siena, 21, 50, 97, 223, 224, 227–8, 247
  Republic and People of, 66, 83, 84, 106, 108, 111, 120, 126, 137–8
  Countryside of, 21, 31
Siena, Girolamo da, 208
Signorelli, Luca, 225, 243
Silesia, 83
Silk, 59, 61, 63, 65, 70, 71, 76, 77, 80, 84, 85, 86, 94, 118–19, 253
  Silk production, Mulberries, 17, 19, 21, 22, 24, 25, 27, 28, 31, 33, 39, 40
  Silk Manufactures, 27, 36, 37, 38, 40–2, 54–5, 57, 63, 251; Brocades, 40, 42; Camlets, 62, 71; Damasks, 42, 71; Taffetas, Satins, Velvets, Ribbons, 42
Simisso, 60
Simonetta, Giovanni, 159
Sinope, 60
Sixtus IV, Pope, 17, 19, 49, 83, 104, 108, 111, 124, 128, 147, 186, 191, 192, 197, 198, 200–3 passim, 243, 247
Skiathos, 60
Skiros, 60
Skopelos, 60
Slaves, 31, 45, 63–4, 65, 69, 95, 98, 109
Smallholdings, Market Gardening, 16, 19, 26, 31
Soap, 61, 65, 77
  Industry, 16, 53, 191
Sobieski, Jan, of Poland, 129
Soderini family, 102, 140
  Niccolò, 139, 143
  Pagolantonio, 102, 142
  Piero, 86, 110, 116, 119, 142, 210
  Tommaso, 140
Sofia, 66
Sokotra, 43, 67
Somaschi Order, 215
Soranzo family, 71
Soto, Domingo de, 176
Southampton, 45
Spain and the Spanish, 17, 24, 32, 35, 42, 43, 53, 58, 61, 66, 71, 76, 77, 82, 84, 86, 87, 89, 90, 94, 95, 97, 98, 103, 108, 113, 116–19 passim, 129, 200, 201, 203, 246, 248, 250, 251
  Spanish Influence in Italy, 18, 27, 33, 38, 106, 107, 111, 112, 115, 116, 119, 132, 142–3, 148, 189, 197, 199, 200, 206, 247, 250, 252
Spalato, 61, 65
Spannocchi family, 83, 97, 137
Spello, 135
Speroni, Sperone, 164, 170
Spices, 62, 63, 66, 68–71 passim, 75, 76, 78, 80, 85, 86, 87, 94, 95, 118, 126
  Cloves and Cinnamon, 67
  Ginger, 67, 75
  Nutmeg and Mace, 67, 71
  Pepper, 66, 67, 71, 75
Spinola alberghi, 31, 81, 98, 133, 134, 135
Strasburg, 85
Strozzi family, 50, 64, 97, 106
  Alessandra Macinghi, 91
  Palla, 167
Styria, 204

Sudan, 77, 88
Sugar, 19, 61, 62, 71, 106
    Industry, 43, 53, 62
Suleiman II, Sultan, 61, 125
Sumatra, 67
Switzerland and the Swiss, 25, 85, 88, 116, 120, 121
Syria, 40, 41, 64, 70, 71, 74, 109

Tabarca, 69
Talamona, 84
Tana, 40, 60
Taranto and Altamura, Prince of, 16
Tartaglia, Niccolò, 172, 175-7, 181, 186-7
Tauris, 40
Tavoliere of Apulia, 17
Taxation, 26, 39-40, 98-106 passim, 138-9, 145, 146, 147
Technological Advances, 41, 52, 194-5
Textual Criticism, 149, 151, 172
Thames, River, 80
Theatines, 215
Theophrastus, 187
Thiene, Gaetano da, 174
Thiene, Gaetano da (St Cajetan), 213, 215
Thomas, William, 32-3, 170
Thrace, 63, 65
Tiber, River, 49
Ticino, River, 50-1, 59
Tigris, River, 67
Tin, 69, 80
Titian, 231, 240-1, 244, 245; 21, 23
Tlemcen, Kingdom of, 77
Toledo, Pedro de, 48, 131, 250
Tolfa, 44, 47, 63, 77, 80-4, 89, 110, 248
Tolls, 17, 22, 103, 133
Tolomei, Claudio, 170
Tor, 67, 70
Tornabuoni, Lucrezia, 140
Torni, Bernardo, 174
Torre, Marcantonio della, 174, 194
Tortona, 40
Tours, 53
Trapani, 19
Trebizond, 40, 60, 66
Trebizond, George of, 166, 181
Trent, 46, 88
Treviso, 55
Trezzo, 51
Tripoli, 77
Tripoli in Syria, 62, 70, 71
Trismegistus, Hermes, 184-5, 219, 249
Tura, Cosmè, 229
Turocmans, Prince of, 109
Turin, 50
Turkestan, 40
Turks, see Ottoman Empire
Tuscany, 24, 31, 33, 36, 43, 132, 221
    Grand Duchy of, 90, 143, 148, 228
Tyre, 70, 71
Tyrol, 68
Tyrrhenian Sea, 46, 59, 85, 110

Uccello, Paolo, 224, 225, 230
Udine, 204, 205
Ukraine, 109
Umbria, 19
Universities, 53

Bologna, 20, 169, 174, 180, 186, 190, 192, 193, 195, 217
Florence, 166, 169
Oxford, 172, 175
Padua, 161, 164, 166, 167, 170, 174, 177-80, 185, 188, 192, 193, 195, 217, 247
Paris, 172, 173, 175, 177
Pavia, 50, 217
Perugia, 195
Rome, 166
Salerno Medical School, 190
Urbino, 174, 225, 243, 255
Ursulines, 215
Usury, 91-2, 105, 106, 242
Uzun Hasan, Shah, 125

Val di Chiana, 19
Valencia, 76
Valla, Lorenzo, 151, 165, 181, 216-17
Valli di Comacchio, 21
Valona, Pasha of, 127, 128
Var, River, 69
Varazze, 46, 52
Varchi, Benedetto, 170
Varro, 151
Vasari, Giorgio, 174
Vendramin family, 144, 252
Venezia, Giovan Tommaso da, 195-6
Venezia, Paolo da, 179
Veneziano, Domenico, 223, 231
Venice, 19, 21, 27, 28, 30, 36-41 passim, 47-8, 50, 53-6 passim, 61, 62, 68, 69, 82, 84, 87, 88, 93, 97, 126, 147, 164, 166-7, 168, 177, 181, 188, 189, 205
    Republic and People of, 16, 24, 27, 28-30, 33, 34, 37, 38, 40-7 passim, 53, 58-66, 68-89 passim, 94, 95, 97-102 passim, 106, 108-13 passim, 115-29 passim, 137, 146, 147, 148, 154, 157, 159, 161, 162-3, 164, 166, 187, 188, 190, 194-5, 200, 203-6, 207, 211-16, 231, 247, 249-52 passim, 256
    Patricians of, 30, 34, 120, 144-5, 146, 148, 164, 166, 187, 189, 204, 205-6, 255
    Terraferma of, 16, 28-30, 33, 34, 36, 39, 41, 46, 56, 59, 74-5, 99, 100, 116, 122, 124, 132-3, 145, 146, 147, 203, 204, 205, 231
    Public Debt of, 97-8
    Constitution of, 141-5 passim, 156-7, 162
    Patriarchate of, 203-4, 205, 211
    The Arsenal at, 46, 55
    Lagoon, Islands, 29, 30, 46, 48, 189, 203;
        see also Murano
Venturi, Girolamo, 84
Vergerio, Pietro Paolo, 207
Verme, Count dal, 132
Vermigli, Peter Martyr, 207
Vernia, Nicoletto, 218
Verona, 36, 41, 57, 65, 89, 145, 205, 21-, 215, 230
    District, 28
Verona, Guarino da, 153, 163-4
Verrocchio, Andrea del, 236
Vesalius, Andreas, 172, 192, 193
Vettori, Francesco, 127
Vicenza, 41, 65, 89, 145, 204, 215, 238
Vienna, 85

Vigevano, 24, 40, 51
Vigo, Giovanni da, 190
Villach, 88
Villages, Hilltop, 16, 22
Villani, Filippo, 152
Vinci, Leonardo da, 50, 51, 174–5, 176, 186,
    194, 195, 225, 233–7 passim, 239, 244; 17
Vineyards, 21, 24, 27, 29, 31
Virgil, 209
Visconti family, 26, 36, 50, 99, 113
    Filippo Maria, 41, 51
    Giangaleazzo, 113
Vitelli family, 120
Vitruvius, 48, 195–6, 225–6, 227, 236, 237–8
Vivaldi albergo, 134
Vives, Juan Luis, 170, 180
Volterra, 82, 201
Voltri, 52, 53

Wage-earning, 25, 26, 54–5
Wagons, 32
Wax, 80
Welser family, 74
Wildlife, 16, 19, 27, 32

Wine, 17, 18, 22, 27, 31, 32, 56, 61, 62, 64,
    69, 77, 80, 99, 104
Wood, 57
    Firewood, 30, 69
    Timber, 17, 18, 30, 46, 76, 109
    Cypress, 61
    Oak, 16
    Sweet Chestnut, 18, 31, 46
Wool, 17, 57, 66, 69, 76, 77, 80, 94, 96, 106
    Industry, 27, 35–9, 40, 41, 42, 54–5, 57, 79,
        251, 252
Worms, Diet of, 205, 213–14

Ximenes, Cardinal, 167

Zabarella, Giacomo, 177, 179
Zaccaria, Sant'Antonio Maria, 215
Zante, 61
Zara, 61
Zeeland, 84
Zeuxis, 226, 239
Zorzi, Bartolomeo, 43, 63, 82

DATE DUE

NOV 28 '67	JUN 21 '89		
DEC 11 '67	JUL 6		
DEC 4 '68			
Tue'B, 12:00			
NOV 17 '72			
NOV 26 '73			
DEC 5 '73			
JAN 15 '74			
DEC 11 '74			
NO 28 '77			
MR 2 '79			
SE 23 '81			
OC 5 '81			
OC 19 '81			
NO 2 '81			
NO 16 '81			
NO 7 '83			